PACIFIC WARBIRD

*To Fred and Jan
with love from
your old friend,
Bob Hamilton*

PACIFIC WARBIRD

Coming of Age in World War II

Bob Hamilton, Navigator

Copyright © 1999 by Bob Hamilton.

Library of Congress Number: 99-89469
ISBN Numbers   Hardcover: 0-7388-0289-1
                Softcover: 0-7388-0290-5

All rights reserved. No part of this book may be reproduced or transmitted in any form or by any means, electronic or mechanical, including photocopying, recording, or by any information storage and retrieval system, without permission in writing from the copyright owner.

This book was printed in the United States of America.

To order additional copies of this book, contact:
Xlibris Corporation
1-888-7-XLIBRIS
www.Xlibris.com
Orders@Xlibris.com

CONTENTS

Preface 7
Dedication 13
Introduction 17

1. Flying Off to War 21
2. Getting There 35
3. Sidetracked 47
4. Ready for Combat 61
5. First Combat Mission 75
6. Search for a Lost Plane 88
7. Jungle Boot Camp 98
8. Bull Session 111
9. Minor League Players 120
10. Lure of the Lake 139
11. Naked on a Life Raft 150
12. Major League at Last 161
13. Bomber Barons 174
14. Three Engines and a Prayer 193
15. Bombing Borneo 210
16. Three Musketeers 227
17. Catwalk in the Sky 244
18. Dangerous Darkness 258
19. Death Before Dawn 273
20. Skeletons 289
21. Dead Drunk 305
22. Ordeal Ahead 319
23. Shot Down Over Borneo 336
24. Victory! 354

25. Peace in the Pacific 371
26. Off-Base Adventures 383
27. Sunset and the Golden Gate 405

Postscript 427
Bibliography 431

PREFACE

This book was written to tell a good story about one man's adventures overseas in World War II. The author, a young navigator on a ten-man B-24 bomber crew, flew with the Thirteenth Air Force (the "Jungle Air Force") in the southwest Pacific during most of 1945, the final year of World War II. He flew twenty-four combat bombing missions against Japanese targets from New Guinea to Formosa (Taiwan) before the war ended. This book is his memoir of that period.

STYLE:

This book was written to read like a novel, to enhance the storytelling aspect of the memoir. The novelistic style is part of a fairly new genre called "creative nonfiction" or "dramatic nonfiction," which adds interest to nonfiction accounts. The dialogs, of course, were created by the author, since there were no tape recorders in 1945. There are no fictional characters in this book. All the names mentioned were real people, really present at that time.

DOCUMENTATION:

It may read like a novel, but this book is not fiction. It is solidly grounded in fact, based first of all on the memories of the author and other veterans of his bomber crew, or their squadron or bomb group, who have shared their memories with him. It is also documented by official Air Force historical records, squadron histories written at the time and classified "secret" until 1983, when they were declassified. The author made several trips to the Air Force

Historical Research Agency at Maxwell Air Force Base, Montgomery, Alabama, and photocopied some 500 pages of relevant records from World War II. The story is further documented by the original letters written by the author to his family and friends, which are now in his files, and by photographs given him by members of his crew, many of which appear in the book.

COMING OF AGE:

In a letter written to his parents on September 3, 1943, at the end of his army pre-cadet training at Knox College, the author (age 18) wrote: "It's been an interesting three months I've spent here. I've learned a lot, not just about math and physics, but about men, and girls, and people, and life. Edgar Guest said, 'It takes a heap o' livin' to make a house a home,' well, I think it takes a heap o' livin' to make a boy a man. I'm beginning to get some of that living here. I'm beginning to find out what men are really like, how they treat each other, and how they get along with each other. I think that's one of the few big rewards of army life—learning how to get along with all sorts of people." This book tells more about the "heap o' livin' to make a boy a man," hence its subtitle, "Coming of Age in World War II."

FAMILIES:

This book is written for the children and grandchildren of the veterans of World War II, to bring to life for them a vital era that they never knew. It tries to share with them how people like themselves, who lived through that great formative event of the twentieth century, thought, felt, behaved, lived, and loved. It may help those children and grandchildren understand the older generation better, and open avenues of dialog between generations. Family ties are mentioned frequently in the book.

Aviation Cadet **HAMILTON** in 1943, age 18.

PROFANITY:

Since the book was written for family readership, the author tried to clean up the language by eliminating most of the casual profanity which characterized military dialog. Some profanity was retained to emphasize moments of tension or high drama, where it was needed for realism. Some readers may feel that the dialog is too clean; they are invited to use their imaginations to add their own profane additions as they read (translate it back into the original "soldierese").

ACKNOWLEDGMENTS:

The author wishes to thank the many people who helped him with this book. First of all, his wife, Jeanne Hamilton, was his most helpful critic and source of encouragement in a five-year project. Secondly, his surviving crew members, copilot Jim Cordell, ball gunner Richard Herrema, tail gunner Jim Hill, radio operator Tony Imhof, and engineer Bob Pieper, who have gotten together in two reunions in recent years, reminded the author of many incidents he had forgotten.

Thirdly, his former wife, Persis Mary Hamilton, generously read and corrected those segments of the book in which she appears. And our daughter, Susan Sisson, helped revise several chapters. Fourthly, the surviving veterans of the ordeal described in Chapter 23, "Shot Down Over Borneo," Tom Capin, Dan Illerich, Jim Knoch, and John Nelson of the Air Corps, and Robert John Graham of the Navy, all contributed greatly to the accuracy of that story. Also, the chapters set in Nadzab, New Guinea, were checked for geographical accuracy by Dan Rath, a Bible translation supervisor in Papua, New Guinea.

Furthermore, members of the Novel Critique Group of the Village Writers Group (Atlanta, GA) including Nikki Beach, Don Boles, Bill Coulton, John Cunningham, Saribenne Evesong, Dudley Hinds, Bill Hunt, Donna Ing, Emily Kisber, Swarna

Krishnamurti, Meredyth Leaptrot, Barbara Lucas, Paul McHenry, June McNaughton, Alice Parsons, Maggie Righetti, David Rybeck, Pete Young, and Maureen Zent, all provided valuable critiques that helped mold the author's first drafts into the more readable prose in the book. Also, the staff of the Air Force Historical Research Agency, including Carl Bailey and Lynn Gamma, gave the author access to the historical records needed. Last but not least, members of the editorial staff at Xlibris (Princeton, NJ), Brian Bishop, Julie Duffy and John Feldcamp, created the book's final shape and appearance. The author's sincere gratitude and appreciation goes to all of the above.

BOB HAMILTON
Jackson Lake, Georgia
May 1999

DEDICATION

This book is dedicated to the memory of my fellow flyers in the Fifth Bomb Group, Thirteenth Air Force, who were killed in action in our B-24s during the events described in it:

Donovan G. **ADAMS**, Staff Sergeant,
    Assistant Radio Operator-Gunner   April 30, 1945
Edwin C **AUSTIN**, Technical Sergeant,
    Assistant Radio Operator-Gunner   April 30, 1945
Elvin J. **BARKHUFF**, Staff Sergeant, Nose Gunner   November 16, 1944
Paul L. **BARLOW**, Corporal, Engineer-Gunner   June 11, 1945
Robert W. **BARNES**, Second Lieutenant, Pilot   June 11, 1945
Frank **BEANLAND**, Staff Sergeant,
    Assistant Engineer-Gunner   July 4, 1945
David E. **BECK**, Technical Sergeant,
    Radio Operator-Gunner   November 16, 1944
Louis D. **BEDGOOD**, Corporal, Engineer-Gunner   March 9, 1945
Leo R. **BENDER**, Staff Sergeant, Nose Gunner   April 30, 1945
Zane R. **BERNEY**, Staff Sergeant, Nose Gunner   April 30, 1945
Clyde R. **BODKIN**, Second Lieutenant, Navigator   June 17, 1945
Philip Y. **BOMBENEK**, Captain, Bombardier   July 4, 1945
Roland **BOOTH**, Corporal, Nose Gunner   June 11, 1945
Frederick **BRENNAN**, Second Lieutenant,
    Navigator   November 16, 1944
James J. **BROWE**, Technical Sergeant,
    Radio Operator-Gunner   July 4, 1945

Howard S. **BROWMAN**, Technical Sergeant,
    Engineer-Gunner — April 30, 1945

Carl H. **CALLOWAY**, Technical Sergeant,
    Engineer-Gunner — April 30, 1945

Robert W. **CHAIN**, Flight Officer, Bombardier — June 17, 1945

Albert T. **CHAPMAN**, Sergeant, Gunner — November 16, 1944

Thomas M. **COBERLEY**, Second Lieutenant, Pilot — November 16, 1944

Robert L. **COMFORT**, Flight Officer, Navigator — June 11, 1945

Russell E. **CROSS**, Technical Sergeant,
    Assistant Engineer-Gunner — November 16, 1944

Charles D. **CRUM**, Staff Sergeant,
    Radio Operator-Gunner — November 16, 1944

Charlie H. **DEAVER**, Staff Sergeant,
    Radar Operator — November 16, 1944

Manuel A. **DIAZ**, Technical Sergeant,
    Radio Operator-Gunner — April 30, 1945

William **DUNN**, Staff Sergeant, Tail Gunner — April 30, 1945

Cecil J. **ELLIS**, Corporal, Radio Operator-Gunner — June 11, 1945

Hobart Y. **ETTER**, Corporal,
    Radio Operator-Gunner — June 17, 1945

Thomas E. **GALLEGHER**, Corporal,
    Assistant Engineer-Gunner — March 9, 1945

John M. **GIANGRECO**, Second Lieutenant, Copilot — April 30, 1945

Harley C. **GRIGGS**, Staff Sergeant,
    Assistant Engineer-Gunner — April 30, 1945

Deunet S. **GURMAN**, First Lieutenant, Copilot — July 4, 1945

Nathan **HANN**, Second Lieutenant, Bombardier — April 30, 1945

Grant N. **HANSEN**, Second Lieutenant, Copilot — November 16, 1944

Isaac J. **HAVILAND**, Colonel,
    Pilot, Commanding Officer Fifth Bomb Group — July 4, 1945

Francis H. **HEBERT**, Staff Sergeant,
    Assistant Radio Operator-Gunner — July 4, 1945

William E. **JOHNSON**, Corporal, Nose Gunner — March 9, 1945

Albert J. **JUSSIER**, Corporal,
    Assistant Radio Operator-Gunner — June 11, 1945

Anthony J. **LORIA**, Corporal, Nose Gunner	June 17, 1945
Robert E. **LUMM**, Corporal, Assistant Radio Operator-Gunner	March 9, 1945
John S. **MASTEKO**, Corporal, Engineer-Gunner	June 17, 1945
Henry D. **MAYE**, Corporal, Assistant Engineer-Gunner	June 11, 1945
William F. **McCLELLAND**, First Lieutenant, Aerial Observer	November 16, 1944
Everett E. **MOORE**, Technical Sergeant, Engineer-Gunner	November 16, 1944
Robert **MULKEY**, Corporal, Assistant Radio Operator-Gunner	June 17, 1945
Robert A. **NELSON**, Second Lieutenant, Copilot	April 30, 1945
Wayatt A. **NORRIS**, Second Lieutenant, Pilot	November 16, 1944
Edward S. **OLSZEWSKI**, Sergeant, Armorer-Gunner	July 4, 1945
Melton D. **PATRICK**, Sergeant, Assistant Radio Operator-Gunner	November 16, 1944
Elmer **PHILLIPS**, Sergeant, Aerial Photographer	November 16, 1944
Rocco **PILIGNO**, Staff Sergeant, Assistant Engineer-Gunner	April 30, 1945
Charles D. **PILJ**, Flight Officer, Bombardier	June 11, 1945
Ernest B. **POLONIO**, First Lieutenant, Navigator	July 4, 1945
Edwin M. **POND**, Jr., Staff Sergeant, Tail Gunner	July 4, 1945
Carroll V. **RITTNER**, Corporal, Tail Gunner	March 9, 1945
Donald L **RICHARDS**, Corporal, Assistant Engineer-Gunner	June 17, 1945
Jerome **ROSENTHAL**, Second Lieutenant, Copilot	November 16, 1944
Ira R. **ROTE**, Tech Sergeant, Engineer-Gunner	July 4, 1945
Arthur **RUBENSTEIN**, Second Lieutenant, Navigator	March 9, 1945
James A. **SAALFIELD**, Major, Pilot, 23rd Squadron Commander	November 16, 1944
Conover B. **SARVIS**, Jr., Second Lieutenant, Copilot	March 9, 1945

Franklin C. **SCHULZ**, Second Lieutenant, Pilot	June 17, 1945
John D. **SCOGGIN**, First Lieutenant, Bombardier	November 16, 1944
Dominic **SERRANO**, Technical Sergeant, Radio Operator-Gunner	April 30, 1945
James E. **SHALLENBERGER**, Flight Officer, Bombardier	April 30, 1945
Arthur B. **SOBOL**, Flight Officer, Navigator	April 30, 1945
Benjamin B. **SMITH**, First Lieutenant, Pilot	April 30, 1945
Kenneth R. **SMITH**, Second Lieutenant, Pilot	March 9, 1945
James W. **STACK**, Corporal, Radio Operator-Gunner	March 9, 1945
August A. **STASIO**, Flight Officer, Navigator	April 30, 1945
Richard L. **STRICKLAND**, Staff Sergeant, Tail Gunner	April 30, 1945
Richard M. **VAN GALDER**, First Lieutenant, Copilot	November 16, 1944
Robert W. **WICKHORST**, First Lieutenant, Navigator	November 16, 1944
Benjamin R. **WHITEKER**, First Lieutenant, Pilot	April 30, 1945
Ahti J. **WUORI**, Staff Sergeant, Tail Gunner	November 16, 1944
Frederick S. **ZIMMERLI**, Second Lieutenant, Bombardier	November 16, 1944
Joseph E. **ZUZGA**, Second Lieutenant, Copilot	June 11, 1945

May the memory of the seventy-seven heroes enshrined above live long in the hearts of their fellow Americans!

INTRODUCTION

THE B-24 IN THE PACIFIC WAR

by

Lieutenant General George C. Kenney
Commanding Officer, Far East Air Forces

As a heavy bomber for use in the Pacific during World War II, the B-24 (Liberator) was the best thing we had until the B-29 was ready. The B-24 carried more bombs than the B-17. It could be flown while greatly overloaded, so it had much greater range than the B-17. We repeatedly hit targets over 1,200 miles from the take-off point. Although designed for a take-off weight of around 50,000 pounds, on our long range missions our take-off weight was over 70,000 pounds. The B-24 was well-built and would take a surprising amount of punishment and still stay together. In formation, and especially after we installed a power-operated turret with a pair of .50-caliber guns in the nose, the airplane could give an excellent account of itself in combat with the Japanese fighters. However, like all bombers, it needed, and wherever possible we provided, fighter escort on daylight missions, to keep from taking losses that in the long run might prove destructive to morale.

As an individual airplane, it was not as nice a flying machine as the B-17. It never seemed ready to take off by itself no matter how far you let it run. You simply built up your airspeed high enough and then pulled the airplane off the ground. Its performance at high altitude was inferior to the B-17, but that made little difference to us in the Pacific where all our combat operations were either on the deck or around 6,000 feet, just above the small arms fire but too low to be a good target for the heavier (anti-aircraft) guns of 77 mm and up.

The nose of the B-24 originally came with individual .50-caliber machine guns mounted to fire through eyeball sockets. Only one of them could be used at a time and the field of fire was quite limited. With these guns, plus a navigator and a bombardier, the nose cockpit was too crowded. When the Japs found out that we had good defensive fire power to the rear, they made their attacks head on from the front where the B-24 was weak. Accordingly, we took a tail power-operated turret from a wrecked B-24 and installed it in the nose. As soon as we tried it out in combat and found it to be highly successful, we remodeled all our B-24s in the same way as fast as we could get extra tail turrets, and asked General Arnold to have all future production of B-24s in the United States fixed up the same way. This was done and the B-24 bomber crews became quite enthusiastic about their ability to survive attacks by the Japanese fighters. The records certainly proved it.

In order to save weight and give better take-off and flying characteristics, we took out all waist guns as our studies showed that they never hit any Jap planes anyhow and therefore the gunner, his guns and his ammunition were simply dead weight. Some squadrons did away with all armor, saying that they never saw any of it with even a dent and therefore it, too, was just weight.

All things considered, our bomber crews were quite happy with the B-24. They didn't boast about its flying qualities but they appreciated its range and load-carrying capacity. And, after all, those were the qualities that really counted in getting the job done.*

---

* (Quoted in *The B-24 Liberator* by Allan G. Blue, 1976, Ian Allan Ltd., Shepperton, TW178AS, England, page 165. Used by permission.)

B-24 FLYING ON MISSION TO BORNEO.

This latest-model B-24-M with Emerson electric nose turret is so new that it lacks the squadron insignia and airplane number which will be painted on the rudders. The ball turret is still retracted; when approaching enemy territory, the ball turret will be lowered from the belly below the star painted on the side of the waist

1. Flying Off to War

At 10,500 feet, our formation of eleven B-24 Liberator heavy bombers flew past Japanese- occupied Brunei Bay, Borneo, and over the swampy green flatlands of the northwestern Borneo coast. We were the "Bomber Barons," the Fifth Bomb Group of the Thirteenth Air Force. We had taken off at dawn from Samar Island in the Philippines on May 18, 1945, the final year of World War II. I was the navigator on my bomber crew, seated in the nose of B-24 number 650, "Little Judith Anne," named after the crew chief's daughter.

Our southwesterly course would send the big silver airplanes across the shoreline and over a shimmering stretch of the South China Sea to a point north of Sibu, where the group would turn left at high noon to bomb Japanese war planes and soldiers on Sibu Airfield.

Suddenly I heard in my earphones, "Waist Gunner to pilot, smoke from number one!"

"Pilot to Waist, say again, over."

"Number one engine smoking bad!"

"Yep! Number one oil pressure way down! Feather number one!"

I looked out the left nose window to see smoke pouring out of the left outboard engine, and then watched the propeller slow down and stop as the pilots turned the blades feather-edge into the slipstream. The smoke thinned out and ended. The other three engines roared louder as the pilots increased power on those.

"Pilot to Navigator, how long to primary target? Over."

"Forty-five minutes if we keep up with the formation, over."

"How long to the secondary, Bintulu? Over."

I did a quick calculation. "Twenty minutes to secondary. You can barely see Bintulu on the coast ahead, ten o'clock low, over."

"Pilot to Crew, we can't keep up with the formation on three engines. We're going to peel off and bomb the secondary target. Navigator, give me a heading, over."

"One-eight-zero, due south," I replied.

Our plane nosed down to drop below the formation, then rolled to the right to peel off and turn south. We leveled off as the pilots pulled back the throttles to lower the roar of the engines to high cruising power.

"Pilot to Bombardier, arm the bombs, open the doors. Prepare for solo bomb run, over."

"Bombardier to Pilot, wilco" (will comply). Lieutenant James, my neighbor in the nose compartment, unplugged his interphone connector and crawled into the bomb bay to unhook safety wires from twenty napalm bombs.

"Pilot to Gunners, we're alone and vulnerable. Keep your eyes peeled for enemy fighters. They love to jump wounded birds like us. Test-fire your guns now."

The airplane shook and rattled briefly as ten fifty-caliber machine guns fired noisy, powerful bursts. The smell of gunsmoke filled the plane.

Lieutenant James reappeared in the nose from the bomb bay and plugged in his interphone. "Bombardier to Pilot, all bombs now armed—twenty great balls of fire!"

"Pilot to all Crew, we're coming up on target fast. Put on your flak vest and helmet now, and keep your parachute handy!"

I lifted my body armor off the floor, and put on the flak vest and heavy steel helmet. My chest-pack chute was hung on a wall clip beside my navigation table.

"Nose gunner to Pilot, flak ahead, two o'clock low!"

I looked over the bombardier's shoulder. There it was, two ugly puffs of black smoke, low and to the right. There's another!

"Navigator to Pilot and Bombardier, we're now over the I.P. (initial point) for bomb run on secondary, over."

"Pilot to Bombardier, commence bomb run! You're in control."

James knelt over the bombsight, with his hands on its dials and his eye glued to its telescopic sight. He now controlled the plane's direction; the pilots maintained only the altitude and airspeed. Whenever he turned the bombsight to the left or right, the autopilot turned the airplane the same direction. Although flak was starting to rock the plane, no evasive action was possible during the bomb run.

James looked through the bombsight at the approaching target, and delicately adjusted the angular speed of the gyromotor that slowly cranked the sighting angle down to keep the crosshairs on the aiming point. When the sighting angle reached the preset release angle, the bombsight automatically released the bombs in rapid-fire sequence, producing a "string of bombs" that "walked" across the target area at fifty-foot intervals.

"Bombs away!" James called on the interphone. "Closing bomb bay doors." He pulled up on the big red bomb bay door handle.

"Let's get out of here!" said Lieutenant Seitz, our pilot, as he rolled the big bomber into a steep right turn. A close flak burst rocked us hard, and shell fragments tore through the plane's aluminum skin as we turned. For the next few minutes we dodged flak as Seitz zig-zagged the plane for evasive action. Without the formation, we had much more freedom to move.

I could not navigate during evasive action; I just sat at my chart, feeling queasy. While I waited, my mind flashed back to another flight on a different plane, ten weeks earlier, where no evasive action disturbed my stomach, because no flak shells burst nearby.

That flight had been on an Air Transport Command C-54 (four-engine cargo plane) leaving northern California with forty army flyers as passengers. On March 4, 1945, I was a nineteen-year-old second lieutenant in the U.S. Army Air Corps, navigator for a newly-trained B-24 heavy bomber crew of four officers and six enlisted men. Three other B-24 crews were also on board, heading overseas to fly our first combat missions.

This C-54 had no airline-style rows of seats; instead, long benches lined both sides, the space between them filled with baggage tied to clips on the floor. We sat side by side in two long rows facing each other, none of us knowing what part of this worldwide war would be our final destination.

I looked around the cabin. All forty passengers were dressed in Army Air Corps summer khaki uniforms under brown leather jackets for warmth. Every face in sight was young, clean-shaven, white and male. American military units in World War Two were rigidly segregated by race and gender, a reflection of American society then. We were also segregated by rank, except in line of duty. Officers were told, "Don't fraternize with enlisted men."

"Here we go at last," said Second Lieutenant Howard James, bombardier on my crew. Black-haired, small and slender, he looked like a schoolboy, though he was really nineteen.

"Yep, we're finally on our way into combat," said First Lieutenant Marvin Seitz, our pilot. He had blond hair, a stubby nose, and an Iowa farmer's weather-worn skin. "Been looking forward to this for a long time."

I agreed, "We're all eager to get there."

"Wish we knew where we're goin'," said Flight Officer James Cordell, our husky copilot, stroking his curly brown hair.

"We're headed west," I said. "It should be pretty obvious that we're going to the Pacific."

"The Pacific is a mighty big spread," Cordell replied. "Be nice to know where."

Two of the six enlisted men on our crew were looking out the windows, watching the California landscape go by.

"Hey, guys, look outside," called Corporal Williams, nose gunner. "We just crossed the shoreline—we're out over the ocean now."

"Hot stuff!" said Corporal Herrema, ball-turret gunner.

"That's the Pacific you're looking at," said Corporal Pieper, engineer-gunner, "so now we're going to the South Pacific for sure."

"I didn't want to go to Europe, anyway," said Corporal Imhof, radioman-gunner.

"Why not?" asked Corporal Gerson, armorer-gunner. "Think of all those gorgeous girls in France!" He put a fat finger to his thick lips to blow a kiss. "Ooo-la-la!"

"Think of all the hula girls in Hawaii!" said Corporal Hill, tail gunner. He began to wave both hands to mimic a hula dance and sing, "I wanta go back—to my little brown shack—in Molokai, Hawa-ii..."

"Yeah," Pieper said, "the hula girls will meet our plane and put a lei around the neck of each one of us."

"Great," said Williams, "I could use a good lay!"

"Dreamer!" Cordell said. "We'll only pass through Hawaii on our way to the war zone. We'll probably end up in Fiji, where the girls are all kinky-haired and black!" He shuddered.

"It could be worse than that," James said, "we could end up on Lackanooki Island, with no girls at all!"

"We'd better get used to life without girls around," Seitz added. "We're not going to England or France. In the Pacific, we can focus on winning the war without distractions."

"Some distractions I hate to give up!" Gerson said.

"I'm glad we had a few distractions on our last leave from Hamilton Field," said Herrema.

"You had a hot date?" I asked.

"No—just pleasant company."

"Yeah," Imhof agreed. "Herrema had a cousin—nice girl—in Alameda. She had a friend—another nice girl nearby. Herrema and I stayed at his cousin's place, and dated those two nice girls. Went to movies, did some eating out—had a good time hanging around together."

"Didn't try to lay 'em?" asked Gerson.

"Heck no!" Imhof said. "I'm engaged to my home-town sweetheart, Marian Bear. I'm not about to spoil a good thing now!"

"How about you, Hamilton? Any distractions on that leave?"

"A very pleasant distraction," I said. "I had the names of two sisters, Pat and Persis, at Stanford University. When we got to Hamilton Field, I called 'em up to ask for a blind date. Pat told me she's already married—to a Lieutenant Dahlin, driving a tank into Germany now. But I did talk her sister Persis into a blind date with me. I rode a Greyhound bus down to the Stanford campus and took her out—in her dad's Oldsmobile, no less. We had a great time together."

"Sounds like a lot of us have pleasant memories to see us off to war," Hill said.

"Hold on to those memories," Seitz said. "We may need 'em to see us through whatever we're headed for next."

I opened the *San Francisco Chronicle*, picked up before boarding, to catch up on news of the war. It was full of good news: American forces advancing eastward through Germany had just taken the city of Trier. The Ninth Army had reached the Rhine river. Russian armies were sweeping westward through Poland toward eastern Germany.

In the Pacific, General MacArthur's forces had just invaded Palawan, the westernmost island in the Philippines, after B-24 heavy bombers from the Fifth and Thirteenth Air Forces had bombed Japanese defensive positions there. Naval Task Force 58 had just sent 600 carrier-based planes to attack Okinawa. Also, 150 B-29 "Superfortress" bombers from the Twentieth Air Force had dropped firebombs on "strategic targets" in Tokyo again.

"Hey, guys, listen to this," I said. "Here's a news report that Lieutenant General Harmon and two other generals from the command staff of the Far East Air Forces are missing—their C-87 transport plane, a converted B-24, failed to complete a long over-water flight. Search planes have found nothing after two days of covering all likely areas of the Pacific."

"How about that!" said James. "The big brass hats got their pants wet!"

"How could an important B-24 like that be lost at sea?" asked Seitz.

"Do you suppose enemy ships or planes shot them down in mid-ocean?" Cordell suggested.

"Like we did, when Thirteenth Air Force P-38s shot down Admiral Yamamoto's plane near Bouganville," I added.

"Most unlikely," Seitz replied. "You know they'd do everything possible to take care of V.I.P.'s."

"Could the navigator have lost his way until they ran out of fuel?" James asked.

As a navigator, I replied, "Of course not! They would put the best navigator in the Pacific on the general's plane—somebody like me!"

"Listen to that conceited bastard brag on himself!" Cordell said.

"Hey, be glad that I'm good—your life may depend on it."

Pieper asked, "Could two or more of the four engines have failed at once?"

"Almost impossible," Seitz replied. "Think about all the dependable B-24s we flew at Tonopah."

I thought about that. From October 27 1944 to February 16 1945, our crew had gone through "B-24 Phase Training" at Tonopah Army Air Base in the middle of the Nevada desert. There we had been introduced to the big four-engine heavy bomber with high wing and twin rudders; there we learned to fly it and make it work for us, and most importantly, we learned at Tonopah how to work together as a crew.

Before Tonopah, we had each been going through specialized flight training in our separate specialties. We happened to graduate in the same month, and were assigned together to form a new B-24 crew. At Tonopah, we spent the next sixteen weeks learning to be a team.

Now Seitz continued, "We flew 144 hours of B-24 training missions at Tonopah without any major mechanical problem."

"Then it must have been bad weather," I concluded. "General Harmon's plane must have run into extreme turbulence in some Pacific thunderhead, and broken up."

"Turbulence would do it," Cordell agreed. "Any plane's wings can fall off if you shake 'em hard enough."

"Remind me to stay out of weather like that when we get over there," Seitz added.

OUR CREW AT TONOPAH, NEVADA, 1944
Left to right: back row: copilot Cordell, bombardier James, navigator Hamilton, pilot Seitz; front row: armorer-gunner Gerson, radio operator Imhof, flight engineer Pieper, tail gunner Hill, nose gunner Williams. (Ball gunner Herrema not in picture.)

My memory drifted back to Tonopah, a hastily-built airbase in a desert valley near an old western mining town surrounded by the rugged, barren Sierra Nevada mountains. On my first weekend leave, I rented a room in the Mizpah Hotel in Tonopah. A pitcher of water and porcelain wash basin sat on the dresser across from a double bed with a brass-rail headboard; the public bathroom was down the hall. Downstairs was an 1890's style bar and a small "casino" with slot machines and poker tables.

Down the street was "Ruby's Resort," the local whorehouse. (Both gambling and prostitution were legal businesses in Nevada.) The Longhorn Cafe offered steak dinners that were a welcome change from mess hall meals, and there was a little Methodist church that I visited on some Sunday mornings. Apart from that, I found that there was little to do in Tonopah except drink, gamble, or visit Ruby's—none of which appealed to me—so I spent off-duty hours working out with a punching bag in the base gym or seeing a movie in the base theater. Whenever I left the base, it was to hike alone up those rugged mountains behind Tonopah; over the months, I climbed most of the ones in sight.

After sixteen weeks of B-24 training there, our crew joined 420 airmen leaving Tonopah by troop train to go to Hamilton Field, California, just north of the Golden Gate bridge, to be processed for shipment to secret destinations overseas. The Assistant Train Commander was First Lieutenant Marvin C. Seitz, our pilot; his infantry background and regular army attitude invited such responsibilities.

Hamilton Field really impressed me with its beauty. Green lawns and attractive permanent buildings were very different from all the ugly temporary air bases I had seen before, and the green hills and large trees of Marin County were much prettier than the rocky bare mountains of Nevada. When we got leave time from Hamilton, I fell in love with the scenery of the whole San Francisco Bay Area. Like many other soldiers out of the multitude passing through California, I thought, *Someday I'll come back here to live.*

Now the engines of the transport plane droned on, hour after hour, over the empty ocean. Two long rows of passengers looked up whenever the crew door opened to let one of the flight crew go through the cabin to the toilet in the rear. Passengers bantered with passing crew members to relieve boredom.

"Hi, you're the pilot of this bird, aren't you? Now that we're on the way, why don't you tell us where we're going?"

"To the north pole, of course! Don't you see the icebergs in the water down below?"

Before departure, the dispatcher had told us that this would be a long flight, and after six hours we could help ourselves to one of the box lunches stacked in the galley. After three hours, the hungrier passengers began reaching for them, and soon the others followed suit to keep from being left out. I put mine under my seat for a while.

"I'm starved!" said Corporal Gerson, opening his box. "Not gonna wait no six hours to eat!" Benjamin Gerson, armorer and upper-turret gunner, was a carefree twenty-year-old from Brooklyn, a short, beefy man with dark hair, a big, round, grinning face, and a knack for avoiding hard work.

"You may be sorry later on," warned Imhof. "If this turns out to be a long flight, you could get pretty hungry toward the end of it!" Corporal Anton Imhof, radio operator, waist gunner and aerial cameraman, was a serious, brown-haired, twenty-year-old from Saint Louis.

"Yeah," Pieper agreed, "the man said to wait six hours to eat, so the flight'll be twice that long—maybe twelve hours!" Corporal Robert Pieper, flight engineer and waist gunner, was a big, well-built, crewcut blond from Racine, Wisconsin. He looked much younger than twenty-two.

"Well, Gerson," said Herrema, "long as you're eating yours early, tell us what's on the menu?" Corporal Richard Herrema, ball-turret gunner from Grand Rapids, Michigan, was a nice-looking twenty-year-old with square jaws and a short brown crewcut.

Gerson put down a half-eaten sandwich. "We got two sandwiches, tuna salad and ham and cheese. Not exactly kosher, but I'll never tell my rabbi. And one piece of fried chicken, and a paper cup of fruit salad." He took another big bite.

"Bet that's a luxury meal compared to what we'll get at the end of the line," Pieper said.

"Not bad!" said Williams, grinding out his cigarette in an ashtray. "I might take a nibble at mine, too." Corporal Robert Williams, nose-turret gunner, came from Canton, Ohio, where his wife Donna and one child waited for him. His face was thin and old-looking for a man of twenty-five, but the spark in his eye suggested a wild wolf heart.

"I got an idea," said Hill. "Eat one sandwich now as a hold-me-over, then eat the rest later when we're hungry again." Corporal James Hill, tail-turret gunner, was medium size, blond, handsome, and twenty-five. His relaxed manner and quiet good humor put people at ease. His wife Anne was also in Canton, Ohio, with their young daughter, Jackie.

"Good idea, Hill," I said.

While the hours crept by, I thought about the members of my crew as I had come to know them at Tonopah. The bombardier, James, had been my roommate. A friendly kid from Topeka, Kansas, he was the youngest on the crew. He had gone to work in an egg-powdering factory right out of high school. After we tasted powdered eggs overseas, we kidded him frequently about his role in making the stuff.

Our pilot, Seitz, was commanding officer of the crew by his status as first pilot and also by his natural leadership. I admired him as a role model and father figure, though he was only three years older. He had earned his rank in the infantry before he transferred to the Air Corps for pilot training. He carried his shoulders back and his spine straight, making him seem much taller than his five foot nine. I thought he showed unusual maturity and stability for a man of twenty-two. His wife Doris and their baby, Marvin Junior, were in Council Bluffs, Iowa.

Cordell, our copilot, came from Ashville, North Carolina, with a slightly Southern accent to prove it. He wore blue bars instead of gold, symbol of his rank of flight officer, one grade below second lieutenant. About one-fourth of all army flyers graduating then received that lower rank, frequently for no discernable reason. At twenty-three, he was the third oldest member of the crew.

The one I appreciated for his interests, similar to mine, was Hill, the tail gunner. As a serious artist who painted in oils and one who knew a lot about classical music, Hill had won my admiration and respect at Tonopah. But the military segregation of officers and enlisted men prevented us from becoming too friendly.

The other men on our crew, Williams, Herrema, Gerson, Pieper, and Imhof, had relationships with me that were primarily professional, though cordial and friendly. We trusted each other to do our assigned jobs and pull together as a team.

Part of the military tradition was to call everyone by last name only, instead of first name. On our crew as well, it was seldom "Jim," or "Marvin," or "Bob." Using the last name sounded more military and helped to keep our relationships professional enough to maintain respect, particularly between officers and enlisted men. Our sense of teamwork gave us a bonding deeper than any light use of first names could provide.

Confidence in each other, and knowledge that we made a good team together, were two reasons why we felt so little fear as we flew off to war together. True, we felt an underlying anxiety about the possibility of being shot down, killed, or injured, but considered it unlikely. I, for one, felt that destiny and my faith in God would carry me through any ordeal. And at nineteen, I shared the universal invincibility of youth.

Our C-54 Skymaster slowly chased the sun westward over the Pacific, but the sun outran us. It finally set in a blaze of crimson glory ahead, and we flew on through the darkness.

In the lighted cabin, Cordell looked at his watch in disbelief.

"Do you realize that we've been in the air for more than fourteen hours?"

"Gee!" said James. "I didn't know that any plane could fly as long as that!"

"Oh, yes they can," Seitz replied. "With extra fuel tanks in the bomb bay, our B-24s can fly a whole lot longer than that!"

I was looking through the windows at the darkness outside. Suddenly a flash of light caught my eye. "Hey, guys, look out there! I think I see a flashing airport beacon ahead!"

All eyes peered out through the darkness.

"Yes," said Hill, "I can see it, too!"

"We're coming down, now," added Gerson. "Don't you feel your ears popping?"

"Look—lights of a town off the right wing!"

We watched the glowing jewels in the black velvet landscape flow past the right wing as the plane flew south of an island shoreline. Tiny automobile headlights moved slowly along a street close to the beach, reflecting off the white surf. City lights glowed in the distance. When we finally landed, my watch read ten P.M. California time. Our flight had taken fourteen and one-half hours. The engines stopped. We heard portable metal steps being rolled up. The door opened, admitting a rush of warm tropical air. Into the cabin came a sergeant in summer khaki uniform.

"Welcome to Hickam Army Air Base, Honolulu, Hawaii," he said in a business-like monotone.

"Where are all the hula girls with leis?" someone asked.

"I want a good lay!" said Williams. Laughter followed.

"Daddy, are we there yet?" came a falsetto voice from amidships.

"Do you need any bomber crews here?" General laughter.

The sergeant looked stern. "We have a war to fight, men! This plane will remain overnight and leave at 0730 hours tomorrow for the next leg of your trip. You will all spend the night in our transient barracks. Be back in your seats on this plane by 0700 hours tomorrow!

"Next item: We have to bump six passengers here, to make room for a high-priority team leaving tomorrow. The following six men—" he paused to look at a clipboard—"on Lieutenant Seitz's crew—will *not* go tomorrow: Corporal Gerson, Corporal Herrema, Corporal Hill, Corporal Imhof, Corporal Pieper, and Corporal Williams. You men take your bags with you to the barracks, and wait there for a later flight."

What? Leave our enlisted men behind? I don't like the sound of that at all! Our crew is being divided by a mindless stroke of army bureaucracy. Who knows how long this split will last, or what its consequences might be?

I left the plane with an uneasy feeling about this unwanted turn of events and its possible effect on the fate of all of us.

2. Getting There

By seven next morning, all four bomber crews had returned from a brief overnight in the transient barracks and were back in their seats on the C-54 Skymaster. The warm Hawaiian climate made our khaki summer uniforms feel quite comfortable.

The other three crews were complete with ten men each, but our crew was missing all the enlisted men. A high-priority party of six officers now took their seats.

"I sure hate to leave our men stuck in the barracks here," Seitz said.

"Could be worse," said Cordell. "At least they're near Honolulu—a nice place to visit."

"But who knows how long it'll be before our crew's reunited?" I said. "It could really delay our part in the war!"

"Maybe that's not all that bad," James said.

"You don't mean that!" said Cordell.

We roared down the runway to depart Hickam Army Air Base at seven-thirty local time on March 5, bound for our still-secret destination.

This was not my first visit to Hawaii. I had crossed the Pacific Ocean by steamship five times during my childhood in China, as my missionary parents had taken their family on furloughs to America and back. Each trip included a brief visit to Honolulu, most recently in January, 1941, when I was fifteen. The scenery of Honolulu was familiar enough for me to identify its features on this beautiful Hawaiian morning.

I watched the sunlit waters of Pearl Harbor slide by under my cabin window, and thought about all those battleships and cruisers that had been sunk there three years earlier (December 7, 1941). Many of them had since been refloated, repaired, and returned to action against Japan, but some were still down there in the bay below us. *Here's where it all began.*

Thinking of Pearl Harbor reminded me of my recent date with Persis. My memory went back one week to our booth in Auten's Stone Cellar, a favorite hangout for college kids, on El Camino Real near Stanford University. We were sipping "Rum and Coca-Cola" (suggested by the song we heard as we ordered drinks), and listening to a juke box playing Glenn Miller's "In the Mood." A whole week had gone by, but the music in my mind was so vivid, it seemed like only yesterday.

Then she told me, "I watched the attack on Pearl Harbor."

"Really? How did that happen?"

"I was in high school in Honolulu at the time. My Dad, Albert Tangemann, was sent to Hawaii by Hawaiian Pineapple Company in the fall of 1941. Dad leased a gorgeous home in Tantalus Heights, above the old volcano crater called Punch Bowl. From our deck we had a panoramic view of Honolulu, all the way from Diamond Head to Eva Plantation beyond Pearl Harbor."

I lit my pipe to impress her. I had learned to smoke it only a few weeks earlier, believing that it made me look mature and distinguished. "So what happened?"

"December seventh, 1941, was a Sunday morning. Dad was sitting on the deck waiting for Mom, my sisters, and me to get ready to go to church. The night before, my sister Pat and I had gone on our very first dates since arriving in Hawaii. We were planning to meet our dates at church and wear the leis they had given us the night before. I heard the roar of an unusual number of airplanes, but didn't pay much attention to it until Dad called out to Mom, 'Allie, come look at this! They've painted a Japanese rising sun on some of our planes!'

"Dad was peering through his binoculars at the planes streaking in from Diamond Head and flying west at our eye level toward Pearl Harbor. 'They must be practicing war games.'

"Soon the whole family was gathered on the deck, watching, wondering. By then we could see huge clouds of smoke rising in the distance. Mom said, 'If those are practice war games, they sure look real to me!'"

"Gosh, Persis! You mean, you watched the whole show from your house?"

"That's right. We forgot about church and stayed there all morning."

"What happened next?"

"Dad went into the house and turned on the radio to see if the announcer would give any information, but it was just normal Sunday morning programming. He left it on, and we all sat there, listening expectantly. More than a half-hour later, an announcer told people to stay home. Pearl Harbor had been attacked, he said. They would keep us informed as they got more news.

"We all went back on the deck, watching, waiting. It was unreal, like a movie, or a play. I didn't feel any fear; I didn't feel at all. Perhaps it was shock, perhaps ignorance.

"Dad said very little. That was his way. He turned the volume up on the radio so we could hear it outside, and we waited. No more planes flew by our house, not Japanese, not American. Off in the distance, the black smoke of all those burning ships rose higher and higher."

I lit my pipe again, trying to keep my anger under control. "Those bastards!"

"Later that day, the radio announced that all schools and businesses would be closed until further notice. About a month later, my father was appointed Civilian Coordinator of Defense for the Hawaiian Islands. It seems the Army, Navy and Coast Guard were in such competition with one another that a civilian was needed to mediate between them."

"Gosh! What an experience! Thanks for sharing your Pearl Harbor day with me. You made it seem so vivid, it made me feel like I was there to see it too."

By the time this scene had replayed in my mind, we had flown far beyond Pearl Harbor. I looked out the window for anything to indicate our location or direction. There was nothing in sight now but empty ocean. But I did notice that the morning sun was to the left rear of the plane, which meant that we were heading southwest. Southwest from Hawaii would take us right into the South Pacific, just as I expected.

I opened a current copy of **Readers Digest**, and read a few articles. Time crept by on caterpillar feet.

After a while, I noticed that air pressure was increasing on my ears. *We're going down. I wonder where?*

I looked at my watch, and saw that it was only eleven Hawaiian time. *This is a short flight, not yet four hours.*

We flew lower and lower, now just skimming the waves, with no land in sight on either side. *Does the pilot think that this is a seaplane?* Just when it looked like the pilot was dropping the plane into the waves for sure, land appeared on both sides, and we touched down on a tiny island. *What a relief!* The plane rolled to a stop, and the rear door opened.

"Welcome to Johnston Island," said the man in the doorway. "This is a short refueling stop on a short little island. You can grab a quick bite in the mess hall, but be back in thirty minutes."

I joined the crowd going down the stairs to the chow line. The air was noticeably warmer than it had been in Hawaii. We walked to the half-round front of a Quonset hut mess hall beside another Quonset hut terminal building. (A "Quonset hut" was a prefabricated metal building with half-round front and rear walls, and barrel-shaped roof and sides made of corrugated sheet metal over semicircular metal trusses. It was widely used in World War II for rapid erection.)

The mess hall was serving hot french toast and syrup, with hot coffee. It made a welcome meal, quick to eat. I had time to swing through the terminal next door to look at the map on the wall, discovering that Johnston is 830 miles southwest of Honolulu. I looked at what lay ahead. The Marshall Islands and the Gilbert Islands lay astride our probable course, about 1600 miles ahead. The next flight would be a longer one.

I got back on the C-54 with a satisfied feeling that I knew more now than I did before.

We took off again promptly at eleven-thirty A.M. local time, and continued on a southwesterly course. I settled down for a pleasant after-dinner nap.

Four hours later, I woke up thinking about the international date line. Had we crossed it yet? Outside, it was mid-afternoon and bright.

One of the ATC flight crew entered the cabin and headed for the toilet. I noticed that he wore navigator wings, not pilot's. I got up and walked to the rear, and waited for him to emerge.

"You're navigating this C-54, aren't you?" I asked.

"Yes, I am."

"I'm a navigator, too—on a B-24. I notice from the relative position of the sun that we're flying southwest from Johnston, so we'll be crossing the international date line sooner or later. Can you give me an E.T.A. (estimated time of arrival) for it?"

He laughed, "Got it all figured out, haven't you! So why don't you tell me?"

"I don't have any of the data in your log. But you could tell me, as a professional courtesy between navigators."

He looked at his watch. "Just between us navigators, we'll cross it in about fifteen minutes."

I looked at my watch. "That'll be about four-ten Johnston time."

"You got it!" He went forward and out of sight again.

I returned to my seat, filled with pleasure at my new knowledge. I waited until my watch showed four-ten, then said to the other three on my crew, "Hey, guys, we're just crossing the international date line now."

"Oh? How do you know that?" Cordell asked.

"I was talking to the navigator on this flight crew, and he said that we would cross the date line at four-ten Johnston time. Well, it's ten after four right now!"

"How does that date line work?" asked James.

"It's the 180-degree meridian. West of the date line, it's always one day later than east of it. A minute ago, it was four-ten on March fifth, but when we crossed the line, it became four-ten on March sixth."

"Well I'll be darned!" James said. "That's a neat trick."

We settled back to a quiet state of half sleeping, as the droning of the engines lulled our minds into semiconsciousness. My mind floated back again to my recent date with Persis, back to the big band swing music coming from the juke box in Auten's Stone Cellar, as Dick Haymes sang "You'll Never Know" with Harry James' band.

I love swing music and enjoy dancing. It didn't take me long to invite her out on the dance floor. The singer crooned, "You'll never know just how much I love you..." Persis was a good dancer. Her natural rhythm harmonized with mine. "You'll never know just how much I care..." Her soft, sweet presence in my arms was intoxicating.

Soon the music changed to Benny Goodman playing "The One O'Clock Jump." Two sailors and their girls started jitterbugging nearby.

"Can you jitterbug?" Persis asked me.

"A little," I answered, "Would you like to try it?"

"Why not?"

I led her through some slower jitterbug routines. Over our shoulders we could see the sailors really going to town with very fast steps, spinning their partners like tops, and sliding them under their legs and swooping them up again.

"Wow!" I exclaimed, "That's quite a performance!"

She smiled. "Sailors always seem to take the cake when it comes to jitterbugging!"

Soon after came Glenn Miller's signature piece, "Moonlight Serenade," and I drew Persis close to me for slow dancing. My height was almost five feet eleven and she was about five eight, so her chin rested comfortably on my shoulder, and our bodies seemed to fit together nicely, as we swayed gently to the music. *Oh, this is lovely! Let's have slow dancing all night!*

I felt the gentle pressure of her soft breasts against my chest, and the tender touch of her thigh against my foreleg; I smelled the sweet, subtle fragrance of her perfume. So many pleasurable sensations swept through me that I was floating, almost intoxicated. I wanted that moment to last forever, but it ended all too soon.

As we drove back to the Stanford campus, she said, "Let's go by the rose garden near the chapel. It's a beautiful place, and I'd like to share it with you."

"Fine," I replied. "Lead the way."

We parked near the rose garden and walked in. It really was a beautiful place. Each planting plot was filled with well-tended rose bushes of many varieties. Bricks and stones paved the walks in interesting patterns. Distant streetlights cast a soft, romantic glow over the scene.

We strolled around, holding hands, as Persis pointed out one highlight after another. Soon we were at the far end of the garden, in a secluded place. We stood facing each other, holding both hands. Her honey-blonde hair caught the dim light, looking like a halo around her face, emphasizing her innocent expression. Her blue eyes and round cheeks reminded me of Ingrid Bergman, one of my favorite movie stars.

Should I kiss her? Why not? She led me to this secluded place, so she must want us to do something in private. This would be the perfect place to kiss her. No, I can't do it! I never kiss a girl on the first date. It just wouldn't seem right!

Instead, I gave her a brief, tender hug, holding her close for as long as I dared, then released her. The moment of sweet intimacy passed, and we walked back to the car.

Now, as the ATC plane droned westward over the dark Pacific, I remembered that moment again and again, trying to change the ending to include a tender kiss, but somehow my imagination could never quite change history, so the kiss never quite came. It left me feeling incomplete, full of longings unfulfilled.

I have some unfinished business with Persis. When my overseas tour is done, my way home will surely go back through California again. Aha! Another date with Persis.

I came to life some time later with air pressure building up in my ears. We were on our way down to land, but where?

A glance at the windows showed that darkness had come. My watch read seven, Johnston time, but I knew it would be earlier here at the place where we were landing. The air in the cabin grew warmer and more humid.

We descended steadily through the darkness toward the empty sea below. After twenty minutes, runway lights appeared, and our wheels touched down on a "swiss cheese" perforated-metal runway surface with a whining roar from the tires. The plane taxied up to a dark olive-drab tent with a sign reading "Tarawa Operations."

When the cabin door opened, a wave of very warm air rushed in. A man entered, wearing a short-sleeve khaki shirt and no tie.

"Welcome to Tarawa Atoll, in the Gilbert Islands," he said. "This is not your destination, only a rest and refueling stop. A.T.C. aircrews are required to take at least an eight-hour rest stop each day, so you can grab a little sack time too. Supper's available in the flight line mess hall. Then walk to the transient tents and look for an empty cot. You won't need a blanket."

He looked at his watch. "Be back in your seats in exactly eight hours for departure. Don't be late, unless you want to spend the rest of the war on this God-forsaken hunk of coral."

We departed Tarawa promptly at two-thirty local time, climbing back up toward the welcome coolness of cruising altitude. It was a beautiful night. The stars were bright jewels on a black velvet sky.

The stars were my friends. As a navigator, I had learned the names and positions of all the stars bright enough to be useful for celestial navigation. I could look up into the night sky from anywhere on earth and feel at home, because some of my friends would be up there to greet me.

Which ones are up there tonight? Let's see—it's the first week in March, so Orion should be out in all his glory.

Looking out the windows on the left, I saw the bright constellation of Orion overhead, with the three stars forming Orion's sword pointing down to Sirius, that very bright blue star below Orion's feet. Then, as my eyes swept a giant circle clockwise around Orion, I named them in my mind, *Sirius, Procyon, Pollux, Castor, Melinkalinam, Capella.* Coming straight down from Capella, my eyes fell on Betelgeux, the great red star in Orion.

Ah, Betelgeux, if I were the navigator on this bird tonight, I would be shooting you with my trusty A-14 octant, you, and Sirius, and Capella, for a perfect three-star fix. (A "fix" meant fixing the location of the aircraft. The A-14 octant was the sighting device used to measure the altitude of stars, which enabled me to calculate the fix.)

The rectangle of Orion pointed generally south, off the left wing. That confirmed that we were flying westward over the Pacific. Moving to the windows on the right, I recognized Polaris, the north star, just above our right wingtip. That meant that we were heading almost due west, about 265 degrees.

"That settles it," I said to the other crew members. "We are definitely going to the South Pacific. Our heading out of Tarawa is 265 degrees true, and that points straight to the broad expanse of the South Pacific."

"Well," said Seitz, "Navigator Hamilton has just revealed his secret x-ray vision. He sees right through the crew compartment wall to read the compass heading at 265 degrees."

"Maybe he saw it in his crystal ball," laughed James.

"Maybe he dropped his pants and saw two crystal balls!" Cordell chuckled.

"No crystal balls, dummy!" I retorted. "I studied the stars! From the position of Polaris just behind the right wingtip, I calculated that our present heading is about 265 degrees true."

"Well, Hamilton, you're a fountainhead of information!" Cordell said. "A good man to have around!"

"Always tells us more than we need to know," said Seitz.

"Certainly more than we want to hear!" James added.

My mind rejected their comments. "South Pacific, here we come!"

"Well, Smarty, have you also figured out where we're going to, out of all the South Pacific?" asked Cordell.

"I'm a navigator, not a prophet." I snapped.

"It'll be Lackanooki Island, of course!" said James.

The weather did not stay nice very long. The stars disappeared behind thickening clouds.

We settled back to many more hours of listening to the engines drone on and on. The weather got worse, with towering thunderheads lying in wait. The plane ran into rainstorms and turbulence, vibrating and shaking badly as it bounced us up and down in our seats.

We had not experienced much bad weather during our crew training in Nevada, so this rough air was nerve-wracking for me. I began to fear that the plane would fall apart in such shaking. I thought of General Harmon's lost B-24, broken by turbulence, gone forever. Fear and anxiety gripped my stomach.

I was also afraid that the rough weather might make me airsick, as it had done in navigation school the previous year. It would kill me to throw up in front of my crew mates. My fear of airsickness added to my fear that the plane would come apart, so I had a time of combined terror for a while. Finally, I got a grip on myself, and rode out the storm without any disasters.

Later we would learn that rough weather was typical for the equatorial region; the heat and humidity led to unstable air, thunderstorms, violent turbulence and rain. Flying in the South Pacific was no picnic. The weather could be a more deadly enemy than the Japanese.

Daylight dawned through the clouds after we had flown four hours. The weather seemed less threatening by the light of day. At least the pilot could see some of the thunderheads and fly around them. In spite of a queasy stomach, I finally ate one of the box lunches from Tarawa–not nearly as nice as the ones from California.

Hours later, our plane began to descend. Our ears told us so, as we felt the air pressure changing. Once again we flew low enough to skim the waves, but this time I saw that we were approaching a large piece of land with tree-covered mountains and jungle.

Quite a big island.

We approached an airport hacked out of the jungle on the south side, and landed noisily on another "swiss-cheese" perforated-metal runway.

"Marston matting," I told Seitz, "that's what they call this perforated-metal runway surface that makes the tires whine. Our engineers use it to build quick new runways all over the world."

"How did you learn that?"

"I asked about it at Tarawa."

As we taxied toward the flight line tents, I looked at my watch. This third leg had been nearly thirteen hours. We had left California nearly forty-three hours ago.

Looking out the window again, I saw the burned-out hulks of of several Japanese aircraft littering the fringe of the taxiway. They had been pushed into the edge of the jungle.

"Look at those wrecks," I said to James. "This place must have been the scene of recent fighting."

"Yeah," he answered, "but look out the window on the other side! There's a whole row of B-24s!"

I looked eagerly out the far side windows. Sure enough! There stood a long row of big silver airplanes—B-24 Liberators! The sight gave me a sudden thrill, a rush of adrenalin.

"Oh, man!" I said. "Let's jump into a B-24 and fly our first combat mission!"

"I'm ready now," Cordell said. "Let's go!"

"We can't," said Seitz, "we don't have a full crew."

Our plane came to a halt. The rear door opened again, and another rush of hot, humid air came in. A sergeant and two privates entered the cabin. Their bright, round, shoulder-patches read "5th Air Force."

"Well, men, this is the end of the line," said the sergeant. "You made it to your secret destination in time for lunch. Welcome to the island of Biak in the Dutch East Indies."

He looked at his watch. "You can reset your watches to the local time: it's twelve-fifteen, fourteen hours ahead of New York.

"My two helpers here will release the snaps on your baggage tie-downs while you respond to my roll call, and then you can each grab your own bags and follow me into the Operations tent."

I had mixed feelings as I waited to pick up my bags. On one hand, I felt a sense of completion; we had arrived in the war zone in the South Pacific. We were now poised at last to strike the enemy as we had been trained to do. And the sight of those wonderful, shiny, familiar B-24s on the flight line told me that this was just the place to do it.

But on the other hand, I was keenly aware of more unknowns. First of all, where were we? Where in the world is the island of Biak? And what adventures awaited us in this strange, hot, jungle airbase? In spite of the heat and fatigue, I was filled with an air of anticipation and excitement as I wondered what would come next.

There were also emotions other than excitement. We were going into mortal combat. Underlying the excitement was an unexpressed dread of being shot up or killed, but that was something we never talked about. After all, we were real men now, even as teen-agers, and "real men never show fear!" Myth or not, we believed it. A little swagger covered up a lot of fear.

3. Sidetracked

We were hot, sweaty men in soiled khaki uniforms when we got off the C-54 cargo plane in the noonday heat of the jungle. Walking past a wrecked Japanese airplane, we left the long row of silver B-24s on the flight line behind us, and carried our bags toward the Flight Operations tent on Biak.

We crowded into the Operations tent, and saw a plywood counter with a large round Fifth Air Force logo on it. The four pilots, leaders of the four crews, stepped up to the counter. Behind the counter, a sergeant said, "Looks like a planeload of fresh meat!"

"We won't stay fresh very long in this heat," Seitz said. "Is it always this hot here?"

"Welcome to the Fifth Air Force, sir," the sergeant replied. "This is just a normal day for the south Pacific."

"We'll feel better when we can get out of these sweaty uniforms," another pilot said. "We've been riding that cargo crate forty hours in the air, plus twenty hours of stops en route."

"Sir, this is a combat base, not a pleasure resort. But we do have trucks to take your crews to transient housing, where you'll find empty cots. Chow call is going on now. Soon as you get comfortable, you can walk to the nearest mess hall for lunch. You're free to hit the sack until orientation in the briefing tent at 0900 hours tomorrow."

After a cold shower and a change of khakis, we went to the mess hall for lunch. There we sat across a table from some tanned flyers with Fifth Air Force patches on their shoulders. My skin suddenly looked very pale compared to theirs.

"I see you guys are with the Fifth Air Force," Seitz said. "What kind of planes do you fly?"

"B-24s," said the dark-haired pilot across the table.

"We're in B-24s, too, fresh from the states."

The pilot chuckled. "Fresh meat."

"That's what they seem to call us. How many combat missions have you flown?"

"Yesterday's mission makes fourteen."

Seitz put down his fork. "Where'd you go yesterday?"

"Zamboanga. MacArthur's men are about to invade the big island of Mindanao, and we bombed the airfields on the Zamboanga Peninsula to keep Jap airplanes off their backs."

"How'd it go?" I asked.

"Great! We laid a beautiful pattern of hits all over those runways. The B-24s from the Thirteenth Air Force hit the target first, and then we came along and finished the job. The Thirteenth think they're hot stuff, but the Fifth Air Force is the one you read about in the papers. We're the best in the Pacific!"

"You don't suppose the Fifth's publicity staff has anything to do with that news coverage, do you?" Cordell asked.

"Course not. We're just hot news."

I gazed in awe at these veteran flyers.

Fourteen combat missions! Fifth Air Force! Zamboanga! It sounded wonderfully adventuresome and romantic. I felt intoxicated to be near them.

We were awakened soon after sunrise the next morning by the overpowering roar of many B-24s screaming down the runway, one after another, as they took off for their morning mission. It was an exciting sound to me. I sat up in my cot and looked around the large transient housing tent, where twenty officers were crowded in. The others were beginning to stir.

"Where do you suppose they're going today?" I asked.

"Back to Zamboanga again," Seitz answered. "Last night I spent a little time at Operations, and heard about it."

"But they hit those airfields already. Why go back today?"

"They're after some Jap warehouses this time."

Never before had I been that close to a real combat mission. Just hearing them take off made my day!

We gathered in the briefing tent before nine in the morning. After a good night's sleep, my spirits were soaring with the exciting thought of manning one of the beautiful B-24s outside to join the Fifth Air Force on their next combat mission to Zamboanga. But first we had to get our crew together. We could not fly anywhere without our enlisted crewmen, who were still at Hickam, as far as we knew.

Promptly at nine, three men entered the tent, two captains and a sergeant. The sergeant called loudly, "Group, at-tensh-HUT!" We all jumped to our feet.

"At ease, men, be seated," one of the officers said. "I'm Captain Griffin from Fifth Bomber Command Personnel Section, here to brief you on where you are and what's happenening to you. First, we need to find out who's here. Let's simplify the roll call. You aircrew commanders look around the room and make sure your crew is all present. I'll just call your names and get your report for the whole crew."

The sergeant passed a roster clipboard to the captain.

"Second Lieutenant Caris T. Hooten, is your crew all here?"

"Yes, sir," Hooten answered.

"Second Lieutenant Lockwood B. Scoggin, is your crew here?"

"All present except Corporal O'Brien, our tail gunner. Oh, there he is now, just coming into the tent."

"Your tail gunner is last over the target, and last into the tent," said the Captain. "Is he last in the chow line, too?"

"No sir, he's pretty prompt at chow." General laughter.

"Second Lieutenant Duane D. Stanley, is your crew here?"

"Yes, sir."

"First Lieutenant Marvin C. Seitz, is your crew present?"

"All officers are present, but our six enlisted men are still back at Hickam, sir."

"See me about that later, Lieutenant; it could be a problem. Meanwhile, let's get on with the briefing.

"Biak is an island north of New Guinea in the Netherlands East Indies." He pointed to it on a hanging map. "It's located only one degree south of the equator. That gives it this hot, wet, jungle climate you now enjoy. Daytime highs range from 100 to 110, but it cools down to 90 at night. Humidity is high all the time, of course, because it rains a lot. The heat and humidity can make you sick, so I brought our flight surgeon, Captain Nussbaum, to brief you on jungle medicine. Go to it, Doc!"

A plump Captain Nussbaum sat down on top of the desk with his feet dangling. He put on a very serious expression.

"Jungle health and medicine is serious business, men. Here's the first rule to remember: FLIES SPREAD DISEASE—keep yours buttoned up!" Groans mixed with laughter followed.

"Seriously, men, the jungle is full of bugs, including lots of mosquitos. Mosquito bites can give you malaria, which causes recurring chills and fever. We fight malaria with a drug called atabrine, a yellow pill that looks like this."

He fished in his shirt pocket for a big yellow pill, which he held aloft between his thumb and forefinger.

"You will take one of these atabrine pills in the mess hall chow line every day for the rest of your stay overseas. Atabrine won't keep the mosquitos from biting you, but it will repress the symptoms of malaria, so you can go on functioning as long as you take it.

"Atabrine is also a yellow dye, and it gradually dyes your skin yellow. When you look at all the dark tans on the jungle veterans around you, you see a color that's half atabrine and half suntan. You may envy the tan, but don't try to get it all at once! This tropical sun is strong enough to kill you, so don't over-expose your pale stateside bodies.

"There's another pill you also need to take with your meals—salt. The jungle heat causes so much sweating, it depletes your body salt. To replenish it, we take salt pills that look like this." He held up a big white pill for us to see.

"You'll find a bowl of salt pills in every chow line beside the other bowl of atabrine pills. You need to take from one to four salt pills every day, depending on how much sweating you do.

"Later on we'll brief you on tropical diseases like cholera, dysentery, dengue fever, malaria, and "creeping crud" fungus. But for now, just remember to take atabrine and salt pills every day." He slid off the table top.

"Thank you, Doc," said Captain Griffin. "Back to the briefing. Biak is forty-six miles long and twenty-eight wide, with a mountain spine and jungle lowlands. The Japs occupied it until ten months ago, when General MacArthur's troops invaded. Dutch and Australian jungle troops did the dirty work, supported by planes from the Fifth and Thirteenth Air Forces. There are still some Jap defenders trying to survive in the hills above us, but at this point we usually leave each other alone and try to get on with the war.

"Biak is in Dutch territory. Army policy requires that all Post Exchanges use the money of the host country where the base is located, so when you go to the P.X. here, you'll find that they won't accept American money. You have to change it into Dutch guilders first. That'll give you a chance to start your short snorter with some Dutch money. What's a short snorter? Ask the local airmen.

"Biak is home base for the Fifth Air Force, which commands three fighter groups and six bomber groups. Each group has three or four squadrons. That's more airpower than you can fit into one island, so we have some of those groups operating out of other islands.

"Let me brief you on the other air forces in the Pacific. There's the Thirteenth Air Force, based on Morotai. It's not as big as the Fifth, and of course we think it's not as good. The Thirteenth also has its bomber and fighter groups operating out of several different islands. Both the Fifth and Thirteenth Air Forces are part of the Far East Air Forces, commanded by Lieutenant General George Kenney. General Kenney used to command the Fifth Air Force, and still favors us when he can. He makes sure we get credit for all the strikes we fly, and then some.

"There's also the Seventh Air Force, flying B-24s from islands north of us, covering the central Pacific under Admiral Halsey's naval command. They're in a separate world from us, like the Twentieth Air Force that flies B-29s to Tokyo.

"Now, where do you fit into this picture? How many of you are ready to climb into those shiny new planes outside, and start flying combat missions with us today?"

Every man in the tent put his hand up.

"Glad to see that you're all eager beavers, but I've got news for you. That's not going to happen, at least, not yet."

A groan of disappointment filled the tent.

"General Kenney's Far East Air Forces also includes the Combat Replacement and Training Center at Nadzab, New Guinea. It's located in the eastern half of New Guinea, right here–," he pointed on the map, "in Australian territory, near the port of Lae. Nadzab's where you'll go next, for a few more weeks of combat training, before you join a front-line air force."

There was another deep groan of disappointment.

"Take it easy, men; this is for your own good. We know you're well-trained in handling the B-24, but how much do you know about combat? In the early years of the war, we rushed aircrews straight into front-line units, and let them learn combat the hard way. We lost a lot of men and planes in the process. Last year we created the Combat Replacement and Training Center, and brought together combat veterans of all types to teach new crews how to fly in combat before they join a front-line unit. Now we lose fewer men and planes than ever before."

I began to feel a little better about getting sidetracked to another training unit.

"Any questions?" asked Captain Griffin.

"Yes, sir," I said, standing up. "How do we get to Nadzab, and when do we go?"

"Nadzab will send its own C-47 cargo planes to pick you up

here when they're ready. Maybe this afternoon, tomorrow, or the next day. Aircraft commanders are responsible for checking with Operations. Before each meal's a good time, then spread the word to your crew. Chow call's an easy place to find 'em."

"What will the rest of us do until then?" I asked.

"Anything you want—write letters, play volleyball, go to the beach. Any more questions?"

Seitz stood up. "Our crew has a problem, sir. Our six enlisted men are still back at Hickam. They were bumped from the flight. What'll we do?"

"Check with Operations frequently for word on their arrival. If they delay too long, your crew will be disbanded; you'll be individual replacements to fill vacancies in other crews. Any more questions?" Seitz sat down; no one moved.

The sergeant stepped forward. "Group, at-tensh-HUT!" We rose to our feet again. "Dis-missed!" They left.

"Hey, that's bad news!" I said. "If our crewmen don't get here soon, our crew might be broken up!"

"I sure don't like the sound of that!" Sietz shook his head.

James scowled. "After training together all that time, we want a chance to fly together!"

Seitz went to Operations to check on when our crewmen might arrive. The rest of us were worried, but soon realized that we could not help the situation by just standing there. Cordell headed for the beach, while James and I found a volleyball game starting in the transient housing area, and joined it. We stripped down to our shorts to let the morning sun toast our pale skin, and played for an hour or more. By then we were not just toasted, we were baked– tropical sunshine, hot air and exercise made us red as boiled lobsters.

The cold-water outdoor shower felt good when the weather was so hot. After showering, I headed back to my cot to write a few letters. I found the leather writing kit my girl friend Sandy gave me when I graduated from Navigation School. In it was the fancy stationary engraved "Lieutenant Robert H. Hamilton," a graduation gift from another girl friend, Pauline. Using their gifts brought warm memories of both.

I made a mental list of letters to write to family and friends. I had written them all from Tonopah not long ago, but now I wanted to contact them again. In unfamiliar settings, I needed the reassurance to be gained by reaching out to people I knew.

Seitz came by with word that our crewmen would not be arriving this afternoon, and that it was time for mid-day chow call.

After lunch, I wrote to Dad, pastor of the Little Brick Presbyterian Church in Knoxville, Tennessee, telling him that I had arrived overseas at a Pacific location which I was not permitted to reveal, but I was glad to be in the war zone at last. I told him not to worry about me, because I would be training for combat during the next month. And I told him to give my love to Mother and all the family.

Not a bad letter. I'll use it as a model for some letters to my friends.

First I wrote a letter to the girl who had given me this stationary, Pauline Bowles, in Galesburg, Illinois. I had met her as a pre-cadet army student in the College Training Detachment at Knox College in Galesburg. Pauline and I had been writing for more than a year. I felt quite tender toward her, though not overly romantic, so I kept the tone fairly light.

Next, I wrote another letter to "Sandy," Evelyn Sanders, of Pine Bluff, Arkansas, whom I had dated for several months in 1944 as a navigation cadet at Selman Field near Monroe, Louisiana. I added some romantic touches to this letter, because I still felt that Sandy was the real love of my life, though I hadn't seen her for more than half a year.

Then I wrote another letter to Persis at Stanford University. *Keep it light. You've only had one date with Persis, so just be friendly.* (Only one date–but her memory haunts me still.)

Finally, I wrote other versions of the letter to several other pen pals who had written me in recent months: Harold Giedt, my high school roommate at Shanghai American School, and Bob Worth, my cousin and roommate at Davidson College, and Edith

Phillips, girl friend of my buddy Robert Walker from Atlanta; she seemed to enjoy writing to me also.

Composing those letters, I felt strong bonds of friendship connecting me with many supportive, loving people. It gave me a feeling of elation, contentment, and peace. I felt spiritually connected with them all, rather like bamboo trees or clumps of grass, which reach out with long lateral roots under the surface to connect themselves with other clumps of grass or bamboo trees. The same life juices flow through them all.

I thought of psychologist Carl Jung's description of spiritual life as a rhizome, or root system, connecting the individual unconscious mind in each person with similar minds in others, thus forming the "collective unconscious" of the human race. Jung seemed to equate God with this collective unconscious. I was not sure that I agreed with him about God and the whole human race, but as for friendship and love with my own family and friends, I felt very connected indeed.

Everyone knew that incoming mail was important to the morale of soldiers, and Uncle Sam went to great lengths to keep it flowing. Mail call was more important than chow call. What I had not realized before, though, was that outgoing mail was just as important as the incoming. The act of writing to my special people strengthened me.

Later, at supper, I asked a Fifth Air Force pilot what a "short snorter" was.

"It's a roll of paper money, with samples of money from every place you've visited," he answered. "Look at mine."

He took a roll of bills out of his pocket. As he unrolled it, I saw different kinds of money represented, fastened end-to-end with Scotch tape. There were signatures on some of the bills.

"You ask your friends to sign it," he said, "and strangers, too, if you meet famous people. It's a souvenir of the places you've been and the people you've met."

"I like that," I said. "Thanks a lot! I'm going to start one right away."

And I did, with a trip to the P.X. to change some American dollars into Dutch guilders. My own short snorter began with a dollar taped to a guilder. Then I remembered that I had some Chinese money in my writing kit, brought back from China in 1941, and added it on.

I'll add to this short snorter with every place I visit. What a wonderful souvenir!

The roar of powerful warbirds screaming down the runway was our wake-up call again the next morning. The sound was still exciting to me, but less romantic. I saw that this was a daily event, so it would soon become as routine and humdrum as chow call.

After breakfast, we started playing volleyball at the court nearby. We peeled off our shirts and trousers for action. This time, all four of the officers on our crew participated. No enlisted men were here, of course; the army segregated us on the playing field as well as in our quarters. There was another volleyball court near the enlisted men's transient housing.

After we had been playing for an hour, I was hot, tired and careless. I was playing at the center net position when the center on the opposing team jumped up, reached over the net, and slammed the ball down toward me. The full force of the ball struck the end of my little finger.

"Ow!" I yelled, and fell to the ground. The game stopped, and players started gathering around my writhing body.

"What happened?" asked Seitz, coming over to see.

"I don't know," I moaned, "but it hurts like crazy! That guy just broke my finger."

"Hey, it wasn't my fault," said the man who slammed it. "You caught the ball wrong!"

"Let's see what it looks like," said Seitz, gently pulling my wounded right hand out of the protective clutch of my left. The little fingertip was bent over backward at an odd angle.

"Gosh," said James, "what a crooked joint!"

Seitz released my hand. "I think you'd better get over to the medics, and have that finger set. Can you walk?"

"Of course he can walk!" said the perpetrator. "It's not that serious! He's just putting on an act!"

"Shut up!" said Seitz. "Show a little sympathy for my wounded crew member." He pulled on my good left hand to help me up from the ground.

"Wounded in my first week overseas!" I said, pulling on my shirt and trousers. "Disgusting!"

"Some people are killed in their first week overseas," my opponent taunted. "Consider yourself lucky."

"Thanks a lot!" I exclaimed, glaring at him. "Who pulled your chain to bring out such a big flush?"

"Go to hell!" he retorted.

I walked to the mess hall to ask the way to medical aid.

"Right down the road that way. Look for the tent with a red cross sign in front of it."

I found it, walked in, and joined the sick call waiting line. After a half-hour wait, I got a chance to show my pitiful finger to a medic.

"Looks broke," said the corporal. "Lemme get the Doc for that one." He went through a curtain wall, and came back with a captain wearing flight surgeon wings, who took my hand in his.

"It's not bleeding, and the skin's not broken, so we can't give you the Purple Heart," he said, "but we can straighten it, and tape it to a splint until it sets."

He bent it back straight, which made me jump out of my seat with pain, and then wrapped it in a gauze bandage, placed it between two wooden tongue depressors for splints, and held them in place with adhesive tape.

"There," he said, "just keep it out of mischief for a week or two, and it ought to be good as new."

As I walked back to transient housing, I was glad that I had written all those letters before this accident. Writing would be awkward with a splinted finger on my right hand.

Next morning, March 10, Seitz went to Operations before breakfast and returned with the news that a C-47 was on its way here from Nadzab. Our crew would leave on it at 12:30.

"Before our crewmen show up?" Cordell asked.

"They're sending us on ahead, to wait for them at Nadzab."

After lunch, we were in a cluster of men waiting at the airstrip for the C-47 pilots to show up and fly us to Nadzab. When they appeared, we followed them over to a twin-engine cargo plane, and climbed on board.

From Biak to Nadzab was a five hour flight in a C-47. New Guinea is a very large island, 1700 miles long and 530 miles wide, and this trip covered half its length. The weather was rough, with tropical thunderstorms and bumpy flying, and soon I started feeling queasy again.

Our plane flew southeast through the lush green Taritatu River valley in western New Guinea past the Japanese base at Wewak, then picked our way between high mountain ranges, to drop down into the broad Markham River Valley at sunset, and land on a perforated metal runway at Nadzab Army Air Base.

We followed the C-47 crew into the Operations tent. The pilot laid a report on the counter. "Here's another planeload of fresh meat from Biak."

The sergeant behind the counter turned to the newcomers. "Welcome to Nadzab. Our local time is an hour ahead of Biak, so reset your watches."

Soon we got trucked to transient housing, had a late supper in the mess hall, and went to our cots. We noticed that the air was cooler and dryer here.

"This weather is a pleasant change from Biak," said Seitz. "I think a blanket will feel comfortable tonight."

"Yeah," James said, "that breeze sure feels good!"

"But we're still in transient housing," Cordell said. "We're crowded into a big tent with all these other officers."

"That won't change until we get our crew together," Seitz said, "and if it doesn't happen soon, we may never fly together."

Next morning we gathered in a classroom tent with other newly-arrived trainees, crews for many different kinds of warplanes. Empty bomb crates were set out in rows to serve as our seats. Promptly at eight, two officers walked in.

"Attensh-HUT!" called the lieutenant.

"At ease, men, be seated." said the major, a lean, sun-tanned man with a dark mustache. "I'm Major Hundt, Director of Training, here to brief you on our program.

"Nadzab is the Far East Air Forces Combat Replacement and Training Center. You will be with us for combat training until you are needed as replacements by a combat group in the Fifth or the Thirteenth Air Force. Our curriculum is set up for four weeks of combat training, but you may be with us shorter or longer, depending on when a combat group calls for you.

"We have ten different courses in Combat Ground School, each class taught by combat veterans who will share their special knowledge with you.

"We also have three sections of Combat Flight Training here: Fighters, Bombers, and Troop Carriers.

"Fighter pilots will learn dive-bombing, strafing, and mast-head bombing, where you attack a Jap warship at 75-foot altitude. We built a full-scale replica of a Jap cruiser on the Markham Valley floor for you to attack. We also set up a conventional bombing range on an empty coral atoll east of Lae for you to dive-bomb and strafe.

"Fighter jocks will also be taught to intercept bombers. Since the Japs haven't sent us any of their bombers lately, we use our own. Every time we send our B-24 heavy bombers out on a mission, we expect our fighters to scramble and intercept them on their return trip, to engage them in mock combat."

The words "mock combat" brought snickers, chuckles and groans from the listeners.

"B-25 medium bomber and A-20 light bomber crews will

also learn masthead bombing, attacking the mock Jap warship."

I was growing uncomfortable with the thought that we were merely in another training program. I raised my hand, and asked, "What about attacking the enemy, sir?"

"Just getting to that, Lieutenant," he replied. "There are two major concentrations of Jap forces near here: a big army base at Wewak, on the north coast of New Guinea, and a combined army-navy fortress at Rabaul on New Britain Island. We attack one or the other every day, and sometimes both. You will all go on those missions before you leave for your front-line unit."

I began to feel better about being here. Combat after all!

"B-24 crews will get bombing practice on real missions over Wewak or Rabaul. You will practice tight formation flying too, because tight formations are so important in combat. Don't leave enough room for fighters to fly through your formation!

"The Japs used to defend both Wewak and Rabaul with fighter aircraft as well as flak (anti-aircraft fire), but our constant attacks have reduced their resources to the point that we never see fighters, now, and seldom draw much flak.

"Last but not least, the Troop Carrier crews. You guys will train by flying C-47s and C-46s all over this part of the South Pacific, carrying our mail and cargo as well as personnel to wherever they're needed. Be nice to our Troop Carrier trainees, men; they're the ones who'll fly you to your combat unit."

We'll never fly to a combat unit until we get our crew together! Where are those darn enlisted men now? Have they left Hawaii yet? Will they get here in time to save our crew from being disbanded? Oh, God, let it happen!

4. Ready for Combat

Our anxiety increased during the next few days as we four officers waited for our enlisted crewmen to arrive in Nadzab. The more threatened our crew status became, the more intense our crew loyalty. We really wanted to fly combat together!

Three times each day, Seitz went to Group Operations to check on news of our crewmen, only to be disappointed. Each day he went to Communications, hoping to send tracer messages to locate his men, only to learn that the backlog of priority traffic precluded much hope of sending the kind of messages we needed.

"Let's get started in ground school classes," I said to the other three officers. "At least it'll take our minds off worrying about when they'll get here."

"I already asked for that," Seitz said. "The army doesn't want to enroll us until our crew is complete."

James looked indignant. "That's just stupid! We still need the training, whether we go as individual replacements or as a crew!"

"Seitz, go back and explain that to 'em!" Cordell demanded. "Ask 'em to reconsider! Don't take no for an answer!"

Seitz went off to pursue that request, and later returned with a smiling face.

"I went straight to Major Hundt, Director of Training. He saw the light and put us into ground school, beginning tomorrow!"

Our classes included jungle health, combat flight operations, bomb strike photography and photo interpretation, personal equipment for combat, and weather in the south Pacific.

The south Pacific weather class brought me new anxiety, because the instructor said that rough weather was typical of the whole equatorial region. From eight degrees north of the equator to eight degrees south, a belt a thousand miles wide and stretching around the world, the equatorial heat and humidity generated unstable air that made stormy weather much more common there than in regions farther away, whether north or south. There hurricanes were born.

The fact that rough weather was so common here worried me, because I had a history of motion sickness. As a child when my parents were stationed in China, I had been very seasick on my first four trips across the Pacific by ship, although my fifth trip across did not make me sick at all. My friends told me that I had finally "gotten my sea legs."

Again, in Navigation School at Selman Field, Louisiana, in the summer of 1944, I had been airsick on my first fifteen student navigation missions. My instructors called me in to "wash me out" for airsickness, but I asked for one more chance. I told them that I had "gotten my sea legs" on my fifth ocean voyage, and I hoped to "get my air legs" on my next flight.

It worked. On my next mission, I did not throw up at all. On all subsequent flights, I was able to work effectively in spite of feeling queasy occasionally, when the ride got rough.

But would I be able to work well if the ride turned out to be rough every time? I had noticed my queasy feeling as a passenger on both flights near the equator, from Tarawa to Biak, and from Biak to Nadzab. Would the tension of combat help to suppress my latent motion sickness, or make it worse? Had I come this far in my preparation, only to fail the test of south Pacific weather? *Absolutely not—(I hope).*

On March 16, our enlisted crewmen finally arrived, carrying their duffel bags. They found us in the evening chow line, and reported to Seitz.

"Am I ever glad to see you guys!" Seitz said. "How'd you get here?"

"A.T.C. finally put us on a plane out of Hickam," Pieper said.

"It was a C-87, a converted B-24 with seats instead of bomber gear," Imhof added.

Herrema grinned. "It flew to Johnston, then Tarawa, then Biak."

"That's the same route our C-54 took," I said.

Hill set down his duffel bag. "Then today, a C-47 brought us here from Biak."

"We were really sweating you out," Seitz said, "because our crew has to be complete before we can fly here. If you guys hadn't come in time, our crew would have been broken up. We would have all been individual replacements to fill vacancies on other crews."

"That's awful!" said Williams. "After we've trained together for so long, we ought to fly together in combat!"

"And now we can," I said. "The crew's together again!"

"Well, not quite all together," Pieper said. "Didn't you notice? Gerson is missing."

"What?" Cordell snapped, "Where's Gerson?"

"He was still in the hospital at Hickam when we left," Hill said. "He came down with a heavy dose of clapp. They've been giving him shots of penicillin every four hours."

Williams frowned. "He wouldn't use a rubber. I warned him, but he wouldn't listen."

"So Gerson got gonorrhea!" I said.

"I'll kick his butt, the stupid butt-head!" James screamed. "Because of him, our crew is still not ready to fly!"

"Oh, no!" Pieper groaned, "is that true? Is our crew status still in doubt?"

"I'll check into that right away," Seitz said, "but I'm afraid we're still vulnerable. Meanwhile, let's have some chow, and you guys plan to join us for ground school tomorrow."

Next day at ground school, Seitz asked the men about how long Gerson had been treated, and when he would be released. They said that Gerson was to be released the very day they left, but not in time for him to make their flight.

"He should be along on the next flight," Pieper said. "We

expected him to get to Biak before we left there for Nadzab, but he didn't make it before our C-47 left yesterday."

"I'm going to see Major Hundt again," Seitz said. "Maybe I can talk him into saving our crew status until Gerson comes, since he's probably on his way."

Later Seitz returned, looking grim. At the next class break, the crew gathered around.

"Major Hundt was about to issue the order to disband our crew today," Seitz said. "When I told him that Gerson should be on his way already, he agreed to give us two more days."

Imhof looked relieved. "Tomorrow and Monday?"

"No. Today and tomorrow. If he's not here by tomorrow night, our crew will be dead meat Monday morning."

Seitz's last sentence was almost drowned out by the roar of powerful aircraft engines and propellers. This happened often in ground school, as many kinds of bombers and fighters took off on various missions. There's a unique high-pitch whine to the sound of big steel propellers revving up, and it filled me with excitement every time. It's a special whine—very different from the ear-piercing "whoosh!" of jets today. It was a classic World War II sound. It made me think of the chorus of a popular Air Corps marching song:

> "When you hear the motors roaring,
> And the steel props start to whine,
> You can bet the Army Air Corps
> Is along the firing line!"

Except for the missing Gerson, we were all focused on one goal, hoping that *we* would be on the next warplane to fly "along the firing line."

Gerson did not arrive that evening on the last plane from Biak. The next day was Sunday, our final day of grace. We attended ground school classes as usual, since the war went on seven days a week We grew more anxious as the day wore on without any sign of Gerson. Our crew seemed to be doomed.

Evening chow call came, and our crew was standing in the chow line when a jeep drove up to the mess hall. A Military Policeman with a pistol on his belt got out, calling, "First Lieutenant Marvin Seitz! Are you here?"

"Over here!" Seitz answered, stepping forward.

"Sir, I have orders to deliver a prisoner to your custody, a Corporal Benjamin Gerson."

"Where is he?"

"In the jeep. Guard, bring the prisoner here!"

Another M.P. climbed out of the jeep, pulling a sweaty, rumpled Gerson with him. They walked over to Seitz.

"Here he is, sir. Sign this release document, please."

Seitz signed the clipboard. The two M.P.'s saluted and left. The whole crew crowded around Seitz and Gerson expectantly.

Seitz looked grim. "Well, Corporal, why are you under guard? Where HAVE you been?"

Gerson wiped the sweat off his face with a pudgy hand. "The other guys had flown away by the time I got out o' the hospital. A.T.C. told me to come back next morning for my flight, but I didn't make it. Drank too much beer, slept late. Then the M.P.s came looking for me. They took me to a M.P. captain—he asked why I missed my flight. I said, 'Why hurry to get into combat? I like it fine here in Hawaii.' He chewed my ass out, and growled, 'My M.P.s will put you on the next flight out, under guard!' And they did. Every stop, M.P.s met the plane–took me off, put me on rough-like. They make me feel like garbage!"

"Good," Seitz said, "you ARE garbage! Where's your sense of responsibility? Where's your loyalty to the crew? Your actions almost cost us our status as a crew! If you hadn't arrived tonight, our crew would've been disbanded tomorrow. We'd only be replacements to fill vacancies on other crews. Is that what you want? Don't you care who you fly with? If you want to fly with me, buster, straighten up and fly right!"

Seitz' eyes were cold grey steel fixed on Gerson's flushed face. "I'm taking you back as a crew member for one reason only–I need to have a complete crew tonight. But you are strictly on probation with me. If you want to stay on my crew, you'll have to earn a place by acting responsibly. Is that clear?"

Gerson saluted. "Yes, SIR!"

"Go get some chow. The boys'll show you where to bunk. Be at ground school tomorrow without fail!"

Next morning I got up at reveille with some news. "Guess what, guys–today's my birthday."

Seitz rubbed his eyes and sat up. "Well, happy birthday! How old are you today?"

"Twenty," I answered. "I was born on March 19, 1925, in China."

"China?" Cordell asked. "Were you born with slant eyes? Are you a Chink?"

I put on my khaki shirt. "If a cat had kittens in an oven, would they be biscuits?"

"Oh, yeah, I remember," James said, "your parents were missionaries in China."

"You got it."

Seitz stepped into his khaki trousers. "So, Hamilton's no longer a teenager! Now we have only one teenage officer left on my crew."

"But not for long!" James said. "I'll turn twenty in May."

Cordell used his falsetto voice, "We're all getting so old, I don't know what we'll do!"

"You get one wish for a birthday present," Seitz said. "What'll you wish for?"

"To fly a combat mission tomorrow."

"Congratulations!" Seitz said. "You just got your wish! You'll fly in combat tomorrow!"

"Really?" asked James, "We're scheduled so soon?"

"You're kidding!" Cordell said. "Our crew just got completed last night."

Seitz grinned knowingly. "Not our crew–just Hamilton. Another crew has a sick navigator, and he's the replacement. Your pilot will be Lieutenant Morgan. Briefing tonight at seven."

"Wonderful! That's the best birthday present I ever got!"

Classes that day took on a fresh urgency, as I tried to absorb everything I could before tomorrow's mission. When seven came, I was in the briefing tent with Lieutenant Morgan's crew, seated on empty bomb-fin crates for stools, part of a crowd of a hundred and thirty men involved in tomorrow's mission. We had pencils and scratch pads ready in our laps, eager to take notes.

At the front of the tent was a curtained structure which looked like a large window with draw drapes in front of it. A spotlight on a tent pole illuminated the closed drapes. We looked at it expectantly, like theater-goers waiting for the curtains to part.

Major Layhee, Director of Operations, entered and strode to the front. Captain Hadley, Intelligence Officer, called loudly, "Group, at-tensh-HUT!" Everyone stood up.

"At ease, men; be seated," said the Major. "Captain, unveil the targets for tomorrow."

Captain Hadley went to the end of the drapery and pulled the cord. Dramatically, the curtains parted, revealing two large maps, one labeled "Rabaul" and the other "Wewak." Red cardboard arrows pointed to targets on each map.

The major opened a folded sheet of paper, and began to read: "Field Order Number 74. This command is directed to strike both Rabaul and Wewak on 20 March 1945. Targets will be Japanese underground shelters and supply dumps near Rabaul, and troop staging areas on the west bank of the But River in the Wewak area.

"The First Composite Bomb Group, using six B-24 heavy bombers, will bomb the Rambau Range underground structures at 828-342 on the Rabaul map. Captain, point out the target."

Captain Hadley used a baton to point to the red arrow on the Rabaul map. "Here."

"Bomb release time will be between 1030 and 1100 hours," the Major continued, "and altitude will be 9,500 feet. Bomb load per plane will be eight 1,000-pound general purpose bombs, fused one-fifth second delay to penetrate the underground bunkers. Ammunition carried will be two hundred rounds per gun.

"The First Composite Fighter Group will maintain an alert for the purpose of intercepting the B-24s on their return. Returning from target, lead B-24 will send us position reports and E.T.A. Nadzab. When B-24s are one hour out, fighters will scramble and intercept.

"The First Composite Bomb Group, using three B-25 medium bombers and five A-20 light bombers, will bomb and strafe the Japanese encampment on the west bank of the But River, from 886-251 to 882-246 on the But West map, Wewak area."

The major paused and turned to Captain Hadley, who promptly pointed the baton to the red arrows on the Wewak map.

"Strike time for Wewak," the major continued, "will be between 1010 and 1040 hours, and altitude will be 75 feet. Bomb load per plane, for both B-25s and A-20s, will be four 300-pound demolition bombs, fused ten-second delay for bomber escape time. Ammunition carried will be maximum capacity. All ammo will be expended over target by strafing.

"Take-off time and route out will be at the discretion of Squadron Commanders. Lead airplanes will take strike photos and send in preliminary strike reports. Returned crews will be interrogated in Squadron Operations.

"By order of Colonel Henebry, 19 March 1945."

Major Layhee sat down, and First Lieutenant Iverson, Squadron Navigator for the B-24s, walked to the map stand and swung out the two target maps. They were each mounted on a plywood panel hinged on opposite sides, so they opened like a pair of shutters. Behind them was a large route map under glass, with a heavy black grease-pencil line on the glass, showing the zig-zag route to Rabaul and back planned for this trip.

He picked up the pointer and began his briefing.

"We'll fly toward Rabaul across the Bismarck Sea, staying north of New Britain all the way, to gain the benefit of surprise. Here's the route:

"Six B-24s will take off at one minute intervals, beginning at 0740 hours. We'll head southeast down the Markham Valley to Lae, and then east along the shoreline to Finschhaven."

He pointed the baton to the east end of the peninsula.

"We'll assemble our formation over Finschhaven at 7,000 feet, from 0816 to 0822 hours, then proceed due north, climbing on course to 9,500 feet, to the northern tip of Umboi Island over here, just west of New Britain.

"At Umboi, we turn right and proceed across the Bismarck Sea on a true course of 068 degrees to the I.P., 30 miles northwest of Rabaul." He gave the latitude and longitude of the I.P.

"From the I.P., we set up the bomb run on a true course of 130 degrees at 9,500 feet, with estimated drop time at 1044 hours. The lead bombardier will sight for range and deflection; all others will toggle on the leader.

"After bombs away, we'll head for the extinct volcano south of Rabaul, regrouping as needed over the volcano," he pointed with the baton.

"Then we head straight over New Britain for Finschhaven on a true course of 243 degrees, then west to Lae and home again to Nadzab. Time outbound should be three hours and four minutes, and return time two hours fifty-one minutes, for a total time of five hours fifty-five minutes, with E.T.A. Nadzab at 1335 hours.

"If bad weather over Rabaul keeps us from hitting the primary target, the secondary target will be the seaplane base at Kairiru, over here."

After that, the Squadron Navigator for the B-25s and A-20s presented their route to Wewak and return. The Wewak mission was not as long as our trip to Rabaul, so their planes would take off after ours left, and land before we returned.

Next came the weather briefing from Captain Smith, Group

Meteorologist. He gave us winds aloft and forecast weather on both routes.

Captain Hadley then stood up once more, to give us the Intelligence briefing. He stroked his black mustache, then spoke with a loud, pompous voice:

"No enemy fighter interception is expected over either target," he said, "but you may encounter light anti-aircraft fire over Rabaul, and moderate small arms and machine-gun fire at the tree-top altitude planned for the attack at Wewak."

Finally, Captain Levi, Communications Officer, briefed us.

"Radio silence will be maintained until strikes are completed." He then gave us our radio frequencies and VHF channels. "Now for the latest time tick, fresh from WLW shortwave. Set your hack watches to—let's see—twenty-thirteen."

We all stopped the hack watches on our arms when the second hand came around to straight up, then set the other hands to 2013 (8:13 p.m.); next we waited more than a minute for the time tick, to push in the stem and start the second hand going. I did the same to my navigator's chronometer (a large pocket watch accurate enough for celestial navigation), except that I set its hands to 1013 to indicate "Zebra"-time (at Greenwich, England), which is used world-wide for celestial navigation. Nadzab (on "King"-time) is ten hours ahead of Greenwich. (There are twenty-four time zones around the world, one for every fifteen degrees longitude. Instead of naming them "Eastern" or "Central" or "Pacific," the military named them with letters of the World War II phonetic alphabet, "Able, Baker, Charlie, Dog, Easy, Fox, George, How, Item, Jig, King" time zones, on through "Zebra" time at Greenwich.)

"Time tick countdown," continued Captain Levi,"—five, four, three, two, one, hack! It's twenty-thirteen King."

At the word "hack," a hundred and thirty watch stems were pushed simultaneously with an audible click, and our watches were all synchronized.

Then Major Layhee stood up again, and Captain Hadley called

out, "Group, at-tensh-HUT!" Everyone rose to attention.

"Well, men," said the Major, "that's our briefing for tonight. Bombardiers and navigators will remain to study the target maps, but all others are excused. Wake-up call will be at 0430. Go fly a good mission tomorrow, and make us all proud of you!"

"Group, dis-MISSED!" shouted Captain Hadley, and people headed out in all directions. Pilots, navigators, and bombardiers went forward to study the target maps for a while, and then headed for their tents.

Seitz looked up from his book when I came in. "Well, Hamilton, are you all briefed?"

"Sure am," I said. "All I wanted to know and then some."

"When's your wake-up call?"

"Four-thirty. I'd better turn in right away."

"Don't wake me then, or I'll kick your butt!" James said.

I lay there, trying to sleep, but my restless mind was busy reviewing all the details of the briefing. *My first combat mission at last!* I had just drifted off to sleep, or so it seemed, when a bright flashlight shone in my face, and a quiet voice said, "Crew call! Crew call! Breakfast in twenty minutes." I got up quietly and dressed in the dark while the others slept. Then I picked up the equipment bags I had packed last night, and carried them to the mess hall.

Combat crews were given a special treat—fresh eggs for breakfast—on the morning of their mission. I had mine fried sunny-side up. It took three cups of coffee to drive my sleepiness away. Then my excitement mounted. *This is the big day I've anticipated for so long! I'll finally fly off into combat!*

I joined Lieutenant Morgan and his crew outside the mess hall, where we assembled our stuff, including .45 pistols, sheath knives and escape kits. A flight line truck came to pick up our crew at five-thirty and drove us to the supply shack, where we were given our parachute harnesses, chest-pack parachutes, and life jackets.

It was before six when we unloaded everything in front of the plane assigned to us. The silver skin of the big bomber reflected the reddish glow of dawn. B-24s always impressed me as huge—more than sixty-seven feet long and one hundred ten feet in wingspan, with four big three-bladed steel propellers nearly twelve feet in diameter. The number 473675 was stencilled in black on both of the two oval-shaped rudders at the tail.

The ground crew had worked long into the night getting the plane ready, and now it was our turn to check what they had done. The crew chief went with Pilot Morgan into the cockpit to go over everything there.

The copilot and the engineer-gunner climbed a twelve-foot ladder to the top of the plane's high wing, and opened each fuel cap to measure the amount of fuel in each tank by plunging a white measuring stick into its depths.

The bombardier and the armorer-gunner inspected each bomb hung in the racks in the bomb bay, checking its fuse setting and safety wire. The other gunners went to all four turrets and the two waist guns to look over the ten fifty-caliber machine guns on the plane and the belts of ammunition feeding them. The radio operator-gunner went to his station to set the day's radio frequencies into the transmitters, and the I.F.F. transponder to the secret code of the day.

I carried all my navigation gear to the navigator's station in the nose of the plane, and got my maps, charts, and navigator's log ready for the mission.

Pilot and copilot together made a final, detailed walk-around inspection of the entire exterior of the airplane, making sure that it was airworthy.

We had all finished our preflight inspections by six-forty, an hour before takeoff, so we gathered under the wing to kill time. Morgan quizzed all of us on emergency fire-drill, bail-out, and ditching procedures for a while. After that, we drifted into the small talk of a bull session.

"How many missions have you guys flown?" I asked.

"Just one, to Wewak," said the copilot.

The bombardier laughed. "That makes us combat veterans."

"So you combat veterans are on your second mission today," I said "Does that make you double veterans?"

"No," said Morgan, "but it does complete our training requirements here. Each crew flies at least one mission to both Wewak and Rabaul."

The bombardier sat down on the left main wheel. "After today, we'll be ready to move on to one of the front-line air forces."

"No more ground school?"

"Naw—we finished all that last week."

"How long have you been here?"

"It'll be a month tomorrow."

Morgan looked at his watch. "Well, men, it's after seven. Let's get on board and fire this baby up!"

I had mixed feelings as we started to enter the airplane—glad to be flying a combat mission at last, nervous about the test of my inner resources which it would pose. And something else as well: *Wish I were flying this first mission with my own crew.*

Nose Gunner **WILLIAMS** in front of his nose turret (Emerson electric turret on B-24-M)

5. First Combat Mission

The way to enter a B-24 is through the bomb bay doors at the bottom, so we all ducked way down under its belly to enter through the open bomb bay doors, and climbed up on the narrow catwalk connecting the front of the plane to the rear, between rows of thousand-pound bombs on both sides. Half the crew went aft to the waist deck, and half went forward to the flight deck.

Outside, a ground crewman stood in front of the number three (right inboard) engine with a fire extinguisher, waiting for the pilot to start it. Inside, the pilots went through their checklist, turning on the many systems, setting flaps, and closing the bomb bay doors. Our radios were on, but silent, as ordered, so we waited for a light signal from the tower to start engines. It came, finally, and our engines roared to life, one by one.

Soon we were taxiing toward the end of the runway, fourth in a line of six B-24 Liberators. The first plane turned onto the runway, waiting for the takeoff signal from the tower. At seven-forty the green light came, and the lead plane poured on full power and roared down the runway. Before it was off the ground, the second plane turned onto the runway, waiting for the green light.

Precisely at one-minute intervals, all six planes departed. From the flight deck, I watched our pilots push the throttles forward all the way, and four big Pratt and Whitney R-1830-65 radial engines poured four thousand eight hundred horsepower into four screaming Hamilton-Standard steel propellers to speed us down the runway. What a rush of adrenalin that gave me!

Takeoff, in any plane, always fills me with excitement. It is the miraculous moment that changes an awkward, heavy, earth-bound machine into a graceful, bird-like creature of freedom. In our B-24, sixty thousand pounds of heavy machinery rolled for a mile or more down the runway, accelerating to flying speed. Then came the moment of truth. The pilot pulled back on the control wheel, and the rumble of tires on "swiss-cheese" metal runway ceased, as we lifted off, one foot high, then two, three, five, ten, fifteen, twenty feet up, and we were flying!

Our squadron of Liberators was a long line of planes a mile or two apart, heading down the Markham River Valley toward the port of Lae. I left the flight deck and climbed down the tunnel to the nose, where my navigation gear was laid out. I wrote "Depart Nadzab 0744" in the log, and started navigating.

Climbing slowly, we reached 2,000 feet as we crossed the seacoast at Lae. Turning forty degrees left, we followed the line of planes ahead eastward, along the sandy shore of the green Huon Peninsula, toward Finschhaven at its far end.

Half an hour into the flight, we could see the lead plane beginning a slow circle to the left over Finschhaven, and the second and third planes turning gracefully to intercept his circle and join him in a V-formation, one on his right, and the other on the left. When we caught up with them, we fell in trail behind the lead plane, and we all swept slowly around another circle while the fifth and sixth planes came up to make a second V-formation, one on our right, and the other on our left.

I love to watch big planes assemble into a formation, because their motions are slow and graceful. It is the opposite of an aerial dogfight, where the maneuvers are rapid and violent. Here we had an aerial ballet, full of grace and beauty.

With the squadron assembled in "javelins in trail" (one Vee behind the other), the leader turned left to lead all of us due north toward Umboi Island. I wrote in my log, "Depart Finschhaven 0826, 7000 feet climbing, compass heading 352, indicated airspeed 150 mph."

Twelve minutes later we reached 9,500 feet, and I wrote, "Level off 0838, 9,500 feet, airspeed 155."

Now the nose gunner came forward to join me. After a brief greeting, he opened the doors to the Emerson electric nose turret, and climbed into his duty station. A blast of cold air blew into the cabin from the clearance gap around the turret, until I closed the doors again behind him. The wind blew my papers off the table.

While I was picking up my chart off the floor, the bombardier came into the nose. He took the padded shroud off the secret Norden bombsight, turned on his bomb control panel, and started his inflight procedures. The nose got pretty crowded when all three of us were working in there at once.

A few minutes later I could see Umboi Island ahead, a bright green oval thirty miles long, set in a deep blue sea. Ten miles to the east I could see the green jungle-covered western tip of New Britain Island, and I knew that Rabaul was at the other end of New Britain, 400 miles away. Suddenly I felt that I knew my way around this part of the South Pacific. It felt good!

As we reached the north tip of Umboi Island, our formation wheeled gracefully seventy-two degrees to the right, and we headed out across the Bismarck Sea on the longest outbound leg of the flight. I wrote, "Depart Umboi 0856, 9,500 feet, heading 064, indicated airspeed 155 mph, true airspeed 157 knots."

Any long over-water leg requires more sophisticated systems of navigation, because there are no visible checks on position. Fortunately, there were a couple of tiny islands in the Bismarck Sea that lay just to the north of our intended track and halfway to the I.P., so they offered a good check point.

When we came to where the first one should be, there was a build-up of clouds below us which completely obscured the island. But a few minutes later, I spotted the second tiny island through a break in the clouds. We were five miles left of course and three minutes ahead of flight plan, from which I calculated the wind aloft, stronger than forecast.

Radio silence did not keep us from using the interphone to talk with fellow crew members on the same plane. We all wore a pair of earphones and a strapped-on throat mike with a push-to-talk switch, so the interphone was like a party-line telephone. The whole crew listened to what anyone said. Now I used it to share my navigational update.

"Navigator to Pilot, over."

"Yeah, Navigator, go ahead."

"Just spotted a tiny island through a break in the clouds. We're five miles left of course and three minutes ahead of flight plan. That makes our wind aloft 200 degrees at 35 knots, a bit more southerly and stronger than forecast, but it's a tail wind. Over."

"Good work, Kid! Keep it up!"

"I'm not a kid anymore—I had my twentieth birthday yesterday!"

"All right, Old Man—get back to navigating!"

Now there were no other check points between us and Rabaul, and the I.P. was only an imaginary spot on the ocean. How could I verify our position? If this flight had been at night, I could have used my octant to shoot three stars for a good fix. By daylight, I could shoot the sun for a single line of position, but it takes two or more lines of position intersecting to produce a fix. And now even the sun was disappearing behind increasing banks of higher clouds.

There was a loran receiver at my navigator station, a bulky black box full of complex electronics, designed to receive special radio navigational signals which could generate lines of position to produce a fix. But the loran receivers of that era were very complicated to use, and I had never seen one before. At navigation school, we had learned the theory of this new system, but at that time, airborne loran equipment was brand new and in short supply, so it all went to the war zones, with none left over for schools at home. Nadzab had a loran school to train people like me, but that was no help to me on this first mission.

The lead navigator, though, had already finished Nadzab's loran school, and he was using his loran set to take us directly to the I.P. in spite of the worsening weather that blotted out the sun above and much of the view below. I simply tracked him by "dead reckoning" (heading, speed and time).

The ride started getting bumpy, as we passed in and out of occasional flight-level clouds. The pilots of all six planes spread the formation out so that there was more space between planes, to avoid possible mid-air collisions from unexpected motion. They did this without breaking radio silence, by seeing a wing-rocking signal from the lead plane.

"Pilot to Ball Gunner, over," the interphone crackled again.

"Ball Gunner reading you, over."

"Lead plane just lowered his ball turret. Why don't we do the same?"

"Wilco—I'll go drop my big ball now!"

"But don't drop your little balls!" added the copilot.

The Sperry Ball Turret was a motorized plastic goldfish bowl barely big enough to hold two machine guns and a gunner seated in near-fetal position (knees high). It was designed to hang down from the belly of the plane, to shoot at enemy fighters attacking from below. It was retracted, of course, for takeoff and landing, and extended when the plane approached enemy territory.

"Pilot to all Gunners."

"Nose Gunner here." "Tail Gunner reading you." "Upper Turret Gunner." "Ball Gunner, balls and all." "Radio Gunner here." "Waist Gunner, too."

"Test-fire all guns, but don't waste ammo. You only have 200 rounds in each."

"Roger (got your message)." "Wilco." "Coming up."

Now the bomber vibrated as ten fifty-caliber machine guns fired short bursts from every part of the plane. Then silence.

"Hey, that was fun!" came through the interphone.

"Bring on the fighters!"

Now the bombardier put his head near mine, and shouted, "What's your E.T.A. for the I.P.?"

I did a quick calculation. "Ten twenty-six."

He looked at his watch. "That's only twenty minutes away!"

"Bombardier to Pilot, over."

"Go ahead, Bombardier."

"Navigator tells me we reach I.P. in twenty minutes. Our bombs are still clean. Gotta pull the safety wires. How about now?"

"Permission granted."

The bombardier unplugged his interphone cable, and ducked

through the tunnel to the bomb bay. Until the safety wire was removed from each bomb, it would not explode on impact, even if the whole plane crashed. With the safety gone, the bomb was ready to drop. It was also ready to explode in the plane, if flak came through the bomb bay and hit it.

A few minutes later, he returned to the nose and plugged in his interphone cable again.

"Bombardier to Pilot, over."

"Go ahead, Bombardier."

"All bombs are now dirty. Eight thousand pounds of live dynamite!"

"Roger."

The copilot's voice came on. "Don't forget to open the bomb bay doors before you drop 'em. We don't want any live ones rattling around in our cage!"

"Shut up, Copilot, or I'll rattle your cage!"

"Cut it out, men!" came Morgan's voice. "Back to business."

Soon the lead plane turned slowly to the right, and the whole squadron followed. I wrote in my log, "I.P. 1026."

Immediately after turning onto the bombing run, the lead plane rocked its wings to signal "tighten formation." The other five airplanes moved in much closer, and the whole tight formation settled into the tense business of the bomb run.

The lead plane opened bomb bay doors, and all others did the same. Our bombardier opened ours with his big red lever in the nose. Now his bombardier's control panel was lit up with indicator lights showing all bombs armed, ready to drop. He was kneeling under the nose turret with the bomb release toggle switch in his hand, peering through the bombardier's sloping window at the lead plane ahead. When he saw the bombs drop from the lead plane, he would toggle that switch to drop our load.

I was looking over the bombardier's shoulder at the sea and shoreline ahead, trying to see the target through the large holes between clouds. We were flying southeast over the great bay of Rabaul's Simpson Harbor. I could see the volcano in the distance to the right, and the city of Rabaul on its promontory into the bay on our left ahead, but clouds in front of us hid the target. Then another hole in the clouds opened up to reveal it. There lay the Rambau Range of foothills where the underground storage dumps were, dead ahead.

Suddenly there was a puff of black smoke below us, ahead and to the left. Then another, and another! Anti-aircraft fire!

"Nose Gunner to Pilot, flak ahead at ten o'clock low!"

"Ball Gunner to Pilot, I see the flak too! Six bursts so far, under number two plane, 500 feet low."

"Hope he doesn't get our range while the bombs are still on board and dirty."

Now everything depended on the lead bombardier, who was busy sighting his Norden bombsight on the target, and making minor corrections in heading to keep the motorized cross hairs on the aiming point as it came closer. The bombsight was connected to the autopilot, so as he turned the bombsight, it turned the plane, and the rest of the formation turned to follow. During the bomb run, the lead bombardier was actually flying the whole formation by moving his bombsight to the left or right.

The Norden bombsight made calculations for groundspeed, wind, altitude, temperature, pressure, bomb type and trajectory, and set up its own predetermined angle of release. The bombardier kept the aiming point in the crosshairs by adjusting the rate motor that depressed the sighting angle to follow the moving image of the target as it came closer. When the sighting angle reached the preset bomb release angle, the bombsight itself released the bombs automatically.

"Bombs away!" shouted our bombardier. "Closing bomb bay doors!" I checked the time–10:36.

We could see the bombs dropping below all three of the planes ahead. We could also see the black smoke of flak shells getting closer. The lead plane rolled into a fairly steep bank to the right, turning toward the volcano, and we all followed.

Then a shell exploded ahead of us, between the lead plane and us, and several pieces of shrapnel made shatter-marks on the nose turret's thick cylindrical plexiglass, while others creased grooves in the skin of the nose, and one came through into the tunnel behind me. The wind started whistling through the hole.

The next shells exploded to the left, where the formation would have been had it not turned right. Some of the pieces clattered against the skin of our plane.

The pilots of all the planes had pushed their throttles forward for maximum power, to speed away from the danger area. We were rapidly moving away toward the volcano, and the shell bursts trailed behind us, and then stopped coming. The pilots then throttled back to cruising power.

The air got bumpy as we flew over the volcano and turned right thirty degrees to head for Finschhaven. We were thousands of feet above the volcano, but the wind blowing up its southern slope made turbulence up to our flight level.

The rough air made me aware of the fact that I had been going through some turbulence for the last hour or more without noticing it. The excitement of combat displaced my queasiness.

Looking ahead, I saw a line of towering cumulus clouds over the mountain range to the left, and thunderstorms building up ahead. We could fly around the worst of those, but the ride home would definitely be rougher than the ride out. I started feeling queasy again.

Stop that now. You don't have time to be sick. You've got work to do.

I wrote in my log, "Bombs away 1036, altitude 9500 feet. Over volcano 1044, altitude 8500, heading 235, airspeed 160." We were lighter and faster without the weight of bombs and half the fuel. Now it was 420 miles to Finschhaven, which should take two hours sixteen minutes to fly.

"Navigator to Pilot, over."

"Go ahead, Navigator."

"Bombs away at 1036, eight minutes ahead of flight plan.

With the headwinds we have up here, I show E.T.A. Finschhaven at 1300, and Nadzab at 1327. How's our fuel? Over."

"Engineer and Copilot are working on fuel readings and cruise control charts right now. If our fuel consumption follows the standard curve, it looks like we'll have dry tanks around 1430, so we should have about an hour to spare."

"Good," I said, "let's hope it stays that way."

But it did not, of course. The lead plane started a series of detours which took the squadron around the major thunder-storms, zig-zagging to the right for five or ten minutes, then to the left, and so on. This kept me busy plotting all those short legs on the chart. The added distance made our return flight longer, of course, and reduced our margin of surplus fuel time.

I searched in vain for possible check points on the ground below, but clouds under us obscured most of New Britain Island. After an hour, there was finally a large break in the clouds just when I needed it, because I could see, on our left, the town of Hoskins on the lush green northern coast, and off to our right was the town of Talasea on its forested peninsula jutting to the north into the Bismarck Sea.

What a beautiful sight!

I pushed the intercom button. "Navigator to Pilot, over."

"Go ahead, Navigator."

"I just got a fix on the town of Hoskins on the north coast. We're six miles right of course, and seven minutes late. If all this detouring around thunderheads keeps up, we won't get to Nadzab until 1345, or maybe later. How's the fuel supply now?"

"That's going the wrong way, too. Our fuel consumption turns out to be running higher than expected. We may have dry tanks as early as 1400."

"Hell's bells!" I said. "Our reserve fuel time may be down to only fifteen minutes or even less!"

"That's a mighty slim margin! If it's a real squeaker at the end,

I might shut down the number two engine, and mush along on three engines to stretch out the gas."

"Better not do that any sooner than you have to, because it will slow down our speed, and make the flight that much longer."

"I never shut down an engine unless I have to."

We continued our detours around thunderheads, but had to fly right through a lot of peripheral clouds that gave us a bumpy ride and occasional rain. I was grateful that this was a daylight mission, so we could see the thunderstorms to go around; if it were night, and we flew right through them, we could encounter violent turbulence and hail big enough to smash our windshield.

I was also grateful that the rough ride had not made me airsick. *I still have my air legs, after all!*

The clouds below us were thinning out. Soon I could see the southwestern coastline of New Britain ahead, and the empty sea beyond. The port of Kandrian lay off our left wing. I wrote in the log, "2 miles right Kandrian 1230."

"Navigator to Pilot, we're leaving New Britain now. I just got a fix on Kandrian. We're four miles left of course, and twelve minutes behind flight plan. Our E.T.A. Nadzab is now 1340. How does the fuel time look now?"

"It's a little better—dry tanks at 1410, so that gives us a half-hour reserve, based on your new E.T.A. We'll get there on all four engines, after all!"

"Hallelujah!" I exclaimed.

Thirty minutes later, over the open sea, I sighted the New Guinea coastline in the distance, with the tip of the Huon Peninsula dead ahead. We were on course for Finschhaven, only ten minutes away, when suddenly—

"Nose Gunner to Pilot—fighters at twelve o'clock high!"

I stood up to look through the astrodome overhead, and saw them—six P-47 Thunderbolts, diving on our formation from straight ahead, high.

"Ball Gunner to Pilot—more fighters at twelve o'clock low!"

I looked down through the bombardier's window, and saw those too—three twin-engine P-38 Lightnings zooming up from straight ahead, low.

"Pilot to all gunners—remember, these are friendly fighters, our guys. So keep your guns on safety."

First the P-47s flashed down through our formation from above, and a few seconds later, the P-38s flashed up through the bombers from below. Our gun turrets were busily turning and tracking the fighters all the way.

"I shot down one of the P-47s for sure!" shouted the nose gunner on interphone.

"So did I!" claimed the upper turret gunner. "Got him long before he reached us!"

"And I riddled one of the P-38s," the ball gunner added, "while he was coming up from below!"

"Heads up! They're regrouping for another pass from six o'clock!" called the tail gunner. "Now it's my turn to get one."

They zoomed past our planes from the "six o'clock" position at our tail.

"I got him!" shouted the tail gunner. "Scratch one P-38!"

"And I got a P-47!" the ball gunner claimed.

"I wonder how many of our bombers they shot down?" asked the copilot. "Those were pretty impressive passes!"

"Heads up again! They've regrouped to our left, and they're coming in at nine o'clock level!" (from the left wing tip)

"Now it's my turn!" said the radio operator manning the left waist gun.

The fighters flashed through us on that third pass, and also for a fourth pass from the opposite side. Then they headed home. All of our gunners claimed to have shot down one or more.

"Between us and the gunners on the other bombers, we got 'em all!" the engineer-gunner announced. "There weren't no fighters left for that fourth pass!"

(After we returned, we heard that the fighter pilots claimed to have shot down all six of our bombers!)

Meanwhile, we passed Finschhaven, headed due west toward Lae, and started our descent on course. Eighteen minutes later, we flew over Lae at four thousand feet, turned right forty degrees, and followed the broad Markham Valley home to Nadzab. There we circled the airport high, while the bombers peeled off in landing sequence, and touched down one by one.

I closed my log with the entry, "Land Nadzab 1344." My first combat mission had taken exactly six hours.

We piled out of the bombers into the waiting trucks for a quick ride to B-24 Operations, where two intelligence officers were waiting to interrogate us at two tables at opposite ends of the tent. Our six bomber crews made two lines, waiting our turn to be asked to describe what we saw–the results of the bombing, the flak we flew through over the target, the weather there and en route, any Japanese ships we saw in Simpson Harbor at Rabaul, the fighter interception on the way home, and anything else we may have seen which could possibly affect the war effort.

Squadron Intelligence combined all our answers into its Mission Report, complete with strike photos then being processed, to submit to Group and Air Force Headquarters. All 48 of our bombs hit in the target area, so our mission was deemed "successful."

(Mission Reports from every combat group gave higher staff officers data to evaluate progress and plan the war at that time. These records were preserved, but remained secret until they were declassified in 1983, giving historians like me, decades later, access to data needed for a factual basis for our accounts.)

We left Squadron Operations to turn in our parachute harnesses, chest-pack chutes, and "Mae West" life jackets at the supply tent, and then rode toward our tents through the afternoon heat. I felt enormous relief to have the mission completed.

"This Markham Valley scenery sort of grows on you," I said. "It's good to be back here again."

"In one piece!" the bombardier added.

"You guys did a swell job," Morgan said. "I was really proud of my crew today, including our relief navigator."

"Glad to be with you," I said. "This was my first mission—it changes my status forever. I'm no longer a recruit—now I'm a combat veteran."

6. Search for a Lost Plane

"Wake up, guys, we fly today!" Seitz yelled as a bugle sounded reveille. The sky outside our tent had the rosy glow of dawn over Nadzab. It was March 21, the day after my first combat mission.

"Training mission today?" asked James, raising his head off his pillow.

"Yeah," said Seitz, "that new B-24-M that Hamilton flew to Rabaul needs a compass swing."

"That won't involve the whole crew," said Cordell, sitting up on the side of his cot. "All we need for a compass swing is pilots and navigator–you, me and Hamilton–and Pieper as engineer, and Imhof for radio."

"That leaves me out," said James, rolling under his blanket. "I'll go back to sleep!"

Seitz pulled on a khaki shirt. "We'll pick up another man from Base Intelligence to help look for the missing plane,"

"What missing plane?" I asked, crawling out from under my rough army blanket.

Seitz ran a comb through his blond hair. "Three weeks ago, twelve B-24s left Nadzab to bomb Wewak. Soon after, one plane left the formation to turn back to base. Weather was nasty, he never made it back—just disappeared. Today the weather's good, so we get to expand our compass swing to include a search. We'll get briefed on where to look when we go to Base Intelligence."

"It ain't combat," Cordell said as he stepped into his khaki trousers, "but a search mission is more exciting than just a compass swing."

We ate a leisurely breakfast, to allow time for all the day's combat missions to take off ahead of us. Breakfast featured imitation scrambled eggs made from powdered eggs and water, a tasteless mush. Our bombardier caught a lot of kidding because he had worked in an egg-powdering factory before enlisting. Every time we ate powdered eggs, we reminded James how much we loathed his handiwork. James was not with us this morning, but we cursed his powdered eggs anyway. They symbolized the "mess hall mess."

Any chow line overseas took some getting used to; it was far more primitive than "stateside" chow. Fresh meats or vegetables were just not available in many locations. Powdered milk, powdered eggs, and dehydrated potatoes were each mixed with water to produce imitations of the real thing, but without much flavor. One answer was to use lots of salt and pepper.

Even overseas, our mess halls were semi-permanent buildings screened against flies, and kept clean and sanitary by kitchen personnel. Everyone went through the same chow line to a serving line in the center of the building that divided it into two dining spaces. Tables for officers were on one side, tables for enlisted men on the other.

"C-rations," or canned bulk foods, were the rule overseas, healthy to eat but not very appetizing. Canned meats like Spam were a frequent treat, whether in sandwiches or as a meat dish entree. Bread was baked locally wherever possible, though not frequently enough; it was often old and stale. Stale bread made acceptable toast, however. French toast (dipped in powdered-egg batter) alternated with powdered eggs for breakfast. A lot of toast also appeared in a recurring entree of canned corned-beef-chips in gravy on toast, which we called S.O.S. (shit on a shingle).

Chow lines in the states had a big sign saying "TAKE ALL YOU WANT, BUT EAT ALL YOU TAKE." (That slogan seemed so sensible to me that I repeated it, later, to my children and grandchildren.) Overseas, that rule still applied, but the poor taste of the food there caused many to change their minds about finishing what they took. I always cleaned my plate as a matter of principle, but I was shocked to see how much wasted food was scraped off the plates of other men around me. The overflowing garbage cans behind mess halls overseas were frequently surrounded by poor native war refugees who fed on whatever they found there.

We each had been issued a folding aluminum mess kit and cup. We had to bring them to the mess hall and eat out of them. (Some pressed-aluminum dinner trays were available for visitors.) The last step in any meal was to go by the clean-up line outside, where we scrubbed our own mess kits, first in a tub of hot soapy water, and then in a tub of hot rinse water. Then we carried our mess kits back to our tents until the next meal.

After breakfast this morning, our five essential crew members went to the Intelligence tent to learn about the search.

"We're about to search for the missing B-24," Seitz said to Captain Hadley, Intelligence Officer. "Can you tell us how it happened?"

"Let me read to you from the report on Mission Number 57," said Captain Hadley, a pompous man with a large black mustache. I recognized him from the briefing before my mission.

"On 28 February 1945, C.R.T.C. bombers were directed against the Wewak area for their targets. Twelve Liberators proceeded to the But River Encampment Area, bombing at 9,000 feet. En route to target, aircraft number 981 was last seen turning left into a cloud bank just south of Dumpu. On return from target, one aircraft made a search for the lost plane, but no information as to its whereabouts has been received as of 0915, 1 March 1945."

"Did they call for help on the radio?" asked Seitz.

"All planes are under orders for radio silence before they strike, so nobody knows what happened. The eleven men on board are listed as missing in action. We sent another plane up to search for them again the next day, and again a week later, with no success. Since the crash was not far away, we waited to see if any survivors would walk home, but none have shown up in three weeks."

Captain Hadley spread out a large-scale chart of the Nadzab area on a table. "Here's where the plane was last seen." He pointed with a fat finger. "There's the village of Dumpu, only forty miles west of Nadzab. The whole formation was climbing, probably reached 3,000 feet by then, when this plane turned left into a cloud bank and disappeared. That would put him on the south side of his outbound course.

"If he'd made a standard U-turn, he'd have headed right down the middle of the Markham Valley with no mountains to hit. But if he turned too slowly—took too long—he could've run into this little mountain right here, eight miles south of his course. It rises to 3,642 feet.

"And if he missed that one, he might have run into one of this pair of hills southwest of Nadzab, one nine miles away at 3,000 feet, and the other eleven miles away at 4,000 feet. They seem to be connected like two humps on a camel's back. Remember, he was flying in and out of clouds, and clouds may have hidden all these mountains."

"Why don't we follow where he went?" Seitz suggested. "Let's fly to Dumpu at 3,000 feet, turn left where he did, and look over those hills close up. After that, we can climb to 5,000 feet and fly the full circle compass swing in the same area, while we keep looking for the crash site from higher up."

"Exactly what I was about to say myself," Hadley boomed. "I'll go with you as Search Director. I'll take charge of the search phase of the flight."

"Yes sir!" said Seitz, but he gave Cordell a strange look, and shrugged his shoulders. Imhof and Pieper noticed that, and exchanged glances of concern.

This day's combat strikes had flown away, of course, so we had the runway to ourselves as we took off into a beautiful clear morning. I gave the pilots a heading of 280 degrees to Dumpu, and then left the flight deck for the nose. Captain Hadley followed me, dragging his fleshy body through the tunnel with difficulty.

"As Search Director," he said, "I'll climb into your nose turret for the best view in the house."

"Go ahead," I said. After he squeezed in, I closed the turret doors behind his plump body. "Search Director to Pilot," I heard his deep voice on the interphone, "I am now seated in the nose turret, where I can do the most effective job of telling you where to go."

I'd like to tell you where to go, you pompous big shot!

Hadley continued, "I see the village of Dumpu now, at one o'clock low, in the clearing at the edge of the rice paddies."

"Pilot to Search Director, I see that too," Seitz said.

"Pilot, start the search with a left turn here."

"Roger, wilco."

We made a slow, graceful U-turn at 3,000 feet, as all eyes searched the valley below for any signs of a wrecked airplane.

"Search Director to Pilot, there's that first hill he could have hit, at two o'clock level, about six miles away. It looks like an old volcano, rising out of the valley like a flat-bottom ice cream cone upside down."

"Roger, Search Director. We'll head straight for it."

We slowly circled the old volcano at 3,000 feet. Through my side window, I looked at its rounded top rising above us. The slope was forested, with some naked spots where large boulders protruded, but none of the trees looked burned or broken from impact, and there were no gashes in the forest.

"Search Director to Crew, looks like he didn't crash on that mountain. Radio Operator, go back to the waist gun hatches and open them. Engineer, go back and help him search from the waist. Keep your eyes on the ground below while we fly to the next hill. He could have gone down anywhere along the way, so look for breaks in the brush and vegetation on the valley floor."

"Radio, roger," Imhof said.

"Engineer, wilco," said Pieper.

"Navigator, what's the heading to the next mountain?"

"One hundred degrees," I replied, "and we'll get there in fifteen minutes."

"Search Director to Pilot, take a heading of one hundred degrees."

"Pilot, wilco."

Soon I could see the twin peaks of the next mountain, just west of the Wampit River which flows north into the Markham River at Nadzab.

"Search Director to Pilot, can you see that mountain ahead that looks like two humps on the back of a camel? The little hump on the left is 3,000 feet high, and the big hump on the right rises to 4,000 feet. I want to circle each one close up."

"Roger. I'll fly over the saddleback between them, and do a figure-8 around 'em both."

We flew over the saddle and turned slowly left to circle the lower hump. At 3,000 feet, we were level with its top, which was rounded, like the previous one. These cone-shaped mountains appeared to be old volcanos, old enough to have the crater eroded away. They were all covered, somewhat unevenly, with tropical trees and brush. We searched in vain for evidence of a crash.

Completing a full circle to the left, we flew through the saddleback again and started circling to the right around the higher peak. Looking through the plexiglass bubble on my right, I studied the peak a thousand feet above us. It was not rounded like the lower one, but flat on top.

"Search Director to Pilot, look at the flat top to this peak we're circling. That indicates the presence of a well-defined crater. Obviously, this volcano is geologically younger than its neighbor, because the crater has not yet eroded away. I want you to climb up high enough to look down into the crater. It's just possible that the missing plane might have crashed into the bowl of the crater."

"That may be a long shot, since it was probably lower than the 4,000-foot crater," Seitz said, "but it won't hurt to look."

We climbed to 5,000 feet and headed straight over the top.

"Yes sir," said Seitz, "this one has a real crater."

"And look at what's in the crater," said Hadley, "a lake!"

"Wow!" I said. "Who would think of a lake in the top of a mountain?"

"It's like Crater Lake, Oregon," said Pieper, "except this lake is a little smaller, and there's no island in it."

"Hey, that lake is beautiful!" Imhof said. "Look at that luscious blue water!"

We had passed over the top of the mountain; the pilot started a slow circle around it.

"Does anybody see evidence of a crash up here?" Seitz asked.

"I see something on the west edge of the crater," Hadley said. "See the gap in the treeline at the rim? It looks like the rocks there are fractured. Maybe the plane clipped the edge of the crater, taking out those trees, and then crashed into the lake. Let's go down closer to the rim, and check it out."

We went down to make a pass over the west edge of the rim at treetop height, studying the trees and rocks.

"Well, there is a gap in the tree line where the plane could have clipped the rim," Seitz said.

"I don't know about that," Cordell replied. "Where are all the broken trees it would have left behind?"

"I see a few downed trees and branches laying around," Imhof said, "but I can't tell whether they're broken or just dead."

"The rocks on the rim do look a bit clipped off," I said, "but I see no evidence of fire."

"Of course not," said Seitz. "If the plane clipped the rim, it would nose down immediately and plunge into the lake!"

"Can anyone see the wreckage down deep in the water?"

"Not from up here. The reflection of the sky is too bright."

"How deep could it be? That water looks pretty clear," said Pieper.

"Very deep," Hadley replied. "This is the throat of the volcano; it could easily be 500 or even 1,000 feet deep."

"Pilot to Search Director, are we through with these hills? We still have another job to do. I'm taking this bird back up to 5,000 feet, and we'll go through the whole compass swing."

"Search Director to Pilot, compass swing approved. While you do that, I want all crewmen to keep looking for the crashed plane in the valley below. We don't know whether it crashed into that lake or not."

The doors to the nose turret opened, and Captain Hadley emerged. "I'm going back to the tail, and observe from there."

I took the astrocompass out of its box and set it up in the clear plastic astrodome overhead. Then I adjusted it for latitude and the local hour angle of the sun, so that the shadow it cast would show the direction of true north.

"Navigator to Pilot, let's start with a heading of 360, due north, and then turn 45 degrees to the left eight times, for eight successive headings around the circle. We'll stay on each heading for two or three minutes while I record all the readings. Then I'll signal you when to go on to the next heading."

"Roger, Navigator. We're now on heading 360, due north."

I read and recorded the compass heading and the true heading on the astrocompass. The difference between the two should equal the local magnetic variation indicated on the local map. If not, the compass was in error, and the purpose of the compass swing was to determine the amount of that error on eight headings around the circle. Then the pilots could correct for known errors.

"Navigator to Pilot. Let's go to heading 315, northwest."

I had to reset the astrocompass for each new reading, because the local hour angle of the sun changed one degree for every four minutes of time that passed.

"Navigator to Pilot. We're ready for heading 270, due west."

Again, I reset the astrocompass, read and recorded the data.

"Navigator to Pilot. Okay now for heading 225, southwest."

After we had flown all eight headings, I prepared a chart of the compass deviation to post in the little chart holder near the compass, and the compass swing was completed.

"We've finished our work, so let's have a little fun." Seitz's voice on the interphone sounded lively. "Cordell doesn't believe you can safely dive a B-24 at 6,000 feet per minute, so I'm going to give him a little demonstration. Hang on, everybody!"

He rolled the nose down into a 45-degree dive, and held it

there briefly. Everything in the plane seemed to be suddenly weightless; my navigation computer rose from the table and floated in the air, along with a pencil and paper, chart and plotter. I felt my whole body rising from its seat.

"Look at that rate of descent increasing," Seitz called excitedly, "3000, 4000, now 5000–come on, baby!–now 6000 feet per minute! I told you we could do it!"

"But look at the airspeed! Up to the red line!" Cordell screamed.

"But not over it!" Seitz yelled back.

Looking ahead through the nose windows, I saw the ground rushing up toward us frighteningly fast, and the propellers and motors were winding up to a high-pitch scream. The pilots began pulling up the nose, and everything floating inside the cabin came crashing down on the floor. I felt like a giant hand was squashing me down in my seat, and my blood drained from my head to my feet. I began to lose consciousness, dimly aware that we were levelling off without plunging into the ground. Gradually everything seemed to return to normal, including my heartbeat.

"We came through that okay," Seitz's cheerful voice came through the interphone. "Wasn't that fun? Is everybody all right?"

"I hope so," I replied weakly.

"This is Imhof, back in the waist. When you started that dive, a whole row of parachutes rose up from the floor and floated through space! They just hovered in mid-air until you pulled up, and then they crashed to the floor!"

Pieper added, "Captain Hadley was halfway through the door of the tail turret when you started diving! He may be dead, now!"

"I AM dead!" Hadley roared. "You gave me heart failure!"

"Sorry, Captain," said the pilot, "I wanted my men to experience this because we may have to do some violent maneuvers in combat. They need to be ready for anything! But now that we're close to the ground, we'll go back to the base and land."

It didn't take long to touch down. "Flight time two hours thirty minutes," I noted in my log.

Captain Hadley was pale and much less pompous when we

reported the results of our search to Base Intelligence. The crew was divided in opinion; some thought we had found the crash site in the crater lake, others did not. Since the evidence was not conclusive, the eleven men were still listed as "missing" rather than "killed" in the Group records at the end of March.

"Come on, Seitz, level with me," I said as the five of us walked to the mess hall for lunch. "Did you pull that heavy dive stunt for our benefit, or Captain Hadley's?"

He flashed a rare mischievous grin. "Kinda fun to set a big shot on his ass when you can!"

Cordell clapped him on the back with a broad grin. "We sure set him on his ass, all right!"

Imhof and Pieper exchanged grins too, and touched palms in a "high five" salute. It was a moment of crew celebration, and we all relished it.

7. Jungle Boot Camp

Our crew began Jungle Training School on the day after our search for the lost plane. Sixty airmen gathered in the briefing tent to hear Major Hundt, Director of Training, tell us how important our jungle training would be for our survival if we ever came down in any jungle. Then he introduced a tall, sunburned officer wearing a greenish khaki uniform and a broad-brimmed safari hat.

"Here's Captain Gillespie of the Australian Army. He's head of our Jungle Training School."

Captain Gillespie stepped forward, and spoke with a very noticeable Australian accent. (Aussies pronounced "A" like "I," so "today" sounded like "to die." Their usual greeting, "Good day, mate!" sounded like "G'die, mite!" And "lieutenant" sounded like "leftenant.")

"Good day, mates! My Australian English may sound a bit different from what you Yanks are used to, so I'll try to speak slowly while you get accustomed to it.

"The Jungle Training School is taught by many jungle-wise Australian instructors. We all speak this same way, which we think is very proper, of course. Your Aussie tutors will teach you how to survive in the jungle when you bail out into it. Jungle school gives you training we hope you never need, but if you do, it'll save your life! Think of this as your jungle boot camp.

"We'll leave this area now to climb aboard the lorries to go to the jungle. There you'll meet 'Leftenant' Brook and his corps of Aussie tutors who'll take you out into the jungle today and teach you how to survive there."

Outside the tent we found the "lorries," big trucks which took us for a forty-minute ride into the jungle. We parked and unloaded in a clearing.

"Let's go into the jungle, mates!" shouted Lieutenant Brook.

With the "leftenant" were a dozen sergeants and corporals dressed in Australian khakis (a shade more greenish than our tan khakis) and wearing their characteristic broad-brim safari hats with one side turned up. All of these Aussies had leather-like skin, with a dark color from deep suntan and yellow atabrine.

The Aussie leader raised both arms overhead to get our attention, and then set the scene for our jungle training:

"Here's the picture, mates. Your plane was shot up, you bail out over the jungle. Your chute brings you down into trees like these, but it gets hooked up in the branches. You hang there, twenty or thirty feet up, and what do you do? You unhook your harness and drop to the jungle floor, spraining an ankle in the fall. So you lie there for a bit, and try to collect your wits.

"Now, what? First and foremost, you want to survive in this jungle. Then you want to start moving toward friendly territory, as soon as your ankle heals enough to move about. Meanwhile, you want to hide from any enemy patrols.

"Let's address the first problem, surviving in the jungle. What makes the jungle dangerous, mates? Only your ignorance of it! Once you know its dangers and its resources, the jungle can be a rather friendly place. You don't have to worry about the cold of the arctic or the heat of the desert. There's plenty of food and water in the jungle if you know where to look.

"So our objective here is to dispel your ignorance and replace it with knowledge—what to look for and what to avoid. To do that, we'll break up into small groups. Each group will be led by one of my jungle-wise instructors, these good sergeants and corporals you see here before you. Each instructor will lead his group off through jungle trails for the next few hours to show you which plants and animals are good to eat, and which are poison.

"Tomorrow, we'll return here to these same small groups, and your instructor will ask you to point out to him things you remember from yesterday's lesson. Then he'll show you how to build a simple shelter to live in, made out of materials found all over the jungle. You'll each practice making a shelter.

"After that, you'll be ready for the big test. We'll take each one of you to a different part of the jungle, and leave you out there, all alone, for twenty-four hours. You'll build your own shelter and sleep in it, and eat only jungle food and water. You'll find that you *can* survive alone in the jungle.

"You'll be unarmed except for the knife you were issued. So, if any of the surviving Japs who live in these hills send a patrol through your part of the jungle, hide from them. They'll have guns. If you can't stay hidden, then surprise them from behind, and attack with your knife. Surprise can be a great advantage.

"We can't let you take guns into the jungle, mates, because you'd be shooting at each other whenever you wandered near your neighbor. We know you Yanks are too bloody trigger-happy.

"It may take us a couple of days to put you all through the solo survival test. We do have to scatter you about, you know. But be sure that you'll each go through the solo survival test before you graduate from Jungle School. Is that clear?" We nodded agreement.

"Now, the instructor for each small group will call out the names of his students. Gather around your instructor, and follow him into the jungle. Don't worry about lunch. Your instructor will teach you how to gather your lunch today from the resources of the jungle."

The five names in my group all began with "H," including Hamilton, Herrema, and Hill from our crew. We followed Sergeant Archibald Murdock into the jungle that he knew so well, and watched with intense interest as he pointed out all the things to eat, edible plants and small animals and grubs, and also the poisonous ones to avoid, both plants and animals.

"What do you think of all this?" Hill asked during a break. He lit a cigarette.

"I appreciate the practical info he's dishing out," I said.

"It reminds me of Boy Scout camp," said Herrema, "except it's more intense."

"You bet it is!" Hill agreed. "If we come down in parachutes, our lives'll depend on remembering this stuff. Did you ever feel that way about Boy Scout camp?"

"Heck, no!" Herrema replied.

During the course of the day, my fear of the unknown was reduced and gradually replaced by a feeling of familiarity. I began to see that I *could* survive alone in the jungle.

After a long truck ride back to base and supper in the mess hall, I headed for the P.X. (Post Exchange) to buy a coke and a candy bar. I handed a quarter to the man at the counter.

"We can't accept American money here," he said.

"Why not?"

"You have to change it into Australian money first."

"Why?" I asked.

"We're in Australian territory, that's why. Army policy says that all personnel use only the money of the host country."

"What's Australian money like?"

"Like English money—pounds, shillings, and pence. Take your money over to the exchange desk over there, and they'll fix you up."

I did so, and got a quick lesson in Aussie money. Their one-pound bill was worth five dollars, each shilling was worth a quarter, and each of their big pennies was worth two cents.

Their paper money looked very different—printed in glowing colors of red, orange, brown, blue and purple—more like works of art than money.

On the following day, all five of us were back with Sergeant Murdock to learn how to build a shelter using jungle materials. We all worked together as the instructor watched.

My feeling of confidence from the previous day now grew into a conviction that I really could live in this place. I was beginning to feel almost at home in the jungle.

"How do you feel about the jungle, now?" I asked Hill, as we looked at the completed shelter.

"I think we're going to make it okay," he said. "I can survive in a shelter like that."

"What about the jungle food selections?" I continued. "I like the fruits and herbs, but what about the grubs and worms?"

"Those fat white cutworms and caterpillars?" Hill laughed. "The man said, 'Just pinch off its head so it can't bite you, and swallow it whole. It's a good source of protein, you know.' Well, I don't think I could even swallow a critter like that. I'd gag on it! It'd make me sick!"

"Remember, a few years ago, when fraternities had contests to see who could swallow the most live goldfish?" I asked. "Well, I swallowed one live goldfish, and it wiggled all the way down! I couldn't do that again if I were starving to death!"

"I guess you and I will just have to be jungle vegetarians."

At the end of that day's instruction, Sergeant Murdock made a brief announcement before dismissing us for the ride home.

"If any of you chaps would like an opportunity to acquire an authentic native souvenir of New Guinea, meet me at six-thirty outside the P.X. I've found something of great value, which you might want to take home with you."

That aroused my curiosity, so after supper I went to the P.X. at the appointed time. Sergeant Murdock was there, and asked me to wait a few minutes to see if others would come. Two others did show up, Herrema and Hill. Murdock led us around the corner to a more secluded area and spoke in a quiet confidential voice, as if revealing a secret.

"I've brought with me something extremely rare," he said. "It's an authentic ceremonial axe used by the aboriginal native headhunters of New Guinea. I have it here in this duffel bag. If you're interested, I'll bring it out for you to see."

"Bring it out, Sarge," said Hill, "let's see it."

He opened the bag and brought out a striking trophy. It was

indeed a ceremonial axe, about two feet long, on a wooden handle thirty inches long. It had a thin blade of polished grey stone, four inches high by six inches long, set into a bound reed socket which joined it to a flat curved tail of dark wood, decorated with carved designs. It impressed me immediately.

"I wouldn't show this to anyone else," he said, "but I'll let you chaps hold it, and pass it around to inspect, because you've been such good students in my jungle seminar."

The three of us took turns looking it over.

"Do you want to sell it?" asked Hill, trying to be poker-faced, though his wide blue eyes betrayed his interest.

"I'd be very reluctant to part with this rare trophy," Murdock answered. "It's my prize possession! But since you Yanks are doing so much to help defend my native Australia against the wicked Japs, I think I'll show my appreciation by letting you purchase this wonderful stone-age weapon for the paltry sum of ten pounds."

"Ten pounds!" exclaimed Herrema, almost dropping the axe. "That's fifty dollars! That's more money than I get to spend out of two months' pay!" He passed it over to Hill.

"I like this thing, but I sure can't afford it!" Hill said, and passed it to me. "Maybe Hamilton can afford it with his big officer's pay." (At that time, a corporal got $35 and a second lieutenant $150 per month, plus 50 percent more for anyone on flight duty.)

The two corporals walked away.

"How about you, Leftenant?" the Aussie asked. "I can see that you are a man of great intelligence! Surely you can see the value of such a wonderful souvenir!"

"I can indeed," I replied. "I'd love to take it home with me, but I'm afraid I don't have ten pounds to spare."

"How much do you have?" he asked.

I took out my wallet and looked inside. "I think I see five one-pound notes, but that's only half the price you set. So I'm afraid that I can't buy it either."

"Well, now, Leftenant, let me think about that for a moment. You know what? I think I'll do you a big favor! Since you're making such an important contribution to the Allied war effort, I'm going to allow you to purchase this magnificent souvenir for only five pounds!"

"I'll accept your offer, Sergeant!" I said, handing him the money. "And thanks for all the things you taught me in the jungle!"

I was elated to have gotten such a bargain. As I carried my prize back to my tent, I visualized a circle of naked headhunters brandishing that axe in exotic ceremonies. I could hear them chanting in my mind, so I held my axe aloft as I entered the tent.

"What in the world is that thing?" asked Seitz, sitting on his cot. Cordell and James were lying on their cots, reading. They sat up to see, too.

"This is my prize souvenir of the South Pacific!" I replied.

PACIFIC SOUVENIRS
Hamilton's bolo knives, carved water buffalo horns, coconut-shell ukelele, and carved ceremonial stone axe (lower right corner of picture, stone blade pointing right).

"This is an authentic ceremonial axe used by the aboriginal native head-hunters of New Guinea! Isn't it beautiful?"

"Where did you get it?" asked Cordell suspiciously.

"I bought it from Sergeant Murdock of the jungle school instructor corps."

James lifted his dark eyebrows. "How much did you pay for it?"

"He wanted ten pounds for it, but since I didn't have that much, he allowed me to get it for only half the price. I was glad to get such a bargain for only five pounds!"

"Five pounds!" exclaimed Seitz, "that's twenty-five dollars! You think that's a bargain? I think it's a lot of money to pay for a souvenir!" ($25 could buy a suit of clothes then.)

"Not for this souvenir!" I replied. "I got a bargain!"

"How do you think the Aussie got that thing?" asked James. "He probably bartered it from some native in exchange for a few beers or cigarettes! I bet it didn't cost him more than a few shillings! And you got a bargain at five pounds?"

"Yes, I did," I insisted, "because a bargain is when both parties are satisfied!"

"Well, that's a new definition!" said Seitz. "'A bargain is when both parties are satisfied!' Don't tell that to Doris—my wife—or she'll find bargains every time she goes shopping!"

I packed my trophy away lovingly in my B-4 bag.

Before leaving Hamilton Field, California, each flight crew member had been issued his personal equipment for overseas use, including a folding mess kit, a .45-caliber automatic pistol with holster and shoulder strap, and a dagger-like sheath knife. That big, razor-sharp knife would be useful in the jungle.

During the next two days, we looked at the training rosters on the bulletin board, almost dreading to see our names on the list for the 24-hour solo survival test for the following day. My name appeared on the roster for March 24. I met with fifteen students and an equal number of Aussie instructors who took us one on one to stake us out, each in our own part of the jungle. Corporal Fitzhugh was my guide.

"We take you out in midday," he said as we walked into the jungle, "because that's when you strike your targets in your daylight bombing raids, so if you come down in the jungle, it'll be about that time. We go before lunch, so you'll be hungry at the start of your 24 hours, to motivate you to eat the jungle foods as we taught you."

In a few minutes we were out of sight of all other men, in a quiet world apart. We continued through the jungle, dodging the underbrush and lifting vines for half an hour, and then he stopped and looked around.

"This is it," he announced. "This is where your parachute brought you down. Here's where you'll live for twenty-four hours. Now, don't roam around very far. When I come back to get you at this time tomorrow, I expect to find you within a hundred feet of this spot. Good luck, Leftenant!"

He disappeared through the jungle foliage. For a while I just stood there, listening, and looking all around. The only sounds were bird calls and the cries of several kinds of wild animals, but even those were muted by the stifling noonday heat. It was a quiet time of day for the jungle.

Well, Bob, you're really on your own, now. Let's explore this neighborhood and pick a spot to build your shelter.

I took out my knife and carved a slash mark in the bark of a tree to mark the spot where my guide had left me. On second thought, I carved some more, to turn the slash mark into an "H" for Hamilton. *There! That should help me identify the place to come back to tomorrow.*

I started moving slowly and cautiously through the jungle, pulling back the vines and branches to let me go through. Soon I saw a spring of water, and stopped for a drink, scooping it up in my hands. It was cool and refreshing.

That's my source of water. I'll build my shelter near it, but not too near—I don't want to be too close to jungle animals who may use this as their watering hole.

Next, I spent some time checking the prevailing breezes, to see which way the average wind was blowing. Then I moved to the downwind side of the spring, about a hundred feet away, to locate my shelter, so that my human scent would not drift toward the watering hole, but away from it. The sounds and scents of any animals at the spring, however, would drift on the breeze toward me at that location, which would help alert me to their presence.

Now I was ready to build the shelter. I took out my big knife and started cutting small tree branches for structural members, palm leaves for roof and siding, and small vines for cord to bind things together.

The architectural design was a small lean-to, three feet by seven feet, with a roof sloping downhill parallel to the long dimension. Two small trees, three feet apart, held up the high end. The entry was between the two trees, where I had a large palm leaf, fastened on one side only, to serve as a door.

Inside the shelter, I put a thick bed of palm leaves on the ground to serve as both ground cover and pad. After lying down to test it, I went out and brought back more palm leaves to make the pad thicker and more comfortable. *But not too comfortable. You don't want to sleep so soundly that you'll not be aware of possible danger.*

I cut some peek-holes convenient to where my head would be, so that I could see out in three directions without moving much. Then I draped some large vines and leaves over much of the exterior, to camouflage the whole thing.

With my home base completed, I moved out in search of food. In a short time I found all I needed: wild fruits and berries, papaya, coconuts, breadfruit, young bamboo shoots, wild onions and other herbs, to take back to my shelter and eat there. I decided not to gather any edible grubs and worms. *I hate to eat anything that wiggles!*

While I was gathering food, I could see the sky darkening as the usual afternoon thunderstorms were gathering. I had barely made it home when the rain started—a real tropical downpour. I lay on my bed to listen to the rain pounding on the palm-thatch roof, happy to have a shelter. Yes, there were a few small leaks, and a little water came in, but it was a whole lot drier inside than outside.

The rain changed gradually from downpour to light drizzle, then back to downpour, and then to drizzle again. I rolled over on my belly and propped up on my elbows so that I could eat my supper while the rain continued. After I had eaten enough, I rolled over on my back again, and rested comfortably while the sound of gentle rain lulled me to a dreamy trance.

My mind drifted to the last time I went camping outdoors—eight or nine years earlier, in China, where my missionary parents allowed me to make an Indian teepee with my friend Tommy Brown, son of our missionary neighbors. Tommy and I camped all night in that canvas teepee, scared to death by every animal sound we heard. It seemed that morning would never come!

Ah, the joys of home! It's been two years since I've seen my family. Wonder when their letters'll catch up with me here in the jungles of New Guinea—and letters from all my friends and sweethearts. Bet they're replying now to the letters I wrote 'em two weeks ago.

I thought of Pauline, in Galesburg, Illinois, petite brunette with laughing brown eyes and quick wit; I longed to laugh with her again. And Sandy, in Pine Bluff, Arkansas, with honey-colored hair, big blue eyes and a sweet smile. Our special song was "I'll Be Seeing You," and I sighed to see her again. And Persis, in Stanford University, California, with a beautiful face like Ingrid Bergman, and a radiant smile. *How nice it would be if she were lying here in my arms—in my arms—in my arms—in my arms—*and I drifted off to sleep.

When I woke up, the rain had stopped and the daylight was gone. Looking through a peek-hole, I could see that there was still a faint glow of twilight left. The jungle brush prevented me from seeing as far as the watering hole a hundred feet away, but the sounds coming from that direction told me that there was significant animal activity there this evening. I heard grunts and snorts of what sounded like wild pigs near the water.

Wild pigs! Wow! Wild boars can be dangerous! I had seen them in the woods in south China. The males—wild boars—had long, sharp tusks that could slash you wide open. It made me very nervous to hear them so near.

Overhead, there were many kinds of bird calls, and the sound of wings flapping as birds settled into the trees. I could hear the distant cries of many jungle animals I could not identify. The whole texture of animal sounds filled me with increasing anxiety that slowly grew into fear.

I wish now that I had smuggled in my forty-five. Previously, in Texas, I had won the "expert" medal from my scores with the .45-caliber automatic pistol. Now I felt unarmed and afraid without it.

Then I began to realize that my bladder was painfully full, and that I would have to leave the cozy safety of my shelter to relieve it. Cautiously I opened the palm-leaf door and crawled out.

In the darkness, I grasped a nearby tree for support while I drained my bladder. I began to sense that countless eyes were looking at me from every direction. I looked all around, seeing little or nothing at first, but gradually perceiving eyes—more eyes—many eyes of all sorts of dangerous animals, fierce green eyes glowing in the dark, all focused on me, threatening me, filling me with growing alarm.

Just then I heard a voice calling "Haiyaku, haiyaku, haiyaku." Like a lightning bolt exploding in my brain, I remembered that "haiyaku" is Japanese for "quick."

Is a Jap patrol coming near? Where's my knife? My right hand found the sheath and closed around the handle of my knife. Cold sweat broke out on my forehead.

Suddenly the snorting of wild pigs at the watering hole grew much louder. Peering intently into the dark jungle in the direction of the noise, I began to see a horde of immense wild boars rushing toward me with fierce, glowing eyes and gleaming tusks, ready to slash me to pieces.

I've got to hide! I turned and dove headlong into the shelter in a state of sheer panic.

"God, help me now!" I cried, as my body shook with fear.

8. Bull Session

I lay in the shelter that night, all alone in the New Guinea jungle, wide eyed, and shaking all over. My body muscles were shivering and my teeth were chattering from stark fear.

What's happening to me? I've never behaved like this before!

Then I began to realize that my body was out of control because my mind was out of control, short-circuited by fear of so many unprecedented dangers.

O God! Help me get a grip on myself! Help me control this mindless fear! Help me make it through this awful night!

Time passed slowly without any of the disasters I feared. My heartbeat slowed to normal, and my breathing came easier. Gradually I began to realize that those countless glowing eyes could have been imaginary—had I actually seen a single one? And the sound of wild pigs, though real, could have been greatly exaggerated by my fearful state of mind, and generated visual images that may not have been real at all. Furthermore, that sound of "haiyaku, haiyaku, haiyaku," may have been a strange bird call instead of a Jap soldier saying "quick, quick, quick!"

As I reflected on the groundless basis of my fear, my panic left, my fear subsided. My body stopped shaking, and peace of mind came to me. Then I lay there for hours in a peaceful state of consciousness between sleeping and wakefulness. I listened quietly to the jungle sounds, prepared for possible danger, but no longer disturbed by the possibility.

You thought your enemies were all out there, but those aren't the ones that'll kill you. Your worst enemy is in here, lurking within you, ready to seize you and destroy you. Your worst enemy is fear—sheer panic—stark, immobilizing fear! You met your worst enemy here tonight, for the first time in your life, and with God's help, you conquered it!

The jungle announced the coming of dawn by a great increase in the noise of bird calls and animal cries. I gradually woke from my restful trance, aware of the growing light that filtered through the cracks in my shelter. I crawled through the entrance, stood up, stretched my arms and legs, and moved around. It felt good to be alive!

The light of day brought a new perspective on everything. My fear, which had loomed so large in the dark, now seemed insignificant in daylight retrospective. Now I found a new residue of confidence within me, rebounding from the challenges of the night.

That night really wasn't so bad, after all!

After eating more of my jungle food for breakfast and drinking all I wanted from the spring, I spent the morning roaming through the brush, looking for the tree with the "H" carved on it. Finally I found it, and sat on my heels beside it to wait for the return of Corporal Fitzhugh. He approached so quietly that he startled me.

"Good day, Leftenant Hamilton! You're back on the same spot where we parted yesterday. Good show, mate! How was your jungle experience?"

"It was a piece of cake!" I bragged.

That was the same report I gave to my friends back in camp, and their reports were all similar. Their solo survival tests had also been "no problem," "a breeze," or "a piece of cake!"

After supper, Hill got me alone for conversation.

"Tell me the truth," he said, looking me straight in the eye, "was your solo jungle experience really a piece of cake?"

I looked at him intently. He was asking me to bare my soul. But it was also an invitation to meaningful trust. I wanted that.

"The truth is that I was scared to death!" I said.

"I was, too," he echoed quietly.

In that brief exchange of truth, we trusted each other with a gift of self-disclosure that gave us a special bond. We never talked about it later, but I knew it was always there.

The next day our crew moved out of the big transient tents into two crew tents, one for the four officers and the other for the six enlisted men. The crew tents had been vacated by another crew just transferred to the Fifth Air Force.

Each tent was square, fifteen feet on a side, with a center pole holding up a pyramid-shaped canvas roof. It held a cot for each of us and a place to put our bags, nothing more. But it seemed luxurious to have our own space after being crowded with a lot of other men in the big transient tents. We rolled up the tent sides and let the breeze blow through.

The following day we went back to the classroom tent for the technical aspects of ground school. The thought of flying combat missions filled us with fresh hope and excitement. I felt that we were leaving the Jungle Training School with a new sense of inner strength that made us better prepared for whatever challenges we might find in the combat missions that lay ahead.

We continued in those ground school classes, all together as a crew, for the next four days, and then we separated to attend classes appropriate for our specialties.

All pilots and copilots went to Link Trainer classes, to practice instrument flying on that early simulator. Gunners went to a gunnery simulator quite advanced for its day; it used several movie projectors simultaneously to throw images of attacking fighter planes on a full semi-circular screen all around a row of gunners, each swiveling his machine gun to point at the fighters. Radio operators went to code and blinker classes, bombardiers to bombsight classes, and navigators went to Loran School.

I was glad to attend loran classes at last, to get my hands on the scarce loran receivers we had never seen in the States. "LORAN" stood for "LOng-range RAdio Navigation" using very low-frequency radio waves that curve around the world. Created years earlier for surface vessels in the navy, smaller airborne units had just been made for aircraft use. Now I could finally master the art of using the complex equipment which would help me plot position fixes when nothing could be seen outside the plane.

Pilots reading this today may ask, "What's complicated about loran?" The loran receivers in planes or boats today have built-in computer chips and circuits that do all your navigation work automatically, and give you the coordinates of your position as a completed "fix." They are truly wonderful! And technology has moved so fast that even our modern loran sets have now been replaced by G.P.S. (Global Positioning System), which gives even better fixes from satellites.

But fifty years ago, loran receivers were quite primitive. They were difficult to adjust and complicated to use. The bottom line was that it took five days in Loran School to learn how to use the equipment.

After my Loran School was over, the whole crew had the next day off.

"Let's go to the Officers Club and have some beers," Seitz suggested.

"Good idea," Cordell said. "We can sleep late tomorrow if we want to."

James and I followed the two pilots to the Quonset-hut Officers Club. We took our beers to an empty table for friendly conversation. Soon three more officers sat down at the next table and started talking about B-29 missions to Tokyo.

I turned around to face them. "Mind if we listen in? I'd like to hear about those B-29 missions, too."

"Guess not," said a red-headed first lieutenant. "We're intelligence officers who debrief crews after missions, and—"

"I remember you—you debriefed me after my March 20 mission to Rabaul. I'm a B-24 navigator."

"Yeah, we met. Well, the captain here just flew in from Guam, where he debriefed the crews on that big fire-bomb raid on March 9."

Seitz put down his beer. "Well, Captain, tell us about that raid. We heard the radio news story, but none of the details."

The captain pushed his horn-rim glasses up into place. "The crews thought it would be a suicide mission, because General LeMay sent them in at low altitude—5,000 feet—in the middle of the night. The first planes dropped firebombs all around the edges of the target area, lighting up the whole perimeter. The rest of the planes just dumped their bombs anywhere inside the burning perimeter. Three hundred twenty-four B-29's dropped almost four million pounds of incendiaries, creating a firestorm that burned out sixteen square miles of south Tokyo."

"Good bombing mission!" said the red-head. "What are our Intelligence estimates of enemy casualties?"

"We think sixty to eighty thousand Japs died that night. The fires started all the way around the outside of the target area, so there was no escape for those inside. At 5,000 feet, the crews all smelled the sickening odor of burning flesh." The captain took a long swig of beer.

Cordell looked uncomfortable. "But those are civilians! Why are we killing civilians?"

"Yeah," Seitz added, "why are we burning up old men, women and children in the middle of the night?"

"They're the enemy, that's why!" said the red-head. "The only good Jap is a dead Jap!"

"Hear, hear—amen," said the other first lieutenant.

"For some of the Jap military, that's true," I said. "I was there when the Japs invaded China in 1937. They committed terrible atrocities. The rape of Nanking destroyed hundreds of thousands of innocent Chinese civilians."

The captain looked at me through his owl-like horn-rims. "You were just a kid in 1937. What were you doing in China?"

"I was born and raised there—my parents were Presbyterian missionaries. But I was a teenager at the Shanghai American School until 1941, old enough to see what the Japanese army was doing. I hate 'em! But does that justify our killing their families in Tokyo?"

The captain took off his glasses and leaned back. "The millions of people in Tokyo are not innocent bystanders in this war. They're all war-workers in the Jap war machine. General Tojo and his buddies have recruited the whole nation in fanatical support of their military conquests. They're all war-workers!"

"Yeah," the red-head added, "and we Intelligence officers also know that the Japs have dispersed a lot of their war production factories into small shops scattered all through their residential neighborhoods. The only way to shut 'em down is to burn 'em out!"

"It's called 'strategic warfare,'" said the other intelligence lieutenant. "Destroy the enemy's production facilities, and you end the war. War-workers have to go with their factories."

"It's called murder on a large scale, if you ask me," Seitz said.

Cordell nodded agreement. "We ought not to attack civilians like soldiers. It ain't right!"

I lit my pipe and drew a good puff. "Even soldiers are human when they're off duty. I met some individual Japanese soldiers and officers in their visits to my parents' home in Hsuchow (see map on page 204). Even Jap soldiers can act like good people when they're with you personally. Colonel Tanaka, Captain Watanabe, and Sergeant Miyasaki drank tea with us, laughed and joked like real people, and told us about their families in Japan. My mother could speak Japanese, and she translated."

"What did your good Jap colonel think of America?" Seitz asked.

"He put on quite a show of friendliness, but he knew we would be his enemies before long. Their plan of conquest guaranteed it. Dad visited their headquarters in 1940, and Colonel Tanaka showed him a map on his wall, labeled "JAPAN AT LARGE." It showed the Japanese home islands in red, and then showed five phases of expanding empire in different shades of pink. Phase One took over

Formosa, Korea and Manchuria. Phase Two annexed all of China. Phase Three added French Indo-China, Burma, Malaya and Singapore. Phase Four included the Dutch East Indies and New Guinea, the Philippines and all Pacific Islands as far east as Hawaii, plus half the Aleutians in the north. Finally, Phase Five occupied all of Australia."

"What a ruthless, bold-faced plan for aggression!" the red-head snarled. "Shows what cold-hearted bastards they are!"

The captain put his glasses on again. "You mean to tell me that back in 1940, the Japs had already decided to conquer Hawaii and Australia?"

"Absolutely! And they almost completed Phase Four when we started pushing 'em back." (Colonel Tanaka's map of expansion was documented by Joel Huff's interview with Dad in the *Atlanta Journal*, November 28, 1943.)

Cordell looked quizzical. "Did our side know about all that?"

"That map was not a secret, or Colonel Tanaka wouldn't have showed it to Dad. He was bragging about it! I'm sure our government knew about Japan's plan for aggression long before Pearl Harbor. There was no excuse for us to be surprised by their attack."

"That's another story," said the captain. "I think Roosevelt wanted to get us into the war to save England and France from Hitler, so he left us exposed to Jap attack. But he thought they would attack the American army in the Philippines, where Jap shipping lanes carried oil from Borneo to Japan. He never thought they would hit his precious navy in Pearl Harbor."

"Bastards!" said James. "How could they act like friends?"

"Their whole aggressive empire has been nothing but evil, but still, those individual Japs visiting our home were our friends. Sergeant Miyasaki became very fond of my kid brother, Billy. He would ride his horse to our house on Sundays, to take Billy horseback riding. He said that Billy reminded him so much of his own son in Japan. Sergeant Miyasaki was a good soldier, but he was also a good man when he was off-duty."

"Why was your family fraternizing with the enemy?" the redhead asked suspiciously.

"The Japs weren't our enemies at that time. It was long before Pearl Harbor, and America was officially neutral in the war between Japan and China. My parents were Americans in China. They felt that the Japanese occupation forces might treat their Chinese Christian converts better if the missionaries were friendly toward the ruling powers. Besides, Dad always gave them some Christian literature to read, and tried to convert them to Christianity."

"Did any of the Japs convert?" asked James.

"I think Sergeant Miyasaki did, but I'm not sure."

The red-headed lieutenant stood up and pointed at me. "Suppose you met some of your good, friendly, Jap soldiers in combat today? What would you do?" He smirked in triumph.

"I'd have to kill 'em. Opposing armies are both trying to kill each other, so both sides can argue that they are acting in self-defense. So I'd have to kill those good Jap soldiers in self- defense." I rose to my feet and confronted him. "But that doesn't mean that I'd be willing to kill their unarmed families in Japan."

"Are you saying that you're not willing to bomb Tokyo?" asked the red-head, wide-eyed.

"It depends on what the target is," I replied. "I'm willing to bomb military installations anywhere, but if the mission is to bomb the whole city without distinction, like the Twentieth Air Force firebombing missions, I would refuse to fly!"

"Refuse to fly?" the red-head crowed. "That would make you a traitor!"

"You'd be court-martialed!" squealed the other intelligence lieutenant.

"Better think that one through again!" the captain advised.

"The consequences could be tough, I know, but I have to live with my own conscience. If other guys can sleep well after killing all those women and children, let them fly missions of mass murder! But as for me, I want to sleep with a clear conscience, even if it's in jail."

I sat down again, and relit my pipe. "I enlisted to help stop evil, not to spread it further."

James stroked his black crewcut. "This is pretty heavy stuff to think about!" He lit a cigarette. His baby face looked older when he scowled; it made his widow's peak as pointed as the one on Mickey Mouse.

Seitz leaned back in his chair and put on his calm, father-figure expression. "Let's keep things in perspective, men. No one's been assigned to fly a mission of mass murder up to now. Hamilton's the only combat veteran on our crew so far. His mission to Rabaul bombed a purely military target. And the missions we'll all be flying soon to Wewak and Rabaul will be the same. As for the future, we'll just have to wait and see."

"Yeah," James echoed, "just wait and see what Hamilton does!"

9. Minor League Players

On Easter Sunday, April 1, I got up before dawn to attend an outdoor Easter sunrise service on the parade ground at Nadzab, New Guinea. The war went on seven days a week, and our crew's combat training program put us in classes again this Sunday. That conflicted with morning chapel services, but a sunrise service would be over before classes began.

Out of nearly 3,000 men at the Combat Replacement and Training Center, some five or six hundred gathered in front of the flagpole for the Easter sunrise service. There were no seats, and no pulpit; only a folding table with a cloth over it to serve as the altar. We simply stood around in a large semicircle, several rows deep, facing the eastern sky, which glowed with pre-dawn light.

The base honor guard came promptly at six, with folded flag and a bugler, for the usual flag-raising ceremony. We all stood at attention and saluted while the flag went up with bugle playing; then the guardsmen and bugler joined the crowd.

The Protestant chaplain was a tall, suntanned captain from Milwaukee. He began the service with a prayer, then invited us to sing the chorus to the first hymn after a soloist sang the verses. The soloist had a good baritone voice; he began to sing quietly,

"Lo, in the grave he lay, Jesus, my Savior,
Waiting the coming day, Jesus, my Lord."
Then hundreds of voices joined in the swelling chorus,
"Up from the grave he arose, With a mighty triumph o'er his foes! He arose a victor o'er the dark domain, And he lives forever with his saints to reign. He arose!—He arose!—hallelujah! Christ arose!"

The chaplain read the resurrection story from the Gospel of

Luke, interrupted by the screech of a giant white cockatoo flying overhead.

Then the soloist led us in singing "Christ the Lord is Risen Today!"

The sky was cloudy, but for one shining moment, the sun rose above the dark hills and below the clouds, to shine through in a moment of radiant splendor, just as we sang that hymn. There it was! Easter Sunrise! We were halfway around the world, but this was a visible sign of a spiritual link with home. It put a glow inside my heart to match the glow in the sky.

The chaplain gave a brief sermon, then invited us all to step up to the altar to share Christ's supper. We did so quietly, in single file, dipping a small piece of hard bread into a large cup of red wine, hearing the words, "this is my body...this is my blood..."

The service closed with our singing "Onward, Christian Soldiers," accompanied by the bugler who had tarried for this. His strong bugle tones floated out over the valley, and gave our hymn unexpected strength and quality. I looked around the circle as we sang. Though I did not know many names, we were not strangers. We were all brothers, linked in a bond of fellowship that strengthened our purpose and raised our morale.

The roar of warplanes taking off began, coincidentally, right after the service ended. I was glad we had time to finish first.

After breakfast, I joined the rest of my crew at ground school. I mentioned the good sunrise service, and learned that Pieper had been there too.

We were in a large tent, listening to a lecture on combat tactics, when Major Hundt entered.

"Now hear this, men. Important news from Armed Forces Radio. They said that Hitler agreed to unconditional surrender for Germany, and General Eisenhower proclaimed an immediate cease-fire! The battle for Europe is over!"

The class erupted with cheering of all sorts. We clapped each other on the back, and whooped in celebration.

"More good news," the major continued. "Right after the cease-fire in Germany, the Soviet Union declared war against Japan, and launched an attack on the Jap army in Manchuria! This will drain Japan's resources and shorten the war."

More cheering greeted that announcement.

"But there's bad news, too," the major went on. "The Third Fleet shelling Okinawa was attacked by five hundred kamikazi planes diving headlong into the ships. The aircraft carrier U.S.S. Princeton burned and sank after being hit by six kamikazi planes. Admiral Halsey went down with his flagship."

So much high-powered news all at once—too much to absorb. We sat there, dazed.

"Go on with your class, Lieutenant," the major said, leaving. "If we get more news, we'll let you know."

Not many of us listened to the lecture for the next half hour; we were preoccupied with the news. Then Major Hundt walked in again, smiling.

"Armed Forces Radio just put out a special bulletin. All news reported earlier this morning came from today's date—April first. In other words, April Fool! None of that news is true!"

The class ended with disgusted groans, and we went out for a break.

Cordell lit a cigarette. "I knew something was wrong with those news flashes."

"I knew it too!" echoed James, lighting up also.

"They sure fooled me!" I said. "I thought of today as Easter Sunday, not as April Fool."

"I should have thought of April Fool," said Seitz. "I could kick myself for being taken in by such far-fetched stories."

"But they're not so far-fetched," Pieper said. "The war in Europe is almost over; Russia did agree to attack Japan after Germany surrenders, and kamikazi attacks on our ships are a new fact of life in the navy."

"Yes, but the details were flawed," Imhof replied. "If Hitler were rational, he'd have surrendered Germany when they lost the Battle of the Bulge, three months ago. But Hitler's a madman, so he'll never agree to any surrender."

"Good point," Hill added. "Hitler loves Wagner's operas—he thinks he's the hero in a Wagnerian tragedy, where the only exit is death. And his nation will die with him."

"Another flawed detail," Seitz said, "Russia couldn't attack Japan so soon—suffered too much in the long German invasion. Russia would have to build up strength, first."

"The third story was flawed, too," I said. "The aircraft carrier Princeton is not Admiral Halsey's flagship. And I remember reading that the Princeton was sunk last October in the Battle of Leyte Gulf."

"My tip-off was just that big news stories never come all at the same time," Williams said. "Any one of the three, by itself, might be believed, but all three happening at once? Never!"

"That bothered me, too," said James.

"Now that we've settled the affairs of the world," Seitz said, "let's go back to class."

For the next three days, our crew had classes in the morning only, with a trip to the flight line each afternoon to fly a brief training mission. We enjoyed flying; this was a welcome change.

The first afternoon we had a one-hour flight to check the B-24's autopilot. After climbing to 5,000 feet to clear the hills, the pilots went through their autopilot calibration. I used the time to plot fixes with the loran receiver—my first chance to try loran in the air since learning how.

Then I saw we were near the camelback mountain. Again I spotted the crater lake we had found in the top of the volcano. *How nice it would be to take a rubber boat to the top of that mountain, and paddle around in that clear, pure lake.*

The next afternoon our training mission was practice formation flying. Again we climbed to 5,000 feet, and joined three other B-24s in a four-plane diamond formation. The instructor pilot standing behind Seitz and Cordell urged them to move closer to the other planes.

"Tighten up the formation!" he shouted. "Don't leave room for an enemy fighter to fly between you! You have more defensive firepower when you're closer together."

The exciting part for me came when we flew over that crater lake once more. Again I felt adrenaline flow at the thought of boating on that beautiful little lake. During the truck ride home, I decided to share that idea with the crew.

"Have you guys noticed that lake in the crater of the volcano? Wouldn't it be nice to go boating in that lovely little lake?"

"I thought of that, too," said Pieper. "It reminds me of my favorite little lake in the woods in Wisconsin."

"And it's so secluded!" Hill said. "Just think how good it would feel to be the first person to reach that lake in a thousand years!"

"It might take a thousand years to reach it!" Cordell said. "That volcano is four thousand feet high!"

"Maybe we could fly over it, drop a rubber boat into it, then parachute in from above," Pieper suggested.

"Have any of us ever parachuted before?" asked James. "That would be a tough place to learn how!"

"We could never get a plane assigned for a paradrop that has nothing to do with the war," Seitz added.

"Mountain climbing really isn't very hard," I said. "While we were at Tonopah, I climbed a lot of those barren Nevada mountains for the fun of it. Couldn't we just carry a rubber boat with us up the mountainside, and launch it at the top?"

"Sure we could!" Hill said.

"Fat chance!" Cordell replied.

"Count me out!" said James, "It's too hot here to climb an anthill!"

Finally the time came for our crew to finish our training by flying combat missions. We were scheduled for three on three successive days, to Wewak on April 8 and 9, and to Rabaul on April 10. On Saturday night, April 7, our crew sat on empty crates in the briefing tent, waiting to be briefed for our first combat mission together.

"Did you officers hear the news?" Pieper said. "Today is Hill's birthday."

"Well, happy birthday, Hill! How old are you?" I asked.

Hill looked embarrassed. "Twenty-seven."

"Gosh, that's old!" James said. (He was still only nineteen.)

"Congratulations, Hill!" Seitz said. "You are definitely the oldest member of the crew."

Hill laughed. "I'm not leaning on a cane, yet."

"With this mission early tomorrow, we can't celebrate Hill's birthday with a beer bust," Imhof said.

Hill smiled. "That's okay, Imhof, I already got my birthday present—a letter from home. Anne wrote that she'd throw a birthday party for me in Ohio with Jackie, our baby girl."

"If she sent you a package, maybe it'll reach you in July," Herrema added.

The briefing began just like the one for my first mission, with a dramatic parting of the curtains over the target map. This time our target was the Japanese Eighteenth Army Headquarters at Mapete, near Wewak. We learned that four different kinds of planes were assigned to go in four successive waves to attack this enemy headquarters.

The first wave would be twelve B-24s to drop high-explosive bombs from 8,500 feet at ten A.M. Three of our planes would each be loaded with four giant "block-buster" bombs, while the other nine would each carry twenty fragmentation (anti-personnel) bombs.

The second wave would be eight P-47 Thunderbolt fighter-bombers, each loaded with a single, large firebomb (1,000 pounds of napalm). These big, single-engine fighters with barrel-shaped bodies were to arrive at 10:10 A.M. and strafe and bomb from tree-top level.

Tail Gunner **HILL** on top of his tail turret.

The third wave would be four P-51 Mustang fighter-bombers, each loaded with two 500-pound napalm firebombs, one under each wing. These trim, slender, single-engine fighters were to arrive at 10:20, and strafe and bomb from tree-top level.

The fourth wave would be six B-25 twin-engine medium bombers, each loaded with eight frag bombs. They were to arrive at 10:30 and bomb and strafe, also at tree-top height.

We got our time-tick to synchronize watches, and a final pep-talk from the C.O. Then we returned to our tents for a few hours sleep before the early morning crew call and breakfast.

The ground crew had worked all night loading our B-24 with bombs, gasoline and other supplies; now it was our turn to check what they had done. Seitz went into the cockpit to go over everything with the crew chief.

Cordell and Pieper climbed a twelve-foot ladder to the top of the plane's high wing, and opened each fuel cap to plunge a white measuring stick into each tank.

James and Gerson inspected the four giant 2,000-pound bombs hung in the bomb bay racks, checking their fuse settings and safety wires. Williams, Herrema, and Hill went to the four turrets and the two waist guns to check out the ten fifty-caliber machine guns on the plane and the belts of ammunition feeding them. Imhof went to his work station to tune the day's radio frequencies into all the transmitters, and set the I.F.F. transponder to the secret code of the day.

I carried all my navigation gear to the navigator's station in the nose and got my maps, charts, and navigator's log ready for the mission.

Seitz and Cordell together made their final walk-around inspection of the entire exterior of the bomber, making sure that it was airworthy.

We finished our preflight inspections about an hour before takeoff, then gathered under the wing to wait for boarding. Seitz quizzed us on emergency procedures for a while. Then came the inevitable bull session.

"Why get us up so early when we have an hour to kill?" Gerson asked.

"Typical army scene—hurry up and wait," said Hill.

Seitz replied, "The army gets us out early so we have some time to correct problems we might find, like errors in fueling."

"Speaking of errors," Cordell said, "remember our first practice bombing mission at Tonopah? James set all his data into that fancy bombsight that can put a bomb into a barrel from 20,000 feet. We flew our first bombing run, and he called out 'Bombs away!'—so full of confidence. 'Gonna be a bullseye!' he said."

Pieper laughed. "I was looking through the bomb bay doors to see where it hit, and I saw his smoke bomb land ten thousand feet off target! Two miles off!"

"A miss is as good as a mile," Cordell taunted, "but with James, it's as good as two!"

"Okay, guys, lay off," said James. "So I used the wrong aiming point for my first bomb run. Nobody's perfect."

"We won't have to worry about that here," I said. "All James has to do is watch the lead plane, and toggle off our load when the lead bombardier drops his."

"Same with the navigator," snapped James. "The lead navigator directs the squadron. All Hamilton has to do is plot where we've been, but who cares about that?"

"Until we lose an engine and leave the formation," I replied. "Then suddenly it's very important that I know just where we are, so I can tell the pilot where to head for home."

"Don't even talk about that!" said Williams. "It might bring on bad luck."

"I think we make our own luck," Seitz said. "We're a good crew, and if each of us does his job well, we'll come through our first combat mission with the same kind of professionalism we had in our later training missions. I'm counting on all of you!"

"You can count on me, Skipper!" Pieper said.

"Me too!" "I'll be there!" "Me too!" "Count on me!"

Seitz looked at his watch. "Well, men, it's time to board. Let's make this baby go!"

Our bomber was one of the three loaded with 2,000-pound "block-busters." It was the first time I had ever seen such big bombs. I touched them with awe as I entered through the bomb bay. *Such great destructive power! What a hole each one will dig!*

The B-24s began taking off promptly at eight A.M. Only eleven planes flew, because one crew discovered major hydraulic problems and never took off.

The weather was cloudy at Nadzab, but it got worse as we flew up the Markham River Valley northwest toward Wewak. There was little to see on this mission but clouds—above us, below us, and frequently all around us as we flew through their mist. The lead navigator was navigating by loran, of course, and I was plotting loran fixes to see where he led us.

Accurate navigation was critical as we followed the two successive river valleys northwest toward Wewak, because high mountain ranges rose abruptly on both sides. Half-way there, not far from the port city of Madang, the highest peak in northeast New Guinea rose to nearly 15,000 feet just a few miles to the left of our intended course. When flying blind in clouds, just a little wandering off course there could end in total disaster.

When we arrived over the target at 8,500 feet, it was completely hidden by clouds. We began circling the spot where loran fixed us over target (probably less than a mile off), hoping a break in the clouds would let us see the target. Our bombs were armed, ready to drop.

Ten minutes later, the eight P-47 Thunderbolts arrived, and dove down through the clouds to low level only to discover that lower clouds obscured the target down there also. They returned a minute later to group under us and drop their firebombs, hoping that we had arrived over the target. They waggled their wings, and left for home. Our B-24s then dropped our loads, too, and also headed home. By the time we landed, our flight lasted four hours thirty-five minutes.

Our crew piled into the big truck that came to our plane to carry us to Intelligence for debriefing. That same red-headed first lieutenant who had argued with me at the Officers Club was our debriefer, but he said not a word about the argument. Strictly business.

Next we drove to the supply tent to drop off our parachute harnesses, chest-pack chutes, and life jackets. Then the truck drove us toward our tents.

I lit my pipe and enjoyed its aroma. "Well, guys, let me welcome you all into the ranks of combat veterans! You're not rookies any more, and I'm no longer the only combat veteran on the crew. Congratulations!"

"These rookies did a good job on their first mission," Seitz said. "I'm proud of each one!"

Later we heard the story of the other phases of our mission. Promptly at 10:20, the four P-51 Mustangs arrived over target at low level, finding the big fires started by the P-47's. Perhaps the heat from the fires helped clear away the lower clouds; the target was visible then, and the Mustangs hit the Japanese Eighteenth Army Headquarters with their firebombs and strafing.

They had just left the scene when the six B-25 twin-engine bombers arrived to find the target partly covered by lower clouds, but open enough for them to bomb and strafe at tree-top level, one plane at a time. Five of the medium bombers got their bombs and bullets right on target before the low clouds rolled over the scene completely, hiding it once more. The sixth plane flew a little higher, circling back above the low clouds, and dropped his bombs anyway, where he thought the target lay.

Intelligence ruled that his bombs were "jettisoned," since he could not see where they went. Also "jettisoned" were all the bombs dropped by our B-24s, and also those of the P-47s. For that reason, the B-24 and P-47 phases of this mission were scored "unsuccessful."

But the mission as a whole was considered successful. The target was visibly hit with eight firebombs from the P-51s and forty frag bombs from the B-25s, and thousands of .50-caliber bullets from both. The Japanese Eighteenth Army Headquarters was demolished. *I hope those block-buster bombs we jettisoned fell close enough to help knock it out. I want our crew to make a contribution toward winning this war on our first combat mission together.*

Our crew flew to Wewak again the next morning, four and a half hours round trip. At the briefing the night before, the Australian Army Liaison Officer pointed out our objectives.

"As you know, mates, the Australian Sixth Division is moving north through the jungle toward Wewak, but they are encountering fierce Jap resistance at this cluster of Ambunti Villages, here, and at the Bukinara Villages, there, and at Fatnea Village, over here." He pointed to the targets on the map.

"Our lads would appreciate your working over those sites with some napalm and demolition bombs, and a bit of splendid strafing with your machine guns. But don't bomb any farther south than half a mile from the targets, to stay clear of our lads. If you have to miss the target, miss it toward the north side, not the south."

When we started engines Monday morning, two B-24s and one B-25 turned back to the ramp and never took off. *Must be mechanical problems.* The lead B-24 took off at seven fifty-four, with the other nine close behind. The weather was much better than the day before, so we expected to see the targets without too many clouds in the way.

Our crew flew this mission in an old-style B-24-D, which had the original greenhouse-style nose instead of a nose turret. It had much better visibility forward without a nose turret in the way, so navigators and bombardiers liked that feature. But it got a bit crowded in the small nose compartment when the nose gunner stepped up to his socket-mounted flexible .50-caliber machine gun while the bombardier tried to use his bombsight and the navigator worked at his table. The gunner had to straddle the bombardier, and rub shoulders with the navigator, while shooting..

The fighters were so much faster than our bombers that they took off an hour and a half after we did, and still arrived first at the target, as planned. As we came in sight of the Ambunti Villages, flying at 9,000 feet, I saw the fighters beginning their attack down at tree-top level. That lovely greenhouse nose gave me a good view of the twelve fighters below.

There were six P-38 Lightnings, those graceful, twin-engine, twin-boom fighters, each with a single large firebomb and lots of machine gun bullets. They went in with guns blazing and dropped their napalm bombs, which turned into giant mushrooms of orange-yellow flames. Two of those big bombs were right on target, but four fell beyond it to the north. Big fires were blazing, then, on target and nearby.

Then came six P-51 Mustang single-engine fighters with frag bombs and lots of bullets. They hit their target with all of their bombs, and strafed the whole cluster of Ambunti Villages.

They had barely cleared the target area when we were on our formation bombing run, with James ready to toggle our bombs away as soon as he saw the lead plane drop its load. Promptly at ten-thirty he shouted, "Bombs away!" Our ten Liberators carried a total of twenty block-busters (twelve hit in the target area) and a hundred frag bombs (fifty-six hit the target). An F-5 photo plane (P-38 with cameras) flew with us, taking pictures of the bomb damage. We could never count all our bomb hits and misses in the air, of course; those figures came only after Intelligence studied the strike photos.

The other villages occupied by Japanese soldiers also were hit well that day. Five B-25 medium bombers dropped forty big frag bombs on the Bukinara Villages, all in the target area.

Four A-20 light bombers dropped sixteen frag bombs on Fatnea

Village, all on target. Both targets were strafed with thousands of bullets, too.

This mission was a great success. The Australian Army's Sixth Division sent a message of thanks and appreciation by radio to their Liaison Officer at Nadzab even before we landed. We heard about it from the Intelligence officers who debriefed us. I felt good about doing something useful for the war effort.

Our crew flew again the following day, this time to the Rabaul area. At briefing the night before, we learned that nine B-24s were to attack Tobera Airdrome, one of three major airfields in the Rabaul area. Since Tobera still had fighter aircraft for its defense, our bombers would be escorted by three P-38 fighters. One F-5 photo plane would go along with us to take pictures of our dirty work.

This mission also ordered other aircraft to attack the Wewak area. Six B-25 medium bombers would attack Pakogo Village, four A-20 light bombers would hit Jama Village, and six P-51 Mustangs strike the Ambunti Villages once more. These were not just training missions for us; they were real strikes to help real Aussie soldiers struggling through that dense New Guinea jungle against a fanatical and cruel enemy. More such help would be given increasingly over the next month, until the Wewak area was overrun by our allied amphibious landings on May 11.

Our crew was flying a B-24-J, the last of the nine to take off at seven forty-five on the morning of April 10. Our bomb bay held four of those awesome one-ton block-busters, the biggest bombs I had ever heard of, and we hoped to put them right on target.

The weather was cloudy at Nadzab, but deteriorating at Rabaul. We hoped that we could still see the target well enough to bomb when we arrived at Tobera Airdrome.

Near Finschaven, we assembled our nine Liberators into a "javelins in trail" formation, three V-shaped, three-plane elements, one following another. Our plane was "tail-end Charlie," the left wing position in the last javelin. We felt even more lonely a few minutes later, when the right wing plane in our javelin peeled off to head back to Nadzab. *Another mechanical problem!*

"Pilot to all Gunners. We're all alone as 'tail-end Charlie.' Keep your eyes peeled for enemy fighters, and test-fire your guns now."

The whole plane reverberated with staccato sounds as all four turrets and two waist guns fired noisy bursts. The acrid smell of cordite drifted into the nose compartment from Williams' nose turret guns.

The presence of friendly fighters to escort us on this mission reassured me. I could see them through the overhead astrodome, in their own formation a thousand feet above us—three twin-engine P-38s in a javelin-V, followed by the F-5 to make a diamond shape. They had to throttle back to minimum power settings in order to go slow enough to stay with our bombers. The graceful shape of the P-38 Lockheed Lightning has always excited my admiration. With its three pointed noses, streamlined body pod, twin slender booms and twin oval rudders, it appealed to me as a masterpiece of design. But it never looked more lovely to me than it did that day when it played shepherd to our flock of bombers.

The route we took on this mission was different from my first trip to Rabaul. Instead of going around New Britain Island on the north side, this time we skirted the southern shore. We headed east over the Solomon Sea until we were thirty miles south of the port of Awio, then turned left thirty degrees to parallel the southern coast of New Britain. Staying about twenty miles offshore, we headed north as we rounded the shoulder, past the neck, to the head of the island. There we saw the top of the volcano between layers of clouds, but its base and much of the landscape of New Britain was hidden by lower clouds. When we arrived over target, by loran fix, Tobera Airdrome was completely obscured. We began circling, to stay over the target, while the flight leader made a decision. No enemy fighters emerged from the clouds below, but anti-aircraft shells began exploding 500 feet below us. Only radar-directed flak would shoot through clouds.

Our bombs were armed, ready to drop on either Tobera Airdrome or the secondary target. On the way in, we had seen the secondary from a distance; it looked almost as obscured as this one. The lead bomber opened his bomb bay doors, and all the others did likewise. He dropped his load at 10:45, and all the others with him, on what we hoped was the center of Tobera Airdrome. The flak was getting more accurate as we closed bomb-bay doors and broke away. I was glad to head for home when we did.

On the trip home, American fighters intercepted us with mock combat, much to the delight of our gunners. For me it replayed the mock combat I remembered from my first trip to Rabaul. We landed at one-thirty. I closed the navigator log with "Total flight time = 5:45."

Our debriefers wrote that we jettisoned all our bombs, so they judged our trip to Rabaul as "unsuccessful." *I hope our bombs did real damage to the enemy airfield, anyway. I hate waste, and the war's had too much of that already.*

Later that afternoon the four officers on our crew sat in the Quonset-hut officers' club, drinking beers and having a relaxed bull session. It helped dissipate the tension of three days of combat missions in a row.

"I'm well pleased with our performance as a combat crew," said Seitz. "Cordell and I have been on top of things in the cockpit, Hamilton has impressed me with his navigation, and James bombed accurately on the practice range, when he did it all by himself, as well as toggling our bombs in formation. Imhoff has handled radio communications well, and the gunners all seem alert and competent. Even Gerson has made more of an effort."

"It sure is satisfying to actually strike the enemy instead of just training for it," I said.

"Are you really satisfied with what we've done?" Cordell asked.

"Why not?," I replied. "After two years of training, I got four combat missions, all in the last month here. You got three, so why are you griping?"

"That's a lot of training, and darn little action!" said James.

"Even the action has been nothin' but minor league games," Cordell protested. "What have we done? Flew a few missions against back-water targets with little opposition, and then we jettisoned our bombs more'n half the time! How's that gonna win the war?"

"Every strike against the enemy, however modest, makes him that much weaker," I said. "That helps win the war."

"Cordell craves dramatic deeds of daring-do," said Seitz. "He wants to be bombing Tokyo, or at least Okinawa, where real live enemy fighters shoot up half our crew on each mission, and our wing man goes down in flames."

"Or *we* go down in flames, instead of the wing man," added James.

"We can take our chances on that," Cordell said. "I want to feel that we're in a major campaign of the war, helping to make a real contribution to front line action where it's important. What's wrong with that?"

"Nothing, if that's where the army sends us," Seitz replied. "But right now, we're needed right here, and doing a good job in our appointed place. The army will send us on when it needs us."

"Every major league baseball club has a minor league team to draw from," James said. "Nadzab is the minor league team for the front line Air Forces to draw from. Why do you think it's named Combat Replacement and Training Center?"

"Well, I'm sure ready to move on to a major league team!" Cordell answered.

"It won't be long, now," Seitz said. "I was talking with Major Hundt a few days ago. Their training program is set up for twenty-eight days. We've been here a month. We've flown four training missions and three combat missions—"

"Four missions for me," I said.

"We've done more than everything in their plan. From now on, they're just holding us here until either the Fifth or the Thirteenth Air Force calls for us as a replacement crew."

"Yay, man!" said James. "Next stop is the major league team! What will it be like when we really get there?"

"We'll find out soon enough," Seitz predicted.

JUNGLE EXPLORER
Lieutenant Hamilton dressed to go exploring, wearing .45 automatic pistol, sheath knife, web cartridge belt and clips, canteen, and pith sun helmet. (Notice his army cot on tent floor behind.)

10. Lure of the Lake

I can see it now—round, blue, cool, and beautiful!

The lake in the crater of the old volcano near Nadzab, New Guinea, had haunted me for three weeks, ever since we flew over it searching for the missing bomber. When I awoke on April 11, after my fourth bombing mission, that little lake filled my mind like a new obsession.

Our crew was scheduled for ground duties during the next three days, but on April 14 (Saturday), we would have the whole day off. I decided that April 14 would be the day for my boating excursion in the crater lake.

I went to see the recreation officer in the afternoon.

"I'd like to organize a little fishing expedition for my crew on the fourteenth," I said. "I think it would be good for our morale. We've flown several combat missions, now, and could use some diversion."

"That's possible," he said. "What do you need?"

"A rubber dinghy and paddles, CO-2 cartridges to inflate it, and whatever you have in the way of fishing gear. Oh, yes, also a jeep to carry it to the bank of the Markham River."

"I can loan you the ten-man life raft your bombers carry, or the little one-man raft the fighters use."

"I'll take the big one."

"All we have for fishing gear is the handline kit for the raft. It comes with artificial lures and hooks."

"That'll do. What about the jeep?"

"Check with the motor pool for that."

At the fenced motor pool I repeated my story to the sergeant in charge.

"Can I borrow a jeep for all day Saturday, to get the life raft to the river and back?"

"No, but we can send a driver with a truck to deliver you in the morning, and go back for you whenever you want."

"Swell," I said. "Can I borrow a jeep now for half an hour or more, so I can drive down to the river bank and look for a good place to launch?"

"Yes sir, we can manage that. Just sign here—name, rank and serial number." I grabbed a pencil and signed, "Robert H. Hamilton, 2nd Lt. Air Corps., 02073118."

"Where's the ignition key?" I asked.

"Jeeps don't have no key, sir; they gotta be ready for any soldier to use in combat. Just turn on the switch, and hit the starter button on the floor."

"Sounds like it'd be easy to steal."

"No sir, not here! You gotta show this pass at the gate to get outta the motor pool." He handed me a pass.

It was my very first time in a jeep. *Feels wonderful to be driving again!* I revved through all the gears like a hot-rodder. *I love this open jeep—it's exhilarating!* I zoomed to the south end of the air base, and then east and west on a trail along the bank of the Markham River.

Looking across to the south shore, I saw where the Wampit River flowed into the Markham on the far side, and I knew that we needed to launch opposite that junction. I found the likely spot to launch, and marked its location in my memory.

Returning the jeep to the motor pool, I set out to recruit members of our crew for my rafting trip. My fellow officers turned me down flat.

"Climb a 4,000-foot mountain—?" Seitz looked quizzical.

"—carrying a life raft to the top?" James blurted.

"In the heat of day?" Cordell asked, wide-eyed.

James broke into a laugh. "Man, that's crazy!"

I hadn't expected much enthusiasm from them. *Not much ap-*

preciation for adventure! They didn't applaud my climbing mountains in Nevada, either.

I walked to the enlisted crewmen's tent. "Hey guys, remember that lovely little lake in the crater of the volcano? How would you like a chance to go boating in it?"

Gerson sat up on his cot. "When?"

"Our crew has the day off this Saturday, the fourteenth. I can get us a big inflatable raft with paddles and fishing lines, and I've lined up transportation with the motor pool."

"Hey, that sounds like an adventure!" said Pieper.

"What's your plan?" asked Hill.

"I've been studying the map," I answered. "On the east side of that volcano, there's a river called the Wampit that flows past the mountain and into the Markham River at the south side of the airbase. A truck will deliver us to the water's edge. We can inflate the raft there, paddle across the Markham and up the Wampit to the base of the mountain. Then we carry the raft between us and climb to the top. There, we launch into the lake, and it's done!"

Gerson lay down again. "You make it sound so easy. Bet it turns out to be a lot of work!"

"How high is that mountain?" asked Williams.

"Four thousand feet."

"Oh, no, that's awful! I'm too old for a climb like that!"

"Cut it out, Williams," said Hill. "I'm the oldest man on the crew, and I know I can make it. You're only twenty-six."

"Another reason for going is to finish our search for the missing B-24," I added. "If it did fall into the lake, we might be able to see it under the water, from a boat."

Gerson sat up again. "I like that! We'd be like detectives!"

Imhof said, "Wish I could go with you, but I'm on the K.P. roster (mess hall) for the fourteenth."

"Darn! So am I!" said Herrema. "I'd much rather go with you than scrub pots and pans!"

By the end of my visit, I had recruited three out of our six enlisted crewmen, Gerson, Hill, and Pieper. Gerson really surprised me by agreeing to come. He was viewed by all as lazy and careless, since his misdeeds nearly broke up the crew.

"Sure you want to work that hard?" Hill asked him.

"This could be my best chance for adventure in the South Pacific," Gerson replied.

I returned to the officers' tent, pleased with plans so far.

"Well, Hamilton, where've you been?" asked Seitz.

"At the enlisted men's tent, recruiting our crewmen for my great rafting adventure."

"How many did you get?" asked James.

"Three out of six," I answered, "Hill, Pieper, and Gerson."

"Gerson?" Cordell asked. "That lazy bum? You're kidding!"

"No kidding. He said he wanted to be in on the adventure. He may be using it for a chance to improve his relationship with the other crew members, after he screwed up so badly in Hawaii."

"I don't like your plan at all, Hamilton," Seitz said. "It sure seems to me like you're fraternizing with the enlisted men!"

"Shame on you, Hamilton!" said Cordell, wagging his finger at me. "Let's not be fraternizing with the troops, now!"

"I keep hearing that, but it doesn't make sense. What's really so bad about officers fraternizing with enlisted men?"

"It undermines the army's system of command," Seitz replied. "Command and obedience are based on respect for ranking authority. If officers are too friendly with their men, the men will lose respect for them as superior officers, and disrespect could lead to disobedience at a crucial time. Every legitimate order given by competent authority must be obeyed without question! The whole army depends upon it!"

Cordell clapped his hands. "Listen to a true blue regular army officer!"

"Well said!" echoed James.

I sat down on my cot. "As a general principle, I agree, but I think that the Air Corps is a special case. For example, our crew spent sixteen weeks training together at Tonopah, learning to work together as a close-knit team. Our success in combat depends on how well we work together and trust each other. That kind of trust breeds a special relationship that is more like friendship than respect for rank."

"An aircrew is different," James agreed. "It has its own loyalty—a special relationship."

"It's okay to be friendly and loyal to our crew, but don't carry this togetherness stuff beyond reasonable limits."

"Okay, Seitz. But we *will* be together on the rafting trip."

On the morning before the trip, I woke up to the realization that the date was April 13 (Friday).

"I'm glad I didn't plan the trip for today," I said. "It's Friday the thirteenth."

"Cut it out, Hamilton!" Cordell said. "Don't tell me an intelligent man like you would believe in that old superstition!"

"Well, I really don't. I know that Friday falls on the thirteenth once each quarter, so it's really a natural occurrence. But it's fun to pretend to believe it. Then, when things go wrong, you say, 'A-hah! It's Friday the thirteenth!'"

"We're not flying today," said Seitz, "so what could go wrong? Some disaster in class?"

"Let's go to breakfast," James said. "Maybe he'll drop a pitcher of coffee in the mess hall."

During breakfast, a loudspeaker came on with news from Armed Forces Radio.

"Attention all hands! Now hear this! The White House just announced that President Roosevelt died less than an hour ago at his country home in Warm Springs, Georgia. I repeat, President Roosevelt died—of a massive stroke at 3:18 p.m. at Warm Springs, Georgia, where he frequently went for swimming and physical therapy. Meanwhile, in Washington, Vice President Truman has just been sworn in as President. He pledged to lead America on to victory over Germany and Japan, following the plans laid down by our late, great President Roosevelt."

That announcement was followed by somber funeral music.

We all sat in stunned silence at that incredible news.

Then James said, "A-hah! It's Friday the thirteenth!"

We all laughed.

"True, it's Friday the thirteenth here," I said, "but we're a day ahead of the States, so back where it happened, it's only Thursday the twelfth. I guess we can't blame it on the date."

"I can hardly believe he's dead," Seitz said. "He's the only President I can remember. He's in his fourth term!"

"Same with me," James agreed. He poured himself more coffee.

Cordell reached for the coffee pitcher and refilled his cup. "I voted for him last November. We were at Tonopah then, but I voted by absentee ballot."

"I did too," I said. "It was my first election ever."

"How did you get to vote?" James asked. "I was too young, and you and I were both only nineteen then."

"I'm from Georgia. A few years ago, Georgia and one other progressive state—Wisconsin, I think—reduced the voting age from twenty-one to eighteen. Of course I voted for Roosevelt. He's been like a father-figure to me all my life."

"He's been that to me, too," James agreed.

"Where I come from in North Carolina," Cordell said, "people think of him as almost a God-figure."

"Where I come from in Iowa," said Seitz, "people think of him as more like the Devil! Naturally, I voted Republican, for Wendell Wilkie."

"Whatever we thought of Roosevelt," I added, "I think we can agree that we'll all miss him, especially his leadership in the war."

"I'll drink to that," Seitz said, raising his cup. James lifted his to meet it with a clink.

The day finally came for the great rafting trip. I got up at six to welcome sunrise on a morning that was clear, for a change. After a hearty breakfast meant to last, I walked down to the motor pool and got the truck and driver I had reserved. Then I directed him to the enlisted men's area to pick up Pieper, Hill, and Gerson.

Hill had an old duffel bag to carry our refreshments. We each brought two or three bottles of coke or beer, and a couple of candy bars for lunch. They all went into the bag.

Next we checked out the equipment, drove to the Markham River, and unloaded there. Telling the driver to return for us at six, we inflated the raft and launched it.

The place I had picked to launch was about a hundred yards upstream from the mouth of the Wampit. As we paddled across the width of the Markham, its current flow carried us downstream at an angle to meet our goal. The current was a bit more swift than I expected, but we paddled furiously at the end, and came right into the mouth of the tributary stream.

"We made it, men!" I said. "Welcome to the Wampit River!"

"This is a smaller stream," Gerson panted. "Maybe it won't flow so fast."

"No, but we have to paddle upstream here," Pieper said. "How far do we have to go?"

"On the chart it looked like five or six miles," I said, "depending on where we choose to go ashore to start the climb."

"Five or six miles upstream?" Hill said. "We'd better settle down to a comfortable paddling rhythm for the long haul."

"Good idea, Hill," I agreed. "Something like this:" stroke—(pause), stroke—(pause), stroke—(pause), stroke—(pause). "A regular rhythm we can keep up for quite a while."

As I noticed how the men looked to me for leadership, it occurred to me that I was in command for the first time in my life. *This isn't a Boy Scout activity; it's a military unit on a field maneuver, and I'm in command! I'll exercise my command rationally—give reasons for decisions—let the men understand, not just give orders.* I felt a new weight of responsibility.

The banks of the Wampit slowly drifted by as we made our way steadily upstream. The Markham valley was broad, flat, marshy ground, with rice paddies filling much of it. Various kinds of reeds, rushes, cattails, and marsh grasses lined the banks, with brush and trees visible in the distance, where the ground sloped up to form hills and mountains.

The morning was mostly quiet, with sounds of frogs croaking, insects buzzing, and distant bird calls, punctuated by the splash of our paddles. Periodically, these were drowned out by the roar of heavy aircraft taking off from the runways across the river behind us.

"Glad we're not on those planes taking off today," said Pieper. "After three missions in three days straight, this is a pleasant change."

"It's a change all right," Gerson agreed, "but whether its pleasant is another question."

"How long do you think it'll be before we reach our landing place?" Pieper asked.

"Let's figure it out," I said. "This stream appears to be flowing about one or two miles per hour, and our water speed may be three or four miles per hour, which would give us a net speed of about two miles an hour. At that rate, it would take us three hours to go six miles."

"Three hours?" Gerson moaned. "I'll never last that long!"

"Not three hours more, dummy, three hours total," said Hill. "One hour's behind us already."

Time went by to the regular splashes of our strokes.

"Look ahead," I said. "You can already see the camel-back mountain in the distance on the right. The peak in front is the old, rounded volcano without a crater. It's hiding the one behind, the younger, taller volcano with the crater lake on top. As we get closer to the side we want to climb, the one in front will appear to move to the right, and the one behind will seem to move to the left and emerge from hiding. Then we'll see it clearly."

"Good!" said Hill. "Now that our goal is in sight, maybe that'll motivate us more."

"I hope so!" said Pieper. "We need something to offset the sweat we're working up."

"Why?" Hill asked. "Healthy sweat is good for you!"

"What I wouldn't give for an outboard motor!" said Gerson. "Nobody in New York ever sets foot in a boat without a motor."

"They're missing half the fun of boating," Pieper replied. "In Wisconsin, we specialize in canoes and kayaks. The double-ended paddle is what makes 'em go."

"Wish we had a canoe right now!" I said. "It would sure be a lot easier to move a streamline shape through the water than this tub we're pushing with single-ended paddles."

"These really aren't paddles at all," Hill added, "they're aluminum oars that we're using for paddles."

More time went by, and our visual angle gradually changed. The taller volcano did emerge from behind the one in front, and got closer and more encouraging all the time. The sky behind the peaks was a beautiful azure blue, with fair-weather cumulus clouds punctuating the blue, like white swans gliding across a blue lagoon. And the sun, shining through and around those clouds, had warmed up to its mid-morning heat. The heat began sapping our strength.

The final half-hour of paddling was the worst. We were all young and healthy, but three hours of paddling through increasing heat had taken its toll.

We finally came opposite the base of the mountain, pulled over to the bank, and climbed out. Gerson lay down in the tall grass for a few minutes of rest, and the others squatted to light cigarettes. We were all lightly clothed in olive drab fatigues over shorts, with fatigue caps, socks, G.I. boots, wrist watches and dog tags, nothing more. But the olive color really absorbed the heat of that tropical sun. We stripped down to the waist, putting the shirts into the duffel bag.

"Come on, guys," I said, standing up. "Let's go up that mountain before the sun gets any hotter."

"Should we deflate the dinghy now, and carry it?" asked Pieper.

"Anything to make it easier," Gerson replied.

"It might be easier to carry if we leave it inflated," Hill said.

"More people could help bear the weight."

"Just pull it along by the rope," I said. "It should float over this tall grass, almost like water."

It did. We put the oars and the duffel bag in it and pulled, and it floated along behind us, across a sea of tall marsh grasses. But we lost the grass when the ground sloped up toward the mountain, and scrub brush took its place.

The dinghy no longer floated, so we lifted it up and carried it on our four shoulders. That worked well in the brushy area, but not when we came to the trees. As the ground got steeper, the trees got closer together, too close for the dinghy to pass through in that horizontal position.

"We'll have to turn the dinghy on edge," I said. "Gerson, carry the oars and the duffel bag, while the rest of us carry the dinghy in a vertical position."

We turned the dinghy on edge, with me at the front end, Pieper, the largest, in the middle, and Hill at the tail end. Gerson trailed along after us, with four oars under one arm and the duffel bag over a shoulder, like Santa with his sack. I led the way between trees, up a slope that got steeper as we went higher.

Soon the trees got so thick it became increasingly hard to find a way between them, even with the raft on edge. Then we found that vines of all sorts were growing up the trees, and as the trees got closer together, more vines were hanging across the open spaces in between. I had to pull them down, or break them, or lift them up, to wiggle the raft through.

"Wait a minute, men!" I said. "This isn't working any more. We need somebody with a sword or machete to go in front and cut these vines away. Pieper, you're the biggest and strongest. Take one of the aluminum oars and walk in front to chop away at the vines."

"Good idea," Pieper agreed, going to get the oar. "Let's see how well this baby can cut these vines."

"Hill and I can carry this boat between us, with me at the nose, where the navigator belongs, and Hill at the rear, where the tail gunner goes."

"I'll be your path-finder aircraft," said Pieper, as he walked ahead of us to slash away with the oar.

"I'll be the fighter escort in the rear," said Gerson.

Pieper was successful as path-finder for a while, chopping away the smaller vines, and lifting up the larger ones. We pushed on up the ever-steepening slope another hundred yards. But the thicker vines became more numerous, and even though Pieper chopped with all the strength of both hands together, he could no longer clear the way.

"This aluminum oar is no sword," Pieper said. "It's too light to really swing hard, and the edge is too dull to really cut the thick ones."

"And the slope has gotten too steep to take another step," Gerson panted. "Just look at us! We're staggering!"

"The forest has developed into a full-fledged jungle," Hill added.

"We need a change of strategy," I said. "Take a break while I survey the situation."

Hill and Gerson lit cigarettes. I walked downhill a little way to find an open place where I could see the landscape. I studied the neighboring 3,000-foot peak (the other hump of the camelback mountain), and compared it with what I could see of the mountain above us. It was discouraging.

We've climbed to an altitude of only 1,000 feet on a mountain 4,000 feet high. The toughest climb is still ahead. We'll never make it to the top without leaving the dinghy behind. Unthinkable! I'm committed to boating in that crater lake.

Frustrated, I rested my eyes on the view of the landscape below. The Markham River, winding peacefully through its broad valley southeasterly toward the sea, gave me a totally new idea. Excited now, I climbed back up the slope to share it with the crew.

11. Naked on a Life Raft

"Listen up, men! With all this effort, we've only climbed one-fourth the height of this mountain. We have to face the facts. We'll never make it to the top unless we leave the boat behind."

"I was afraid of that," Pieper said.

"We have options," I said. "We could pick our way to the top, but without the boat, we couldn't enjoy the lake much."

Hill dropped his cigarette butt and stepped on it. "It wouldn't be worth the effort."

"But the trip doesn't have to be a total loss," I added. "We could take the dinghy back downhill, drift on the Wampit downstream to the Markham, and then let the Markham take us downstream to the sea, where we could fish in the ocean."

Gerson's eyes grew wide. "Hey, that's a swell idea!"

"I like two words you said—'downhill' and 'downstream'!" said Hill.

"Where does the Markham River meet the sea?" asked Pieper.

"At the Port of Lae, which has an Aussie Army camp nearby. I think we can hitch a ride back to Nadzab on an Aussie truck, or 'lorrie' as they call it."

"Ahoy, there, mate!" Hill mimicked, waving his thumb, "Can you give us a bit of a lift in your lorrie?"

"Let's do it!" said Pieper, to a chorus of agreement.

Going downhill was so much easier than going up that it was positively exhilarating. While at first we had to move carefully through the thicker woods, we soon reached the thinner part where we went faster. Then we came out of the trees to the scrub brush and almost ran downhill to the sea of marsh grass. There we floated the dinghy on the tall grass again, and pulled it to the river.

"Hooray!" shouted Pieper as we cast off downstream.

"Now we got it made—in the shade—with pink lemonade," Gerson added, in his thickest Brooklyn accent.

"There's no shade and no lemonade," said Hill, "but there is warm beer and warm coke and melting candy bars in the bag, and I'm ready to reach for something."

"Pass me a beer and a candy bar," Pieper requested.

"It's eleven thirty, and I'm hungry," I said. "Pass me a candy bar and a coke."

We all had something to eat and drink as we relaxed and drifted down the stream. Our spirits and good humor returned with nourishment and rest. The sunshine felt good, and our hopes for enjoyment soared.

"How long will it take us to reach the Markham?" asked Hill.

"If we just drift with the current, it'll take three hours," I said. "Or we could paddle lightly, and cut the time in half."

"That sounds like the thing to do," said Pieper. "We have to paddle a little anyway, just to steer away from the banks."

So we started paddling lightly, enough to keep us in the center of the stream and add to its speed without tiring us. Time passed pleasantly, and by one P.M. we reached the Markham.

"There's the airfield across the river," I said. "If you want to go home, we can paddle straight across. If you want more adventure, we'll go to the middle and let the strong current carry us down to the sea. But we have to decide right now."

"Anybody want to chicken out now?" asked Pieper.

"Well, uh, maybe," said Gerson doubtfully.

"Aw, come on, Gerson, you won't have to paddle here!" Hill said. "Besides, the truck won't come back for us for five more hours. We'd have to hike in from the river."

"Okay—I guess," Gerson agreed weakly.

"We'll go for it!" I decided, and turned downstream.

"Good!" Pieper shouted.

In high spirits, we welcomed the grasp of the strong current of the Markham as we watched the airbase beyond the north bank slowly fade from view.

Suddenly I saw it—something unusual in the water ahead, halfway between our raft and the north shore. Two dark semi-circles rose a foot above the surface, parallel to each other, like the dorsal fins of two large sailfish swimming in formation just below the surface.

"What is that?" I asked, pointing to the pair of fins. The other men looked carefully at the strange sight.

"Looks like the fins on a pair of big fish," said Hill.

"But they can't be fish, because they don't wiggle or move," Pieper said. "See the ripples in their wake? The current's flowing by, but they're standing still."

"Fish don't stand still," said Gerson. "It's impossible!"

"You don't suppose they could be the top part of the twin rudders of a B-24, do you?" Hill asked, "I mean, if the rest of the plane was under water, out of sight?"

"That's it!" I exclaimed. "The missing plane!"

"What missing plane?" asked Gerson.

"The one we thought might have crashed in the crater lake," I shouted. "Start paddling, men! Move this boat over to where we can grab hold of it! Hurry, before it's too late!"

We started to paddle vigorously, moving the boat northward across the current toward the object. As we got closer, the circular tops of B-24 rudders became unmistakable. But reaching the plane would be nip and tuck. I thought we would make it, but then the swift current carried us downstream faster than we could paddle across. We were still twenty feet away when the current swept us by, and once we had passed it, there was no turning back.

"Darn!" said Hill, "we were so close!"

Disappointed and weary, we put down our paddles and watched the twin rudders grow smaller and finally disappear from view.

"Hill and Gerson were not on the search mission, when we went looking for that plane three weeks ago," I said. "Something went wrong on a bombing mission to Wewak six weeks ago, and one B-24 turned back. They tried to make it to Nadzab in lousy weather, but the plane disappeared."

"They almost made it," said Pieper. "They fell into the river only two miles from the runway."

"How many men were on board?" Gerson asked.

"Eleven," I replied, "ten crew members and one instructor."

A sobering silence followed. We felt the presence of death.

"There, but for the grace of God, go I," said Pieper.

"Amen," I agreed.

"Amen again for my wife and child," Hill said.

"That's one advantage to being single," Gerson added, "I don't have to worry about that."

I'm single, too, but I want to get back to see Persis again.

"When we return to base," I said, "we'll go to Intelligence and tell them what we saw."

"Yeah," Pieper added, "they'll send a team to the river to recover the bodies."

"How much would be left of bodies after six weeks in a warm tropical river?" I asked. "Flesh would rot away by then."

"Or be eaten away by hungry tropical fish," said Hill. "There may be nothing left to recover but bones and dog-tags."

We paused to see the scenery, lost in private reflections. As far as the eye could see, there was no evidence of human habitation. We quietly drifted between the widely-spaced banks of the river, with only reeds, rushes, cat-tails, and marsh grasses in view on any side, except for the dark mountains that rose in the distance.

"This tropic sun sure is hot!" Pieper exclaimed. "I'm going to take off all my clothes and cool off in the river."

"Good idea!" Hill agreed.

"I'll do it too," said Gerson.

Soon all three were in the water.

"I'd like to jump in, too," I said as I stripped naked, "but I'd better wait until one of you comes back. We need one person on board at all times, to make sure the boat doesn't get away."

Yes, that's all we need now, to have the dinghy get away while we're all in the water! Then we'd have to tread water all the way to the ocean, and emerge naked at the Port of Lae, if we could make it that far! God forbid!

The three in the water were splashing each other, shouting friendly insults, and laughing.

Soon Hill climbed on board, saying, "Go ahead and jump in! I'll relieve you."

"Thanks, Hill!" I said, and dove overboard. The cool water instantly refreshed my hot body, giving me fresh vigor. I swam over to the other two, and joined their friendly water-fights.

In a few minutes, Gerson climbed back on the raft, and Pieper followed soon. Not long after, I climbed aboard myself.

I noticed that the other three were drying in the sun, still naked. I looked through the duffel bag for my shorts.

"Why put anything on?" asked Gerson. "There's nobody around to see us out here."

"Yeah," Hill agreed, "and as soon as you get too hot in the sun, you'll dive in the water again, so why not stay prepared?"

"Good point," I agreed.

So we spent that afternoon naked, all the way to the sea. There was room for one man to lie down while the other three sat, and we took turns for the prone position. Periodically, we got hot enough to dive in the water, always with one man on board.

"Do we need to look out for crocodiles?" asked Pieper.

"I don't think so," I said. "We haven't seen any sign of crocodiles in either river today. But it won't hurt to look out for them."

We all had good suntans on our arms, legs, and faces before this trip began. The heavy dose of sunlight we got on this trip simply darkened the tan in the areas where it was already well established. But there were other places, unaccustomed to sunshine, which turned uncomfortably red before the day was done.

"This'll be quite the adventure to tell my old man about, after I get home," said Gerson. "Did I ever tell you guys that my old man is a diamond-cutter? He works in a jewelry store, in Brooklyn. Whenever you need a diamond ring, just come to Brooklyn. My old man will cut you a swell stone for a real cheap price, if you tell him that you're my buddy."

"Thanks, Gerson, but we all live so far from Brooklyn, not many will take you up on the offer," said Pieper.

"I need a change—where's that fishing kit?" Hill asked.

"Right over here," I said, handing it to him.

"We don't have to wait 'til we're in the ocean to drop a hook in the water," Hill said. "Maybe a fish'll bite here." He took out the handline, fastened an artificial worm on the hook, and threw it into the water.

"That's such a primitive rig," Pieper said. "I really miss the good fishing rods and reels I left at home."

"Fly fishing or bait casting?" asked Hill.

"I have both, but I really miss my fly rod most."

"I never had a fly rod," I said, "but I really enjoyed bait casting for drumfish in Florida. I spent three months with Uncle Liston on Amelia Island in 1941. He's a great fisherman, and we went out every day, through Harrison Creek to the Amelia River, just above the place it flows into the Atlantic. There we heard those big drumfish making their deep grunting sounds under water—'baroom, boom—baroom, boom!' We'd catch big drumfish with fresh crabs on a large hook, and bring 'em back to Aunt Minnie to cook. They sure tasted good, fresh and hot! I still miss that, four years later."

"You're making me hungry," said Gerson. "Pass me another candy bar and a beer."

"I'm ready for another round, too," Hill agreed.

"I guess good food is what we all miss most about being overseas," Pieper said.

"And a good bed, for a good night's sleep!" I said.

"And a good woman, to share the bed with!" Hill added.

"That's an appropriate remark for you, Hill," I said. "You're the only married man on this boat."

"But any of us could have said it, with a little wishful thinking," Gerson said. "We'd all like a little nooky now."

"I miss music, my record collection, classical and popular," Hill said, "and my art supplies, to paint some pictures again."

"I miss having a choice of good movies, not the B-grade flicks they show here nightly," Pieper said, "and I miss the friends I used to see 'em with."

"Friends, girls, and families, that's what we all miss most," said Hill. "I miss my wife, Anne, and little Jackie."

"I miss taking a girl to the beach," Gerson said. "We used to go to an open beach on the Jersey shore, and lay on the warm sand watching the sun go down. Then, when it got good and dark, we'd roll over and snuggle real tight, and enjoy some long, slow, passionate sex! Wow, did that ever feel good!"

"Down, boy!" said Pieper. "Don't get all worked up out here in the wilds of New Guinea, without a woman in sight."

Hill pulled on the handline. "Hey, I just felt a fish nibble the bait on this handline. There he goes again. Darn! I jerked the line to set the hook, but he got away."

"Patience," said Pieper, "maybe he'll be back soon."

"I miss a hot shower," I said. "We're lucky to be in the tropics, where cold showers aren't too frigid, but there's nothing like a hot shower to relax and soothe sore muscles."

"We're lucky to be in the Air Corps, with any showers at all," said Pieper. "For soldiers in the field, like the Aussies moving through the jungle toward Wewak, the only chance they get to bathe is when they can jump into a river like this one."

"It could be a lot worse," Hill agreed. "Before we complain about any conditions, we ought to ask, 'compared to what?' There are always other guys who have it worse than we do."

"And our casualty rates are so much lighter than others," I added. "I saw the casualty report for March. Nadzab lost one A-20 light bomber and two fighters to enemy fire last month, plus four more planes to accidents, including that missing B-24 we just sighted. That's only twenty men dead out of two or three thousand here—less than one percent. I'll bet those Aussies in the jungle lose more than one percent in a month."

"That's why we joined the Air Corps," said Gerson.

"Not me; I joined the Air Corps because I wanted to fly," Hill said. "I was an aviation cadet, accepted for pilot training, when they cut back the program 'for the convenience of the government.' They'd trained too many pilots. They said, 'We still need gunners,' so here I am."

"Same thing happened to me," said Pieper, "but I was halfway through pilot training, with eighty hours of flying time, when they washed me out of Basic flight school. 'Be a gunner, or stay on the ground,' they said. But my pilot time did help me get into flight engineer training after gunnery school."

"It happened to me, too," I said. "I was in Primary flight school with forty hours of flying, when they washed me out. 'Too many pilots,' they said. But I had also qualified for navigator training with the highest possible score, so they gave me a chance to go through that."

"Everybody wants to be a pilot," Hill chuckled.

"Everybody on our crew signed up for pilot training," said Pieper, "except Gerson, who didn't want that much work."

"And also James," I added. "He only qualified for bombardier, not for pilot or navigator."

"We can all learn to be civilian pilots on our own, if we want to," Pieper said. "I plan to get my pilot license after I get out of the army."

I said, "I'll do that too, soon as I get settled." (I earned my private pilot license in 1950.)

"I hope I can afford that," said Hill.

The hours went by as we drifted down the river, cooling off in the water whenever we got too hot. As the sun got lower in the west, we looked ever more anxiously to the east, expecting to see the ocean appear beyond each bend in the river.

"Not there yet?" said Gerson, "I thought it would be around this bend for sure!"

"Well, Navigator, do we have an E.T.A. for Lae?" Hill asked.

"Let's figure it out," I said. "It's twenty-three miles from Nadzab to Lae by air, so it'll be twenty-five to thirty miles along the winding river. This strong current is flowing at five or six miles per hour, so the trip should take from four to six hours. We turned into the Markham at one, plus four to six hours would put our arrival at five to seven p.m)."

"My watch says five-thirty already," Pieper said, "so you can scratch that early E.T.A."

Hill shaded his eyes with his hand, looking west. "The sun is mighty low now. We have less than an hour of daylight left."

"Too late for fishing in the ocean," Gerson said.

"It would be dangerous to ride the waves after dark," I said. "As soon as we see the mouth of this river, we'll turn left into the harbor at Lae."

The sun set with flaming gold and red at six-fifteen. The climate seemed cooler immediately; my sunburned body felt a chill. We all reached for our clothes and dressed.

Twilight in the tropics is brief; it lasts for only ten or fifteen minutes, instead of lingering on. By six-thirty it was pitch black.

There was a flash of flame as Hill lit a cigarette, then the red glow of its tip gave enough light to dimly see the faces in the boat. Beyond the dinghy was absolute darkness. A few stars were visible between clouds, but most of them were hidden.

Darkness brought a whole new perspective on life. Instead of the fun of adventure that seemed natural by daylight, now we felt quiet, more contemplative, more dependent on each other, more anxious about possible danger lying ahead in the dark.

The red glow of Hill's cigarette was joined by two others as Pieper and Gerson lit theirs off his burning end. Their young faces were lined with anxiety, exaggerated by the darkness. I shared their anxiety, and felt the additional burden of command. I was responsible for getting us all into this dangerous situation, and I was expected to lead the way out.

The silence ended with Pieper's excited whisper, "Listen—can you hear that?"

"Hear what?" We all listened intently.

"The sea—don't you hear it? The sound of surf—waves breaking on the shore."

Hill cupped his hand around his ear. "Surf?—yeah—think you're right. Sounds like we're approaching the sea at last."

"Our long ordeal is over!" said Gerson.

"Over? Heck, no!" I said. "For the first time today, we could be in real danger! We were supposed to get here by daylight, but here we are, in pitch black darkness, on a river whose current is strong enough to shoot us miles out to sea!"

"We could drift all night at sea," said Pieper.

"Or capsize in the waves, and drown!" added Hill.

"Please, don't even talk like that!" Gerson moaned.

"Everybody grab an oar! Start paddling!" I commanded. "We've got to get out of the strong current in the middle. Pull to the left, toward the north bank. This river is half a mile wide at its mouth. We can't see the north bank, but it's over there in the dark, somewhere to our left."

As we paddled, we heard the sound of waves growing ever louder. The crash of surf pounding a beach became more distinct.

"Come on, men, pull harder!" I shouted. "We've got to make it to the north bank before we're swept into the ocean!"

"But where is the north bank, really?" asked Pieper. "If we keep paddling to the left, we'll just go around in big circles in the middle of the river."

"Oh, no!" Gerson groaned. "And all the time, we're being carried downstream to be swept out to sea!"

"Paddle, men, paddle!" I ordered. "We'll never get there by drifting!"

We paddled with renewed vigor, on and on through the dark. But we could see nothing to guide us, so we might have been going in large circles to the left, just as Pieper had said.

I wonder whether we really are getting any closer to the north bank?

The clenched muscles around my stomach told me that my anxiety was turning into fear. *What can we do?*

Suddenly, we were plunged into the waves, and the boat started rocking violently, pitching up and down in the darkness.

"Oh, no!" cried Gerson.

"Oh, shoot!" Hill said. "We got to the sea too soon!"

"Big ocean waves we're riding now," said Pieper. "Looks like a long black night at sea."

For a moment, I felt a flash of anger sweeping over me, anger at the turn of fate that put us here, with all my plans gone wrong. Then the anger dissolved into a sense of utter helplessness.

Please, God, get us out of this mess! What in the world should we do now?

12. Major League at Last

"We're on the ocean now," said Gerson. "Why paddle any more? It does as much good as farting in the face of a hurricane!"

"No, we're still in the mouth of the river," I said, "and we need to get out of the strong current in midstream. It could shoot us miles out to sea!" Voicing the danger snapped me out of my brief spell of helplessness and fear, and set my mind to problem-solving. I felt that I was back in command again.

"These big waves sure feel like the ocean," Pieper said.

"This river mouth is half a mile wide, so the ocean waves roll into the river quite far," I said. "But the darkness tells me that we're still in the river. We haven't seen the harbor lights yet."

"What harbor lights?" asked Hill.

"The port of Lae is just north of the river's mouth, hiding behind the dark north bank, on the left." I replied. "When we do get out of the river, we'll see the harbor lights."

"What should we do now?"

"Keep paddling to the north! The current is not as strong along the shore, and the eddies will help whip us around toward the harbor."

"But which way is north?" asked Pieper, resting his paddle. "How can we tell in the dark?"

I had a flash of insight. "By the sound of the surf—it's in the east, so north is left of that."

We paddled north, steering by the sound of the surf. A few minutes later, the current carried us past the dark end of the river's north bank, and we saw the lights of Lae's harbor.

"Lights!" "Yay!" "We made it!" They all cheered.

"We haven't made it yet," I said, "but at least we can see the target."

We were a quarter-mile away from the harbor lights, and the dinghy was being swept out to sea.

"Come on men," I urged, "give it all you've got!"

We paddled like demons, and slowly the distance grew less. Then the raft came out of the strong current into the eddies near the shore, which whipped us around closer to the harbor.

Hill began to sing, "I see those harbor lights...."

"Let's aim for the first chunk of beach in sight," I said.

We landed, pulled the dinghy up the beach, and deflated it. Then I led a little parade to the waterfront town, as Pieper carried the folded raft, Hill carried the oars in his duffel bag, and Gerson followed behind.

We entered a waterfront bar, full of Aussie soldiers and sailors celebrating Saturday night with good spirits. Some of them let us squeeze in to join them at a table, where we bought a round of full-flavored Australian beers, and some long bread rolls called "Crullers," which were hard, but good for dunking. With our bellies full of bread and beer, we felt much better.

"We're American flyers based at Nadzab," I told the Aussie sergeant beside me. "We just came ashore here in our life raft, after spending all day on the water. Do you know where we could catch a lorry back to Nadzab?"

"Just come ashore in yer life raft, mate?" He repeated.

"Yes, and we need to get back to Nadzab before they start to worry about us," I added.

"Well, leftenant, you're in luck! I have a lorry outside, what brought me mates down here from camp. I'll take your crew to Nadzab now."

"Wonderful! Thanks so much!"

"What's your name, Sarge?" Hill asked, "and what do you do?"

"Me name's Curly Edwards, from Adelaide, Australia. I run the lorries here, but I'm really a prizefighter."

"Curly, I'm Jim Hill, from Canton, Ohio. Glad to meet you!"

He gave Curly a hearty handshake. "Come out to my camp soon and teach me some of your prize punches. I've got some American cigarettes there to give you."

"With pleasure, mate!" said Curly, "let's do it tonight."

So we rode back to Nadzab in a U.S.-built army truck, given to the Australian Army by American lend-lease, now returning the favor to us by the generous spirit of an Aussie sergeant, who thought he was helping to rescue airmen downed at sea. Hill sat up front with Curly in the cab, forming a friendship that blossomed into more visits between them during the following week. On his next visit, Curly would sell Hill an Aussie jungle uniform, with broad-brimmed safari hat, bush jacket and trousers—Hill's major souvenir of the war.

Meanwhile, Pieper, Gerson and I rode in the back of the truck, jolting along the bumpy road from Lae to Nadzab.

"I'll check in for us at the orderly room—the truck sent to meet us at six would report us missing," I said.

"Don't want 'em to think we're A.W.O.L.," Pieper said.

I lit my pipe and relaxed. "This adventure didn't turn out like I planned. We didn't make it up the mountain to the crater lake."

"We had some hairy moments at the end, but we did have fun on the river," said Pieper.

"And we're all going home alive and healthy," Gerson added. "May all our trips end so well!"

One week after the life raft trip, our crew departed Nadzab, New Guinea, as a replacement B-24 crew assigned to the Thirteenth Air Force. It was April 21, Saturday morning.

We had climbed aboard a twin-engine C-47 cargo plane with twenty passengers, two B-24 crews. Our destination was the Thirteenth Bomber Command on the island of Morotai, just north of the larger island of Halmahera in the "Dutch East Indies" (now Indonesia).

Our take-off was delayed by the unusually large number of warplanes leaving Nadzab on the morning mission to Wewak. We watched dozens of bombers roar off the runway, including B-24 heavies, B-25 mediums, and A-20 light bombers, followed by P-38 twin-engine and P-47 and P-51 single-engine fighters.

"This is the biggest strike ever mounted from Nadzab," Seitz said. "I talked to one of the flyers after briefing last night; he said they planned fourteen fighter and eighty bomber sorties against Wewak today."

"How did they find that many bombers at Nadzab?" said James.

"They didn't. The returning bombers will be reloaded with fresh crews, and sent out on a second mission this afternoon. Eighty sorties is the total of both."

"Why the big push at Wewak, now?" Cordell asked.

"They want to smash as many of the Jap positions as possible before the big invasion. It seems that General MacArthur's troops are going to land soon and take Wewak." Seitz's steel-blue eyes lit up with excitement.

"Well, doggone!" Cordell scowled. "Just when the action gets exciting, we get transferred!"

"Yeah," said James, raising his dark eyebrows, "but look at where we're going! To the Thirteenth Air Force!"

"Right!" I said. "No matter how exciting the action at Nadzab gets, it's still in the minor league. But in the Thirteenth Air Force, we'll be in the major league at last!"

After all the warbirds had taken off, we finally had our turn. We flew in the same direction, northwest up the familiar Markham Valley route toward Wewak. All the warplanes ahead were faster than our C-47 cargo plane, so they had time to attack their targets and then fly past us on their way back to Nadzab, before we came near Wewak. Looking ahead to the right, we saw many columns of smoke rising from the fires they had started all around the Wewak area.

"Looks like our flyboys did a good day's work," Cordell said. He lit a cigarette and lazily blew a smoke ring.

"More damage than both our missions put together," James agreed, reaching for his own cigarette pack.

"And the afternoon strike is yet to come," I added.

"Those Japs will sure be softened up before MacArthur's troops land," Seitz said.

We flew to the west of Wewak, twenty or thirty miles inland, over the swampy Sepik River valley. While we ate a lunch of packaged army field rations, I enjoyed seeing the long, lush-green Taritatu River valley pointing our way toward Biak. In the distance to our left, I saw the rugged central mountain range of New Guinea, with cloud-capped peaks rising to 16,500 feet. After flying five hours, we landed for a refueling stop on Biak Island, just off the northwest coast of New Guinea.

"Biak again," Pieper said. "Brings back some memories."

"Here's where we thought we were joining the Fifth Air Force," Cordell said. "Now we're headed for the Thirteenth."

"Here's where somebody broke my little finger playing grand-slam volleyball," I said, holding up my right hand. "Look at that crooked joint! It never did grow back straight!"

"Here's where we started sweating over our crew status, when Gerson fouled up the whole crew with his no-show," James said.

"Forget Biak," Seitz said. "We're off to make some fresh new memories now."

"Memories are all we'll have, when we go home from the war," said Hill, running his fingers through his blond hair. "There'll be some snapshots, and a few trinkets, too, but memories will be our real souvenirs."

"Wartime memories can be either good or bad," Imhof warned.

"Let's hope we end up with memories to cherish," Hill said, "not with nightmares to escape."

"I'll drink to that!" Imhof agreed.

From Biak we flew on in the same direction, west-northwest, this time over the darkening ocean for three more hours before landing at Pitoe Airfield on Morotai soon after sunset. We had traveled nearly fifteen hundred miles since leaving Nadzab.

Morotai is a small, oval-shaped jungle island with a 4,100-foot mountain in the middle. At the south end, its three runways were hacked out of the jungle and paved with hard-packed crushed coral, chalky white in color. The engineers who built these runways were a combination of Army Engineer Battalions and Navy Construction Battalions, called "C.B.'s" or "Sea Bees," who were always there with bulldozers as soon as the Marines moved off the invasion beaches.

Morotai was as hot and humid as Biak. In contrast to the cool air we had enjoyed at cruising altitude, the hot, muggy night air of Morotai swallowed us up like a mind-numbing sauna while we carried our bags to the operations tent.

Inside, a sergeant stood behind a plywood counter painted with the circular logo of the Thirteenth Air Force: a red and white star with golden wings curling upward around a big white number "13" on a blue background.

"Welcome to the Jungle Air Force," the sergeant said.

"You sure have the jungle climate to go with that name," Seitz said. "This heat could get a man down."

"You get used to it after a while, and then it don't bother you no more." His suntanned face was yellow from atabrine pills, like all old-timers on South Pacific islands.

"I hope you're right! We're a couple of B-24 replacement crews from Nadzab, on orders to the Thirteenth Bomber Command. I'm Lieutenant Seitz, and that's my crew over there, and this is Lieutenant Quirk, with his crew."

"Which Group are you ordered to? The Thirteenth has two B-24 Groups, the 307th, here on Morotai, and the Fifth Group, based on Samar in the Philippines."

"We haven't been told that yet."

"Then we'll just put you up in our transient housing tents until we find out, maybe tomorrow. Thirteenth Bomber Command will decide which Bomb Group you each will go to."

Lieutenant Quirk spoke up, "We've been riding that cargo crate all day; how about some chow?"

"The nearest mess hall is three blocks down the road. Here are some meal chits to get you a late supper, and when you get back, I'll have a truck take you over to transient housing."

Next morning at dawn, we were awakened by the familiar sound of a dozen B-24s warming up their four dozen 1200-horsepower engines, and then screaming down the runway, one at a time.

"Sounds like the 307th Bomb Group has a mission today," said Cordell, rolling over in his cot.

"Wonder where they're going?" said James.

"Borneo, the big island," Seitz replied from his cot. "I heard it at Operations last night. An important target on the east coast of Borneo called Balikpapen."

"Balikpapen!" I rose up on one arm. "That's the biggest oil refinery in the Dutch East Indies. If it's shut down, Jap ships and planes will starve for fuel. I heard we've bombed it several times, with heavy losses. It's well-defended."

"Great!" Cordell exclaimed, sitting up. "We really are in the major leagues now!" His face lit up with a boyish grin.

Seitz got up and put on a khaki shirt. "Let's get a bite of breakfast, and then hike down to Operations to find out which group we're assigned to."

After breakfast, we were hiking toward the flight line under a blazing hot tropical sun, when Seitz asked, "Does anyone know if there's much difference in climate between here and the Philippines? Would it make any difference whether we're assigned to the 307th here, or the Fifth Bomb Group on Samar?"

"Ask Hamilton," said James, "he's up on that sorta stuff."

"Yes," I answered, "I did look over the maps last night. Morotai is only two degrees north of the equator, but Samar is twelve degrees north. That's ten degrees difference in latitude, the same difference between Jacksonville, Florida, and Philadelphia. The climate at Samar should be significantly cooler than Morotai."

"Dear God, let it be Samar," said James, putting his hands together in a prayer-like gesture. "I just don't function well with sweat running down my face like this."

"The only time you have to function well is on the bombing run," said Seitz, "and up there it's cool enough so sweat is no problem."

"Maybe so," James mopped his brow, "but it sure would be nice to have it cooler on the ground, too."

When we reached the Operations tent, Seitz put the question to the man behind the counter. He looked at his message board and said, "Lieutenant Seitz, I'm afraid you won't be staying here with us after all. Your crew and Lieutenant Quirk's crew have both been assigned to the Fifth Bomb Group on Samar."

Seitz tried hard to keep a straight face, but Cordell, James and I turned to each other to flash beaming smiles.

Seitz asked, "How do we get there, and when do we leave?"

"They'll send a C-47 here to pick you up, maybe tomorrow, maybe later in the week. It's about three and a half hours each way. They usually arrive around noon, in time to have lunch in our mess hall, then fly back in the afternoon."

"Okay, I'll alert my crew to be ready for possible departure tomorrow noon."

We left Operations, and paused to look over the flight line. Two long rows of B-24s stretched to the right and left of us. Each was parked in a separate "hardstand," a parking spot cut out of the jungle to face the taxiway. A row of hardstands was on each side of the taxiway, which connected them with both ends of the two runways. Sunlight gleaming from the silver surfaces of the bombers made a brilliant contrast to the dark green jungle around them. Even without the dozen bombers that were away on the mission to Balikpapen, there were forty B-24s in sight. Ground crews and mechanics were busy servicing many of them.

I have an incurable attraction to airplanes, and this sight gave me an emotional high. "I think I'll stroll down the flight line," I said, "and see what I can learn about the nuts and bolts of a bomb group."

"Go ahead," said Seitz. "I'm going to hang around Operations for a while, and learn a little about running a bomb group."

"I'm not gonna learn anything!" said James. "I just want to celebrate the news that we're leaving this hot place for a cooler climate!"

"While you're celebrating," Seitz said, "how about finding some of our enlisted men, and spread the good news to them."

"Roger, wilco."

"I'm gonna go to the beach," Cordell said, "and enjoy my prepaid vacation on this lovely Pacific paradise."

We all went our separate ways. I headed down the flight line, going from one hardstand to another, watching ground crews drive gasoline trucks up to the wings to refuel the planes, and mechanics climb ladders to remove the oval aluminum cowlings from around the engines, to work on whatever needed fixing.

"Hello," I said to an older mechanic, who was standing in front of one plane to direct two younger mechanics on ladders who were working on a engine. "Are you the crew chief?"

"Yes sir, sure am." His lined face was dark from suntan and atabrine.

"Do you mind a little conversation while you work?"

"Guess I can handle that." He lit a cigarette.

"What are your boys doing?"

"Replacin' the hydraulic pump on number three engine. Our bird had a hydraulic problem lately."

"Shot up in combat, or just normal wear and tear?"

"Combat this time. Caught a piece of flak over Borneo—punctured a hydraulic line and lost all the fluid. The pump ran dry all the way home, and burned out. Lucky it didn't set the durn engine on fire!"

"Is combat damage increasing or decreasing overall?"

"Decreasin', for sure. A year ago, we lost planes on every mission, and half the ones comin' back was shot up somewhere. Now, don't often lose a plane, and mostly our maintenance work's normal wear'n tear."

"You've got all these planes lined up in a row. Isn't that an invitation to Jap intruders to bomb or strafe this flight line? It looks like such an easy target."

"Well, yes, but it don't seem to happen no more. When our

group got here, come last October, Jap bombers come over every night to hassle us with a few bombs. They don't hit many planes usually—their aim wern't too good in the dark. But that was a problem too—ya never know where the bombs'd fall. We had to dig foxholes close to all the tents. When the Jap planes come over, we all dive into the foxholes."

"A few bombs every night? Could that hurt us much?"

"It adds up over time. Japs destroyed or damaged seventy-five of our planes durin' eighty-two bombin' raids on Morotai. That's countin' from September '44, when we invaded, to the last raid, come February '45. Worst raid come in November, night before Thanksgivin'. Nine Jap planes knock out twenty-three of ours— fifteen destroyed, eight damaged, all on the ground. Some Thanksgivin'!"

"That was only six months ago! Wow! This war sure changes fast. I didn't hear any bombs last night."

"You won't, no more. Jap bombers're mighty scarce since we bombed all thirty Jap airfields within four hundred miles o' here. That's about the range o' their bombers. Haven't had a single raid since February. But you should have been with us when it was really rough, back on Guadalcanal!"

"Did the Thirteenth Air Force fly out of Guadalcanal?"

"Durn right! Two years ago, we flew out o' Henderson Field, where Jap gunners shot at us from the hills by day, and Jap planes come bomb us by night. Back then, we scattered our own planes far apart as we could, so one bomb or shell don't get too many of 'em. We had lots fewer planes then, o' course. Now we got B-24s a-comin' out our ears, so we make our parkin' spots pretty close together. If the Japs ever do come back and hit some of 'em, we'll just push 'em aside and use 'em for spare parts. We just don't worry about that no more."

"Sounds like our major league teams are winning this game faster all the time. I hope I have a chance to get in on some big plays soon. I'm navigator on a replacement crew."

"Our team is winnin' all right, but you got plenty o' time to step up to bat. There's a lot o' heavy fightin' ahead, before all the innings are over."

I walked slowly away from the flight line, thinking about the sweep of history behind the war in the Pacific. My mind reviewed how Japan began acquiring an empire fifty years earlier, when it took Formosa (Taiwan) from China in the war of 1895. Then it seized Korea and much of Manchuria after winning a war with Russia ten years later. Japan swallowed up the rest of Manchuria in 1932, and invaded China in 1937. I had my own vivid memories of that, since I was a student at Shanghai American School at that time. It was the beginning of World War II.

Next, World War II spread to Europe in 1939. Hitler's blitzkrieg defeated France in 1940, allowing Japan to occupy all of "French Indo-China" (Vietnam, Laos, and Cambodia) without opposition. Soon after, Japan launched its knockout blow on the American Pacific Fleet at Pearl Harbor on December 7, 1941.

Within six months after Pearl Harbor, Japan invaded almost all of the Pacific Islands north of Australia and west of Hawaii. In that brief time, Japan's overwhelming forces defeated thinly-spread defending forces of Americans (in Philippines, Guam, Wake Island), British (in Burma, Hong Kong, Malaya), Dutch (in Dutch East Indies, west New Guinea), and Australians (in east New Guinea, New Britain, New Ireland). Cousins of those Americans, British, Dutch, and Australians joined as allies in General MacArthur's army to resist the Japs.

This was the fastest, most amazing imperial expansion in world history. In the whole half-century, Japan never lost a battle until May 1942, when a large invasion fleet headed for Australia was turned back by American and Australian naval forces in the Battle of the Coral Sea. Then in June, 1942, another major Japanese fleet tried to invade Midway Island on their way to Hawaii. American aircraft carriers, still alive because they happened to be away from Pearl Harbor when the Japanese struck, went to the Coral Sea and to Midway to defeat both invasion fleets. Those two victories stopped the Japanese expansion and turned the war around.

Then came three years of American and Allied Forces pushing back the rim of Japan's vast empire, beginning with the American invasion of Guadalcanal in August 1942, and slowly progressing from one island to another, westward across the Pacific. General MacArthur's forces invaded the Philippines last October (1944), and Admiral Nimitz's forces invaded Okinawa just this month (April 1945). Major battles were still raging around Okinawa, and minor ones in the Philippines, while I waited on Morotai. I grew more excited as I thought of the role of our crew.

We'll be part of this great sweep toward Japan, and maybe part of the final invasion of Japan itself!

Thinking about the whole big picture helped me feel a sense of purpose that made all of the struggle seem worthwhile. It felt good to be doing something important as well as exciting.

Next morning, we were awakened again at dawn by the noise of a dozen B-24s taking off for another Borneo strike by the 307th Bomb Group, who called themselves the "Long Rangers." They lived up to their name by their repeated strikes all the way to Borneo.

After breakfast, Seitz went down to Operations, and returned soon with the good news that a C-47 from Samar was really on its way here to pick us up for a 12:45 departure. We packed and got our bags to the flight line by 11:30, and went for midday chow.

We gathered again at Operations after lunch, along with the same crew who had flown with us to Morotai two days earlier. We were scheduled to leave together now for Samar.

A tall, dark-haired pilot came into the Operations tent and called out, "Lieutenant Quirk and Lieutenant Seitz, are you here?" They stepped forward to meet him.

"I'm Lieutenant Wildey from the 394th Squadron in the Fifth Bomb Group. I'm here to take your two crews to Samar. Are you guys ready to go?"

"You bet we are!"

"Okay, have your men pick up their bags and follow me over to C-47 number 950. We're on our way to the Bomber Barons!"

The Bomber Barons! Thirteenth Air Force! This is it—we're in the major league at last!

13. Bomber Barons

Lieutenant Wildey led his twenty passengers to a twin-engine C-47 cargo plane with a big blue stripe painted from nose to tail. The words "Bomber Barons Airliner" paraded in large blue letters above the stripe.

"Who are the Bomber Barons?" asked Seitz.

"The whole Fifth Bomb Group," answered Lieutenant Wildey. "It's our proud nickname." We left Morotai at one P.M. on April 23, climbing into a sky already overcast with afternoon thunderstorms. We headed north-northwest over the open sea, dodging the big thunderheads for three and a half hours.

Halfway along, our route took us parallel to the east coast of Mindanao, second largest island in the Philippines. We followed its colorful shoreline for an hour. Between clouds, sunbeams lit up the golden sand of its beaches and the whitecaps on dark waves rolling into foaming surf.

Descending over Leyte Gulf, we saw the southernmost tip of Samar Island. A long, narrow finger of land pointed southeast into the sea, with a runway cut through the jungle across the entire width of the finger, next to the little town of Guiuan. Water lapped at the beaches just twenty feet below both ends of the runway, so there were no obstacles in our flight path as we landed.

We passed long rows of silver B-24s facing the taxiway, wingtip to wingtip. Behind the planes, service vehicles and dark green flight line tents stood in a row. Beyond the clearing for the airstrip, tall palm trees formed a jungle-like backdrop as far as we could see on both sides. Our plane rolled up to an empty parking space where the engines died. The pilot got out, and we followed him into a big tent marked "5th Bomb Group Operations." He stepped up to the counter.

"Lieutenant Wildey, 394th Squadron, back from Morotai with a plane load of fresh meat."

"Two more new crews, sir?"

"Yeah, Lieutenant Quirk and Lieutenant Seitz."

"We'll call the roll, and put 'em in transient housing. The Old Man will want to meet 'em in the morning, along with the other two crews who came in yesterday."

At nine-thirty the next morning, the four new crews were seated on empty bomb-fin crates in the large briefing tent. Our multiple conversations died when two officers entered.

"Group, at-tensh-HUT!" called the captain.

We all jumped to our feet.

"At ease, men, be seated," said the colonel. "I'm Lieutenant Colonel Haviland, commanding officer of the Fifth Bomb Group. Let me welcome all of you to the Bomber Barons! Congratulations for joining the best team in the Thirteenth Air Force! Give yourself a round of applause!" He led the clapping himself, with a smile.

I liked this man instantly. He was tall and well-built, with dark hair, handsome face, square jaw and prominent chin. His open earnest face and good looks reminded me of movie star Cary Grant.

"Let's see who we have here today." He took a clipboard from the captain to read, "First Lieutenant Milford V. Peck."

"Here, sir!" said Peck, rising to his feet.

"Have your crew stand up, so we can see them!" the colonel said loudly. The other nine flyers stood up with him.

"Your crew will be assigned to the 23rd Bomb Squadron. There are four squadrons in the Fifth Bomb Group, so each of these four crews will go to a different squadron. I believe in fair play for all! Okay, men, sit down."

The colonel read from the clipboard again, "Second Lieutenant Daniel H. Quirk."

"Here, sir!" Quirk replied as he rose.

Colonel Haviland said, "Okay, men, will the rest of Quirk's crew please stand up?" They rose to their feet, looking embarrassed.

"This crew will join the 31st Bomb Squadron. When they do, they'll tell you that the 31st is the best damn squadron in the group! If they don't, I'll kick their butts! I believe in competition with enthusiasm! Okay, men, sit down.

"Second Lieutenant Sheldon L. Dauchy."

"Yes, sir!" said Dauchy, "on your feet, men!" His crew rose beside him.

"Very good, Lieutenant! You catch on quick. Your crew will go to the 72nd Bomb Squadron. And when you get there, what'll you say about it?"

"Best damn squadron in the group, sir!" Dauchy replied.

"That's the spirit! Sit down, men."

The colonel turned over the page on his clipboard, and read, "First Lieutenant Marvin C. Seitz."

"Here, sir!" said Seitz, jumping to his feet. Cordell and I jumped up next, and without a word, the whole crew stood up.

"All right!" the colonel exclaimed. "I see a learning process going on here. That's good! I want every one of you to be eager beavers, eager to learn something new at every turn! This crew will join the eager beavers of the 394th Bomb Squadron. Okay, men, be seated.

"You are all Bomber Barons of the Fifth Bomb Group now. Each one of you is an important member of this team! Be proud of it! We'll depend on every one of you to DO YOUR BEST to make it the best damn team in the whole Pacific!

"I demand excellent performance from every man in my group! I will not accept sloppy work! If you are careless or lazy, you'll find that I'm a tough C.O., but if you give me your best, I'll give you my best! That goes for every kind of reward in my power—promotions, medals, honors, better food, housing, the whole works! Are there any questions?"

I held up my hand.

"Stand up, Lieutenant, and ask your question."

I rose to my feet. "Sir, what is our present tactical situation?" I heard some snickering from men nearby. "I mean, where is the group bombing now, and how often? How many squadrons, and how many crews, go on a typical mission?" I remained standing.

"We are currently bombing in two areas—close at hand, in the Philippines, and far away, in Borneo. Our close-in strikes are ground-support missions against Jap troops being attacked by our ground forces in neighboring islands like Mindanao, Negros, and Cebu. These are short missions, only three or four hours round trip, so we can mount two missions a day, if needed. "Our distant strikes are strategic missions against the Jap oil fields of Borneo, like Balikpapen and Tarakan, or against the many Jap airfields in Borneo. Those are very long missions—twelve, thirteen, or fourteen hours. You can expect to have a night take-off before dawn, fly all day to the target and back, then face a night landing when you return. Those missions separate the men from the boys!

"In general, this group flies one combat strike every day, but that varies with the needs of the war, of course. We use two squadrons per day, with six planes and crews from each squadron, so we'll send out twelve bombers on a typical mission. The other two squadrons will fly on the following day. Each squadron has twelve or more crews, and six of them fly a strike every other day, so you can expect to fly a combat mission about every fourth day. Does that cover your question?"

"Yes, sir, thank you, sir," I said, and sat down.

"Any more questions?" Colonel Haviland said.

Another man stood up to ask, "What about our living area? Is it by squadron or Group? Are we four teams, or one?"

"Each squadron has its own living area and its own mess hall, with separate tenting areas in each squadron for officers and enlisted men, of course. Within the Group, we are four teams, because the four squadrons compete against each other for top honors in the Group. But when it comes to the outside world, we are all one team—the Bomber Barons of the Fifth Bomb Group, and proud of it! Got the picture?"

"Yes, sir," the man replied, and sat down.

Colonel Haviland continued, "Speaking of living areas, you men are going to have to put up your own tents. The Fifth Bomb Group moved here from Morotai only six weeks ago, so we're still building up our base. Each crew can draw two tents from Supply—one for officers, one for enlisted men—and ten cots, blankets, pillows, and mosquito nets—but no lumber.

"There's no lumber on Samar for the army. The U.S. Navy controls this island, and the only lumber here is in the Sea Bee yard, for the navy. So if you want to build a wood floor for your tent, like most of us do, you have to steal the lumber from the Sea Bees! It's called 'moonlight requisitioning.'

"Our Bomb Group has an unofficial, off-the-record, on-going agreement with the Chief Sea Bee himself. His men will always look the other way while my men take the lumber we need for essential construction. Of course, I give him something he wants in return—free use of our Bomber Baron Airliners, which just happen to fly wherever he wants to go.

"So, just borrow a truck from our motor pool, drive down to the south tip of Samar and over the bridge to the Sea Bee yard on Calicoan Island, and take what you need without asking. If you ask, that makes it official, and they have to say no. But wear a Thirteenth Air Force patch on your shirt, so they'll know you.

"Any more questions?" No one moved.

The captain came forward. "Group, a-tensh-HUT!" he said. We all jumped to attention. Colonel Haviland walked out.

"Dis-missed!" the Captain called, and followed him out.

The crews in the tent started a buzz of many conversations. Our crew clustered together for our own comments.

"Well," said Seitz, "the Old Man seems to be a straight shooter!"

"Yeah," James agreed, "he really laid it on the line."

"No ifs, ands, or buts, or he'll kick your butt!" Cordell added.

"I like that man," I said. "He's the kind of leader I'll follow anywhere."

"With his gung-ho attitude, he'll be promoted to full bird colonel very soon," Cordell said. "A group commander should be a full colonel, anyway."

"Let's go over to the 394th Squadron area," Seitz said, "and look over the sites available for our tents. Then we can figure out how much lumber we need to build two tent floors, and when to grab it from the Sea Bees."

When we got to the 394th Squadron area, we found that the whole area was a series of gentle hills, which made for good drainage of rainfall—not like the flat surface of Morotai, where rain water made lakes around the tents. We selected two vacant sites, one in the officers' area, the other in the enlisted men's section.

We looked at the tents already erected. One end of the floor rested on the grade while the other end was elevated on wood columns and girders, so the floor was level while the ground sloped away below it. We measured the size of the tent floors, and counted the pieces of lumber they contained.

During the next few days, our mornings were spent in orientation classes with the 394th Squadron, while the afternoons were free to work on our tents.

Officers and enlisted men on our crew worked separately as two teams to steal from the Sea Bees the materials needed, and to build the floor platforms. It was slow work, because Cordell and Imhof were the only ones good at carpentry, and we had no power tools to help us.

After the two platforms were built, we brought the whole crew together again to raise the heavy tent over each one.

"Okay, men," Seitz said, "let's spread the tent out over the floor, and one or two men pull on each corner to straighten it." We did it, pointing the doorway to the front.

"That's good!" Seitz went on, "Now let's get the two biggest guys—Pieper and Cordell— you guys go inside with the tall center pole, and lift up the center of the roof."

Cordell, with tall, husky body and curly brown hair, lifted the tent at its door while Pieper, our big, blond athlete, ducked under it, carrying the center pole. They both crawled under the hot tent to find the center pole socket, and slowly raised the pyramid top of the tent. I pulled up on the door front, to let the strong breeze blow in and give them some air to breathe.

"Hey, that breeze feels great!" said Pieper from inside.

"And the wind is helping to lift the tent," Cordell added.

Just then the wind increased from a stiff breeze to a strong gust which filled the tent like a big balloon, raising it up and off the center pole.

"Look out!" cried Williams, grabbing the nearest corner.

I caught the canvas door flap, holding it for a moment; others reached for whatever they could grab, but the wind gust overpowered us, and jerked the tent loose. It rose up overhead like a balloon, and sailed downwind twenty or thirty yards before falling. Cordell and Pieper stood like statues, holding up the center pole in the middle of the naked floor.

"Come on, guys, let's go get it!" I said. Imhoff, Hill and Herrema chased after the tent with me. Seitz and the others were cracking up with laughter, watching us. We rolled up the tent where it fell, and brought it back to the wood floor.

"Spread it out over the floor again," Seitz ordered, "but this time, tie down the ropes at the four corners before we raise the roof."

After securing the corners, we let the wind fill the tent to help raise the center pole. This time it couldn't fly away.

Finally, at each site, a fully-erected tent stood over a sturdy wooden floor, with a tall pole in the center and four shorter poles holding up the four corners. The roof was shaped like a pyramid, and four canvas side walls could hang straight down or be rolled up for ventilation. A canvas doorway was in the middle of the front. Tension ropes were staked to the ground at the four corners and on both sides of the doorway.

HERREMA (left) and **IMHOF** near tent.

Now we could move out of transient housing and into our new tents. Inside were four cots in the officers' tent, and six in the enlisted men's tent. We hung a mosquito net over each one. Empty ammunition crates and bomb-fin crates served as furniture, providing seating and storage units to supplement our flight bags.

Cordell sat on a crate. "I'm gonna build me an easy chair, soon as I find the lumber."

I lounged on my cot, enjoying our new home with a sense of belonging. "I feel like I just built my first new house."

"Reminds me of camping in a tent with my wife and kid," Seitz added. "Doris would love this—for a day or two, then she'd want to go home."

"Feel that lovely breeze," James grinned. "It's so much cooler here than Morotai!"

"For two reasons," I added, "the temperature's not as hot here, but also we have this breeze. At this latitude, we're in the trade wind zone, with a ten to fifteen knot wind from the northeast blowing most of the time. It used to blow the Spanish galleons here from Mexico, when Spain ruled the Philippines."

"Thanks for the information, Hamilton," Cordell said. "You always tell us more than we want to know about any topic that comes up! We're so lucky to have you around!"

I was taken back by his comment. *Do I really tell them more than they want to hear?*

Seitz changed the subject. "We're part of a major league team, now. Wonder what the major league games will be like?"

"Yeah," said Cordell, "'specially those all-day-long missions to Borneo, with night take-offs and landings! They sound like real killers!"

"Just what you've been asking for," James said. "Now step up to bat."

Next morning Seitz said, "It's the 30th of April—the day the eagle shits!" (The last day of the month was always payday.)

Cordell ran a comb through his short, curly, brown hair. "Last month it was Australian money because we were in New Guinea."

"But here in the Philippines," I said, "we'll be paid in Filipino money."

(Filipino money was easy for us to understand—100 centavos made one peso, and each peso was worth half an American dollar at that time.)

James buttoned his short-sleeved khaki shirt. "Where do we go here to collect it?"

"To the orderly room," Seitz answered. "The squadron adjutant serves as paymaster; he's Captain Pigeon."

James chuckled. "Little Pigeon will help big eagle drop his load."

After breakfast, we went to the tent where a sign read "394th Bomb Squadron Orderly Room." There were thirty or forty men already standing in line outside the tent.

"How many men are there in our squadron?" I asked.

"About six hundred," Seitz replied; "less than half are flyers; the rest support personnel."

I did a quick calculation. "If it takes one minute to pay each man, it would take ten hours to pay six hundred men."

"Maybe it takes less than a minute," Cordell said. "This line seems to be moving along." In a little while we were inside the tent, where I saw a desk with a name plate, "Captain Alfred W. Pigeon." On top of the desk was a loaded .45 automatic pistol. Seated behind the desk was a slender officer with dark hair and a small mustache. His dark, beady eyes were intense behind wire-rimmed glasses, but his face wore the dead-pan look of a poker player. Behind him, a tall sergeant with another pistol on his belt stood beside an open file cabinet.

When my turn came, I stepped up to the desk and saluted. "Lieutenant Hamilton, Robert H., 02073118," I said.

"At ease," the captain said, returning my salute. "Sign here." I signed the pay roster while the sergeant found my name on an envelope in the filing drawer. He handed the sealed envelope to the captain, who gave it to me. I saluted again and left. The whole transaction took about forty seconds.

Outside, I tore the envelope open to see Filipino money and a pay voucher. I took out a one-peso note to add to my "short snorter." Thus far it had samples of Dutch, Australian, and Chinese money. Now I would add Filipino, and start passing it around for friends to sign.

Two days later, at supper, we heard some upsetting news: Two of our crews did not return last night from a mission to Borneo. Two days earlier, six B-24's from our squadron had joined the Group on a short mission to a target in the Philippines, to be followed by overnight at Morotai and then a long mission to Borneo, with return to Samar. But two of our planes collided in mid-air while returning to Morotai. The accident destroyed two bombers and killed twenty men. The surviving four crews from our squadron stayed overnight at Morotai and flew the Borneo mission yesterday along with the other three full squadrons. *What caused the fatal collision?*

"Let's go by the Officers' Club after supper and hear what really happened," Seitz said.

The bull session on the accident was already going on when the four of us entered the 394th Squadron Officers' Club, which at that time was only a large tent on the hilltop. Fifteen or twenty officers were gathered around the tables at one end, where Captain Gaston, a tall, dark-haired lead pilot, was telling the story slowly, with suppressed emotion:

"The Fifth Bomb Group sent all four squadrons on the April 30th ground support mission to Davao Gulf, Mindanao. Colonel Haviland was Group Leader, flying in front with the 72nd Squadron. Captain Luketz was 394th Squadron Leader, flying as pilot with my crew—I was flying as his copilot. We expected to land at Morotai, to stage for a mission to Borneo next day.

"The 394th was the second squadron in the Group Combat

Box. We were descending in a tight formation toward Pitoe Airfield. Colonel Haviland had been chewing our ass on the radio to tighten our formation, and make it super-tight when we arrived over Morotai. Haviland wanted to impress some big shots from Washington who were visiting Thirteenth Bomber Command there. But we were flying in and out of scattered clouds as we came down, so a tight formation was dangerous.

"At 2,500 feet, Haviland turned the group to the right, and Luketz pulled back our throttles to slow the squadron down, since we were inside the turn as number two squadron. But he didn't just ease the throttles back—he chopped 'em! It was all I could do to keep my hands from reaching out and shoving 'em forward again! The planes behind were overrunning us. We nearly stalled!

"Then Haviland turned the group to the left, and we had to firewall the throttles to catch up on the outside of the turn. All this slowing down and speeding up and turning both ways while we're descending through clouds—we had a mid-air collision. Lieutenant Smith in 541, flying number five position, came out of a cloud and turned left to tighten the formation. He ran into number four plane, Lieutenant Whitaker in 869.

"It was a bad mid-air. Smith's propellers cut Whitaker's fuselage in two at the waist windows, and both parts of his plane fell into the sea. We saw men falling out of it on the way down, but no parachutes. Smith's plane continued turning left while it broke up and exploded in the air. Its pieces fell into the sea. No chutes from that one, either."

"Were there any survivors?" I asked.

"No—the crash boat from Morotai picked up one body, floating in its life jacket. Nothing else was found except some floating debris, like oxygen bottles."

"What dirty tough luck!" someone said. "Twenty of our buddies dead in one sickening minute!"

"It wasn't tough luck, it was lousy leadership!" said another. "Didn't you hear him blame it on the Group Leader?"

Captain Gaston went on, "Right after the collision, I heard

one of the pilots say on the radio, 'I hope that sonovabitch is satisfied!' Of course it was Haviland's fault, for tightening the formation too much! Him and Luketz, who over-controlled the throttles in our squadron lead plane. But don't quote me on whose fault it was, or I'll swear I never said it!"

"Wait a minute," said Seitz, "at Nadzab, our instructors kept telling us to tighten our formations, 'cause we need 'em tight in combat. They said, 'Don't leave room enough for a fighter to fly between your bombers!' Maybe a tight formation wasn't too much to demand."

"There's a time and place for everything," Gaston replied. "Tight formation over target, sure, but not when you've gotten back to base, and you're coming down through clouds for landing."

Another pilot said, "They had the four surviving crews practice formation flying today, but the ones who should have been up there practicing were Haviland and Luketz!"

The discussion broke up into several smaller conversations. The four in our crew naturally clustered together.

"It's bad enough to be killed by the enemy," James said, "but it's worse when we kill ourselves."

I said, "Maybe Colonel Haviland isn't the white knight in shining armor I thought he was."

"He's only a gung-ho leader who demands performance," said Cordell. "You can't fault him for that."

"Finding fault won't help anything, "Seitz said. "This just shows us that flying bombers in combat conditions is dangerous business."

"Maybe that's the difference between this front-line unit and the minor leagues," I said; "front-line flying could be intrinsically more dangerous."

"We'll find out when we do it," said Cordell. "We still haven't flown our first mission with the Bomber Barons."

By May 4, our crew had completed the orientation classes required by the 394th Squadron. We were now ready and eager to get into action.

The next day Colonel Haviland flew with our 394th Squadron to lead the whole Fifth Group on a long mission to bomb Keningau Airfield on Borneo. It was a ten-hour mission, spanning more than 1500 miles. "The Colonel had to lead the first tough one available, to restore respect for his leadership, after that mid-air disaster," Cordell said.

"I volunteered for a combat mission tomorrow," Seitz told us at suppertime on May 5.

"Wonderful!" I said, "where do we fly?"

"You don't go anywhere," Cordell answered with a smug expression. "This is just for Seitz and me."

"What do you mean, just for Seitz and you?" asked James. "We do everything together!"

"This is an exception," Seitz said. "Our crew hasn't been assigned to a mission yet, but the copilots on two of the crews flying tomorrow got sick—jungle diarrhea—so Cordell and I volunteered to fill in as replacement copilots on those crews."

"Well, you lucky guys!" I said. "Aren't there any sick navigators that need replacing?"

"How about finding a sick bombardier?" James said.

"Some other time," Cordell taunted us. "The best get called first. You second-stringers wait 'til later."

"Go suck your thumb!" James snorted.

Our two pilots headed for the briefing tent after supper, while the rest of our crew strolled over to the Bomber Barons' outdoor theater for the nightly movie The theater was on a gently-sloping hillside with a natural bowl shape. Palm tree trunks for benches lay in a semicircular pattern like seats in a Greek theater. At the front stood a covered platform stage backed by a large screen made of plywood, painted silver. Partway up the hill, in the middle of the seating, was a small shack for a projection booth, to keep the frequent showers off the equipment.

BOMBER BARONS OUTDOOR THEATER
Palm tree logs for open-air seating. A small officers' section in front of the projection booth was covered by an awning. The stage was also covered to protect live performers from showers.

Every night some Hollywood feature-length film on sixteen-millimeter reels was shown soon after sunset. Usually the movies were second-rate flicks we would not have bothered to see back in the States, but here in the jungle they drew large audiences. The only competition to the films was letter-writing, drinking, small poker games, bull sessions and other private pursuits.

Tonight we hit the jackpot—we saw Spencer Tracy, Van Johnson, June Allyson in "A Guy Named Joe," a first-class movie with an Army Air Corps setting—P-38s in the south Pacific. I loved it! A rain shower came when it was halfway through; those with raincoats put them on, while those without them stayed there and got soaked. This film was just too good to miss!

Next morning, Seitz and Cordell got up early to go on their combat mission as replacement copilots, while James and I slept late. Two days passed before they returned to our tent in the heat of the afternoon. Both pilots looked rumpled and fatigued as they dropped their gear on the floor.

"That was a mighty long mission," I said. "Where did you go?"

Seitz sat on his cot and lit a cigarette. "Well, the first day we flew to the north tip of Borneo to bomb Kudat Airfield. From there the group flew to Palawan, to spend the night there."

"Where's Palawan?" James asked.

"It's the westernmost Philippine island," Cordell said, stowing his flight gear under his cot. "We staged through Palawan because it's that much closer to the coast of China."

"Next morning we flew all the way to Saigon, in French Indo-China, (now Vietnam) to bomb Thu Dau Mot Airfield," Seitz continued. "Then we returned to Palawan again for another overnight stop. This morning we flew home in time for lunch."

"How'd that mission to Saigon go?" I asked.

"It was a long one—1700 miles round trip, eleven hours flying—"

"And hairy, too," Cordell interrupted. "Jap fighters all over the sky, and flak on the bomb run! We got several holes in our plane, and I think most o' the others got shot up, too. Lucky we all came back, the way those fighters came boring in on our nose from twelve o'clock level! Three of their fighters went down in flames, but our bombers all made it back. For some, they barely squeaked into Palawan on three engines."

"What an exciting mission!" I said. "Just what Cordell's been asking for! And to think he got it on his first flight with the Thirteenth Air Force!"

"It was a historic mission," Seitz said, "the farthest westward penetration ever for the Thirteenth Air Force, and the first to reach the Asian mainland. I'm glad I got in on it."

"I sure want in on the next one," I said. "When can we fly together as a crew?"

"Soon," Seitz said, "maybe day after tomorrow. Our crew has finally been put on alert for a mission on May 10—day after tomorrow."

"Great!" James said. "Where will we go?"

"We won't find out until briefing, tomorrow night."

Officers and enlisted men ate separately on opposite sides of the mess hall, but everyone left through the same exit, beside the garbage cans and wash tubs, where we dipped our mess kits into hot soapy water first, then into hot rinse water. James and I were leaving after supper that same evening, when we ran into three of our crewmen cleaning their mess kits.

"Hi, Hamilton," said Hill. "Did you know that today is Pieper's birthday?"

"Well, Pieper, happy birthday!" I said.

James dipped his mess kit into the suds. "How old are you?"

"Twenty-three."

"Gee, Pieper, you sure don't look that old," James said.

Imhof rinsed his mess kit. "That so-called meal we had wasn't much of a birthday dinner, was it?"

Pieper shrugged his shoulders. "Can't expect a mess hall to celebrate birthdays."

"I'll help you celebrate," I said. "I'll drop by your tent tonight with a beer for the birthday boy."

"But don't tell Seitz," Hill added. "He'll think you're fraternizing again."

For the previous week, Armed Forces Radio had been bringing us news stories about the end of the war in Europe. On May 2, the Russian Army captured Berlin, and Hitler was nowhere to be found. Rumors said that he had died in Berlin the previous day. Fighting continued in many places in Germany.

Finally, the radio told us, German generals signed the documents for unconditional surrender at General Eisenhower's headquarters in Reims, France, at 2:41 A.M. (French time) on May 7, and the cease-fire order for Europe followed immediately. (That was 9:41 A.M. in the Philippines, where the war against Japan continued without a pause.)

The war in Europe was not officially over, however, until the surrender documents were ratified in Berlin the following day. The world waited for the Allies to proclaim "Victory in Europe." Then on May 8, 1945, at Russian Army headquarters in Berlin, Field Marshal Keitel, head of the German Army, ratified the surrender and gave his sword as a token to the Allied generals waiting there.

It was then mid-morning in Berlin, only four a.m. in Washington, but President Truman was dressed and waiting to give an immediate pre-dawn press conference and live radio broadcast. He proclaimed "Victory in Europe" to the nation, and crowds of people waiting in New York City poured into Times Square to start celebrating in the early morning darkness. That was six P.M. on May 8 in the Philippines, where we stayed in the mess hall after supper to hear Armed Forces Radio bring us the President's voice and also descriptions of celebrations there.

"The flags of freedom fly all over Europe," President Truman announced. "The West is free, but the East is still in bondage to the treacherous tyranny of the Japanese. Let there be no doubt of our unshakable resolve. We shall fight on in the East until God grants us the inevitable final victory!"

I had mixed feelings about the occasion. I was glad to hear that the killing was over in Europe, but I knew that our war would only intensify as Allied resources were shifted to the Pacific. Also, I felt grateful that our crew still had the opportunity to participate in major-league action before we won the victory over Japan. After all, our crew had just moved up to the major league. *Give us a little time to enjoy the game!*

14. Three Engines and a Prayer

"V-E Day" was hardly celebrated at all in the Pacific. There was no holiday from the war; it was "business as usual." On May 8th evening, assigned crews gathered in our Group Briefing Tent to prepare for tomorrow's mission. The only official gesture toward a celebration was an announcement that all four Squadron P.X.s would give out free cokes all evening. But there were quite a few small, informal gatherings.

I joined a small group celebrating over beers in our 394th Squadron Officers' Club. I overheard Lieutenant Ken Gutheil, one of our B-24 pilots, reminiscing with a bombardier, Lieutenant Pete Kanduros, about a mission they had flown two months earlier. It had been a pre-invasion ground-support mission on March 9, the day before the U.S. Eighth Army invaded Zamboanga on western Mindanao.

"It was my first mission after the Fifth Bomb Group moved here from Morotai," Gutheil told the men around his table. I brought my beer over to listen to his story.

"Just after our group dropped our bombs on Zamboanga, I looked up and saw another B-24 group two thousand feet higher. Hey! They're dropping their bombs, too. Holy smoke! Those bombs are falling straight toward our squadron! Looks like they're all coming right into my cockpit!" He gestured with both hands.

"One of 'em hit the bomber in front of me! Both the bomb and the airplane exploded right in my face!" He raised both hands in front of his face, as if to shield it.

"Great balls o' fire!" said one of the listeners. "What happened to your plane?"

"Flying junk from the exploding plane hit us all over. Punched seven holes in our wing's leading edge. Knocked two feet off our left wingtip! Damaged number one engine and cocked it up toward the left. Cracked the nose turret glass and smashed both waist windows. Flames from the explosion burned the fabric off our left aileron and left rudder. It was all I could do to control the plane and keep it in the air, but that cockeyed old B-24 flew us home to Samar on three engines, a twisted wing, and full of holes!"

"The B-24 is one great airplane!" another listener said.

"When we landed, the nose wheel collapsed, and we bent the nose on the runway. They towed that bird off to the bone yard, but at least it got us home."

"Were any other planes hit by those bombs?" someone asked.

"No, but the explosion of that one bomb blowing up one unloaded airplane damaged every plane in the squadron but two. Lucky the hit didn't happen a minute sooner, when our bombs were still on board! That could've made an explosion big enough to destroy the whole group!"

"Who dropped those bombs?" I asked. "Who were those idiots in the other B-24s?"

"The 307th Bomb Group, the 'Long Rangers' from Morotai."

"Shoot!" I said. "The Thirteenth Air Force has only two heavy bomb groups to deal with, one on Morotai, and one on Samar. Are you telling me they sent both of 'em to bomb the same target at the same time? How could that possibly happen?"

"Easy," another man said, "just a case of SNAFU" ("Situation Normal, All Fouled Up").

"Another SNAFU mission! And it won't be the last!"

"But that's not the end of the story," pilot Gutheil went on. "Wait'll you hear what Kanduros tells you. He was the bombardier on the plane that exploded!"

"What?" I gasped. "How could anyone survive an exploding airplane?"

"Here I am," Lieutenant Kanduros smiled. "I had put on my flak jacket and helmet before the bomb run—that helped protect me in the blast. I had just dropped our bombs, when a great ball of fire filled the plane like a thunderclap. The nose section was blown clean off the plane—it went spinning down by itself, with me inside! Centrifugal force pinned me to the ceiling.

"All the glass was blown away, and the nose turret doors, too. I could see our nose gunner, Corporal Bill Johnson—his clothes were blown to shreds and his skin was red. I don't know whether he was dead or alive, but I saw him slip out of the turret and disappear."

"Gosh!" said a listener. "What could you do?"

Kanduros' suntanned face turned redder, veins bulging at his temples.

"My chest-pack chute was clipped to the wall beside me, so I grabbed it and tried to put it on. Then I saw that I was still wearing my flak jacket over my parachute harness! How stupid can you get? I tore off the flak jacket first, and clipped the chute onto my harness. Then I threw away my flak helmet, and decided it was time to bail out!"

"Way overdue!" said a listener.

"First I tried to climb out through the astrodome hole in the ceiling, but with the chute on, I was too big to go through it. That was sure dumb! There I was in a broken-off nose section— nothing but empty space behind me—and I tried to climb through the astrodome!" The listeners chuckled and groaned.

"When I moved down from the ceiling, the slipstream sucked me away from the wreckage. But my foot got caught in the ammunition belt to the nose turret—the wreck spun me around two or three turns before I could kick free. When I was really clear, I pulled the ripcord. The chute popped open with such a jerk, it pulled my boots off! Then I floated down for only a few seconds, and dropped into the water."

"Gosh!" someone said, "you were that low when it opened?"

"You had a guardian angel working overtime," said another.

Kanduros continued, "I slipped out of my harness and deflated the chute. I pulled it under water to get it out of sight—I was only a few hundred yards offshore from Jap-occupied Mindanao. Then I saw some American ships about three or four miles away, so I began swimming quietly toward them."

"How badly were you hurt?" I asked.

"How'd you feel?" asked another.

"I noticed that the salt water burned my skin—I had a lot of minor cuts. Later I learned that I had third degree burns in several places. While I was swimming, I saw a half-naked body floating nearby in a life jacket. It was my radio operator, Corporal Jim Stack. He had a deep gash in his neck, and his skin was burned to a crisp. It made me sick to look at him."

"How'd you get rescued?"

"I swam half a mile offshore—thought it was safe to inflate my Mae West (life jacket) and start splashing to make myself more visible. Somebody on a ship must have been looking my way with binoculars—it wasn't long before I saw a cruiser launch a float plane from a catapult. It was a Kingfisher seaplane, and it flew toward me. Then two F4U Corsair fighters appeared out of nowhere. They strafed the shoreline while the Kingfisher landed on the water to pick me up.

"The float plane flew back to its cruiser, the USS Phoenix, and landed beside it. A crane swung out over the water and hoisted the plane back up to its catapult. We climbed out, and they took me to sick bay to treat my cuts and burns. I was a guest of the navy for a while, but they got me back to the 394th Squadron after a few weeks. Navy chow is a lot better than army chow!"

"Wow!" I said. "What an unusual experience!"

(Unusual, but not unprecedented. Air Force records reveal similar accidents in both Europe and the Pacific. Only recently, the long-kept secret of the disappearance of the great jazz band leader Glenn Miller was revealed December 15, 1994, at a 50th-anniversary memorial service at the American Military Cemetery in England. On December 15,1944, Glenn Miller and some of his band were flying from England to France in a small army plane, UC-64 Norseman, when it was hit in mid-air by a bomb dropped by a British Lancaster bomber overhead, which released its bombs over-water before returning to base because of bad weather. *Flying*, March 1995 issue)

I went to bed that night wondering if any of the adventures which lay ahead for me could come close to what I had just heard. *Probably not. But I'll take all the adventures I can get. If I don't find enough in combat, I'll look for some more on my own.*

The following night I went to the briefing tent, along with more than a hundred other flyers, to learn about our mission for the following morning, May 10. It was my first briefing with the Thirteenth Air Force, and I was struck by how similar it was to the briefings we had experienced at Nadzab.

The target was Japanese Army installations in the town of Malaybalay, on the southern Philippine island of Mindanao. My fifth combat mission would be a half-day ground-support strike to help the U.S. Eighth Army retake Mindanao.

The 394th Squadron would lead the Fifth Bomb Group this time, and our Group C.O., Lieutenant Colonel Isaac Haviland, would fly the lead plane. The colonel was a man I admired. *His leading the Bomber Barons on my first mission with them is a good omen for me.*

At seven A.M. on May 10, a dozen B-24's started engines on Guiuan Airfield, Samar, and taxied toward the west end of the runway, ready to take off east into the prevailing trade winds. Six planes were from the 394th Squadron and six from the 31st Squadron; the other two squadrons had the day off.

At 7:10, the first B-24 roared down the runway. The others followed at one minute intervals. Our crew took off at 7:15 in number 199, with the name "Daisy Mae" and a half-naked picture of Li'l Abner's comic-strip girl friend painted on its nose.

We flew the last plane in our squadron, but the six planes of the 31st Squadron took off after us. The planes circled the field until all were airborne, and then slowly wheeled into the "Group

Combat Box" formation. Each squadron made two three-plane Vees one behind the other. The trailing squadron flew behind and to the right of the lead squadron. The Group formation would provide maximum defensive firepower against potential enemy fighter attack.

The group departed on a true course of 205 degrees (south-southwest), climbing on course to 9,000 feet. We flew right over tiny Hibuson Island in southern Leyte Gulf, a good checkpoint for navigation.

As I looked down at this little island through the bombardier's nose window, the natural beauty of Pacific islands fascinated me. This one was only three miles long and two miles wide, covered with deep green foliage, and edged with a golden sandy beach that shone in the brilliant morning sunlight. A little lighthouse stood on the north end, with a cluster of native huts nearby, and outrigger boats pulled up on the beach.

All around the island stretched the sea, in concentric circles of different shades of blue, from pale transparent blue at the shore, through bands of light, medium and dark blue as the water got deeper, to midnight Prussian blue in the ocean beyond. Dancing off the dark waves was a band of shimmering sunlight, sparkling from the low morning sun. The scene was more beautiful than a glistening jewel displayed on dark blue velvet. Its beauty filled my mind.

"Pilot to Navigator," crackled in my earphones, "what's our E.T.A. for target?"

I snapped out of my reverie and looked at my navigator's log.

"Navigator to Pilot, E.T.A. target 9:02" I answered, and got back to work.

Williams and James both came forward and took up their duty stations. The nose was crowded again with a full work crew.

The islands of the Philippines, large and small, stretched out in all directions as far as I could see. Southern Leyte was on our right side, its tip directly ahead. On the horizon beyond Leyte, I saw Cebu a hundred miles away, with some smaller islands in between. Bohol Island, south of Cebu, was closer in, ahead to the right. All of them had forest-covered mountains and lush green plains.

Dinagat Island was now on our left a few miles away, with striking coral reefs all around it and around the hundred little mini-islands between Dinagat and the north tip of the big island of Mindanao, ahead to the left. Such colorful contrasts—both light and dark green foliage, bright sandy beaches, white coral reefs, and in the water, multiple bands of different shades of blue. What a feast for artistic eyes! I wanted to capture those scenes somehow, but in 1945 color photography was just beginning, not yet in common use, and my skills in painting were much too limited to do it justice.

I'll have to talk about these scenes with Hill. He's an artist who paints in oils—he'll appreciate the beauty he sees from the tail.

We flew just left of little Camiguin Island and its mile-high mountain, crossing the shoreline of Mindanao at Talisayan Point. Then we turned twenty degrees left to follow the coastline south to Bugo at the foot of the bay. There we turned left again to head southeast toward the target, Maylaybalay town, thirty-six miles ahead. No enemy fighters appeared to challenge us.

At Bugo, we also changed the group formation from "Combat Box" to "Squadrons in Trail," with the 31st Squadron trailing directly behind our 394th Squadron as we headed for the bomb run. That allowed the two squadrons to bomb independently, promoting a healthy rivalry between squadrons to produce the best bombing results. No flak came up to distract us today.

Bombardier James opened our bomb bay doors and squinted through his bombsight. The lead bombardier of each squadron was now guiding his formation as he sighted for deflection, aiming for a large building in the center of the town. But each bombardier was sighting for range, so each plane's bombs were dropped by the skill of its own bombardier, instead of all releasing their bombs when the lead plane did.

Our plane carried twenty 300-pound bombs set for sequential release to strike the ground at 90-foot intervals. James was aiming on the first cross street on the near side of town, which would make our bombs fall in a string 1800 feet long, the length of the entire town. Our twelve planes planned to drop 240 bombs in twelve such strings, blowing up the whole town. At briefing, Intelligence officers had told us that Japanese soldiers had displaced all of the Filipinos when they occupied the town, so bombing it would harm only enemy soldiers, not the natives.

When our bombs dropped at 9:01, they did a good job. Most of our bombs fell within the city limits; we destroyed four major buildings and damaged many others. Towering columns of smoke rose from the fires we started. Secondary explosions followed, as Jap ammunition stored in some of the structures blew up.

Radio silence ended with the bomb drop. A strike report went to Thirteenth Bomber Command, and our VHF radios came alive.

"Able Leader from Able Four, over." (Each squadron had a letter in the phonetic alphabet, "Able, Baker, Charlie, Dog....")

"Able Four from Able Leader, go ahead."

"Able Four's bombs failed to drop. Request permission to leave formation and try another bomb run, over."

"Able Four, permission granted for solo bomb run, out."

Lieutenant Grissom in 209 dropped all his bombs on his second run at 9:17, with apparently good results. Meanwhile, Colonel Haviland led the rest of the group in a big circle a few miles away. Then 209 rejoined the waiting group.

From the target area we flew north to Magsaysay Point, then turned ten degrees right to head straight for our home base at Guiuan Airfield at the south end of Samar. The route took us by the northern tip of Mindanao, then over Dinagat Island, where we began to descend. Over the base we peeled off to land. Our plane was the sixth out of twelve, touching down at eleven A.M. for a flight time of three hours forty-five minutes.

After debriefing with Lieutenant Mander of Intelligence, our crew lined up in front of Doc Dolce, our flight surgeon, for the after-mission ration of whiskey given flyers in front-line units. I had never drunk a straight shot of whiskey before. I watched Seitz, Cordell, and others drink their two-ounce shots in a gulp.

"I think I'll pass up my shot," I said. "That was an easy mission, and it's only midday—too early for whiskey in my book. Seitz, would you like to drink my shot as a chaser?"

"Why not?" said Seitz, holding his glass out for another.

"Too early for me, too," Herrema said. "Hill, it's yours."

"Thanks, Herrema," Hill said with a grin.

"I'll pass on mine, too," Imhof said. "You want it, Williams?"

"Sure," Williams said. "Nice to have some light drinkers around."

Our next mission, a week later, was the long-awaited trip to Borneo. It was my sixth combat mission, on May 18. At briefing the night before, we learned that the target was the Japanese personnel and supply area at Sibu Airfield, far down the west coast of Borneo. The secondary target was a similar area at Bintulu Airfield, 100 miles northeast on the same coast.

This was the first time the Bomber Barons had ever gone as far down the west coast as Sibu; it was a fourteen-hour mission covering 2,340 miles, with a night take-off before dawn, an all-day flight there and back, and a night landing long after sunset. Since the target was enemy personnel and supplies, each plane carried twenty 100-pound napalm firebombs instead of the high-explosive bombs used to break up airfield runways.

On this mission, the 394 Squadron would lead the group again, and flying the lead plane would be Major "Pat" Patterson, C.O. of the 394th Squadron. I felt excited all through the briefing—our crew now had a real major league mission at last!

Wake-up call for the duty crews was three A.M., followed by the special breakfast served only to the mission flyers—fresh eggs, cooked to individual order. Then we drew our equipment, went to the airplane, checked everything over, and were ready to start engines by five-thirty. We were assigned B-24 number 650, "Little Judith Anne," named for the crew chief's daughter. "Little Judith Anne" had eighty-nine bombs painted on her nose, one for each mission she had flown. What a combat veteran! Before we boarded the plane, the crew chief, Staff Sergeant Eddie Lorden, had told us, "Be sure to bring her back. She's my little girl."

At 5:48, Major Patterson began his take-off roll down the dark runway into the black night sky. His lead plane was number 199, "Daisy Mae," which we had flown on our last mission. From our position of fourth in take-off sequence, we watched his running lights and the glow of four engine exhausts grow smaller and fainter as he receded into the darkness. The other planes followed at one-minute intervals, cued by a green signal light from the control tower. Our turn came at 5:51 A.M.

Looking out from the flight deck behind the pilots, I realized for the first time how scary it was to take off at night in a heavily-overloaded bomber on a dark runway just a few feet above an inky-black ocean. *There's nothing to see!*

We roared down the full length of Guiuan's 8,000-foot runway before staggering into the air at end of the island, and then there was nothing outside for visual reference, just black sea, black sky, no lights outside, no horizon. The pilots were flying totally on instruments immediately, and roared along only twenty feet above the water for two or three miles before gaining speed enough to climb so slowly that it took six minutes to reach the first thousand feet of altitude.

The slightest dip for any reason during those critical moments after take-off would have caused a deadly crash into the sea. I broke into a cold sweat just to think of it! *This sort of flying is an accident waiting to happen! This long mission's barely started, but that overloaded night take-off over water's adventure enough already!*

We followed the faint glow of the other planes ahead to circle the airfield while all twelve bombers took off; then we slowly formed the "Group Combat Box." By six-fifteen we were ready to depart. The group headed southwest toward Borneo on a true course of 237 degrees, continuing to climb on course as dawn ushered in the daylight. The trip to the target was expected to take seven hours.

Twenty minutes en route, the interphone crackled in my ears, "Waist gunner to Pilot, we're losing tail-end Charlie, over."

"Pilot to Waist, say again."

"This is Herrema in the waist. The plane on our left wing just turned back. His number three engine was smoking up a storm, and he shut it down, over."

"Must have had an oil leak or engine fire. What's his plane number? Over."

"Six-one-eight, over."

"That's Lieutenant Heinz. Well, no one needs to shift places since he was tail end. We simply have a smaller group."

The remaining eleven bombers leveled off at 10,500 feet over the island of Leyte, between layers of clouds. Looking down, half of Leyte was hidden by cumulus clouds with tops 1,500 feet below us. Overhead the sky was almost obscured by another cumulus layer 1,000 feet above us.

The clouds got thicker as we flew through a weather front beyond Leyte. We were in the clouds, flying on instruments, over Bohol Island, and flying through rain and turbulence between Bohol and Cebu. Starting to feel queasy, I focused on my navigation as an act of will, plotting fixes with data from the loran receiver. I stayed too busy to get airsick.

Beyond Cebu, we came out of the frontal system, and found ourselves between layers again; the lower cloud tops were 3,000 feet below us, while the scattered higher clouds were 2,000 feet above us. Looking down through the broken clouds below, I saw the southern end of Negros Island, the last of the Philippines on our way to Borneo. Ahead lay four hundred miles of open water as we flew over the empty Sulu Sea, more than two hours with no scenery. The weather stayed much the same all the way to Borneo.

We crossed the coast of North Borneo at Labuk Bay, near Sandakan. The flat wetlands along the whole northeast coast were covered with vivid green swamps full of mangrove trees, with occasional clearings for villages and towns. We continued on our southwesterly course over the forested mountain ranges ahead. The rugged Crocker Range stretched out to the right, climaxing in Mount Kinabalu, forty miles off our right wing, whose rocky peak rose to 13,455 feet, the highest in all Borneo.

PACIFIC AREA MAP
(Area covered: 3,000 miles east-west,
4,500 miles north-south)

Beyond the mountains, our course drew us ever closer to the northwest coast on our right, and soon we flew near Brunei Bay, a great round harbor thirty miles in diameter, said to be large enough to anchor the whole Japanese navy. It looked nearly empty as we passed it a few miles inland, but only six months earlier, it had sheltered an enemy fleet of three battleships, two cruisers, and nine destroyers.

I had heard stories about November 16, 1944, when the Thirteenth Air Force had sent eight squadrons of B-24s (four from each bomb group) to Brunei Bay to attack that fleet. Heavy anti-aircraft fire from the ships' big deck guns shot down three of our bombers and damaged many more while they were ten miles away, but the planes pressed the attack to claim one cruiser sunk and another damaged. I visualized that attack as I watched Brunei Bay go by.

The Japanese fleet had later been withdrawn and sent north to help defend the Japanese homeland, so I saw nothing but small freighters and native boats in the bay.

Beyond Brunei Bay, our group of eleven B-24s flew over the green swampy flatlands of the northwestern Borneo coast. Our southwesterly course led us across the shoreline and over a stretch of the South China Sea to Igan Point, north of Sibu, where the group would turn left to bomb Sibu airfield. But Little Judith Anne never got that far.

Soon after crossing the shoreline, I heard on the interphone, "Waist Gunner to Pilot, smoke from number one, over."

"Pilot to Waist, say again."

"Number one engine smoking bad, over."

Cordell's voice added, "Number one oil pressure way down!"

"Feather number one!" Seitz' voice commanded.

I looked out the left nose window to see smoke pouring out of the left outboard engine, and then watched the propeller slow down and stop as the pilots turned the blades feather-edge into the slipstream. The smoke thinned out and ended. The other three engines roared louder as the pilots increased power. I checked the time; it was 12:30.

"Pilot to Navigator, how long to primary target? Over."

"Forty-five minutes if we keep up with the formation, over."

"How long to the secondary, Bintulu? Over."

I did a quick calculation. "Twenty minutes to secondary. You can barely see Bintulu on the coast ahead, at ten o'clock low, over."

"Pilot to crew, we can't keep up with the group on three engines. We're going to peel off and bomb the secondary target. Navigator, give me a heading, over."

"One-eight-zero, due south."

Our plane nosed down to drop below the formation, and rolled to the right to peel off. ("Never turn toward a dead engine.") Then we leveled off, heading south, as the pilots lowered the roar of the engines to high cruising power.

"Pilot to Bombardier, arm the bombs, open the doors, and prepare for solo bomb run."

"Bombardier to Pilot, roger, wilco." James unplugged his interphone connector and crawled through the nose tunnel into the bomb bay to pull safety wires.

"Pilot to all Gunners, we're alone and vulnerable. Keep your eyes peeled for enemy fighters. If there are any out there, they love to jump solo birds like us. Test-fire your guns now." The airplane shook with the sound of ten fifty-caliber machine guns as they fired a few short bursts.

James reappeared in the nose from the bomb bay and plugged in his intercom. "Bombardier to Pilot, all bombs now armed. We're carrying twenty great balls of fire!"

"Pilot to all crew members, we're coming up on target fast. Better put on your flak vest and helmet now, and keep your parachute handy!"

I lifted my body armor off the floor, and put on the flak vest and heavy steel helmet. My chest-pack chute was hung on a wall clip beside my navigation table.

"Nose Gunner to Pilot, flak ahead, two o'clock low, over!"

I looked over the bombardier's shoulder. There it was, two ugly puffs of black smoke, low and to the right. There's another!

"Navigator to Pilot and Bombardier; we're now over the I.P."

"Pilot to Bombardier, commence bomb run. You're in control."

James knelt on the floor, bent over the bombsight, with both hands on its controls and his eye glued to the eyepiece. He now controlled the plane's direction; the pilots maintained only the altitude and airspeed. Whenever he turned the bombsight to the left or right, the autopilot turned the airplane the same way. Although flack was starting to rock the plane, no evasive action was possible during the bomb run.

James looked through the bombsight at the approaching target, and delicately adjusted the angular speed of the gyromotor that slowly cranked the sighting angle down to keep the crosshairs on the aiming point. When the sighting angle reached the preset release angle, the bombsight automatically released the first bomb and the intervalometer released the rest in rapid sequence, producing a string of bombs that "walked" across the target area at fifty-foot intervals.

"Bombs away!" James called on the intercom. "Closing bomb bay doors." He pulled up on the big red bomb bay door control.

"Let's get out of here!" said Seitz, as he rolled the big bomber into a steep right turn. A close flak burst rocked us hard, and shell fragments tore through the plane's aluminum skin and rattled around inside as we turned. *That one was close!*

For the next few minutes, we dodged flak as Seitz zig-zagged the plane for evasive action until we got out of range of the guns at Bintulu.

I could not navigate well during evasive action; I just sat at my chart table, feeling queasy. While I waited, I wrote in my log, "Bombs away 1250," and considered our possible destinations. If we could not go all the way back to Samar on three engines, we could divert to Zamboanga, on the western tip of Mindanao, or to Palawan, the westernmost island in the Philippines. Our 13th Air Force now had fighter bases at both places.

"Pilot to Navigator, I don't want to risk flying all the way back to Samar on three engines. What are our alternates? Over."

"Zamboanga or Palawan, over."

"Which is closer? Over."

"Palawan, about a hundred miles closer from here, over."

"Give me a heading to Palawan, over."

"Head northeast, zero-four-zero, out."

Seitz turned the plane northeast, and I calculated an E.T.A. for Palawan. We were flying twenty knots slower without the fourth engine, and I figured three and a half hours to Palawan.

"Pilot to crew, we can't maintain altitude on three engines at reasonable power settings. We have to make the ship lighter. Throw out everything that's not tied down. Start with all the flak helmets and flak vests, and whatever you can think of."

"Bombardier to Pilot, shall I open the bomb bay doors to make it easy to throw stuff out?"

"Crack 'em part way open."

"Waist to Pilot, our waist gun windows are open back here; we can throw stuff out the windows, over."

"Pilot to Waist, do *not* throw stuff out the side windows; it could damage the tail. Open the belly hatch, and throw your junk out through that. If something's too big for the belly hatch, dump it through the bomb bay doors."

We all removed our flak vests and helmets. James carried the ones from the nose back to the bomb bay to throw out.

"Waist to Pilot, what about these swivel machine guns? Over."

"Throw them overboard! We haven't seen a fighter all day, over."

"What about the ammunition? Over."

"Throw it out, too!"

"And the ammunition for the turret guns?"

"Throw it all out!"

"It'll take a while to remove the machine guns mounted in the turrets—you want us to do that, too? Over."

"Sure—all four of you turret gunners, get busy and jettison the guns in your own turret." "What about our parachutes and harnesses? Over"

"We may have to bail out yet—better save them."

"What about this big aerial camera in the waist? Over."

"Imhof, did you get pictures of the bombs on target? Over."

"Yeah, I took five or six pictures through the belly hatch, over."

"Then remove the film pack, and throw out the camera."

Imhof objected, "But they told me this camera is a real hot military secret, and we're over enemy territory. Why not wait 'til we're over water before dumping it? Over."

"I'm giving you an order—throw it overboard now!"

"Yes, sir!"

"Pilot to Ball Gunner, retract your big ball now—we don't need the drag it makes. Then, when you've removed the guns and ammunition in your turret, see if you can find the wrenches to unfasten the whole ball turret and drop it out. That'd get rid of a lot of weight."

"Engineer to Pilot, I'll go back and help him do that, over."

"Good idea—you know where the tools are."

"Pilot to Nose and Tail Gunners, stay in your turrets as lookouts. Imhof, stay with your radios. All other gunners and Bombardier, go to the waist and help lighten this airplane."

I studied the flight instruments at my navigator station in the nose. Our altitude continued to drift downward; we were under 9,000 feet, and our airspeed down to 133.

"Navigator to Pilot, we have a tailwind up here, west at 15 knots, but if we go to lower altitudes, we may lose it. That would lengthen our trip to Palawan."

"Pilot to Navigator, I'm fighting for all the altitude I can get! But I don't want to push the other engines too hard. Gotta keep them from burning out, too!"

For the first time in my combat career, I felt the need to pray in flight.

Dear God, get us safely to Palawan!

Then I felt ashamed that my faith was so shallow that I only talked to God when events got out of control. *I wonder if everyone overseas uses God as a backup parachute?* For the moment, I had a simpler question: *Will my prayer be answered?*

15. Bombing Borneo

As we flew over western Borneo with one dead engine, I used the loran receiver to plot a fix which placed us over the coastal plains near Lutong. We were on course for Palawan.

My earphones crackled, "Radio to Pilot, just received the strike flash our Group Leader sent to Bomber Command. He reported 'ten planes bombed primary target at 1312 from 10,500 feet with good results, 200 bombs on or near target,' over."

"Pilot to Radio, that ends our radio silence too. Now we can send our own strike flash to Bomber Command, quote: 'Able Four lost engine near secondary target, put twenty bombs on secondary at 1250 on three engines, proceeding to Palawan for repairs,' over."

"Radio to Pilot, say again while I copy, over."

Seitz repeated the message, slowly.

"Radio, roger."

"Pilot to Crew, if you've dumped everything possible, close all hatches and bomb bay doors to give us a clean machine."

Soon we crossed the northwest coast of Borneo west of Brunei City. Flying over water, we passed Brunei Bay again, this time looking at it from the ocean. Our course toward Palawan took us over the South China Sea, thirty miles offshore, almost parallel to the northwest coast of Borneo. Two hours after bombs away, the awesome rocky peak of Mount Kinabalu appeared off our right wingtip again, fifty miles away. It rose nearly two miles higher than our current altitude. We had drifted down to 4,500 feet by then, and I became anxious because our slow descent was continuing.

"Navigator to Pilot, we've lost 6,000 feet in two hours. We still have an hour and a half to go before we reach Palawan. If we continue to drift down at our present rate, we'll run out of airspace before we get there, over."

"Pilot to Navigator, our rate of descent is only 50 feet per minute. Now that you mention it, that does add up to 3,000 feet per hour. But we're getting lighter as we burn off more fuel, and if the men in the waist manage to dump the ball turret, that'll make us quite a bit lighter."

Pieper's voice came on the interphone, "Engineer to Pilot, there's no way we can dump the ball turret in mid-air. Herrema and I've been working on it for quite a while, but we just don't have the heavy tools we need to finish the job."

"Okay, men, thanks for trying."

Two minutes later, Pieper's voice came on again, "Engineer to Pilot, I just looked in the bomb bay and saw something else we can dump. The extra fuel tanks in the bomb bay are both empty now, so we can drop 'em. They're pretty heavy, even when empty."

"Pilot to Engineer, go do it! Good thinking!"

Imhof's voice came on the intercom, "Radio to Pilot, just copied another message from Group Leader to Bomber Command. They just lost another plane from our squadron. Able Five headed for Zamboanga due to fuel shortage, over."

"Pilot to Radio, Able Five's Lieutenant Taylor. That leaves only three out of six planes from our squadron still going home with the group."

"There'll be some unhappy crew chiefs tonight on Samar," Cordell said. "Sergeant Lorden won't sleep well till we bring back this bird, his Little Judith Anne."

Our altitude was only 3,000 feet a half hour later, when we passed the town of Kudat on the northwestern tip of Borneo. The Japanese had an airfield at Kudat, the sixth one we had passed in Borneo, but no enemy fighters rose to intercept us. *We bombed all of those airfields recently, thank God.*

The altimeter showed only 2,200 feet over Balabac Island when I saw the southern tip of Palawan ahead to the left. But our destination, Puerto Princesa, was halfway up the long, narrow island of Palawan, so we still had another hour to fly. We were down to

1,500 feet as we passed Bonobono on San Antonio Bay, then down to only 1,000 feet at Panitan on Island Bay, and still creeping downward. Under 1,000 feet made my mouth feel dry as cotton.

The air inside got warmer as we came down. Suddenly, I felt hot. Sweat dripped off my face and stained the navigator log.

How low will Seitz let us drift before he increases power? Should I remind him again about our altitude? No, my job is only to steer him to destination, not to tell him how high or how fast to fly. I will not remind him again, but if he lets us get much lower, I'm afraid I'll have a heart attack!

The white surf of Palawan's eastern shoreline lay directly below us, stretching ahead as far as we could see. We were down to only 600 feet as we sailed by the jagged ridge called "The Teeth," 5,900 feet high, inland off our left wingtip. Three minutes later, when the altimeter showed only 500 feet, I heard the roar of the three good engines get louder, as the pilot finally increased power enough to maintain altitude. The airspeed rose to 140, and the altimeter held steady at 500 feet. *Thank God! The pilot finally came to his senses!*

"Navigator to Pilot, E.T.A. 1620. I'm coming up to the flight deck now for the landing."

The next ten minutes brought Puerto Princesa Bay in view, with coconut groves behind the city on the shore. The airfield lay beyond it, just south of a Filipino prison identified on the map as "Iwahig Penal Colony." We turned left to cross the narrow waist of Palawan, going out over the South China Sea, then turned right to land into the east trade wind. We touched down at 4:22.

A jeep with a "Follow Me" sign met us at the end of the runway, and led us to a parking space in the maintenance area. The jeep took our pilot to Operations. The rest of us looked for flak holes in the plane while we waited for a crew truck.

"Look at this one," said Cordell, poking a finger through a hole in the side. "We just survived a pretty good mission."

"Yeah," James said, "I got to drop my own bombs! First time in combat I dropped bombs all by myself!"

"And I got to navigate a solo return trip," I added. "That's the first time in combat that I've directed the pilot myself!"

"Our first trip to Borneo," said Pieper, "but not our last."

We didn't mention that it was scary flying on three engines over enemy-held territory and wondering whether we could make it home.

Ours was the only B-24 in sight. There were lots of twin-engine P-38s (my favorite fighter), and twin-engine B-25s (which reminded me of miniature B-24s, since they also have high wings and twin rudders). This was obviously a fighter and medium bomber base. I soon learned that the B-25s were in the 42nd Bomb Group, and the P-38s in the 347th Fighter Group. The Thirteenth Air Force Fighter Command was here on Palawan.

A crew truck drove up and took us away to the transient housing area, the usual large tents crowded with cots. After the evening chow call, most of the others headed for the outdoor movie in the coconut grove, but I was dead tired. I went straight to my cot and slept like a dead man for twelve hours.

The other men were sleepy-heads next morning when I woke up bright-eyed and vigorous. I decided to go exploring alone after breakfast. We were camped at the narrow waist of Palawan, barely two miles wide, so it was not far to either shore. First I headed west, where the waves of the South China Sea broke over rocky coral reefs at the foot of a modest cliff. I found a path down the cliff, and walked over the rocks below to look at the colorful fish, crabs, and moray eels in the tidewater pools of the coral reef. Sea birds wheeled overhead and filled the morning with their vibrant cries.

When I had seen enough of that, I climbed the cliff and walked two miles east through shady coconut groves to the shore of Puerto Princesa Bay. It was a beautiful little bay, a natural circle of white sandy beach one mile in diameter, open to the Sulu Sea on the east. The city of Puerto Princesa was at the north end of the bay, on a promontory into the Sulu Sea. There a tanker ship at the dock was unloading gasoline through a pipeline to shore. The morning sunlight sparkled on the water, inviting me to come in for a swim.

I kicked off my boots and socks to feel the warm white sand under my toes. A minute later my khaki shirt and trousers lay on the beach while I plunged in for a swim, clad only in shorts. The shallow water was warm and pleasant, and the waves rolling in from the Sulu Sea were low and gentle. The sunlight tingled on my skin. *Thank God our plane didn't go down in Borneo! It's a great day to be alive!*

A few minutes later, I swam back to the beach and dried off in the sunshine. Dressed, I walked back to camp to ask when they thought our engine repairs would be completed. Hearing that it would be after lunch or later, I checked out a one-man life raft and paddle, and took them to the beach to explore Puerto Princesa Bay by boat.

Stripping down to shorts again, I launched my little orange dinghy and paddled into the center of the bay. Slowly I cruised around, enjoying the tropical scenery and the warm sunshine on my skin. Then I saw something unusual on the south shore, and paddled there to investigate.

The Filipinos had built several fences out into the water, made of bamboo poles stuck vertically into the shallow bottom of the bay. Each fence went out a hundred feet or so, and ended by bending around to form a large circle, a corral for rounding up fish. As I approached the nearest fence, I saw a pair of small shark fins, one behind the other, above the water near the fence. Both fins moved in unison, as if on a single fish.

Aha! Let's see if I can round up a shark in this corral.

Paddling as quietly as possible, I moved my dinghy behind the fish, and shooed it along the fence into the corral. Then I paddled into the entrance gap, and looked for a weapon to use on it.

I tugged on the last bamboo pole at the end of the fence, and managed to pull it up from the bottom and out of the water. The bottom end had been cut to a point; it was a ready-made spear.

Waiting for just the right opportunity, I speared the fish and brought it up out of the water and into my boat in one sweeping motion, then slammed the paddle against it to pin it down at the far end of the boat.

Boy, was I lucky! I've never speared a fish before—and this is such an impressive catch! I held it with the paddle at the end of the boat for a few minutes until its death throes ceased, then pulled it closer for a good look at what I had caught.

It was a strange fish, only two feet long. It had two dorsal fins one behind the other, each tall and shaped like a shark fin, and a flat, triangular head that was long, thin, wide, and pointed. The head looked like a miniature manta ray, horizontal and flat, with pointed wingtips, and both eyes were on the flat top of its head. But this ray-like head had a shark-like body attached to it.

I'll call it a "ray-head shark." Gotta show this trophy to my crew.

MY RAY-HEAD SHARK
(I drew this sketch in 1945 in my next letter to Dad.)

My fish attracted the attention of several Filipino children and adults who were near the beach when I paddled in and deflated the dinghy. They pointed at it and made approving sounds in their Tagalog language. I decided to give it away after showing it off.

"You—want—fish?" I said to an older boy, gesturing. "You—come along—me, I—give you—fish." He nodded, and smiled.

After dressing, I carried the folded life raft in one hand, and the fish in the other, hanging by the tail. Into the camp I went, followed by the Filipino boy and several smaller children. We made an interesting parade as we approached the tent area.

"Well, here comes the Pied Piper, leading the children," Seitz said, coming out of the transient officers' tent. "What did you drag in from the sea?"

I held my trophy higher. "It's a baby ray-head shark. Isn't it a beauty? I've never seen anything like it before."

"Neither have I," Seitz said.

"It sure is different!" said James, emerging from the tent. "Did you buy it from these Filipinos?"

"Heck no! I saw it from my boat in Puerto Princesa Bay and speared it in the water with a sharp-pointed bamboo pole."

Cordell came out and looked it over. "What'll you do with it? Stuff it and hang it over your fireplace?" He laughed.

"No—I'll give it to these kids to take home for dinner."

I turned to the oldest boy and held the fish out to him. "You—take fish—go home."

He took it with a big grin, held it up like a trophy, and led the parade of children away.

"What are we going to do with you, Hamilton?" Seitz asked with mock severity. "If you're not out climbing a mountain, or paddling down a river in a dinghy, you're out in the ocean spearing a weird-looking shark! What'll you think of next?"

I chuckled with satisfaction. "Anything that adds some adventure to life."

"But our purpose here is to do our job for the war effort, not to pursue private adventure," Seitz said.

"Didn't I do my job on that mission we just flew? I worked as hard as anyone on the crew! As long as I do that, I feel free to pursue private adventure. Can't be serious all the time!"

"Well, okay. Now it's time to get some chow, then fly our big iron bird back to Samar."

An hour later, we took off and headed east across the Sulu Sea. We flew around the usual afternoon thunderstorms, and landed on our home runway at four P.M.

"One-ten to four," I said to James, "two hours fifty minutes from Palawan, for a total of thirteen hours twenty minutes on this whole mission to Borneo. That's our longest mission ever!"

"I feel it," said James; "I'm ready for that after-mission shot of whiskey. And if you want to pass up yours again, I'll be glad to drink yours too!"

"No, this time I'm ready to drink it myself."

Next morning I woke up with the vivid memory of the enjoyment I had experienced paddling around Puerto Princesa Bay. That was so much fun that I wanted more of it here.

"I think I'll build a small boat of my own," I said to my tent mates as we got up for breakfast.

"What?" James asked, "build a boat here? On Samar?"

I put on my khaki shirt. "Sure, a little one-man boat like a kayak. Then I can paddle around the Gulf of Leyte anytime I want."

Seitz stepped into his khaki trousers. "Have you ever built a boat before?"

"Yes—when I was in high school, I spent three months with Uncle Liston on Amelia Island in Florida. He had a little three-horsepower outboard motor going to waste, and I decided to build a little boat to make use of it. I designed a pretty neat boat, and built it out of plywood. It floated okay, but it was so small that my weight and the motor's weight made the boat sit too low in the water. I could hardly turn it without shipping water. One day it swamped and sank in the middle of Harrison Creek."

Cordell tied his shoelaces. "Not a very good beginning for your boat-building career,"

"So I made it too small—at least I built my own boat."

"Thinking of a bigger boat this time?" Seitz asked. He exchanged glances with Cordell, both laughing quietly.

"Twice as big, and no motor to weigh it down, so I'm sure it'll work."

James buckled his tan web belt. "How long will it take to build?"

"I built the last one in about ten days, working full-time. Between missions, I guess it might take me twenty or thirty days."

Cordell's eyes lit up. "Betcha ten pesos you can't finish it by the end of June. That's forty days from today."

"I'd never bet ten pesos—I don't believe in gambling."

James put on his overseas cap. "But you do play penny-ante poker with us."

I laughed. "Penny-ante's not gambling, that's just entertainment."

"So, if the stakes are low enough, you call it by another name," Cordell said. "Then I'll bet you ONE peso you can't finish your boat by the end of June!"

I thought for a moment. "That's small enough to be acceptable. I'll take that bet!"

After breakfast, I sat down on my cot with pencil and paper to sketch a boat design. I wanted to build something like a kayak with a flattened bottom and sides that tapered to a point at both ends. I could build rectangular rib stations out of four straight pieces of wood nailed together, and connect them by wood stringers running from bow to stern. If I could find thin plywood, I'd cover it with that, but if not, I'd add more stringers and cover it all with canvas or aircraft fabric, painted waterproof.

Seitz came back to our tent in mid-morning, looking unhappy.

"Why so grim?" I asked.

"I just had my ass chewed out by Captain Davenport!"

"Who is this captain, and why is he chewing your ass?"

"He's the 394th Squadron Operations Officer. He said that Intelligence was giving him a hard time because we dumped that darn camera over Borneo. He told me that the big aerial camera was classified secret, almost as big a secret as the Norden bombsight. Since I dumped it on land, the enemy might find what was left of it and learn how to copy it. He said I should have waited till we were over water to dump it."

"That's just what Imhof asked you to do, remember?"

"He was right, and I ordered him to throw it out. I was too focused on lightening the plane immediately."

"Well, it's only a rebuke. Your ass will grow back again."

"But every reprimand is a black mark on your record. I want to become Operations Officer myself some day. Now I'll have to work that much harder."

I went back to designing my boat. The design work and list of materials took all morning. Then I joined the chow line for lunch, resolved to search for materials in the afternoon.

I borrowed a jeep from the motor pool for a trip to the Sea Bee lumber yard. It took only a short while to learn that they had no plywood thin enough to bend, so I went for the second plan, a fabric-covered boat, and looked for wood trim stock which would work for stringers. After much searching, I found the materials needed for the rib stations and stringers. I tied them into a bundle, and folded down the wind-shield of the jeep to lay the bundle down flat.

Just then a Sea Bee rode up on his home-made motor scooter. *What a neat rig!* Eagerly I inspected it for ideas. He had made a simple two-wheel scooter frame from scrap metal found in the salvage yard, installed two small tail-wheels from wrecked fighters, and powered it with a one-cylinder "putt-putt" gas engine off the A.P.U. (auxiliary power unit) from a crashed bomber. *It sure is cute!*

I want to build one like it, after I finish my boat. It was nice to discover that there were other men around with creative hobbies, too.

The only tools I could borrow were a hammer and a handsaw, plus a can of small nails. I drove home with my loot and unloaded it under the floor of my tent.

Next morning I started to build the boat, using our tent's wood floor as a workbench. I started on the rib stations (cross-sections of the boat at two foot intervals), cutting 1 x 6 pieces and nailing them together on the floor to make the four sides of each. I sawed a curve on the top and bottom; since I had only a handsaw, this took time.

At eleven-thirty, James came back to the tent. "Seitz sent me to call you. We have to pose for our crew photo at the orderly room."

"That's right, I heard about it yesterday. Today I got busy building my boat, and forgot."

"Well, get your butt down there now!"

We walked together to the 394th Squadron Orderly Room tent, where several crews were waiting in clusters while another crew posed in front of the bulletin board. The photographer, a staff sergeant with a booming voice, snapped two pictures, then called for the next crew. We found our crew grouped in one of the clusters. Williams had a monkey on his shoulder.

"Hey, Williams," I said, "what's this monkey business?"

"Meet Shoo-Shoo, Hamilton. Shoo-Shoo's a Philippine Spider Monkey." He squatted to let the little monkey jump from his shoulder to the ground, but held onto the leash to its collar.

"He sure is a cute little fellow," Imhof said, petting the monkey's head.

"Why do they call it a spider monkey?" I asked.

"He eats bugs—spiders, grasshoppers, things like that."

"I thought monkeys ate bananas," Herrema said.

"He'll eat bananas and peanuts, too."

"Look—no tail!" said Gerson. "What happened to his tail?"
"Philippine spider monkeys are born without tails."
"No kidding? No tail! I'll be darned!" Gerson said.
"Where'd you get him?" Cordell asked.
"I bought him from a shopkeeper in Guiuan. He wanted ten pesos, but I bargained him down to five."
"So, what'll you do with him?" James asked.
"He's my pet—he'll be our crew mascot, too. I'd like to take him along on our flights." "Maybe on a short training flight," said Seitz, "but *never* on a bombing mission! I'll have no monkey business in combat!"

The photographer called for the next crew, and it was our turn. The four officers in the front row sat on a palm tree log, while the six enlisted men stood behind. Williams had Shoo-Shoo on his shoulder again. (See picture on following page.)

After lunch, I returned to my boat project. By late afternoon, I had about half the rib stations built, when Cordell and James came back from playing volleyball.

Cordell turned to me. "Did you know we're flying tomorrow?"

"No. Where to?"

"We won't know till briefing tonight," James said. "Probably another trip to Borneo."

I stowed the boat parts under my cot.

At briefing we heard that the target was way down the west coast of Borneo again, the Japanese supply and personnel area on Bintulu Airfield, the same target that our crew had hit all alone on our previous mission. This was a larger strike; all four squadrons from the Bomber Barons would send six planes each.

Our squadron would be number three in the group formation. Captain Boggess would lead our squadron in plane number 199, "Daisy Mae," while Seitz' crew would fly position five in the squadron in plane number 823, "Shady Lady." This would be my seventh combat mission, and my third with the Bomber Barons.

Next morning, May 22, our crew was on board "Shady Lady" at six-twenty, starting engines. The rosy light of dawn grew brighter, foretelling an imminent sunrise. I felt relieved that this would be a daylight take-off, after the scary night take-off of our previous mission.

OUR CREW ON SAMAR
Left to right: Front row, pilot Seitz, navigator Hamilton, bombardier James, copilot Cordell. Back row: nose gunner Williams (with monkey on shoulder), radio operator Imhof, armorer-gunner Gerson, tail gunner Hill, flight engineer Pieper, ball gunner Herrema.

The first two squadrons had already taken off and were circling overhead when Captain Boggess made his take-off at 6:31. Our crew got the green light at 6:34.

We roared down runway 07 into the glare of the rising sun. We were as overloaded as we had been four days ago on our night take-off, but with daylight around us, I felt a lot less tense. Again we used the whole 8,000-foot runway to get airborne and flew only twenty feet off the water for several miles to gain speed for a slow climb, but now we could see the water, and judge our height above it.

It took six minutes for us to climb to 1,000 feet, the level where the squadron and group formations were assembling over the airbase, and twenty-five minutes from the first take-off to get all twenty-four bombers into the Group Combat Box formation. Then the Bomber Barons departed at 6:44 on a true course of 247 (west-southwest), beginning a slow climb to the cruising altitude of 7,000 feet.

I looked out in all directions at the planes around us, and felt a sense of awe and wonder. Twenty-four big, heavy bombers, with 96 roaring engines, carrying 240 trained airmen, all moving along together in a powerful aerial ballet! I had heard about the giant formations in Europe, where hundreds of our bombers flew together into German skies, but this was the Pacific, and all around me was the biggest formation of awesome air power that I had ever seen. I was filled with pride to be part of it!

We leveled off a half hour later over the middle of Leyte Island and continued on the same heading across the central Philippines. I saw a beautiful day for flying; only a few fleecy white clouds, like grazing sheep, moved under us, and the low morning sun behind us let us see the dark green islands of Cebu and Bohol ahead, and Negros Island on the far horizon. The vivid colors of the islands and the sea filled me with pleasure whenever I paused to look at them.

Between Cebu and Negros, the weather worsened; a squall line of thunderstorms and showers lay across our course, but the turbulence did not last long. We spread out our formation for safety, and flew between thunderheads. Beyond Negros good weather reappeared, except for a high overcast which kept me from sighting the sun for navigation. I used loran fixes to track our path across four hundred empty miles of the Sulu Sea.

Instead of crossing over enemy-occupied northern Borneo, like we did on our previous mission, today we flew around Borneo over the water. We went straight to the north tip of Borneo and turned southwest to fly along the Borneo coastline past Brunei Bay. When we passed Kudat Airfield, we saw smoke rising high into the air. B-25 medium bombers from the 42nd Bomb Group on Palawan had just bombed Japanese defenses there ahead of us.

We climbed to our bombing altitude of 8,000 feet during the hundred miles from Cape Baram to the I.P. The hammering sound and acrid smell of machine gun fire filled our plane when our gunners test-fired all their guns.

As we neared the target, Bintulu, the Group Combat Box formation split into Squadrons in Trail. When each of the four squadrons reached the I.P., an invisible spot in the water eight miles northwest of Bintulu, that six-plane squadron turned left onto the bombing run southeast to target.

The flak we saw at Bintulu Airfield on our previous mission reappeared on this one. It was low and inaccurate as the first squadron dropped its bombs, but its accuracy improved with each squadron that followed. Our squadron came third; a few pieces of shrapnel punctured the skin of our plane and two others. The fourth squadron caught more accurate flak and more punctures, but they were lucky—all of them made it through.

The target was unusually small, an area only 370 by 700 feet containing warehouses and barracks. Each plane carried fifteen 250-pound bombs (360 bombs for the whole group). At "bombs away" time (12:40), we plastered the target. Smoke rose high into the air. Later we heard that two-thirds of all those bombs hit inside the target area, enough for "excellent results," destroying four large buildings and damaging many more.

Radio silence ended with "bombs away," and interplane chatter started on VHF radio. We listened to it on the interphone.

"Able Leader from Charlie Two, over."

"Charlie Two from Able Leader, go ahead."

"Charlie Two's bomb racks malfunctioned. Only ten bombs dropped on target. We still have five bombs hung up. Request permission to leave formation and make solo bomb run, over."

"Negative, Charlie Two, stay in formation. Fuel is too critical to have the group wait for you, and I won't let you fly home alone, over."

"What about our bombs on board? Over."

"Jettison them on safety when we're over water."

"Roger, Charlie Two wilco."

Seitz said to us on interphone, "Charlie Two is the second plane in this squadron— Lieutenant Ellenbecker in 649 straight ahead. Let's watch his plane to see where he drops those bombs."

"Why doesn't he save those bombs and take 'em back to base?"

"Because he might crash on landing, and the bombs could endanger the base."

We flew north from Bintulu Airfield toward the coast, and soon crossed the shoreline out over the South China Sea again.

"Nose Gunner to Pilot, there go his bombs!"

"Yep, I see five going down, so he got all of 'em out."

"They won't make a big splash, 'cause they're on safety," said James.

"Look—one exploded in the water! Made a great big splash!"

"His bombardier goofed—failed to safety wire one of 'em!"

"Can't be true!" said James. "Bombardiers never goof!"

The four squadrons moved into the Group Combat Box formation again, and twenty-four big bombers headed northeast over the edge of the South China Sea. We flew back the way we came, along the northwest coast of Borneo past Brunei Bay to Balambangan Island, then turned right to 067 degrees (east-northeast) across the Sulu Sea toward Samar. The trip out had taken six hours and twenty minutes; the return trip would take almost six hours more. Our only anxiety was the fuel supply, but careful calculations showed that we should make it with a little to spare.

The afternoon sun was behind us, and the weather was good except for the line of thunderstorms lingering over Negros. Going through it between the storm cells, we were in the clear again when we flew by Cebu. These Philippine Islands were looking more familiar every time, and now I had an upbeat feeling that came with a sense of being almost home.

As we passed over Leyte, the sun set behind us, and we flew on for a night landing on Samar half an hour later. This mission took twelve hours and ten minutes nonstop.

"That was a good major-league mission!" Seitz announced as we rode in the crew truck from the airplane to the Intelligence tent for debriefing.

"Very satisfying," Pieper agreed. "We did everything right, caught a little flak, dropped our bombs on target, and made it safely home!"

"Even a twelve-hour mission bombing Borneo can turn out to be a milk run," said Hill.

"Yeah, if they all go like this," Imhof said.

But I know that won't happen. I have a gut feeling our squadron will run out of luck soon.

16. Three Musketeers

On Wednesday, May 23, the morning after my seventh combat mission, the whole crew slept late. Twelve hours of combat flying stretched our nerves and left us bone tired—took a while to get over it. I woke up before the others, and headed for the mess hall to be early in the line for lunch.

"Well, Bob Hamilton! What are you doing here?" a familiar voice called from the line ahead. There stood an old buddy from navigation school, a tall, scarecrow-like figure.

"Bob Comfort! I'll be darned!" I said, moving up to shake his hand. "So now you're Flight Officer Comfort, complete with navigator wings!"

"And look who else is here," said Comfort, turning to the man behind him. A short man with a beaming smile appeared.

"Clyde Bodkin!" I said, clapping him on his shoulder. "I see you're now Lieutenant Bodkin, with navigator wings, too!"

"Yeah, man! We both graduated from Selman Field a month after you did." He gave me a friendly jab with his fist.

"I'm so glad to see both of you here! We can be the Three Musketeers again—"

"—like last year!" Bodkin finished.

"Those were good times," said Comfort. "Remember all the bull sessions we had in the Cadet Rec Center? We solved all the problems in the world!"

"How about the pool games?" I said.

"And the bowling!" said Bodkin.

"And the beer!" added Comfort. We did a three-man handshake with glee.

"Let the good times roll again!" all three said in unison.

"We'll get caught up on our news during lunch."

Second Lieutenant Clyde R. Bodkin was a stocky man with dark hair and a handsome face. I towered over him with my five-foot-ten height, but I looked short next to the third musketeer, Flight Officer Robert L. Comfort, who was really tall, thin, and lanky. He had sandy hair, a plain face with receding chin, and a prominent Adam's apple. He slouched a bit to lower his height, giving him a very unmilitary posture, which was probably why they made him a flight officer instead of a second lieutenant. He just didn't look like officer material!

As different as we were in appearance, we all had sharp, creative minds, some college education, a taste for classical music and arts, global interests in social issues, and we liked to talk about everything. Our conventional companions viewed us as "smart-asses," "odd-balls," or just "different." Comfort was on Lieutenant Barnes' crew, and Bodkin was on Lieutenant Schulz's, both newly arrived on Samar.

"Let me show you my boat-building project," I said as we left the mess hall, carrying our freshly-cleaned mess kits.

"Great," said Bodkin. "Can we go by our tents to hang up these mess kits first?"

By the time we got back to my tent, it was empty; my crew members were probably eating lunch with the late shift.

"Here it is," I said, pulling the boat parts out from under my cot. "These are the rib stations I've built so far. Please excuse the craftsmanship—all I had to work with was a hammer and a handsaw."

"Not bad," said Comfort, "considering your tools."

"Did you say that the boat was like a canoe?" asked Bodkin.

"No, it's an original one-man boat I designed myself along the lines of a kayak. Here are the plans I drew."

We sat down on my cot to study the plans.

"As you can see, the sides are simple curves. They taper from two feet wide in the center to a point at both ends," I traced it with my finger. "But the top and bottom surfaces are compound curves. They taper to the sides and also to the ends."

"What a clean, simple, neat design!" Comfort said.

"Will you use thin plywood for the surfaces?" asked Bodkin.

"I'd like to, but there's none available here. I plan to form the surfaces with 1 x 2 stringers close together, and cover them all with canvas or aircraft fabric, painted waterproof."

"Hey, that's creative!" said Bodkin. "Why don't we work on it right now?"

"You guys want to help me build it?" I asked, surprised.

"Sure!" said Comfort. "We don't have any other commitments this afternoon. We might as well give you a hand."

"That's swell!" I said. "The Three Musketeers, together again!"

So we got busy and completed the rest of the rib stations before evening chow call.

"Tomorrow we can put stringers on," I said. "Then we'll see the boat take shape."

"Clyde and I have classes tomorrow morning," said Comfort, "but we'll be back to work on it in the afternoon."

Next afternoon, the Three Musketeers gave the boat its shape. We moved two cots to give us room on the floor to assemble the full length of the boat, then placed the rib stations in order. Then we connected the rib stations by nailing stringers to them on both sides, top and bottom.

"Hey, that's starting to look like a boat!" Bodkin said.

"It's a beautiful shape, any way you look at it!" said Comfort.

I'm proud of that design.

Cordell and James arrived from the volleyball court, hot and sweaty, dressed only in shorts. Their muscles bulged and glistened from the workout. They reached for towels before heading for the open-air, cold-water showers, and tripped over the cots and storage boxes moved out of place to make room for boat-building.

"What's that thing?" asked James, kicking the boat.

"The framework of my new boat," I said.

"What's the idea of shoving all our stuff aside to make room for a boat?" said Cordell. "This is our home, not a workshop!"

"Get it out of here!" James snorted.

"Cool down, hot-head!" I said. "I'll move it, but don't get bent out of shape!"

My friends and I lifted the boat and lowered it to the ground at the end of the tent. We squeezed it underneath the high end of the floor; the sloping ground barely made room for it.

"That'll keep it dry overnight," I said. "Tomorrow I'll look for a better place to keep it. Thanks a lot, Musketeers!"

"That was nothing," Bodkin said. "Remember our motto—"

"—All for one and one for all!" said Comfort.

Next morning, I looked for a bigger storage place. The sloping ground in the officers' area was not steep; other tents there had no higher crawl space under the floor than our own. Then I remembered that the ground in the enlisted men's area had a steeper slope; maybe I could keep it under the floor of our crew members' tent. I walked there to see.

No, the slope under their tent was about the same as mine, but the slope got steeper beyond it. A new tent next door had lots more space under its downhill side; it would make a great place for the boat, if I could get permission. The ranking enlisted crew member was always the engineer; I would ask Pieper, our engineer, to ask the engineer in the tent next door for permission. Entering our crew's tent, I saw only Gerson lying on his cot, reading a magazine.

"Hi, Gerson," I said, "Where's Pieper?"

"Working on the new Enlisted Men's Club, sir, with the rest of the boys."

"Then why aren't you out there helping them?"

Gerson laughed as he sat up. "They already got more volunteers than they need. Let the eager beavers build it for me. Why should I bust my butt?"

"Where is this new E.M. Club?"

"Right up the hill from here, sir. You can't miss it."

I saw it as soon as I started up the hill. It was the largest building in the area, a rectangular wooden structure about twenty-five by sixty feet, with triangular trusses supporting a corrugated metal roof. The solid walls were only three feet high; above that level, screen wire over posts provided a continuous window. A spacious view deck ran the entire length of the downhill side, overlooking the camp below and the road to the airstrip.

Men in fatigue clothes swarmed the place. Some were painting the woodwork white, both outside and inside. Others were putting screen wire in place, or hauling away scrap and trash. All seemed unusually happy and cheerful for soldiers at work.

Inside, I saw a long, curved bar that occupied one whole corner of the building. It was made of plywood segments that gradually swept around a quarter-circle. Behind the bartender's space was a plywood partition featuring a large, striking mural: An almost-naked lady with a poster-girl figure lay sensuously among tropical ferns and flowers, guarded by a beautiful black panther. It was hand-painted in oil.

In front of the picture stood Williams, caressing the poster-girl's naked breasts, while he had his picture taken by Herrema.

Imhof was leaning on the bar while sanding the inside of a clear plastic half-dome.

"Hi, guys, what're you doing?" I asked.

"Making a frosted-glass lighting fixture out of this old astrodome," Imhof said. "The sandpaper scratches the plastic surface—makes it look like frosted glass."

Herrema finished his picture-taking and joined us.

"It'll hang there, over the bar," he pointed. "We'll tie it under the light bulb at the end of that dangling wire."

"Well, I'm impressed! You guys are really making an elegant place here! And that's quite a picture behind the bar! No wonder

Williams wanted his picture taken with her! Who painted Miss Luscious Cheesecake and the Panther?"

"Would you believe Hill painted that?"

"That's amazing! I knew he's an artist who paints with oils, but this mural is quite an achievement! Where is Hill?"

"Over there, in the far corner, painting another picture."

I walked past half a dozen other men who were painting plywood tables and chairs blue and white, and found Hill in the corner, painting another almost-naked lady on the two-foot wide strip of solid wall on one side of the end. In his left hand he held a crude plywood palette, daubed with many colors, while his right hand stroked with a two-inch-wide paint brush.

"Hello, Hill!" I said. "How's the Great Artist today?"

"Well, hello, Hamilton! I'm fine, but sort of pressed for time. Trying to finish this figure today, and another one like it on the other side tomorrow, before the club opens tomorrow night."

"This girl looks beautiful already. Not much more needed here. Where will you paint the other one?"

Hill pointed with his paint brush. "See the other solid space like this, in the other corner? We want one full-size pin-up girl standing in each corner, to balance this end of the room."

"You're good with tits! Can't get over how great your mural looks over the bar—Miss Luscious Cheesecake and the Panther!"

"Thanks! You have no idea how hard it is to blend good flesh tones out of these crude airplane colors I have here!" He pointed to a few cans of paint on the floor. "And this two-inch- wide brush—the smallest I could find in the aircraft paint shop! I turn it on edge—barely touch the corner—for small strokes."

"You're doing a great job! At the rate you're going, you'll finish both of these figures before noon tomorrow."

"Sure hope so!"

BAR IN ENLISTED MEN'S CLUB
Hill's painting of a naked lady behind a black panther decorates wall.

I remembered my original quest. "Have you seen Pieper?"

"He's up high, hanging parachutes for the ceiling."

"Oh, there he is. Well, good luck!"

The center of a parachute was tied to a roof truss in the middle of one-half of the building, and Pieper was standing on a ladder at the wall, tacking up the skirt of the chute.

"Hello, Pieper," I said at the foot of the ladder.

"Well, hello, Hamilton," he said from the top. "What are you doing here?"

"Looking for you, really, but also checking out your club. Looks like you guys are making this place more elegant than our officers' club."

"I don't know about that, but we are copying you in spreading out old parachutes for a smooth silk ceiling. This one'll cover this half of the room, and then I'll hang another one in the other half."

"That's great! And tomorrow night is the grand opening?"

"Yeah—Saturday night. But why're you looking for me?"

"I have a favor to ask you, Pieper. I'm building a one-man boat, like a kayak. I need a place to store it. I saw a lot of space under the floor of that new tent next to yours. It'd be a good place for the boat. Would you mind asking your neighbor for permission, since you're our senior enlisted man?"

"I can handle that. I'll ask him tonight."

"Thanks a lot! If he agrees, I'll move it tomorrow."

The next morning was Saturday, May 26, the date our enlisted men had been waiting for—the grand opening night for their new E.M. Club. From the morning assignment sheets on the bulletin board, I learned that our crew was scheduled for the bombing mission the following day.

Oh, no! We'll have some unhappy crew members! The briefing tonight will cut into their party time, and they can't drink too much if they're flying tomorrow. I feel for the boys!

After lunch, my two navigator buddies came to my tent to move the boat. We carefully slid it out from its tight fit under my tent floor, and Bodkin and Comfort picked up the boat between them, while I brought the tools in one hand and remaining lumber in the other. We carried all this to the enlisted men's area, to the tent with the extra space under the floor, where I now had permission to keep the boat, thanks to Pieper.

We put the boat in place under the floor, resting it on two pieces of lumber to keep it off the ground. There was room enough to work on the boat without removing it, by bending over it or squatting beside it. We cut and nailed a few more stringers on the top surface, just to make sure that we could work in there. The noise of hammering brought curious spectators out of the tent above it, and out of my crew members' tent next door.

"So this is the boat you're building!" said Pieper.

"Yes indeed," I said, "and thanks for getting permission for me to keep it here."

"Glad to help," said Pieper. "Who're your friends?"

"These are my two buddies from navigation school, Flight Officer Comfort, the tall one, and Lieutenant Bodkin, the short one. And this is my engineer, Corporal Pieper."

"Think of us as Mutt and Jeff," said Comfort, grinning.

"And here come more of my crew members—my radio operator, Corporal Imhof, and my tail gunner, Corporal Hill."

"Nice boat design!" Imhof said.

"Nice workmanship, too!" Hill added.

"Speaking of nice workmanship, Hill, did you finish your third beautiful painting in the new E.M. Club?"

"I guess I did," Hill scowled. "They stopped me!"

"He kept wanting to apply more finishing touches," Pieper said, laughing. "At noon, we told him it was finished, and dragged him away, kicking and screaming!"

"Takes two people to paint a picture," Comfort said. "One is the artist who paints it—"

"—and the other is the man who decides when it's finished,

and drags the artist away!" Bodkin interrupted.

I changed the subject. "You boys know that we're flying a mission tomorrow, don't you?"

"Yeah!" Pieper said. "Isn't that just our luck? On opening night for the new club, we have to go to briefing!"

"And we'll all have hangovers tomorrow, for the mission," said Hill.

"Not if you don't drink much, or stay up too late."

"But we gotta stay up late," said Pieper. "A U.S.O. troupe is putting on *Oklahoma!* at the Bomber Barons Theater tonight, and Colonel Haviland arranged to bring the whole cast over to our club after the show is over! We'll get to see some real live girls close up!"

"That's a nice thing for the Colonel to do," Bodkin said.

"He wants to build up the morale of his enlisted men," said Comfort.

"I'm going on that mission tomorrow, too," said Bodkin. "Lieutenant Schulz is my pilot— his name was on the list. This will be our first combat mission with the Bomber Barons."

"That's swell!" I said. "It'll be nice to know that my old buddy is navigating in the plane next to mine! How about you, Comfort? Are you on for tomorrow, too?"

"No. I'll just have to wait a bit longer."

"It would sure be fun to get the Three Musketeers all flying on a mission together!" I said. "Maybe someday, it'll happen."

At the briefing that night, twenty-four bomber crews, two hundred forty men, gathered in the Fifth Group briefing tent, sitting on empty bomb fin crates. Colonel Haviland spoke first.

"As you all know, the visiting U.S.O. troupe is beginning a performance of the new Broadway musical, *Oklahoma!*, at this very moment. Too bad the war makes us miss some entertainment! You may have heard that I arranged for the entire cast to visit the new 394th Squadron Enlisted Men's Recreation Hall after the performance is over.

"For any enlisted men worried about leaving the party too soon because of the early crew call, I have some good news: Tomorrow's mission is most unusual—it has a mid-morning departure. Take-off is set for 1030, so there will be no early crew call tomorrow! You can all sleep till reveille."

Cheering and applause broke out.

"You might think I set the take-off time for your benefit," the Colonel continued. "I wish I had that power! No—this came down from Thirteenth Bomber Command.

"The target tomorrow is Tarakan, the oil refinery island off the northeast coast of Borneo. The Australian Army invaded Tarakan and ran into tough Jap resistance. This mission is ground support—to break up entrenched Jap positions. The Aussies asked us to hit the target in mid-afternoon, which requires a mid-morning take-off.

"All four squadrons will fly on the mission tomorrow, with six planes from each squadron. Like most ground-support missions, we won't know the precise targets until we get there. The Aussies will fire smoke shells to mark the targets they want you to hit.

"This is a very important mission, requiring absolutely accurate bombing. The lives of our Aussie allies depend on it. So do a good job tomorrow, one that will reflect credit on the good name of the Bomber Barons! Remember, men, we're the best damn group in the Pacific!

"Now Major Armstrong, Group Navigator, will brief you on details of the trip."

Major H.R. Armstrong, veteran of 32 combat missions, was a tall man with dark hair, rugged features, and a Regular Army sense of purpose. He unveiled the route map.

"The Group will assemble over the base, and fly direct from Samar to Boeka Island, fifteen miles south of Tarakan," he said, pointing to it on the map. "Orbit there until Aussie Ground Control gives permission to bomb. Then the lead squadron will fly to the I.P. eight miles west of Tarakan, and turn east for the bomb run.

"As they make that turn, the Aussies will fire a smoke shell to mark the near edge of the target. The lead bombardier will sight on that smoke shell to begin his string of bombs, dropping at 60-foot intervals beyond it. All other bombardiers will toggle their bombs on the leader.

"Then the second, third, and fourth squadrons will follow the same procedure. As each squadron leaves the target area, it will begin the return trip direct to Samar, in squadron formation.

"The code name for Aussie Ground Control is 'Bonding.' Squadron leaders will communicate with Bonding on VHF Channel C, using the squadron letter, Able, Baker, Charlie, or Dog."

Major Armstrong was followed by Captain Herring, Group Weather Officer, for his forecast. Then Captain Woodward, Group Intelligence Officer, told us to expect no fighter interception and little or no flak. He added that the PBY rescue seaplane "Playmate 6" will be on ground alert at Morotai. Finally came the official time tick, to synchronise all of our watches, and then the enlisted men were dismissed. They all dashed out in a party mood, headed for the play and their club's grand opening.

Pilots, navigators, and bombardiers stayed on for target briefing by the Group Bombardier, Captain Harry Suttle, a small, dark-haired, intense veteran of 48 combat missions.

Next morning, May 27, twenty-four big bombers lined up on the taxiway, engines running, ready to take off at 10:30. Today the 394th was the third squadron in the group; Lieutenant Ellenbecker led our squadron, taking off at 10:44. Our crew's plane was number five in the squadron; we took off at 10:48 in number 818, "Ten High," (the number of crew members). I was thankful for another daylight take-off.

In position six was number 674, "Dangerous Dude", piloted

by Lieutenant Schulz, with my buddy Bodkin navigating. This was their first combat mission with the Bomber Barons, which made me feel like an old veteran.

We joined the circling bombers over the field, wheeling into our special place in the Group Combat Box formation, and continued orbiting until the last plane of the fourth squadron had arrived. Then at 10:59, the assembled group headed southwest from Samar, on a true course of 226 degrees, climbing slowly to our cruising altitude of 7,000 feet. The weather was gloomy as we departed, with a solid overcast above us at 10,000 feet, other clouds below us, and visibility limited to five miles in haze.

When I turned on the loran receiver, I discovered that it had a major malfunction; its square-wave generator could not be adjusted, so loran was useless for fixing our position. The thick overcast precluded shooting the sun for celestial navigation; all that remained was "pilotage," the simple process of seeing things on the ground which I could find on the map, thereby fixing our position. Fortunately, today's route was ideal for pilotage; instead of flying across the long, empty Sulu Sea, we would skirt its southern rim, a chain of islands called the Sulu Archipelago, stretching from the southern Philippines to eastern Borneo, so there were lots of things to identify along our intended course.

We flew over the southern end of Leyte, then Bohol Island, and by 12:13 we were over Silla Point, the northwestern tip of the big island of Mindanao. For the next 150 miles, our course took us along the rocky western coastline of Mindanao's Zamboanga peninsula, ending with the major port of Zamboanga, which we passed (ten miles off our left wing) at 1:05 P.M.

A bit earlier, I noticed that I could see the sun through breaks in the overcast, so I started shooting the sun for a "noonday fix" to practice my celestial navigation. During any noon hour, the sun changes its direction rapidly, from southeast to south, then to southwest. Sun shots taken at least half an hour before local noon, then at local noon, then a half hour or more after it, yield lines of position that intersect to make a good celestial fix. My noonday fix gave our 1:09 position as southwest of Zamboanga, harmonizing with our track derived from pilotage.

As we continued southwest of Zamboanga, the weather improved to scattered clouds above at 15,000 feet, scattered cumulus below with tops at 5,000 feet, and visibility up to 20 miles. Furthermore, our tailwind from the east increased to 21 knots, moving us toward Borneo faster than planned.

We flew over the many islands of the Sulu Archipelago to Tawitawi Island, where I saw the giant land mass of Borneo coming into view on the right. We continued off the coast of Borneo for another hour until at 3:06 P.M. we flew past our target, the island of Tarakan (five miles off our right wing), and on to our rendezvous over tiny Beoka Island, 15 miles south of Tarakan. There the group began circling at 7,800 feet, while the squadrons waited for permission to bomb from Australian Army Ground Control, "Bonding."

"Able Lead to Bonding, do you read me? Over."

"Bonding to Able Lead, read you loud and clear, mate, over."

"Able Lead requests permission to drop calling cards, over."

"Permission granted, mate. Drop beyond the smoke, over."

"Able Lead, wilco, out."

We watched the first squadron leave the group formation and head northwest toward the I.P. twenty miles away.

Seven minutes later we heard, "Able Lead turning I.P., over."

"Roger, Able Lead, firing smoke now. Do you see it, mate? Over."

There was a pause, then: "Affirmative; smoke in sight, out."

Five minutes later, we saw many little flashes of bright light on Tarakan, fifteen miles north, as fifty-four 500-pound bombs hit the target.

"Bonding to Able Lead, thanks for a good show, mate!"

"Glad to oblige. Able Lead homeward bound."

The first squadron was too far away for me to see the planes, but I visualized them turning left to head back to Samar.

"Baker Lead to Bonding, over."

"Bonding to Baker Lead, go ahead."

"Request permission to drop calling cards."

"Permission granted, Baker Lead. Drop beyond the smoke."

We watched the second squadron depart for the I.P. Seven minutes later, we heard, "Baker Lead turning I.P., over."

"Roger, Baker Lead, firing smoke now. Can you see it? Over."

"Affirmative, smoke in sight. Oh, no! There's another smoke, a mile ahead and to the right. Which one should we aim for? Over."

"Baker Lead, do NOT drop calling cards! Go around again!"

"Wilco, Bonding, Baker Lead will circle back to I.P. What happened? Over."

"The enemy has mortars and smoke shells too. They dropped one in our camp. If you had aimed at the second smoke, you would have hit your friends instead of the enemy, over."

"Damn! Those Japs are clever little bastards! What signal should we look for now? Over."

"Give us a moment to sort things out."

Three minutes went by. "Bonding to Baker Lead, over."

"Baker Lead to Bonding, approaching I.P. again, over."

"We'll fire two smokes, side by side, 100 feet apart. Disregard any single smoke; aim only at the double smoke."

"Roger, Bonding, Baker Lead at I.P. now. Give us smoke, over."

"Firing double smoke now. Do you see the double, mate? Over."

"Affirmative, double smoke in sight. There goes another one, over where the extra smoke fell before! They did it again! We'll disregard it; bombardier will aim only at the double smoke."

Four minutes later, we saw bright flashes again on Tarakan.

"Bonding to Baker Lead, your calling cards well received, over."

"Baker Lead now taking pigeons home to roost."

The Aussies and the second squadron had beaten the Japanese trickery. Now it was our turn, after circling nearly an hour.

"Charlie Lead to Bonding, request permission to drop calling cards, over."

"Bonding to Charlie Lead, permission granted, out."

Now our 394th Squadron left the last squadron still circling as we turned to 330 degrees, heading for the I.P.

"Charlie Lead, your signal for aiming point will be three smoke shells 100 feet apart in triangle. Disregard any other smoke, over."

"Roger, Bonding, we'll aim only at triple smoke."

A few minutes later, our squadron turned right to head east.

"Charlie Lead turning I.P., ready for smoke, over."

"Roger, firing smoke now. Do you see triple smoke? Over."

A brief pause; then, "Affirmative, triple smoke in sight, out."

In our plane, James was kneeling to see through the bombardier's nose window, bomb release switch in right hand. He saw bombs emerge from the lead plane's belly, and squeezed it.

"Bombs away at 1618!" he called on our intercom. On a sudden impulse, I crawled quickly through the tunnel to the open bomb bay door to watch our nine big bombs getting smaller as they fell toward a landscape of wrecked buildings and twisted oil refinery piping, evidently the area where the enemy soldiers had been able to dig in for their last-ditch defense.

Suddenly, bright flashes appeared in rapid succession all across the area, each flash surrounded by visible shock waves which expanded like ripples around a stone hitting water, only much, much faster. Eight seconds after the flashes appeared, I heard a series of "pop-pop-pop-pop-pop" sounds, like a string of firecrackers exploding. Fifty-four 500-pound bombs had changed the landscape below, hiding it under clouds of debris and smoke.

I thought about what those explosions had done to the enemy soldiers dug into their trenches below. They were human too, sent thousands of miles from home to occupy a hot, unfriendly island. Now they were told to die for the glory of their Emperor, defending that hell-hole. I had brought death and destruction to their midst, and those who survived would soon be killed or taken prisoner by the Aussie soldiers, waiting to rush their positions.

Never before had I watched from the bomb bay as our bombs dropped in combat. Seeing them explode below me made me feel like a murderer. Never again would I watch the bombs go down. I left the bomb bay with a shudder, and crawled back through the tunnel to my navigator station in the nose. My enthusiasm for the mission evaporated.

General Sherman was right: "War is hell!"

17. Catwalk in the Sky

What I had seen from the bomb bay gave me a lingering emotional shock. *We're blowing up people—not just things!* That thought depressed me on the trip home.

We flew northeast; the sun behind us sank into the Sulu Sea when we were halfway home. Beyond my left wing I saw the sixth B-24 in our squadron silhouetted against the crimson sunset glow. It felt good to remember that my buddy Bodkin was navigator on that plane. The thought of his companionship helped me shake off my depression.

After winging through darkness from Zamboanga to Samar, we landed. My flight log showed ten hours eighteen minutes. It was two hours shorter than the previous mission, but I felt more tired after this one. My inner conflict was like a black hole for energy.

First Lieutenant Mander of Intelligence debriefed our crew. Captain "Doc" Dolce gave us our post-mission whiskey shots, and we ate the late supper waiting for us in the mess hall. My mood became more cheerful with good food and drink, and I went to bed satisfied with my professional performance. *Navigating bombers is my duty—I've done a good day's work.*

The next day I slept all morning, and got up for mid-day chow. My two navigator buddies were coming out of the mess hall as I entered.

"Hello, guys!" I said.

"Howdy, Bob!" said Bodkin. "Missed you at breakfast."

"I was sleeping off yesterday's mission."

"Breakfast wasn't much to miss," said Comfort. "Oatmeal and dehydrated eggs."

"When can you two help me build my boat again?"

"How about tomorrow afternoon?"

"Okay—see you then."

After lunch, I went by the mail clerk and found two letters, one from Dad and the other from Sandy, my girl friend from cadet days in navigation school. *Hot dog! A "sugar report"!* I went to the officers club to find a quiet spot to read them, and whipped out my knife to slit open the "V-Mail" self-folding letter-envelopes that were standard then for overseas mail.

Dad wrote that Mom and my three kid brothers and two sisters were doing well and sent me their love. He said that David had joined the Navy, and was a sailor on the battleship Missouri already. If the war went on for another year, Bill would also be old enough to enlist. The Presbyterian church Dad pastored in Knoxville hosted quite a few visiting servicemen each Sunday. Dad had been offered a Captain's commission in the Marines if he would enlist as a chaplain. He was strongly tempted to do it, since he had served in France in World War I and knew the needs of soldiers; but after praying about it, he felt that God wanted him to continue serving the church where he was.

Wow! David in the Navy already! How long have I been gone? Two years. I'm glad Dad didn't join the Marines—somebody has to keep things together on the home front.

Sandy wrote that she was excited about her new job—she was now a teller trainee at the bank in downtown Pine Bluff, and she expected to be promoted to teller soon. Her Mom was busy knitting me another sweater. *She gave me one already, when I graduated from navigation school.* Sandy told her I didn't need a sweater in the South Pacific *(you got that right!)*, but her Mom said I could have it when I came home. And Sandy wrote that she missed me very much, and sent me all her love.

FOUR HAMILTONS
On right, Bob and Minnie; on left, David and Bill. (Not pictured, younger siblings Dorothy and John.)

My memory replayed pictures of these people, which wove a web of warmth and peace inside me. How sweet it had been the previous summer, when Sandy and I danced to the jukebox in the Stardust Cafe in Monroe, Louisiana, near my navigation school. The song we loved the most was "I'll Be Seeing You—in all the old familiar places," sung by Frank Sinatra with Tommy Dorsey's Orchestra. Enjoying slow dancing, I had looked long and lovingly into her glowing, sky-blue eyes. Tenderly I kissed her warm, smiling lips—the world disappeared around us. There was nothing in the universe but that wonderful music and the two of us, floating through space to its rhythm, close, so very close that I felt every gentle, clinging movement of her young, warm, soft, tender body. Yes, "I'll Be Seeing You" was OUR song!

I felt blessed by such rich, loving connections to family and friends. That afternoon, I replied to both letters, bringing them up to date on my adventures. To Sandy I wrote, "Whenever I see this South Pacific moon, I remember the closing words from OUR SONG, 'I'll be looking at the moon, but I'LL BE SEEING YOU!'"

Next morning I was assigned to the censorship crew, a group of officers who censored the outgoing mail of the enlisted men. We gathered in the mess hall after breakfast was cleared away, and poured out the previous day's mail on the tables, each taking a batch to read. Enlisted men were not allowed to seal the letters they wrote; every letter had to be censored. Officers read the mail with razor blades at hand, to cut out anything that might help the enemy learn military information such as the location of our military units, the targets we attacked, the morale of our men, or plans for future missions.

We seldom had to cut out anything, because the men had been warned that any military information would be deleted by a censor. After reading a letter, the officer would seal it and sign his name and rank in the upper right corner of the envelope, where the stamp would go for civilian mail. Soldiers and sailors used no stamps overseas; all wartime military mail was carried free. Officers, of course, signed off their own mail; only enlisted men required censorship.

This effort kept enemy intelligence officers from gleaning useful information from bags of mail that might fall into their hands when our cargo planes were shot down over enemy territory. Posters on our bulletin boards carried slogans such as "THE ENEMY IS LISTENING!" (over cartoon heads of Hitler and Tojo with hands cupped to ears), and "LOOSE LIPS SINK SHIPS!"

After lunch, my two navigator buddies and I walked over to the enlisted men's tent area to work on my boat. We cut and nailed additional 1x2 wood stringers over the rib stations on the curved sides and top.

"Well, Clyde," I asked Bodkin as he drove in a nail, "how did you feel about flying your first mission with the major league?"

"It was easier than I expected," he said, looking up from the boat, "After all, I had your plane to follow all the way."

"I felt good about that too," I said. "I looked at your plane off my left wingtip and knew you were there. I wish our other Bob had been in the plane off my right wing."

"I wish so too!" said Comfort. He took another 1x2 and sawed it to length.

Bodkin drove in the next nail, then asked me, "How did you feel about the mission, compared to others you've flown?"

"It was a good mission—short for a Borneo trip, just a bit over ten hours. We had no opposition, no mechanical problems, and the weather was good. But one thing really shook me up. I went to the bomb bay and watched the bombs go down. Have either of you ever done that?"

"Nope," said Bodkin.

"Nor I," added Comfort. "What was it like?"

"The bombs got smaller and smaller as they fell. Then there were bright flashes of light when they exploded. Visible shock waves—white circles—expanded like ripples around each burst. It took eight seconds for the sound to reach us, then I heard the bombs—'pop-pop-pop-pop-pop'—like a string of firecrackers. Then dust and smoke covered the scene below."

"That's fascinatin'!" Bodkin said.

"Why did it shake you up?" Comfort asked.

"It was not what I saw, but what I visualized in my mind. I thought of the enemy soldiers dug into their trenches and bunkers below me, and I imagined the death and destruction that my bombs brought." My throat felt clogged. I coughed up words, "I watched them die in my mind! It was horrible!"

"But that's why we flew the damn mission—to kill the enemy!" Bodkin said. "Any ground support mission is for the purpose of intervenin' on the battlefield. Look," he drew lines on the ground with a 1x2. "The Aussies are here, and the Japs over there. The Aussies invaded Tarakan here, but couldn't take the whole island because the Japs were too well dug in. Our bombers were sent there to kill the damn Japs, to keep 'em from killin' the Aussies as they advance. Why should that bother you?"

"It shouldn't. I agree with your logic, but I have an irrational gut feeling that revolts against it. I started thinking of the enemy as human beings like us. They must think that they're the good guys, because they're the defenders against our giant attack forces. They're David against our Goliath! And now they're told to die for the glory of their Emperor, defending that hell-hole of Tarakan! I feel sorry for the poor bastards—I don't feel like killing 'em!"

"Your mistake is putting yourself in the enemy's shoes," said Comfort. "Never humanize the enemy—always demonize him! You fear a demon, and hate what he does and everything he stands for. Killing a demon is not only necessary, but right! But for men like us—prone to rational thinking—demonizing the enemy requires an on-going practice of self-deception."

"Well said!" Bodkin clapped his hands. "Couldn't have put it any better myself!"

"On most of my previous missions," I said, "we bombed airfield runways, storage dumps, buildings—inanimate objects. We destroyed facilities the enemy needed to wage war—killing people was not the main purpose. But on this mission, I suddenly realized that killing people *was* the purpose. When I watched my bombs go down into the enemy bunkers, I felt like a murderer! It made me sick!"

"Hey, wait a minute!" said Bodkin. "What do we have here—a real crisis of conscience? Are you goin' to quit flyin'? There are serious consequences to your line of thinkin'! In wartime, you can't let your tender Christian conscience take control!"

"So how will you handle this new feeling?" asked Comfort.

"I'm not sure," I said. "Maybe I'll transfer to Intelligence or something where I wouldn't kill people personally. I'll keep flying for the present, but never again will I go to the bomb bay and watch the bombs go down. If I don't see it happen, I won't dwell on it, and then—maybe I can go back to being a normal, macho, All-American, military hero."

"Sensible resolution!" Bodkin clapped again.

"That's what I like about the Three Musketeers," Comfort said. "We open up and talk about stuff like this. Other men, no doubt, have these problems too, but keep 'em bottled up inside. Generates stress that sometimes cracks 'em up! We talk it out unashamedly, and help to resolve the stress in rational ways."

I was assigned to the mail censoring crew again on the first of June. This time I saw that one of the side effects of censor duty was to serve as an information, rumor, and gossip session for the officers involved. They talked a lot, spreading the very kind of information they were told to cut out of the letters, but here it was all in the family.

I sat down next to a tall, dark-haired pilot I recognized. "Aren't you the pilot who flew me here from Morotai? In a Bomber Barons C-47?"

"Yep, that was me. I'm Lieutenant Wildey—'Wild Bill' Wildey, some people call me." He extended his hand.

"You don't look very wild to me," I said, shaking his hand.

"I'm Lieutenant Hamilton—Bob Hamilton, navigator on Lieutenant Seitz's crew. Are you assigned here to fly the C-47s?"

"Oh, no—I fly C-47s as a hobby. I'm a B-24 pilot, with my own crew. My navigator is Lieutenant Townsend—John Townsend. Maybe you've met him in the navigator get-togethers."

"Yes, I've met Townsend," I said. "He seems pretty sharp."

"Oh, he is! I have a good crew. I brag on my bombardier, Lieutenant Hackenberger—Ernie Hackenberger. He can actually hit what he aims at!"

"That's more'n you can say for a lot of 'em! Did you hear about the secret report on Eighth Air Force combat bombing accuracy? Only forty percent of all their bombs fell within a thousand feet of the target!"

"That's pitiful! Ernie can do a lot better'n that."

Wildey picked up a letter from the pile in front of him. "Did you hear about the staging mission today?"

"No, tell me about it."

"Our squadron has seven B-24s flying toward Tarakan right now, for another ground-support mission. The whole Fifth Group is going."

"Tarakan again!" I said. "The Aussies sure are having a hard time overrunning the Japs there!"

"Those Japs just won't give up! Anyway, our planes won't come home tonight—they'll go to Palawan, and stage out of there for a week, to hit targets on the west coast of Borneo."

"Palawan is closer," I said. "I found that out two weeks ago. We flew to Palawan from the west coast of Borneo when we lost an engine near Sibu."

"Lieutenant Tomlinson will fly our C-47 to Palawan and back today. He'll take crew chiefs and mechanics there to service our airplanes during the week they'll stage from Palawan."

"Why aren't you flying the C-47?"

"There are several pilots checked out in the C-47, so we take turns. It's fun to fly a different plane once in awhile, and a Goony Bird's an easy one to fly."

I raised my eyebrows. "Goony Bird?"

Wildey laughed. "That's slang for a C-47."

The Three Musketeers got together during the next three afternoons to work on my boat. We trimmed the cockpit opening with a splash guard around it. We installed a plywood seat in the cockpit. We added all the stringers needed on all the surfaces, especially the bottom, where they were closely spaced.

Williams came from his tent next door with his pet monkey, Shoo-Shoo, to watch us work. Shoo-Shoo was more interested in catching bugs to eat than in my project. I was grateful for that. All I needed was to have a monkey run off with vital tools or materials!

We finished the wood framework. All the boat lacked was its fabric surface and suitable waterproofing paints, but I had none of either material. So I stowed the boat well back under the overhanging tent floor, where it would be safe until I got the stuff. My next job would be to find out where on Samar I could scrounge the fabric and the paints needed to finish it.

Our crew flew my ninth combat mission the next day, June 4. Captain Boggess led the 394th Squadron, taking off in the dim light of dawn. Two minutes later, we were third to take off in B-24 number 823, "Shady Lady." This was another ground-support mission to Tarakan, to aid the Aussies in their struggle against those stubborn Japanese defenders.

When we reached our destination, we flew past Tarakan to tiny Boeka Island again, where we circled while waiting for permission to bomb. "Bonding" gave permission for Able Squadron to bomb the jungle target marked by smoke shells. Able Squadron left for the I.P and bomb run.

Twelve minutes later it was our squadron's turn.

"Baker Lead to Bonding, request permission to bomb, over."

"Bonding to Baker Lead, permission granted. Call for smoke when turning I.P., over."

"Baker Lead, roger, wilco, out."

Captain Boggess turned our squadron northwest toward the I.P. ten minutes away. 8,500 feet below us lay the dark green mangrove swamps of the Borneo coastal plain. The I.P. was an invisible spot in that carpet of vegetation which navigators found by loran.

"Baker Lead turning I.P., request smoke, over."

"Now firing smoke. Aim at double smoke. Report sighting, over."

"Baker Lead has double smoke in sight, out."

We were now heading 025 degrees (north-northeast) on the bombing run toward bomb-blasted Tarakan Island. Bombardier James knelt on the floor, watching for bombs to drop from the lead plane. Looking over his shoulder, I saw the two patches of smoke the lead bombardier was aiming at. A moment later, at 11:04, a cluster of bombs emerged from the plane ahead. James squeezed his bomb release.

"Bombs away!" he called on our interphone, and then looked at the bomb rack indicator panel at his left elbow. A minute before, forty green lights had indicated forty bombs were ready to go. Now thirty-two lights were out, but eight still glowed.

"Oh, shoot!" James shouted, "bomb rack malfunction!"

He reached for the interphone button. "Bombardier to Pilot, we have eight bombs that didn't go!"

"Pilot to Bombardier, don't close bomb bay doors! Let me check with our leader."

The squadron was turning left for the breakaway.

"Baker Three to Baker Lead, we have eight bombs hung up."

"Baker Leader to Baker Three, do not leave formation. Jettison bombs on safety when over water."

"Baker Three, roger, wilco, out."

"Pilot to Bombardier, we will not make a second bomb run. Go back and safety-wire those bombs, then jettison them when we're over water. If they won't release electrically, trip the racks by hand, over."

"Bombardier to Pilot, roger. I love to stand on the catwalk over open doors, to safety bombs and trip the racks by hand! Over."

"That's your job, man! It comes with your bombardier wings! Over."

"Yeah, but this is the first time I ever had to do it! Out."

James unplugged his headset to go back toward the tunnel. As he passed my navigation table, I called to him, "Better take your parachute."

"Forget it!" he shouted back. "You can't squeeze through the catwalk opening with a parachute on! You know that!"

"I'll follow you with your chute," I said. "If you fall out, I'll throw the chute out after you! Maybe you could clip it on in mid-air." *Maybe he could, if he caught it in mid-air. Fat chance!*

I crawled through the tunnel after him, dragging his chest-pack parachute behind me. We wore our parachute harnesses all the time, but only clipped the bulky chute onto the harness when the need to jump seemed imminent.

The big rolling doors were open, and the wind whirled around in the bomb bay. The noise of the engines reverberated in the room-like space, amplified to a deafening roar. James was out on the catwalk, balancing as the airplane swayed, reaching out with both hands to safety-wire the eight remaining bombs. Looking down, I saw the edge of Tarakan Island pass behind us. Nothing but water was visible below.

"We're over water now!" I shouted to James above the noise. "You're free to spring 'em loose any time!"

"Thanks!" he shouted back. "Can't look down! Makes me dizzy!"

James walked to the front end of the bomb bay to punch the back-up bomb-release switch. Nothing happened. He punched it again and again. Still no movement. "Shit!"

He brought out a big screwdriver and pried up the release lever on the nearest bomb rack. The rack grips opened like steel fingers, and the bomb fell out. My eyes followed it down. It brought back my agony on the last trip to Tarakan when I had watched my bombs explode in the enemy trenches. Again I felt cold sweat all over.

James did the same thing to six more bombs. Only one bomb

remained, the one needing the longest reach. Stretching, he tripped its release with the very tip of the long screwdriver, but as the bomb dropped, James lost his balance. Desperately he grabbed for the upright beam beside the catwalk. He caught it with one hand. A hot flash of fear swept over me as I watched his body slipping down.

James had one hand on the upright and one foot on the catwalk. The other arm and leg hung down in the 180 mile-per-hour slipstream.

"Hang on!" I shouted. "I'm coming!"

Leaving the parachute behind on the tunnel floor, I squeezed between the upright beams and walked carefully along the catwalk, keeping one hand on the nearest upright. A fierce wind whipped around me in the cavernous bomb bay. I tried not to look down at the dark ocean eight thousand feet below.

Carefully I knelt down on the catwalk beside him. I wrapped my left arm around the upright, and reached down with my right hand. He didn't see it. His eyes were closed tight against the stinging flow of the slipstream.

I took a deep breath and shouted, "Give me your free hand!"

His eyes slit open barely enough to see me above him.

"Give me your free hand!"

Slowly he swung his arm upward against the pull of the slipstream. His hand came near mine, and I grabbed it. Slowly I pulled his hand up until his head and shoulders were level with the catwalk. As his head entered the protected space of the bomb bay, his eyes opened wide. He took a deep breath. Then another.

"Can't breathe out there!" he said.

"Rest a minute and breathe in here."

He hooked his left elbow over the catwalk. His right leg still hung down in the slipstream.

"Hang in there, buddy," I said. "You're going to be okay!"

He looked at me, red-faced. The veins stood out on his neck.

"Let go my hand—I wanta grab the upright!" he said.

"Okay—I'm letting go!"

He moved his arms and grabbed the upright with both hands. But the motion changed his balance—his left foot slipped off the catwalk. Both legs hung down, swaying backward in the wind. Another hot flash of fear poured over me. *My God! What'll I do now?*

James held on to the upright with both hands while his whole body hung down on an angle, blowing back like a streamer in the slipstream. Suddenly, I knew what to do.

"Hang on!" I shouted, "I'm going to grab your belt!"

I crawled toward the rear of the catwalk and knelt down over his middle. Holding on to an upright with my left hand, I reached down as far as I could with my right. *Dear God! Guide my hand!* His body swayed up and down, just beyond my reach. On the next upward swing, I lunged down and managed to grab his belt. My right hand clamped onto that belt like a vice. *Gotcha! Thank God!*

I started to lift his body. In order to raise him high enough, I had to straighten my back and stand part way up on my feet, bearing his full weight. *For a skinny little runt, he sure weighs a lot!* By then his hips were a foot above the catwalk level. He lifted his legs and spread them to straddle the catwalk. I lowered him gently on top of it. He lay there a while, resting.

I released my grip on his belt, and waited for him to look up. When he did, I reached my hand under his shoulder to help pull him up, while he strained arms and legs to rise slowly to a standing position. We stood there, staring at each other.

"I dropped the damn screwdriver!" he shouted.

"Shame on you!" I screamed, and suddenly we both laughed. Our laughter grew in volume until we both were nearly hysterical. We balanced on the open catwalk, without parachutes, laughing like idiots. I felt flushed with relief.

"Let's get the hell out of here!" James shouted.

"Roger, wilco!" I agreed. We inched along the catwalk to the front end of the open bomb bay, and crawled through the tunnel to the nose. James went immediately to his red lever to close the bomb bay doors. We both plugged in our interphone cords.

"Bombardier to Pilot, all remaining bombs were dropped on safe. Had to squeeze 'em out by hand! Closing bomb bay doors."

"Good deal, Lucille! Uncle Sam is proud of you!"

Through the intercom we heard the VHF radio come on.

"Bonding to Baker Lead, over."

"Baker Lead to Bonding, go ahead."

"Just received report on your bombing from our aerial observer. Baker bombing was perfect! Every bomb hit assigned target area! Now our lads are ready to roll. Good show, mates!"

"Thanks for the good news, Bonding. Baker Lead out."

I settled down to navigating a routine flight home. We landed on Samar in mid-afternoon, total flight nine hours fifteen minutes.

Captain Nagel, Intelligence, debriefed our crew. Captain Dolce, Flight Surgeon, gave us our usual whiskey. Then on to the mess hall we went for an early supper. Whenever the bomber crews returned, there was a hot meal waiting for them. It was the Air Force way of saying, "Welcome home!"

Later, lying on my cot, I realized that this ground-support mission had not troubled my conscience at all. I had been distracted completely by the catwalk in the sky. *But how will I feel on the next mission, without distraction?*

18. Dangerous Darkness

Three hundred men sat on empty bomb fin crates, talking and smoking. It was an unusual daytime assembly of the Fifth Bomb Group—briefings were held at night. On June 7 half of our crews and planes were flying a combat mission to Borneo. All other crews on Samar, including mine, gathered in the briefing tent at eight A.M. to hear about new ways to fly our bombers.

Three officers entered.

"Group, attens-HUT!" shouted the adjutant. We all stood up.

"At ease, men—be seated," said Colonel Haviland. "Before we start the main business, I want to take a moment to praise the outstanding performance of one of our crews over Borneo yesterday. On the way to the primary target, the Group Leader sent one plane from the 394th Squadron to bomb the secondary target alone.

"The pilot of that plane was Lieutenant Peoples and the bombardier Lieutenant Friedman. They had nine 500-pound bombs on board. Sinkawang Airfield has three runways that form an "A"-shape, but they actually knocked out all three runways with just nine bombs! They made three bomb runs, one down each runway, and dropped three well-spaced bombs right down the middle of each runway! Every one was a perfect hit!

"Lieutenants Peoples and Friedman—where are you?" Two hands went up in the center of the tent. "Stand up so we can all see the pilot and bombardier who gave us the best bombing performance in the history of the Group!"

The two men rose to a roar of applause and cheers. Peoples was tall, thin, and lanky; Friedman heavy-set, black hair, olive skin. Both smiled dubiously, like embarrassed schoolboys.

"Before you call 'em the 'Two-man Air Force,' let's have the rest of their crew stand, too." Eight more men stood to receive more applause.

"A recent study of Eighth Air Force combat bombing over Germany showed that only forty percent of all bombs hit within one thousand feet of the target. Against that record, it's a pleasure to have this example of perfect bombing to inspire us all! Congratulations! You bring honor to the 394th Squadron and to the whole Fifth Bomb Group! Remember, men—the Bomber Barons are the best damn group in the Pacific!"

The ten men sat down amid back slapping and hand shaking from those around them. Colonel Haviland continued to speak.

"We're here this morning to learn how to make the B-24 fly farther and carry bigger bomb loads than its designers ever dreamed. You know that the B-24 was originally designed for a gross weight of only 50,000 pounds. In the states you sometimes took off with 56,000. Out here, we regularly load you with ten thousand more, to 66,000, but General Kenney has just told us to increase that to 70,000 pounds."

Groans and sighs came from many in the audience.

"70,000 pounds!" Cordell muttered beside me. "Hell's bells!"

"General Kenney sent us Major Dooley, Operations Officer for the 307th Bomb Group, to tell us how they take off heavier and fly farther in the Long Rangers. They pioneered these methods."

Whispered comments buzzed around the audience. "More bragging from the Long Rangers!" James said in my ear.

Major Dooley stepped forward. "Thank you, Colonel. Men, they call the 307th 'the Long Rangers' for a good reason—we've been pushing the limits for range and load steadily upwards. General Kenney asked me to share our secrets with all the B-24 Groups under his command, in both the Fifth and Thirteenth Air Forces. Our secrets are simple, but they make quite a difference.

"First, don't start engines until time to taxi—run up your engines while moving toward the runway. After the plane ahead of you starts its take-off roll, turn onto the very end of the runway, set your brakes and rev up to maximum power—WITH FLAPS UP. A few seconds later the tower gives you a green light, you release brakes and roll—WITH FLAPS UP—until your airspeed reads eighty. You accelerate faster with flaps up! At eighty, put down half flaps. Rotate for lift-off at 130 or the end of the runway, whichever comes first, but DON'T TRY TO CLIMB! At this gross weight, you'll stall and crash if you try to climb right after take-off. Stay in ground effect—fly straight and level over the water—until your airspeed gets to 160, when it's safe to climb."

I felt a flash of fear as I thought of flying twenty feet above the waves for miles. *Not all that bad by daylight, maybe, but it'll make those night take-offs even more hairy!*

"You will no longer assemble into formations over base. Each plane will fly separately, at low altitudes, to an assembly point near the target. Fly no higher than needed to clear the terrain—fuel consumption is better at lower altitudes."

If we all fly separately, every navigator will have to direct his pilot—not just follow the leader.

"B-24s fly more efficiently 'on the step.' Get your bird on the step by climbing a couple of hundred feet higher than you want to cruise, then push the nose down slightly and slide down to cruising altitude. The fuel-efficient airspeed to fly outbound to target is 160, since you're still heavy.

"As you approach the assembly area, climb to bombing altitude and enter your squadron and group formations. By that time your planes will be a lot lighter because of all the fuel burned, so climb and assembly will take less fuel.

"The formation will fly only from the assembly point to the target. After bombs away, you don't need the formation any longer unless fighters attack—but that's unlikely over Borneo at this stage of the war. You use more gas jockying throttles to fly in formation than you do when you fly by yourself at optimum power. So leave the formation as soon as the leader permits, and fly home as individual aircraft, preferably at lower altitudes. The best airspeed to fly on the way home is 150, since you're lighter. Any questions?"

A beefy pilot stood up, cap pushed back on his head. "If we gonna fly these birds to target and back by ourselves, d'you mean all these navigators are gonna hafta shift their butts and get to work, instead of readin' comics like the bombardiers?"

General laughter followed as he sat down.

"Sure thing!" said the major. "ALL navigators will earn their keep from now on! We'll see about bombardiers later!

"We're also going to lighten the plane by removing the waist guns and ammunition, and leaving one gunner on the ground. Waist guns are the least effective defensive weapons, and with our low level of aerial combat, we don't need 'em any more. From now on, you'll fly with nine-man crews instead of ten. Put the engineer in the upper turret, three more gunners in nose, tail, and ball turrets, radioman at his radios, plus two pilots, navigator, and bombardier makes nine—no waist gunners. Any questions on that?"

A gunner stood up. "How will you decide which gunner gets left behind? And will the surplus gunners be sent home now?"

More laughter greeted that suggestion.

Colonel Haviland stepped forward. "Major, let me handle this hot potato. The answer to the second question is *no*! The rotation requirement is still 35 missions, but now it'll take some gunners longer to qualify. We'll give every aircraft commander authority to decide who on his crew will fly each mission."

Gunners whispered profanities all over the tent.

Major Dooley resumed his briefing. "If present trends continue, it won't be long before we remove the armor plate behind the pilot seats to save weight, and maybe take out the ball turret too—leave the turret gunner on the ground. But we'll save all that stuff, because we'd need to put it back in place when they move us north to fly against the Jap homeland. There are still lots of fighters in Japan. Any more questions?"

There were none. "Thank you, Major," Colonel Haviland said. "This briefing will be repeated tomorrow for the crews flying today. Twenty-eight crews have been away for a week, staging from Palawan. They'll strike a target in Brunei Bay later today, then head home tonight. Brunei Bay is our new target area, getting ready for the next invasion of Borneo."

"Group, attens-HUT!" shouted the adjutant. We all stood up while the colonel and major left the tent. "Dismissed!"

The audience dissolved into a noisy chaos of small groups.

"Seventy thousand pounds!" Cordell scowled. "I hope we have enough runway to take off with such a load!"

James gave me a playful jab with his fist. "No more reading comics in flight, Hamilton! Now you'll have to work all the time!"

"Look who's talking—you lazy bombardier!" I raised both fists and jabbed him back. "You know I work all the time anyway—I want to be Squadron Navigator one of these days!"

"Lieutenant Seitz, sir—" Pieper came up to the pilot. "Which gunner will you leave behind on our next mission?" Other gunners heard the question, and crowded behind him to hear the answer.

"Well, let's see," Seitz said. "It won't be you—we need an engineer—not Imhof, for the radios, nor Hill in the tail turret, nor Williams in the nose turret, nor Herrema in the ball turret, so that leaves Gerson. We'll leave Gerson behind next time."

"But you can't leave me behind!" Gerson said. "I man the upper turret!" His bushy brown eyebrows collided in a frown.

"You heard the major," said Seitz. "He said to put the engineer in the upper turret, so Pieper'll go there! Most other crews already have the engineer there—closer to the cockpit."

"I used to man the ball turret," Gerson said. "I could go back to the ball, instead of Herrema. Besides, I'm the armorer—you need me to check the bombs and ammunition before flight."

"I'll make Herrema assistant armorer—you can teach him," Seitz said. "Then the two of you can take turns, every other mission—one stays home while the other flies as armorer and ball turret gunner. Herrema, you and Gerson spend the rest of this day on the flight line, learning what you need to know about checking bombs and ammunition. Continue tomorrow, if you need to. I'll take you into Flight Operations late tomorrow, and get you certified for your new specialty."

"Yes, sir!" said Herrema. "Come on, Gerson, let's go do it!" Gerson followed him out with a sudden smile on his fat round face. *He's happy! He really would rather stay home and loaf while we fly the mission! I knew it!*

To inaugurate the new procedures, our squadron commander, Major Patterson, led the squadron on the next day's mission. (My crew was not involved.) The take-off was in the dark, but all the planes got away safely, in spite of the heaviest load we had ever tried.

Last in line for this take-off was Lieutenant Schulz, with Bodkin as navigator. He told me later that they flew separately to a rendezvous point at the northern tip of Borneo, assembled there and flew in formation to bomb the airfield on Labuan Island in Brunei Bay. After bombing, the planes flew home individually to Samar. It was Bodkin's second mission with the Bomber Barons.

Next day Captain Rice led our squadron in a very early night take-off, so the bombers could strike the beaches of Labuan at sunrise to cover the work of Navy SEAL teams clearing the shore of obstacles ahead of the invasion. (Again, my crew was not involved.)

Flying this mission was Lieutenant Barnes, with Comfort as navigator. This was his first mission with the Bomber Barons. "I got excited when I saw the invasion fleet in the distance while we were bombing the beach!" he said later.

My turn came the following day, June 10, "D-Day" for the Australian Ninth Division's invasion of Brunei Bay. Ten B-24 squadrons, four Bomber Barons, four Long Rangers, and two Australian squadrons, converged to bomb the beaches a few minutes before the landings. It was my tenth combat mission—our first with a nine-man crew. Herrema did the armorer's preflight work as we checked the plane over in the dark at 2:30. An hour later we sat in B-24 number 673, "Wild Irish Rose," waiting to start engines and taxi. My excitement grew as I thought about where we were going. *I'm in a real invasion at last! I can hardly believe it!*

Lieutenant Harris led the squadron, taking off at 3:35. We watched his lights fade into the black night as we started our engines. Three more planes piloted by Lieutenants Heinz, Wildey, and Ellenbecker, followed in rapid sequence. We were next.

Seitz turned onto the end of the runway, set the brakes and revved the engines wide open. The tower flashed a green light, Seitz released the brakes, and we roared down the dimly-lit runway. I stood on the flight deck behind Seitz, watching the night take-off with fascination and fear. Pieper stood between the two pilot seats to read and call out airspeed.

"Forty....fifty....sixty....seventy....eighty!"

"Flaps down one-half," Seitz shouted over the noise.

"Wilco," shouted Cordell. "We got half flaps."

"Ninety...one hundred...one-ten...one-twenty...one-thirty."

"Rotate," Seitz said, pulling back hard on the wheel. The nose lifted and the rumble of the wheels stopped.

"Gear up!" shouted Seitz.

"Gear up!" Cordell echoed, left hand lifting the big red lever at the base of the pedestal. "We got three green lights!"

The island disappeared behind us, and we flew into the inky blackness of night. Black ocean merged with black sky—there was nothing outside to see.

I felt nervous sweat drip down my face. *Damn! These overloaded night take-offs are accidents waiting to happen!*

Instruments showed zero rate of climb. The nose-high attitude that lifted us off also generated more drag, so acceleration was slow. *Seventy thousand pounds of men and machine hurtling through the night!* Twenty feet below us, the dark waves were zooming by, but if we dipped down and touched them, they would impact like concrete on the speeding plane. Gradually the airspeed increased, and Seitz slowly lowered the nose with skill, balancing the changing forces to keep us flying level.

"Airspeed one-sixty," Pieper called.

Seitz pulled back gently on the wheel, and the instruments showed a slow climb. We were still headed east over the Pacific; when we reached 100 feet of altitude, Seitz made a gentle U-turn to head us back toward the base. Now we could see the lights of Samar ahead, giving me a great sense of relief.

"Flaps up," Seitz called.

"Flaps coming up," Cordell said, lifting the flap lever.

"Reduce power to 46 inches and 2550 rpm," Seitz said.

"Roger," said Cordell, adjusting the power settings.

I saw the lights of other bombers coming toward us at a lower level. They had taken off after us at one minute intervals, and now we climbed above them, going the other way. The lights of the planes formed a dimly-lit ladder climbing slowly toward the heavens. We reached 1,000 feet as we passed over the base going west. I looked at my watch. "Departure 0345", I noted in the log.

"Outbound heading two-four-seven," I told the pilot. Then I crawled through the tunnel to the nose to start navigating.

Laying out my maps, chart and log on the small navigation table, I turned on the loran set and adjusted it. During the next two hours, with the ground below shrouded in darkness and the stars hidden by clouds above, loran would be my only source of position fixes.

"Navigator to Pilot," I said through the interphone, "let's continue our climb to 4,500 feet to clear the mountains on Leyte. We can hold that altitude for the next hour, then we'll need to go up to 5,500 to get over the mountains on Negros."

"Pilot to Navigator, how much clearance are you allowing?"

"Navigator to Pilot, those altitudes are at least 500 feet higher than any peak within ten miles of our course."

We leveled off at 4,500 feet, and half an hour later, saw the lights of Cebu City directly below. We were right on course.

Great! My first solo navigation mission in combat is off to a good start! It's almost like flying lead navigator.

A few minutes later I told the pilot to climb another thousand feet to 5,500, to clear the mountains on Negros, hidden in the darkness ahead.

Twenty minutes later, my loran fix showed me that we had passed over Negros.

"Navigator to Pilot, over," I said on the interphone.

"Pilot to Navigator, go ahead."

"We've just passed the last Philippine Island—there's nothing below but the empty Sulu Sea for the next two hours. You can safely let down to any altitude you think will save the most fuel."

"Roger. We'll slide down to 2,000 and see if lower altitudes really do help."

Dawn in the tropics is brief; a swift transition from darkness to daylight. I had been navigating in the night. Suddenly the sun rose behind us in a burst of brilliant orange, lighting up the dark waters of the Sulu Sea.

An hour later, we began climbing toward our bombing altitude of 8,000 feet as we approached the assembly point, the northern tip of Borneo, near Kudat. Other bombers were already circling as we arrived at seven-thirty. We moved into our place—fifth plane in the third squadron. The Group left the assembly point at seven forty-two, flying southwest along the coast of Borneo toward Brunei Bay.

"Able Lead to Pipe Dream, over," we heard our Group Leader call Ground Control on VHF radio.

"Pipe Dream to Able Lead, read you loud and clear, over."

"Able Lead approaching Brunei Bay. Request strike permission, over."

"Able Lead, take your Group to the center of the bay and circle there until we clear each squadron, over."

"Roger, Pipe Dream, Able Lead out."

We entered Brunei Bay over the town of Weston, at the northeast shore of the bay. Seven minutes later we reached the center.

"Able Lead to Pipe Dream, now circling at bay center."

"Pipe Dream to Able Lead—Able Squadron cleared to strike."

"Able Lead headed for I.P., out."

We watched the first squadron leave the group, heading southwest across the bay. Our purpose was to help the landing at Brooketon, on the west side of Brunei Bay. Our bombs would clear out Japanese troops from a wooded area next to the beach.

Smoke and haze covered the bay with a shroud that limited visibility to twelve miles. From bay center, I could hardly see the shoreline. Smoke came from the north side of the bay—Fires burned on Labuan Island from shelling by our warships. Through the smoke I saw Navy fighter planes diving low to strafe targets on Labuan while Long Ranger B-24s, higher up, bombed the beaches there. Below me the bay was full of warships and landing craft; their smoke contributed to the haze. The whole scene excited me—my heart pounded faster.

"Pipe Dream to Baker Lead, over," the VHF radio squawked.

"Baker Lead to Pipe Dream, ready to go, over."

"Baker Squadron cleared to strike."

The second squadron left the group and headed for the I.P. The other two squadrons continued circling. Five minutes later, our call came. "Charlie Squadron cleared to strike."

Our squadron headed across the bay to the I.P. seven miles south of Brooketon, then turned north for the bombing run. James opened the bomb bay doors and crouched to watch the lead plane.

Twenty green lights glowed on the indicator panel beside the bombardier, showing twenty bombs armed, ready to go. Each was a 120-pound fragmentation bomb, a "daisy-cutter" designed to spray shrapnel over a wide area. James had set the intervalometer to drop them at intervals of two hundred feet.

We saw the first bomb emerge from the lead plane's belly—instantly, James squeezed his bomb-release toggle switch.

"Bombs away!" he called on the interphone.

James and I watched the twenty green lights go out one by one, as the intervalometer released the bombs a little faster than one per second. When the last light went out, we both gave a sigh of relief. "No hung-up bombs this time!" He said, and closed the bomb bay doors. *(No falling off the catwalk this time!)*

"Bombs away at 0908," I wrote in my navigator log. Below us, landing craft headed ashore toward beaches cleared by our bombs.

Our squadron turned right and flew across the bay to Weston, where our six planes peeled off to fly home individually.

"Pilot to Navigator, give me a heading to Kudat point."

"Navigator to Pilot, heading zero-three-two degrees."

"Pilot to all Gunners, keep your eyes peeled for enemy fighters. There are several Jap airfields on the way to Kudat." *They didn't attack the formation coming in, but those bastards might be tempted to go after a plane going back alone. And all of us are alone now.*

"Bombardier to Camera, did you take strike photos?"

"Camera to Bombardier, affirmative—six or eight of 'em."

"How did the bomb pattern look to you, Imhof?"

"It was a good pattern, James—looked like most of 'em fell inside the target area."

"Great! Makes me feel good to do something right!"

Flying along the Borneo coastline, we passed the Japanese airfield at Jesselton without a challenge.

"Pilot to Navigator, I'm starting a slow descent, so we'll be down to two thousand feet when we reach the end of Borneo. We'll hold that altitude across the Sulu Sea."

"Navigator to Pilot, would you like to hold two thousand all the way home? We can do it if we fly around the south end of Negros and Leyte instead of climbing up over them like we did on the outbound trip. We'll have daylight all the way, so it'll be safe to skirt the edges. It won't add much to the distance."

"Roger, Navigator, sounds good—let's do it!"

We reached the north tip of Borneo at 10:13, and turned right to 073 degrees. No planes rose from the Japanese airfield at nearby Kudat, so again we passed unchallenged. *The Japs must be short of fuel or bullets—I know they still have planes!*

For more than two hours, we flew over the Sulu Sea alone but not isolated. We saw other B-24s at intervals ahead of us and behind, some higher or lower, some to our right or left, all going our way. If one had gone down at sea, others would have seen it and radioed for help.

"Navigator to Pilot, how's our low altitude fuel consumption working out? Do we have plenty to make it home? E.T.A. is 1403."

"Pilot to Navigator, no sweat this time. We won't know the exact figures until we measure fuel remaining after we get there, but it seems to be performing like they said it would."

We flew around the southern tips of Negros, Bohol, and Leyte islands. Their rugged mountains rose far above our altitude just a short way inland; it would not be safe to try this edge-skirting route at night. The afternoon sun was behind us as we flew northeast across Leyte Gulf to land on Samar at 2:05 P.M. All six planes in our squadron landed within a nine-minute time span, almost as if they had arrived in formation. We had flown ten and one-half hours.

Mission accomplished! I felt a great sense of relief and satisfaction. *I finally flew in a real invasion!*

Later that afternoon, I ran into my two buddies, Comfort, tall and thin, and Bodkin, short and stout.

"We're both scheduled for the mission tomorrow," Comfort said cheerfully. "How about you?"

"I just got back from the mission today. We usually get a day of rest between long flights."

Comfort's tall frame slouched even more. "Aw, shucks! We were hoping the Three Musketeers would all fly together at last!"

"Well, maybe next time!" Bodkin said, smiling.

"Do you know which planes you'll be flying?" I asked.

"Number 199, 'Daisy Mae,'" said Bodkin.

"And I'm in 674, 'Dangerous Dude,'" Comfort said.

"Daisy Mae is a lucky airplane—I had my first Bomber Barons mission in 199—it'll give you a good flight, Clyde. But watch out for Dangerous Dude, Bob—Dangerous Dude might be dangerous in darkness—I hate these night take-offs!"

Comfort laughed. "As if a name can make any difference in an airplane's performance!"

"Sometimes it seems to make a difference in an airplane's luck," I said. "Well, good luck to both of you tomorrow! Have a real good flight! I'll be sleeping off my last mission while you're starting your next one."

Next morning I slept late and missed breakfast, but went to the mess hall anyway, to see if I could find a cup of left-over coffee. Wildey, tall, dark-haired, looking a bit rumpled, was standing next to the coffee urn, sipping a cup.

"Hello, Wildey, let me at the coffee," I said, pouring some. "I missed breakfast and need coffee bad!"

"Hello, Hamilton. I missed it too, sleeping off yesterday's mission. Did you hear about the crash?"

"What crash?"

"One of our B-24s didn't get away on today's mission—crashed on take-off."

"No! You're kidding me!" I searched his face for signs of humor. He looked deadly serious.

"No kidding, Hamilton. We really lost one today—crashed into the sea in the dark—another early night take-off, like we both had yesterday."

I felt a growing tightness at the pit of my stomach. "Were there any survivors?"

"No survivors—that's all I heard."

"What crew?"

"I don't know yet. As soon as I swallow this coffee, I'm going down to Operations to find out."

"I'll go with you," I said, gulping mine down. "My two best buddies are navigating two of the planes on this mission—I hope to God it wasn't either of them!"

"One of my buddies is lead pilot this morning, but I don't think he'd be likely to crash. It's probably one of the new crews—not much experience."

"Both of my buddies are on new crews!"

"Come on, let's go find out."

In silence we walked the dirt road to the flight line through a half-mile of palm trees and jungle vegetation. My growing sense of dread cut off any desire for conversation, but I felt comforted by Wildey's presence.

The Flight Operations tent was unusually crowded. Fifteen or twenty men hung around, some at the counter, others talking in small groups. Captain Davenport, Squadron Operations Officer, sat on the edge of his desk, talking with Captain Gaston and Captain Rice, two of our lead pilots. Sergeant Bryson sat at the radio table listening to VHF, while Staff Sergeant Henson and Corporal Capo stood behind the counter. We went to the counter.

"What happened, Sarge?" Wildey asked Henson.

"Our fifth plane took off at 0407 and didn't get very far. The tower saw him go down in the dark—his lights disappeared—and sent the crash boat out after him. After searching a while in the dark, the PT boat found the wreckage in shallow water on the coral reef a quarter-mile from the end of the runway."

"Any survivors?"

"No, but they were able to recover the bodies in that shallow water. Lucky it wasn't further out—beyond the reef, the ocean floor drops way down. Another mile, it's five hundred feet deep. It keeps going on down to the deepest place on earth less than fifty miles away—over 34,000 feet deep! They call it the 'Philippine Trench.'" He seemed proud of his knowledge.

"Enough geography! Which airplane? Who was the pilot?"

"Lieutenant Barnes in 674, 'Dangerous Dude.'"

My guts felt like a boxer punched me below the belt.

"Was his whole crew on board?" I asked.

"No, just nine out of ten. New policy drops one gunner, you know."

I had to get explicit confirmation. "Who was the navigator?"

He read the crew list. "Flight Officer Robert L. Comfort."

For a moment the whole tent seemed to reel around me. I held on to the counter to steady myself.

Captain Davenport, behind the counter, came toward us.

"Wildey, I'm glad to see you. We need to fly the C-47 to Leyte today, to take nine bodies to the military cemetery at Tanuan. Would you like to fly the plane?"

"Sure—why not? It's a sad trip, but somebody's got to do it. Hamilton, want to come along for the ride?"

I felt nauseous and numb. "I'll pass." Wildey's eyes met mine in silent understanding.

"They're loading the bodies on the C-47 now," Davenport said. "You can leave in half an hour."

"Captain Davenport," I said, "what caused the crash?"

"We've been debating that all morning. The crash occurred a quarter-mile offshore. At 130 miles per hour, it took the plane only seven seconds to cover a quarter mile. That's a damn short flight! It would have taken almost that long for the plane to settle the twenty-foot height from the runway to the water.

"Maybe it wasn't really flying when it shot off the end of the runway. Maybe the pilot tried to climb out of take-off and stalled. Maybe it was a mechanical problem, like loss of power in one engine, that made him swoop down a bit too low. It could have been any of several possible causes. We'll never know for sure."

"Maybe seventy thousand pounds is just too much weight to try to lift off in the dangerous darkness of a night take-off," I said.

"Not if the pilots focus on their job," Davenport replied. "Look, in the past four days since we increased the load, the Bomber Barons have launched ninety-six planes—no, ninety-seven, because we launched the standby crew on this mission when Barnes went down. We lost one plane out of ninety-seven. It was just an unfortunate operational accident. Nothing wrong with the policy."

Nothing wrong at all—except an empty place in my heart shaped like Bob Comfort!

I turned and walked away, heading back toward my tent. I felt a desperate desire to sleep away—or drink away—my pain.

19. Death Before Dawn

Death reached out to me at last. For three months I had fought in the Pacific—a hundred hours of combat flying in ten bombing missions—without suffering the death of anyone I knew personally—until today. Now death had snatched away Bob Comfort, my best friend.

Mid-morning, I sat on the edge of my cot and drank a warm beer while I remembered the face of my friend—open, kind, intelligent. He looked like a scarecrow in uniform—tall and thin, slouching shoulders, protruding Adam's apple, hair like unkempt straw. But his mind—curious, sharp, organized, communicative—revealed a soul closer to my heart than anyone else in uniform. I had lost part of my own self!

I needed to talk about the loss with my other close friend Clyde Bodkin, but he was then navigating toward Borneo on the same mission Comfort had intended to fly.

"Mail Call!" Seitz entered the tent with some letters.

Cordell and James sat up in the cots where they had been sleeping off yesterday's mission.

"Looks like all of us got sugar reports today." Seitz tossed letters to each of us. Mine was from Persis in California.

"Dear Bob," she wrote, "Thank you for your good letters. I really enjoy reading them! Sorry I haven't written recently—my classmates and I have been busy finishing our sophomore year on the Stanford campus. Now it's June, and that job is finally done! So many exams! I'm exhausted!

"After a summer vacation, our nursing class will move to the Stanford-Lane Hospital in San Francisco. We'll spend the next three years there before we graduate with R.N. as well as B.S. degree.

The three years of nursing take the place of our junior and senior years on campus.

"San Francisco will be quite a change from Palo Alto. There's no place for a car in the crowded city. I'll leave Dad's Oldsmobile with sister Pat on the Stanford campus—she has another year there. I can ride those cute little cable cars instead—they run close to the hospital.

"One of my good friends is a year ahead of me—already in the nursing school. I went up there to visit her recently, to see what it's like. As we talked, she said one of the hardest things to adjust to was death. You never know when you'll face a '*code blue*,' and one of your patients will die on you while everyone struggles to prevent it.

"She said death seems so strange—so final—it makes you feel so helpless when it strikes. I've never seen anyone die. I think it would put me in a state of shock! But I'm sure that I'll see lots of it before I finish nursing school.

"I hope I can be brave, like you. You're flying bombers over the enemy all the time, and you've never mentioned death to me. I guess you'll see more than you want of death before this war is over. When you do, just remember that you have my moral support and love to strengthen you. And when I do get into nursing, I hope to understand death better, so my support will mean even more.

"I'll write you next from the mountains—my parents have a cabin in the high Sierras. It's a lovely place to spend a summer.

"Goodbye for now. My thoughts are with you every day.

"Love, Persis."

What a shot in the arm! This lovely girl, so thoughtful and serious about death, sent me her moral support and love on the very day I needed it! I thought of her with increasing respect and appreciation.

Next afternoon Bodkin and I headed for the Officers' Club to conduct our own private wake for Comfort. Cold beers in hand, we settled back to grieve his death by sharing memories.

"The Three Musketeers are down to two, now!" Bodkin said.

"I never thought it'd come to this!" I sighed.

"We wanted to get the three of us flyin' together on the same mission."

"That dream won't happen now."

"Back in navigation school, we used to dream of bein' assigned to the same combat base—remember?"

"At least that dream came true," I said.

"We had some good times there at Selman Field—the three of us, together."

I lifted my beer in tribute. "The best of friends for the best of times."

"Yeah! And some of the best times were when the three of us were hangin' around with jolly Jerri and dolly Dora—"

"—our two favorite WACs!" (Women's Army Corps)

"The five of us made a pretty good group, singin' to the juke box at the Stardust Cafe," Bodkin said.

"Remember the time all five of us were strolling along the Ouachita River in downtown Monroe when a beautiful Chris-Craft speedboat pulled over to offer us a ride?"

"Yeah, it was Mr. Noe, the rich old guy who owns a chain of radio stations in Louisiana," he said. "Nice of him to offer."

"So you and jolly Jerri sat in front with Mr. Noe, and Bob and I sat in the back seat with dolly Dora between us."

"Yeah. That old guy had a patriotic heart—gave our group of five soldiers a wonderful hour swishin' up and down the river in his Cadillac of a boat—leather seats, mahogany paneling."

"That Chris-Craft was so quiet, it just purred along—"

"—until we got outside the city limits—then he opened it up and really roared away!"

"Scared Dora to death!" I said. "She clutched Bob and me like she'd never let go!"

"I'll bet that didn't hurt your feelings! You two Bobs were both sweet on Dora!"

"She was sweet on me, too," I said. "Dora gave me a swell

graduation present—fancy navigator wings embroidered with silver thread on khaki, to sew on my dress tan jacket."

"She was sweet on you both, that crazy red-head! 'Bob' must've been her favorite name."

"Too bad we never did anything about it—she was some dish!"

"Well, actually we did do somethin' about it—or Bob and I did somethin' after you graduated."

"You're kidding!" I said. "What'd you do?"

"Well, long as there was five of us, it didn't seem right to pair off. But you graduated and left a month before we did. The four remainin' just sorta naturally fell into two pairs—"

"I know how it split—you and Jerri, and Bob and Dora."

"Bingo!" said Bodkin, grinning, and took a gulp of his beer.

"So what happened? Did the two couples ever couple?"

"Yeah—at our graduation, the end of October. We decided to celebrate by goin' to a fancy downtown hotel—"

"—you couldn't!" I said. "The hotels in Monroe won't rent rooms to young couples unless you sign in as 'Mr. and Mrs.' and you both wear wedding rings! Once I tried to rent a room there for me and Sandy, but couldn't do it. Neither of us were willing to lie about it—so we're both still virgins."

"We didn't have to lie about it—two couples made it easy! Bob and I rented one room, and the two girls rented another. After we got upstairs, we did a switcheroo!"

"Well, I'll be darned! How simple! Say 'hello' to ecstasy! Bye, bye, virginity!"

"We were all virgins then, the Musketeers and the WACs. But we had a glorious comin' of age sexually, on the same day we became 'Officers and Gentlemen by Act of Congress.'"

"Congratulations!" I lifted my glass to clink against his. A sudden rush of jealousy made my guts burn—I had strong feelings for Dora too. But I heard my lips say, "I'm so glad our buddy Bob had that satisfaction before his crash!"

"I'm glad he did, too! And hey—I'm glad I had that experience myself! The war's not over yet, you know. I could crash next week, and you could crash the week after—"

"Stop! Don't say that out loud—it might happen!" I paused for another drink. "But if it did—then you'd die satisfied, and I'd die a virgin. That's life."

"Hey, we're here for Bob's wake, not yours or mine." Bodkin drained his glass. "Time for refills—my turn."

When he returned with fresh beers, I said, "Let's sing the 'Flyer's Toast' to the memory of Flight Officer Comfort."

"Of course!" We interlocked our forearms at the elbows. Each took a long swallow of beer, then we sang a duet:

"Flyers, fellow flyers, we salute you—
The finest men to ever span the sky!
Here's a toast to the ones dead already—
Then we'll drink to the next man to die!"

Arms still overlapping, we each took another long swallow, not quite emptying the glasses, and sang again,

"Here's a toast to the ones dead already—
Then we'll drink to the next man to die!"

The third long swallow emptied the glasses.

"It sounded better when the three of us did this together," Bodkin said, "but that duet wasn't bad."

"That 'duet' was a trio!" I exclaimed. "Bob's arm was right there, intertwined with ours! Bob lifted his voice and his glass with ours, in spirit and in truth!"

"Amen, amen! Now it's your turn to buy the next round!"

Two days later, June 14, I was on my way to Borneo again, flying my eleventh combat mission with Seitz and crew. We started rolling down the runway for another sweat-drenched night take-off at 5:33 A.M. My mind replayed its own creation of the searing sights and sounds of Bob's bomber crashing into the sea. Anxiety mingled with my grief, but somehow I survived the departure.

Now we were flying through stormy skies in B-24 number 650, Little Judith Anne, which had taken us on our first trip to Borneo.

Eighteen B-24s from the Fifth Bomb Group were flying separately toward Balikpapen, the major enemy oil refinery far to the south on the east coast of Borneo. We knew that the bombers were spaced about three miles apart by their take-off sequence, but we saw no other planes outside our windows. They were hidden behind clouds and occasional pelting rainstorms.

After flying through nasty stuff for five hours, we reached Cape Mang-kalihat, a fat peninsula projecting eastward into the sea from the middle of Borneo's east coast. There, a break in the weather allowed our bombers to assemble into squadron and group formations as planned. That took almost half an hour, as each plane emerged from the clouds to join the circling group. In Combat Box formation at 10,000 feet, three squadrons flew southwest two hundred miles to Balikpapen. The bad weather got worse as we went along. We loosened the formation to be safer.

Rain showers, sleet, and moderate turbulence shook our planes as the formation flew in and out of clouds and around thunderheads. Ice formed on our wings, only to be cracked off by pulsing de-icer boots on the wing's leading edge.

We put on oxygen masks as the group climbed to 13,500 feet, seeking a stable bombing level between layers of clouds. At that altitude, the temperature was minus ten degrees Celsius (fifteen degrees Fahrenheit). There were no heaters in our B-24s. so we put on our fleece-lined leather jackets, trousers, boots and gloves.

Our 394th Squadron led the group. The other two squadrons moved behind us as we approached the target area at noon. We were ready to bomb by separate squadrons. Clouds hid most of the ground below.

We flew to the I.P., eight miles south of the target, and turned north on the bomb run. Our target was anti-aircraft guns at Panadjan, close to Balikpapen. Those guns could be aimed at us through clouds by radar, so we put on steel helmets and flak jackets—bullet-proof vests—over our parachute harnesses. Another heavy layer to wear! Under each harness was a rubber "Mae West" life jacket, and under that was the fleece-lined leather jacket, which was over the pistol belt and escape kit, which was over the flyer's jump suit—all together, a bulky combination indeed.

James knelt in the nose ahead of me, bomb release switch in hand. He looked intently at the lead plane, but no bombs fell from the lead plane or ours.

"Able Lead to Able birds," Captain Boggess's voice came over the radio, "hold your eggs! Lead bombardier couldn't see the target. We'll go around and try again."

Little Judith Anne followed the squadron leader as he turned left and headed back toward the I.P. again.

"No flak!" I shouted at James through my oxygen mask.

"What?" he yelled through his, turning toward me.

"No flak! Those guns we're trying to bomb are silent!"

"Great! Hope they stay silent!" He closed bomb bay doors.

Meanwhile, the second squadron was on its bomb run. I saw them on our left as we passed. Suddenly, bombs emerged from their bellies, plunging down into the clouds below.

"Baker Lead, bombs away!" came the radio voice.

"Able Lead to Baker Lead, did your bombardier see the target? Over."

"Baker Lead to Able Lead, don't know if he did or not—he dropped 'em, anyway. Baker Squadron heading home, out."

James turned around to frown at me. "Wasn't supposed to do that," he shouted, "dropping bombs without sighting target!"

"Maybe he caught a glimpse of it," I shouted back.

"—or didn't give a damn! Just unload and fly home!"

"Charlie Lead to Able Lead," the radio crackled again. "Request permission for Charlie Squadron to bomb secondary target. The clouds here look hopeless to me, over."

"Able Lead to Charlie Lead, permission granted. Give us a report on cloud coverage at secondary, over."

"Charlie Squadron proceeding to secondary, out."

I turned to the target data in my briefing notes. The secondary target was the anti-aircraft gun battery at Manggar, fifteen miles east of the primary. *Go there, boys! Bomb 'em to pieces!*

Our lead squadron reached the I.P. and turned left into the bomb run. James opened the bomb bay doors and focused on the lead plane again.

"Tail Gunner to Pilot—we got flak at seven o'clock low!"

"Ball Gunner to Pilot—I see it, too! Three black bursts now, trailing us, 500 feet low, but moving in our direction!"

"Pilot to crew—hang in there! We're on the bomb run now—no evasive action possible!"

Nothing to do now but sweat out the bomb run!

I listened to the muffled "crump! whump!" of flak bursts. *Damn! They're getting closer!* Suddenly I heard the "ping" of shrapnel piercing our plane's aluminum skin. *Shoot! They're starting to find our range!* After two minutes of cold sweat, we passed my estimated bomb release time, but no bombs fell. Our squadron started a right turn.

"Able Lead to Able Squadron—spread formation, use evasive action! We're heading for the secondary target, out."

Flying east, we soon left the flak behind.

"Charlie Lead to Able Lead—cloud cover at secondary is solid undercast. Should we bomb the general area of target anyway? Over."

"Negative, Charlie Lead. Safety your bombs and drop them over water en route base, over."

"Charlie Lead wilco, out."

A minute later we approached the I.P. for the secondary target. It was obvious to me that no one could see through the clouds below us, but our leader turned the squadron onto the bomb run anyway. Captain Boggess was a "by-the-book" perfectionist.

This bomb run was another waste of time, but at least it gave us the possibility of a sighting through a break below.

"Damn it all!" James shouted at me. "Why can't we drop our bombs in the general area of the target? We might hit some enemy features!"

"We'd likely hit native villages," I shouted. "We're not at war with the natives of Borneo— only with the Jap invaders!"

"Able Leader to Able Squadron," said Captain Boggess over the radio, "safety your bombs and drop them in formation on lead bombardier's drop—in ten minutes."

"Pilot to Bombardier," Seitz spoke on interphone, "close bomb bay doors and safety the bombs, over."

"Bombardier to Pilot—wilco."

James pulled the red lever to close the bomb bay doors, then grabbed a walk-around oxygen bottle and plugged his mask into it. He carried the bottle as he crawled into the tunnel to the bomb bay. A few minutes later he returned to the nose.

"No sweat this time?" I asked.

"Naw—it's easy to work in the bomb bay when the doors are closed." He hit the lever to open the bomb bay doors again.

The lead plane's bomb bay doors opened, and James watched for bombs to appear. When they did, he squeezed his bomb release.

I wrote in the navigator log, "Bombs away over water at 1327 from 13,500 feet at 02-20 S, 117-40 E." *What a waste! All these planes fly all this way through all this weather—for nothing!* (Air Force policy prohibited returning to base with bombs on board. A crash on landing would not detonate safetied bombs, but the heat of a burning plane would make them explode.)

"Able Leader to Able Squadron—peel off now and fly home on your own." The formation vanished as we peeled off in sequence. All the planes headed down to lower altitudes, where we could remove our oxygen masks and enjoy warmer air and improved fuel efficiency. But that put us back into the nasty weather we had flown through on the way out. Again, we were in and out of clouds and rain, with frequent detours around thunderheads.

"Able Six to Able Lead, over," came the voice on VHF radio.

"Able Lead to Able Six, go ahead."

"Able Six just feathered number three engine—oil leaking away. Also lost all hydraulic pressure. Must have caught some flak over target that let the fluids piss away, over."

"Roger, Able Six. Where do you plan to land? Over."

"We'll try the new fighter base at Sanga Sanga, over."

"Roger, Able Six—we'll give your regrets to the crew chief, out."

Seitz called me on interphone, "Pilot to Navigator, where's Sanga Sanga?"

I checked my maps. "Navigator to Pilot, Sanga Sanga is a small island in the Tawi Tawi Group at the west end of the Sulu Archipelago. It's only seventy miles from the northeast tip of Borneo. Our boys just built a new fighter airfield there, over."

"Able Six is Lieutenant Johnson,'" Seitz said. "He can land his wounded bird on a short fighter runway, but who knows whether he can get it fixed there? Over."

"Well, that's his problem—glad it's not ours, over."

"But we do have a different problem," Seitz said. "We spent so much time over the target area that we might not have fuel enough to get back to Samar, over."

"We could land and refuel at Zamboanga two hours before we could reach Samar, over."

"We'll do it. Give me a heading, over."

"Ten degrees left to heading 030. E.T.A. Zamboanga 1730."

Seitz called on the radio, "Able Three to Able Lead, over."

"Able Lead to Able Three, go ahead."

"Able Three is low on fuel, will stop to refuel at Zamboanga, over."

"Roger, Able Three. See you later at home base, out."

"Able Four to Able Lead—we're low on fuel too, will also stop at Zamboanga, over."

"Roger, Able Four, out."

Seitz' voice came on interphone, "Pilot to Crew, we'll have some company at Zamboanga. Able Four is Lieutenant Ellenbecker.'"

After two more hours of clouds and rain, we touched down in a rainstorm on the perforated-metal runway at Zamboanga. As Seitz braked to slow down our roll, the wheels slipped on the slick wet metal surface. The plane skidded slowly to the left, where a ditch paralleled the runway. Slowly and gracefully, Little Judith Anne curved around to head straight into the ditch.

"Look out! We're gonna crash!" Cordell shouted.

"CUT ALL ENGINES!" Seitz shouted.

"Wilco!" said Cordell, hitting switches and throttles.

The rest of us froze in place, helpless in a plane out of control. *The next few seconds could end our lives in a flaming crash or explosion of fuel that'd blow us to smithereens!*

With a gentle thud, Little Judith Anne stopped with her nose down in the ditch and her tail high above the edge of the runway.

"Open bomb bay doors!" Seitz shouted. "All crew bail out!"

We all moved fast, but without panic. The six of us on the flight deck climbed the tilted floor behind us to jump through the front of the bomb bay to the ground below. The three in the waist appeared at the rear of the bomb bay and dropped to the ground from there. We ran out through the rain into a wide circle around the airplane, fearing possible fire or explosion.

I looked around the circle. *Thank God! All nine of us got out alive!* My knees stopped shaking.

When no explosion came, we moved in closer to assess damage.

"That's the gentlest crash I ever saw!" said Pieper.

"Look at the propellers," said Cordell. "They're not even damaged!"

"Yep," Seitz said. "The B-24's wings and engines are mounted so high, the propellers never struck the ground. If this had been a B-17, all four props would be busted now."

"Speaking of high, look at the tail!" said Hill. "I opened the rear hatch to bail out from there—then I saw how high I was, and said, 'No way, Jose!'"

Williams inspected the nose turret. "You've put a dent in the nose, and cracked the nose turret glass. But the nose wheel looks okay."

"I think this bird will fly pretty well if we tow it out of the ditch," Seitz said.

A jeep roared up and skidded to a stop. The Operations Officer jumped out.

"Gotta move this bird!" he shouted. "Your tail is blocking our runway!"

"Get something here to tow us out." Seitz said.

"I've got a six-by-six on the way! It'll winch you out."

A big six-by-six truck drove up and parked on the far side of the runway, pointing toward the plane. Two men pulled cables from a pair of winches on the front of the truck, and hooked the cables around the vertical struts of the plane's two main wheels. The driver turned on the winches, which slowly backed the plane out of the ditch. The tail came down with a thump. Crisis over.

We climbed back into the plane, started engines and taxied to the ramp, where there was one other bomber parked among all the P-38s and P-51s of this fighter base. It was B-24 number 651, "No Duds," with a shapely nude girl painted on the nose. Its crew came over to tease us about our accident.

"That was not a very convincing crash," said one. "Go back and try it again!"

"Yeah—let's have a big explosion and roaring flames!"

"Were you guys tryin' to make Little Judith Anne turn a somersault?" said another. "What a half-ass performance!"

"Naw—not a somersault—just a headstand! They put her head down and her ass high, like she's achin' for a makin'!"

"We're lucky we landed ahead of you—otherwise, we'd of run out of fuel circlin' while you clowns block the runway!"

"'Oh, the monkeys have no tails in Zamboanga!' Your bird nearly lost her tail, too!"

That last comment made me curious. I asked Hill, "Is that monkey line a quotation? Where does it come from?"

"It's an old sailor song—haven't you heard it?"

"No. How does it go?"

Hill made a face, but then he sang,

"Oh, the monkeys have no tails in Zamboanga,
  Zamboanga, Zamboanga.
Oh, the monkeys have no tails,
  They were eaten by the whales,
So, the monkeys have no tails in Zamboanga."

I had a sudden flash of insight. "The sailors coming to Zamboanga saw the Philippine Spider Monkey—born without a tail—and created a legend to explain it."

"Yeah—that's why Shoo-Shoo, our mascot, has no tail!"

Hill and I raised our right hands and clapped them together. It was a warm moment of sharing on a dark, rainy day.

The darkening clouds became black, as night settled over the airfield. A few minutes later No Duds finished fueling and taxied out for take-off. Forty minutes later, our plane was also ready. We took off at seven-ten for the two-hour flight back to Samar—a fourteen-hour mission. *All that flying for nothing! Just bombs dumped in the sea! We need planes equipped with radar, to bomb through clouds.*

Two days later our crew was flying back to Balikpapen on my twelfth mission. Again my mind replayed Bob's plane crashing, while we lived through another overloaded night take-off at 3:45 A.M. Again we were flying B-24 number 650, Little Judith Anne. The dented nose and cracked nose turret were still there.

This is our third trip to Borneo in this bird. The first time, she lost an engine and we detoured to Palawan. Second time, she ran low on fuel and crashed on her nose at Zamboanga. 'Third time's a charm'—maybe she'll get us home non-stop this time.

Neither the route nor the weather had changed much in the two days since our last trip. Twenty-four bombers flew separately through nasty weather for five hours to Cape Mang-kalihat on the east coast of Borneo, where we emerged from clouds to assemble our squadron and group formations.

The whole group flew south to Balikpapen, climbing to 15,000 feet for the bomb run on the primary target (to reduce exposure to flak, but heavy flak came up through the clouds, anyway). The cloud layer below was too thick to see the target. No bombs fell on the primary target, which was the flak guns shooting at us there. *(On this mission, we finally have two planes equipped with radar bombing gear, but no trained radarmen to run them!)*

Expecting such weather, Thirteenth Bomber Command had given us five different targets in Borneo—an unusual number of alternates. The whole group turned east to make the next bomb run on the first alternate target, five miles away, with the same results—no bombing. The second alternate, only one mile further east, was also hidden by the same solid undercast, so we passed it by without a bomb run.

The group then flew to the fourth target, Manggar Airfield, sixteen miles from Balikpapen, and made the next bomb run there. Again, no breaks appeared over target, and we dropped no bombs. A lot of flak came up on all three bomb runs. It was enough to scare us, but not accurate enough to shoot down any of our planes.

The group flew next to the fifth target, the shipbuilding area at Samarinda, sixty miles north of Balikpapen. There the clouds parted enough for the lead bombardier to sight the target, so the group finally dropped its 720 bombs on the shipyard below. Then the formation vanished as we peeled off to fly home singly.

Only one plane in our squadron made it all the way home nonstop. The group had spent nearly two hours visiting so many targets in Borneo that most of the bombers ran low on fuel. Five of the six in our squadron had to land at Zamboanga to refuel before going home. *Again, Little Judith Anne failed to get us home nonstop! That's three times out of three!* This time there was no rain at Zamboanga, and no one slipped off the runway.

When we landed on our home base at 7:12 P.M., we had flown more than fourteen hours. Finally, we had delivered our load to one of the assigned targets. *I hope it was worth the effort.*

Instead of sleeping late the next morning, I woke up in time for breakfast. Cordell and James were still sacked out, but Seitz was dressing already.

"You're up mighty early for a pilot who flew fourteen hours yesterday," I said.

He put on his shirt. "Iowa farmers wake up at the crack of dawn come hell or high water."

"Wait a minute—I'll go to breakfast with you."

A few minutes later we sat down on the officers' side of the mess hall to eat "scrambled eggs" made from water and powdered eggs, overdone toast that seemed to use sawdust for flour, and strong coffee with loose grounds and a kick like battery acid—a normal jungle meal. The mess hall seemed deathly quiet—the usual buzz of conversation and laughter was missing.

"Why are we all so quiet today?" I asked, looking around.

"This place is like a tomb!" Seitz said.

Seated across from us, Captain Rice looked at Lieutenant Grissom. "Didn't you hear about the crash?" Grissom asked.

"What crash?" asked Seitz.

"We lost another plane on today's mission to Balikpapen."

"Damn!" I said. "Another night crash on take-off?"

"Yeah," said Rice, "it was number 813, 'Big Iron Bird,' but this time the iron bird didn't fly so good."

"I flew that plane last month," Seitz said. "It flew fine."

"It's not the plane, it's the pilot. This was a new crew."

"Which new crew?" I asked, suddenly worried.

"The pilot was Lieutenant Schulz."

"Oh, no!" I moaned. I felt a heavy weight in my chest.

Seitz turned and looked at me. "Are you all right?"

I could hardly talk. "His navigator—Lieutenant Bodkin—was my good friend—in navigation school."

Seitz looked sympathetic. "Oh, man! That is so sad!" Then turned to the men across the table. "Were there any survivors?"

"Yes, one—the copilot, Lieutenant Aneloski. He was thrown through the windshield into the water. He was badly injured, but the crash boat found him floating in his inflated life vest."

I found my voice again. "How many were on the plane?"

"Nine, of course. The other eight crew members aboard all bought the farm."

"Do you remember the navigator's name? —Was it—Lieutenant Bodkin?" My heart stopped beating for a moment.

"Yeah—Bodkin—that was it for sure."

My heart started beating again, harder than ever. My whole body felt flushed with hot blood and hot anger that turned into rage. Rage against God. *God! How could you do such a horrible thing? Both of my buddies! One right after the other! Shit-fire-damnation!*

Suddenly the mess hall was unbearably hot. I was dripping with sweat from head to toe.

"I've got to get out of here!" I said.

I left my mess kit on the table and went straight out the door. The fresh air felt good. I paused and drew in several deep breaths.

What was it Clyde said last week? "The war's not over yet, you know. I could crash next week, and you could crash the week after." *Shit! The Three Musketeers are going down fast!*

20. Skeletons

I wandered around in a daze after leaving the mess hall, half blinded by rage. I was angry with everything around me. *I'm sick of the damn war—the killing—the army—the lousy food— the hell-fire heat! I'm mad at the damn Japs for starting this damn Pacific war! And God—I'm angry with you! Why the hell did you let my two best friends die?*

Seitz emerged from the mess hall and came over to join me. He carried two mess kits, freshly washed.

"You left your mess kit," he said. "Thought I'd take it home, in case you ever want to eat again." Sunlight lit up the smile on his face.

"Thanks." My thoughts snapped back to earth.

"Sorry your buddy was killed today."

"I don't need sympathy!—But—thanks for caring."

"Your second big loss in a week, isn't it?"

"Yes, dammit! In navigation school, we called ourselves the 'Three Musketeers.' Now I'm the only one left. Who knows how long I'll be around?"

"Don't hand me that stuff, Hamilton. You'll live to see your grandchildren!"

"How do I apply for transfer to another branch of service?"

"Transfer? What for? You want to quit flying?"

"No, but I'm really pissed! I want to make big changes!"

"I was in the Infantry, son, and transferred to the Air Corps. Believe me, this is a better life—lot more satisfying!"

"I wasn't thinking of Infantry," I said. "I'd like to transfer to Army Intelligence for service in China."

"Intelligence? In China? That'd be a double change!"

"Well, I was born in China, and I speak Chinese fluently. If Army Intelligence requires any intelligence, I have lots of that!" *(And I wouldn't have to kill people if I switch to Intelligence!)*

"If you're really serious, go to the orderly room—fill out a request for transfer. It'll come to me for approval or comment, as your immediate superior. Then it goes up through channels. But I won't approve it—I'll comment that you're needed where you are. You're a damn good navigator, Hamilton! I don't want to lose you for some new replacement! After all we've been through together, we really ought to stay together!"

"Right on all counts. But I still want to submit the application. Intelligence work wouldn't involve me in killing people. If transfer orders come through, my conscience will be less troubled. If not, I'll continue to fly with you. Either way, I'll do my duty in the war."

"Meanwhile, nothing changes—you're still my navigator!"

"Right!" He put out his hand. We shook. I felt better.

I went to the orderly room, where cheerful Sergeant Peterson helped me fill out the application. Captain Pidgeon, the Adjutant, studied the form suspiciously, and turned to stare at me with his dark, beady eyes behind steel-rimmed glasses. *(He looks like he ought to wear a black SS uniform and swastika!)*

"Intelligence? In China?" His small black mustache twitched.

"Yes, sir!" *(He makes me sick every payday! I have to salute this Nazi-head every time the eagle shits!)*

After leaving the orderly room, I ran into my tail gunner.

"Lieutenant Hamilton, sir!" Hill saluted.

"Corporal Hill, I presume," I said, returning his salute.

"Hell, no! Look at my sleeve!" He pointed to the new triple chevron above his elbow.

"Well, SERGEANT Hill! Pardon me! When did this happen?"

"Last night. Our whole crew found promotion orders waiting for us when we got back from the mission! All six of us went to the E.M. Club last night to celebrate! We all got drunk!"

"So you're all sergeants now! Congratulations, Hill! You're a good man!" I gave him a clap on the back.

"Thanks, Hamilton. It feels so good to be a sergeant!" Hill left with a beaming smile.

Maybe the world's not completely bad today, after all.

The next day, June 18, my crew flew another bombing mission to Balikpapen. We were in B-24 number 593, "My Irish Colleen," a veteran of over 100 missions and more than 1,000 hours flight time.

This was the thirteenth mission for pilot, copilot and navigator; the rest of the crew lagged one or more missions behind. Some of our crew members talked about "unlucky thirteen."

"Ain't it unlucky to fly a war-weary plane like this on the thirteenth mission?" Williams asked as we waited in the darkness to climb aboard. "The old bird might fall apart from old age."

"On the other hand," said Herrema, "after she's returned from a hundred missions, surely she'll come back again out of habit."

"Look at the nose art," said Hill. The distant floodlight lit up the name "My Irish Colleen" painted above a lovely naked red-head sitting on a large green clover leaf. "That big clover leaf's good luck will offset any bad luck from 'unlucky thirteen.'"

"What we call 'luck' is simply God's will," I said. "May He bless this thirteenth mission."

"We make our own luck," Seitz said. "Do your job well, and your luck will be good."

At 3:58 A.M., I stood on the flight deck behind the pilots watching us roar down the dark runway for another overloaded night take-off. Seconds after lifting off, I thought I saw a face in the blackness outside the windshield. *It's Bob! Good Lord! Here's where he went down!* Then he vanished. I felt goose bumps on the back of my neck. *Damn! Am I cracking up?*

Half a minute later, I saw another face. *It's Clyde! Here's where it happened to him!* A wave of fear brought cold sweat to my face.

Glad I'm not the pilot right now! I'd be too shaken to fly! I blinked hard and looked outside again. *Nothing out there but utter darkness.*

For the next five hours, we flew through nasty weather, pelted by rain squalls, sleet and occasional hail. Turbulence gave us a bumpy ride, with thunderheads all around us, overcast above and undercast clouds below.

The forecast called for similar clouds over target, but this time we had new technology to beat it. Our lead plane was radar-equipped for the first time. When our formation assembled near the target today, Major "Pat" Patterson (my Squadron C.O.) would lead the Group. His plane had a radar operator and H2X radar equipment designed to bomb through the clouds below.

I can't wait to see how well it works!

At 9:10 A.M. we had almost reached the coast of Borneo. Seitz' voice came on the interphone.

"Pilot to Crew, we just lost our lead plane. 618 had a major electrical failure—so Major Patterson turned back to head home. He told Captain Boggess to take over Group lead."

"Navigator to Pilot, there goes the H2X equipment, dammit! No chance to bomb through the clouds today!"

"Bombardier to Pilot, that's pitiful bad luck! Back to the old bombsight. Why can't things go right for a change?"

"Pilot to Bombardier, it's our thirteenth mission!"

Five minutes later we reached the east coast of Borneo at the assembly point. The clouds there were thick. *No luck on the weather here.*

"Pilot to Crew, Group Lead just called all planes to head for Cape Bajor and assemble there. Too many clouds here. Navigator, give me a heading and E.T.A. for Cape Bajor."

"Navigator to Pilot, heading 225 degrees. Cape Bajor is 250 miles closer to Balikpapen; E.T.A.—let's see—ten thirty-five."

At Cape Bajor, it took 25 minutes for our group to assemble. The formation then flew to the primary target at Balikpapen. The layer of clouds below us covered the target completely, but Captain Boggess led the Group on a bombing run anyway, at 11:06. *Maybe his bombardier'll get lucky and see the target. I sure hope so!* But it was a dry run—all our bombs stayed on board.

"Able Lead to Magpie, over," Captain Boggess' voice came through the radio.

"Magpie to Able Lead, go ahead," Strike Control replied.

"Primary target fully obscured. Request permission to bomb secondary, over."

"Able Lead, permission granted. Magpie out."

The Bomber Barons followed Captain Boggess to the secondary target, Manggar Airfield north of Balikpapen, for another unsuccessful bomb run at 11:25.

"Another dry run, dammit!" James shouted to me.

"It's our thirteenth mission!" I yelled back.

The clouds below seemed to be breaking up, however, so Boggess had us circle for a while at 13,000 feet until he could see the target. Then we made another bomb run, this time with success.

"Bombs away!" James called. We both watched fifteen glowing lights on his panel go out one by one as each bomb fell. I checked my watch—11:57—to record the time in my log.

James' voice came through my earphones, "Bombardier to Camera, did you get strike photos? Over."

"Camera to Bombardier, affirmative, over," said Imhof, in the waist.

"How'd it look from up here? Over."

"Looked like most of 'em fell in the target area. Good work! Over."

"Imhof, you just made my day! I could hug you! Over."

"Just call me 'SERGEANT'! That'll make my day! Over."

"Okay—cheers for SERGEANT Imhof! Out."

Later we heard that our bombing was rated "excellent"—the strike photos showed sixty percent of the bombs fell within the target area and the rest within 500 feet of it.

The formation stayed together for the brief flight back to Cape

Bajor, where we peeled off to fly home separately. The return trip took us through the same nasty weather we had flown through earlier. *No joy ride today—this is work!* My duties distracted me from thinking about my two dead friends, but the emptiness I felt added to the fatigue of a long mission.

"My Irish Colleen" landed at 4:58 p.m.—exactly thirteen hours, to the minute, from the time she took off.

"Now hear this," I told the other guys as we rode away from the bomber in a crew truck. "On our thirteenth mission, we flew exactly thirteen hours with the Thirteenth Air Force, and dropped our bombs from 13,000 feet."

"That's 'unlucky thirteen' four times over," Herrema said.

"But we made it back," said Pieper, "so good luck came our way in spite of 'unlucky 13'!"

"It was that big green clover leaf on the nose," Hill said. "That was big-time good luck!"

"Lucky for us, today was Monday the eighteenth, instead of Friday the Thirteenth," said James.

"Let's get one thing straight, men," Seitz said slowly, with emphasis. "We make our own luck on every flight! Today we did everything right—so of course we came back okay! Just keep up the good work, and we'll have many happy returns."

Two days later, June 20, our crew flew to Borneo again on our fourteenth bombing mission. We had all cheered at briefing when we heard that take-off would be after sunrise. Now our turn came at 7:32 a.m., when we pointed the nose of number 209, "Miss Behavin'," down runway 07 on Samar and roared off into the morning sunlight. *No ghosts rise from the water by daylight! What a relief!*

This mission was different in another aspect, too—the Bomber Barons went back to our old custom of assembling squadron and group formations over home base, and flying in formation all the way to the target and back. However, since we had to fly in and out of clouds on the way, the formation was spread out loosely until we reached Borneo. But flying in formation meant that my navigation consisted of plotting where "Miss Behavin'" was led, instead of directing the pilot.

"Dog Four to Dog Lead, over," the radio spoke at 9:50.

"Dog Lead reads you, go ahead," Captain Boggess' voice replied.

"Dog Four requests permission to abort and return to base. Just feathered number two engine—had a pesky oil leak for the last hour—finally lost all pressure."

"Permission granted. Drop your bombs over water, on safety. Dog Lead out."

For the next three hours, we kept punching through clouds in a loose formation until we reached the east coast of Borneo. At Cape Mang-kalihat we spent twelve minutes circling to tighten the Group Combat Box formation, then all four squadrons flew together to Balikpapen above the clouds at 11,000 feet.

Our primary target was a battery of anti-aircraft guns near Balikpapen. They were shooting at us while we were bombing them. It took them a while to find our position in the sky; then their aim improved with each squadron that passed over. But the number of guns shooting decreased as our bombs blasted some of them out of action.

Each squadron bombed separately on the aiming of its lead bombardier. Able, Baker, and Charlie Squadrons bombed in sequence ahead of us. On our Dog bomb run, dust and smoke from their bombs covered much of the target, and shifting clouds below us covered the rest. We plowed through the flak bursts for nothing.

"Lead Dog to all Dogs, hold your bombs. We're going around again." Captain Boggess led our squadron back to the I.P.

On our second bomb run, the dust had settled and the clouds shifted enough for us to see the target. But the target could see us too, and the flak became more accurate. Black puffs exploded all around us. James knelt in the nose, eyes on the lead plane.

"Bombs away!" said James. In rapid sequence, our fifteen bombs were released in only three seconds. The plane surged upward, as always at bomb release, since it suddenly became that much lighter. At that moment, a flak shell burst where we had been just before the uplift. It would have blown us out of the sky, but now we were sixty feet higher than before, so it only punched holes in the aluminum skin. *Bang!* My steel helmet clanged as if hit by a hammer. At the same time—*thud!* Another hammer-blow struck me in the side.

I was numb from the shock of those two blows for a few seconds. When I recovered, I cautiously felt my head and my side. One of the shell fragments had made a dent in my helmet over the left ear, while another one lodged in the webbing of my flak jacket. *Thank you, Lord, for a guardian angel! I guess it's not yet time for the Third Musketeer to go!*

The trip home was uneventful, but fatiguing. For six long hours, I plotted our return track on the chart, showing where "Miss Behavin'" had been led. I was ready to direct the pilot anytime she might misbehave enough to drop out of the formation, but that didn't happen. Her behavior was as beautiful as the naked figure painted on her nose.

Only occasionally did I think about the recent deaths of my friends, but a gut-level grieving sapped some of my energy like a slow, on-going draining of a reservoir. When I thought of my own narrow escape over the target, fear, relief, and gratitude mingled with shock and anger over their deaths. I felt more weary than ever before. We finally reached our home base and landed at 8:36 p.m.— total flying time thirteen hours four minutes. I felt as tired as an old bear yawning for his long winter sleep.

Mail call next day brought me a V-mail letter from Pauline Bowles, my girl friend in Galesburg, Illinois. Seeing her name and return address took my memories back two years, to June 1943, when I arrived at Knox College in Galesburg as a student cadet in the army unit set up in Seymore Hall. I met Pauline and her sister, June, at the welcome dance given by the city for the new class of cadets. The girls invited me to come to their house for Sunday dinner next day.

I wrote about the Bowles family in a letter to my Dad from Knox College, September 3, 1943: "This would have been simply another military station, with all its secret loneliness, if it were not for what the Bowles family has done. They took me out to spend the day on Sundays time after time, so that I came to regard it as a natural part of my life. Theirs was my home. Eating Sunday dinners and suppers with them—having fun with June and Pauline in the afternoons, going for rides out to Lake Storey, or playing badminton in their backyard—chatting with their mom and pop in the evening—just being away from the post as I would sit on their porch in the gathering dusk—all these things meant worlds to me. It almost took away the feeling of being away from home. . . . I'll always have the memory of a family who felt that they were doing to one soldier boy what they hoped someone will do for their sons. One, Paul Bowles, is a chief petty officer aviation machinist mate in the navy. . . . The other, Elvin Bowles, is in the army, in Michigan . . . Paul is twenty, and Pauline is his twin sister. . ."

Pauline was a pretty, petite brunette with black curly hair, big dark eyes, a small, turned-up nose, and a perky, upbeat personality. Her smile always lifted my spirits. At twenty, she was two years older than I, which had seemed like an important difference then.

June was Pauline's opposite in many ways—a tall, big-boned blonde with hazy blue eyes and a moody, downbeat personality. She was younger—seventeen—but her ample figure was fully developed. June had a crush on me that was hard to resist—never before had I been pursued by a girl. She taught me how to "neck"— she was the first girl I had ever kissed with passion. Two months passed before I realized we were incompatible. *In June it was June, but in August it was no longer June.*

So I broke up with June, and went back to being "just a friend" to both sisters. But when I left Galesburg, only Pauline wrote to me. She said that June got another crush on a later cadet, who led her on and then broke her heart thoroughly. Pauline and I had written to each other for nearly two years now, and our friendship had grown deeper and more meaningful.

"Dear Bob," she wrote today, "I'm glad you got your wish to go to a front-line unit and 'fly with the big boys,' but it scares me to think of the constant danger you must be exposed to. Please write me frequently—it gives me so much joy to know that you're still alive and kicking!

"Galesburg is a pretty dead town now, since the army unit at Knox College was shut down. They said that no more flyers are needed now, since the war's supposed to be winding down. That's *not* what Paul writes me from the navy. He says that the worst fighting of all is still ahead—the invasion of Japan! He thinks it'll take another year of hard fighting there before it ends.

"Paul wrote that he would like to enroll in Knox College after the war. How about you, Bob? Wouldn't you like to do that too? I'm sure you could transfer your credits from Davidson. You and Paul could be roommates! I'd love to have my favorite man room with my twin brother! And I'd love to make you feel so very, VERY welcome—you'd never want to go anywhere else!

"Take care of yourself, my sweet flyboy! Love, Pauline."

Pauline, you really boost my morale! Just the thought of your very, VERY warm welcome makes me feel hot all over! Maybe I'll consider transferring to Knox—I did enjoy classes there, and the Bowles family sure did make me feel at home. Maybe I'll even marry Pauline, after a while. The fact that she's two years older makes less difference, the older I get. But on the other hand, I like Davidson too much. And my own Dad wrote "O Davidson" (the college "fight" song) when he was a student there in 1917. No, my roots are too deep—I gotta go back to Davidson.

The next day—Friday, June 22—my crew flew another trip to the Balikpapen area, my fifteenth combat mission. During the latter half of June, the Bomber Barons flew there every day.

We were up long before daylight, as the Fifth Bomb Group went back to night take-offs and separate flights to a rendezvous near target. This time we had number 956, "Raggedy Andy," an old B-24-J with well over 100 missions and 1,000 hours flight time. Rumor had it that "Raggedy Andy" and other old planes would soon be declared "war-weary" and sent to the aircraft graveyard at Biak, replaced by brand new B-24s from the states.

We met the crew chief, Tech Sergeant Bill Maddox, in the darkness of the flight line while we loaded our gear.

"What's this rumor about you running a war-weary airplane?" Cordell asked the crew chief.

"This bird works fine," said Sergeant Maddox. "I'm the war-weary one—been out here thirty-two months. The army ought to declare *me* 'war-weary' and send *me* home, and leave this bird on the flight line. It's got some more good hours left in it yet."

We were the last in our squadron to take off. At 5:35 A.M. "Raggedy Andy" roared along the dimly-lit runway into the dark night sky beyond the end of the island. I tried to control my fear of flying that close to the waves for the whole long minute that we had to skim them. The Twenty-Third Psalm seemed to help. *The Lord is my Shepherd . . . though I fly through the valley of the shadow of death, I will fear no evil . . .*

The weather on the way to the east coast of Borneo was as bad as usual, making my navigation difficult. After four and a half hours, we emerged from the clouds at 9,000 feet near Cape Mangkalihat to assemble our squadrons and group. Our 394th Squadron led the group, with Major Patterson flying the lead airplane. Seitz eased "Raggedy Andy" into the sixth place, at right rear. Suddenly the plane ahead and to our left rolled to the right, crossing in front of us, and dove down out of sight.

"Nose Gunner to Pilot, did you see that? He damn near hit us!" Williams' voice shrilled on the interphone.

"Sure did, Nose. Where'd he go? Over."

"Down and out of sight, over."

"Ball Gunner to Pilot, I can see him from my belly bowl. He's in a twisting dive or spin, going down fast! Over."

"What the hell happened?" James asked on interphone.

"Must've lost control," Cordell's voice replied.

"Pilot to Ball Gunner, can you see him now? Over."

"Negative—just disappeared into the clouds below. Out."

Seitz switched to the radio. "Able Six to Able Lead, over."

"Able Lead to Able Six, go ahead," Major Patterson's voice replied.

"Did you know that Able Four just went down in a spin? Over."

"Are you kidding? What happened? Over."

"He rolled to the right—crossed over in front of us—and plunged down in a twisting dive. Like he lost control, over."

"Can you see him now? Over."

"Negative, he went into the clouds below, over."

"Able Lead to Able Four, can you read me? Over. Able Four, can you read me? Over."

A few minutes of suspenseful silence followed. *Did he go all the way down and crash? Why no reply, if he's still alive?*

"Able Four to Able Lead, over." It was the missing plane, Lieutenant Johnson in 673.

"Go ahead, Able Four. Where are you? Over."

"In the clouds below you, at 4,000 feet, running on three engines. Took us a while to regain control and shut down the faulty systems. Over."

"What happened, Able Four? Over."

"Number one prop ran away—prop governor amplifier failed. The power surge from number one rolled us right. At the same time we lost the power boost on all flight controls. It took all the strength of both pilots to wrestle this wild bird tame. We lost 5,000 feet in the plunge, over."

"Able Four, what's your current status? Are you okay? Over."

"Able Four currently stable. Request permission to return to base by way of Sanga Sanga, Jolo Island, and Zamboanga. That'll give us emergency landing strips if we need 'em, over."

"Permission granted, Able Four. Drop your bombs over water on safety, and proceed to base. Able Lead out."

The group formation continued to fly southwest for another hour and a half to Balikpapen, where the weather had cleared up since my last trip two days ago. We could actually see the ground! The whole massive refinery area lay in ruins from earlier bombings—twisted pipes and burned-out tanks. The group separated into squadrons for the bomb run.

"Able Leader to Pirate Special, do you read me? Over."

"Pirate Special here, read you loud and clear, mate," said a very Australian accent.

"Able Squadron ready to unload. Please confirm target, over."

"Target confirmed as briefed—target number twenty-four, ack-ack guns and personnel area. Good hunting, lads! Pirate Special out."

Major Patterson led Able Squadron to the I.P. and onto the bomb run, which lasted only 50 seconds, thanks to the good visibility. Black puffs appeared near us—flak had started.

"Bombs away!" James shouted on the interphone. We both watched thirty glowing lights on his panel go out one by one.

"Bombs away at 12:12 from 11,400 feet," I wrote in my navigator log. Able Squadron flew back to Cape Mang-kalihat, where we peeled off to fly home separately.

Our crew members started to chatter on the interphone.

"Engineer to Pilot, this is my third mission in a row where our squadron lost a plane before we got there," said Pieper. "I'm tired of seeing only five planes bombing where six ought to be!"

"Bombardier to Pilot, that pisses me off, too! Over."

"Copilot to Bombardier, if you need to piss, use the relief tube in the nose, over."

"Shut up, Cordell!" said James.

"Pilot to Crew, enough idle chatter. Get back to work!"

The flight home was uneventful, but long and tiring, since most of it was through bumpy weather. We finally left the clouds behind when we passed the end of Mindanao. We were just in time to see an orange-red sun drop behind the dark green mountains of Leyte, off our left wing, as we descended over the deep blue Gulf of Leyte. Raggedy Andy landed in twilight at 6:17 P.M., total flight time twelve hours forty-two minutes.

As we rode away from the flight line in the crew truck, we were in a reflective mood. Cigarettes glowed all around.

"After so many missions to the same place, you'd think that they'd all be alike," I said, lighting my pipe.

"But they're not," said Imhof. "Each one is different."

"Yeah—different in some new hair-raising way!" James added.

"Like that near miss we had today in formation," Seitz said.

"Darn near had a mid-air collision!" said Pieper.

"Could of wiped us all out!" Cordell said, crushing a butt.

"We were lucky today," said Hill, as he blew a smoke ring.

"Our guardian angel was working overtime," I said.

That night I skipped the outdoor movie and went straight to bed after supper. My cot had a blanket, pillow, and mosquito net. (I never saw a sheet or pillowcase in my whole tour overseas.) I slept like a dead man until three A.M., when I woke up to pain—throbbing pain—in my right hand. It was hanging down over the edge of the cot, out of the protective cocoon of the mosquito net. I rolled over, sat up in the dark, flicked a flame on a lighter to look at my right hand. It had blown up like a balloon.

Damn! What could do THAT to my hand? I've got to get to the doctor!

Naked except for shorts, I stumbled up the hill to the tent of Captain "Doc" Dolce.

"Doc!—Doc!—wake up, Doc!" I said. "Look at my hand."

A groggy doctor shook his head, got up, turned on the light. "Let's see what you got here, son. Hmmm—really swollen! Does it hurt much when I poke it?" He jabbed it with a rigid finger.

"OW!" I yelled. "Hurts like red-hot needles!"

"Yep, you got bit by a giant bug—either a scorpion or a centipede. Both of 'em grow to nearly a foot long in the tropics. Your hand is full of poison—that's what made it swell up so."

"Do you have a treatment for it? A shot or a pill?"

"Nope, they haven't yet invented any treatment for it. All I can do is give you a shot of morphine to help you sleep it off."

"Sock it to me, Doc! Anything to take away the pain!"

I woke up twelve hours later, in mid-afternoon, alone in my tent. The pain was gone, but my hand was still very swollen. I sat up and started to dress. I picked up a shoe, about to put my foot into it, when I saw something shiny inside. *What's this?* There in the bottom of my G.I.. boot was a giant centipede, a foot long, as thick as my finger, shiny, gun-metal blue! *Good Lord!*

I carried the shoe outside to a big flat rock, and poured it out onto the hard surface. Then I used the shoe as a hammer, and struck the bug repeatedly, smashing it to a pulp. *Take that, and that, and that, and THAT, you sonovabitch!*

Not yet content with the vengeance I had wrought, I brought some lighter fluid from the tent, and poured it over the remains. Striking a light to the fluid, I watched the flames cremate what was left of my midnight attacker. *Ah, sweet revenge!*

At the mess hall for supper, I learned of another accident on take-off early this morning. Lieutenant Taylor, in number 330, bounced hard on his nose wheel during take-off, and his whole nose wheel assembly broke off and fell out as he lifted off.

"What did he do about it?" I asked.

"He flew around nearby for hours, burning away his fuel load. The tower told him to dump his bombs and his bomb bay fuel tank, and shift all movable equipment and crew members to the tail, to make the plane tail-heavy. Then he landed on the main wheels, nose high, and rolled along scraping the tail skid."

"The nose never came down at all," said another, "until all the crew climbed out, and they pulled the nose down with a jeep."

"Quite a show!" I said. "You can skip the movie tonight."

The following day, I took my swollen right hand to the enlisted men's tent area, to look at my boat-building project again. I had not been there since the Three Musketeers worked on it together, before Bob Comfort's crash two weeks ago. There it was, stored under the high floor, just as the three of us had left it.

As I looked it over, I felt pride in the beauty and simplicity of the design—my design. *Look at that structure—simple, strong, logical. Look at that curving shape—it's beautiful!*

All it needed to be completed was to be covered with canvas or aircraft fabric, and painted three or four coats. A few more days of work would finish it. But then, as I looked at it, I was haunted by the presence of my two dead friends. In my mind, I could see tall, gangly Bob, and short, stout, cheerful Clyde, every time I looked at the open woodwork of the boat. Their presence filled me with a yearning for their real company, and made me realize afresh the pain of their loss, and the emptiness I felt without them.

I'll never work on this boat again—I can't stand the pain it brings me! No, it's better to let this skeleton of a boat stay buried here under this tent floor, like their skeletons buried in the military cemetary at nearby Tanuan. This boat skeleton is my monument to the memory of two very special men who meant so much to me.

"Cordell, here's a peso," I said. "I'm paying off my bet. You were right. I didn't finish the boat by the end of June."

"But there's another week to the end of June," Cordell said.

"True, but irrelevant. I changed my mind. I decided to leave the boat unfinished."

"After all the work you and your buddies put into it?"

"Exactly. It reminds me too much of what I need to forget."

Cordell looked at me intently.

Can he see the pain behind my attempt to be cool?

Then his eyes softened. He took my peso gently. I felt close to him for the first time.

21. Dead Drunk

"The question isn't 'where?'—it's 'when?'" said Herrema.

Behind me in the chow line, Hill spoke, "Yeah—for two weeks now the Bomber Barons've hit the Balikpapen area every day."

"It must be building up to something big," Pieper added.

"Two earlier bombing campaigns led to invasions of Borneo," I said, "first at Tarakan, then Brunei Bay—remember?"

"Yeah," Hill said, "Balikpapen's gotta be next to see ground troops come in."

Next day, June 28, our crew's sixth trip to Balikpapen started at three A.M. with another overloaded night take-off. Its terrifying effect had gradually diminished, but it still reminded me how I lost both my friends. Each plane flew separately through rough weather to the assembly point on the Borneo coast. There, twenty-four bombers wheeled gracefully into squadron and group formations and headed for the target, Klandasan Beach, directly south of Balikpapen.

When we got there, it was covered with clouds, so the group headed for the secondary target, Manggar Beach twelve miles east.

We were briefed to fly east along the beach to destroy the enemy defenses against invasion. But the morning sun lit up the thick ocean haze, making the target area hard to see. After two unsuccessful bomb runs flying toward the sun as briefed, Captain Davenport tried something new. He led our squadron on a third bomb run in the opposite direction. That greatly improved our visibility, and we dropped long strings of bombs on the Japanese defenses at 9:32 A.M.

American ingenuity triumphs again!

We saw no enemy fighters or flak; only the weather opposed

us. Flying home through the same heavy storms, we landed in late afternoon. Total flying time was nearly thirteen hours. As navigator, I was the only crew member who had to work all the time. (Pilots trade off for naps.) Fatigued and nervous, I was very ready for that shot of whiskey Doc Dolce gave each of us after landing. It was my sixteenth combat mission.

At supper we learned of a great beer and cigarette issue at the P.X. The supply of both those luxuries had been low for weeks; minimal rations were sold. Today, however, a supply ship arrived with generous quantities; our good Colonel Haviland approved a bonanza issue of three cartons of cigarettes and a full case of 24 beers for each man. Cheers and rejoicing greeted the news. I smoked only a pipe, but bought some cigarettes to trade with the natives for souvenirs. (Anything the army issued us became barter material for someone.)

"Did you hear about the plan for double staging?" Seitz asked at lunch next day.

I lowered my fork into the mess I was eating. "What do you mean—double staging?"

Seitz put on his fatherly expression. "The Bomber Barons have sent two squadrons to Palawan several times, to stay for a few days while bombing Borneo. This time, they'll send two to Palawan, but they'll also send the other two squadrons to Morotai, to stage out of there."

"So the whole Fifth Bomb Group will be out staging at the same time," James said. "Why?"

Cordell took a swallow of coffee. "Bet it's for the invasion of Balikpapen."

"Bingo!" said Seitz. "While we're flying out of Palawan to bomb Borneo, the other guys'll fly out of Morotai to bomb the airfields on Celebes."

"Why Celebes?" Cordell asked.

"Celebes is the next big island east of Balikpapen," I said. "Jap warplanes on Celebes would have only a short flight to attack our invasion fleet near Balikpapen."

James took a big bite, and asked through a full mouth, "When does this double staging begin?"

Seitz sipped his coffee. "Tomorrow, big boy. Our crew is part of the strike."

Next day, June 30, the Fifth Bomb Group divided into two task forces. Colonel Haviland, our "gung ho" Group Commander, led the 23rd and 31st Squadrons on a long strike to Japanese airfields on Celebes, returning to Morotai. At the same time, Lieutenant Colonel Wahlstrom, Group Operations Officer, led the 72nd and 394th Squadrons on a twelve-hour strike to Balikpapen, with a return to Palawan.

Behind the Colonel, Captain Davenport led our 394th Squadron with Seitz' crew. Our primary target was Klandasan Beach again; this time the scattered cloud cover allowed us to see it. We entered the bomb run flying southwest, away from the sun. *Hey, they did learn something from the previous mission!* Each plane had fifteen bombs, which we dropped in a long string on the Japanese defenses along the inner edge of the beach. Barbed wire, sandbags, artillery and machine-gun nests were all blown to bits.

Making the breakaway turn to the left, we saw the invasion fleet gathering in the distance offshore—dark ships silhouetted against the morning sunlight shimmering on the water. Their presence told us that the landing was imminent. I thought of the Australian soldiers on those ships—how the tension must be mounting as they prepared to invade! *Those guys need this beach cleared out before they land! Glad we could help.*

When we landed at Palawan, the mission had taken nearly twelve hours. Waiting for us were the crew chiefs and mechanics for each plane, ferried directly to Palawan by Lieutenants Wildey and Taylor in two more B-24s.

Palawan was familiar to my crew because of our overnight visit six weeks earlier when we had lost an engine over Borneo. This time, however, there would be no opportunity to repeat my one-man dinghy tour of Puerta Princesa Bay. We had to fly every day and be briefed every night, so there was no free time at all.

VIEW FROM COPILOT'S WINDOW
Lead B-24 seen through the curved side window of the number three plane in formation (number two is on the right of lead plane).

Next morning, July first, was D-Day for the Balikpapen invasion. To support it, our assignment was to bomb Japanese airfields on the far southwest tip of Borneo, near Singkawang and Kuching. For the next four days, July 1-4, our two squadrons on Palawan flew a ten-hour mission every day. We took off "by the dawn's early light" to bomb runways with no fighter opposition and little flak, then return by late afternoon. These were all "milk runs"—even the weather was nearly perfect, for a change.

I discovered that combat missions could be boring if nothing unexpected happened. The only tension was knowing that something might go wrong at any time, with possibly disastrous results. When nothing much went wrong on our next four missions, I was grateful to be bored.

The July fourth missions completed the Fifth Bomb Group's staging projects at both Palawan and Morotai. No strikes were planned for our bombers the next day—instead, all four squadrons would return to Samar. No briefing tonight—we were free to celebrate the Fourth of July by attending the outdoor movies for the first time since we arrived.

Many of the Palawan personnel celebrated the Fourth with drinking parties. The visitors couldn't, since our beer was back on Samar. "When we fly home tomorrow," we told each other, "we'll throw a proper celebration with that big beer ration."

After supper our crew joined several hundred other men sitting on coconut palm logs arranged in quarter-circle rows before a stage with a large plywood screen painted silver. The "Palm Tree Palace" was cut out of what had been a thriving coconut palm plantation before the war. (The palm tree plantation on Palawan was owned by Lever Brothers, makers of Palmolive Soap. The U.S. treasury had to pay that corporation fifty dollars for every palm tree cut down to make room for this air base.)

The movie was a second-rate western horse opera, in black and white of course, but it was the only show in town. Swarms of mosquitoes were feeding on the assembled bare flesh of the theater crowd; I slapped several on my neck and arms. They didn't worry us much—we took atabrine pills daily to ward off malaria. But one of those suckers had a good feed on my right hand. When the film ended, I noticed that my hand was throbbing with dull pain. I raised it up to see—*Wow! It's blown up like a balloon!* My hand had swollen again like it had done after the big centipede bite eleven days earlier.

"Holy smoke! Look at my hand!" I said.

James looked puzzled. "What happened? Get another centipede bite?"

"Hell no! My hand was in my lap the whole time!"

"Whatever it was, it sure looks bad," Cordell said.

"Better take it to the medics," Seitz said. "Hope it won't keep you from navigating tomorrow."

I found my way to the local flight surgeon, and told him about my earlier bite. "But this wasn't a centipede! This time it was only a mosquito!"

He studied my hand carefully. "Hmmmm. Residual toxins. They take a long time to flush away. That centipede bite left a lot of toxin in the tissues of your hand, so the mild stimulus of a mosquito bite—in the same place—was enough to trigger this degree of swelling."

"It was swollen for a week last time."

"This recurrence won't last that long—maybe twelve hours, twenty-four at most."

"Good! Maybe I can use my hand tomorrow."

"If you're lucky."

I was lucky. When I got up for breakfast, my swollen hand had returned almost to normal size. Soon all the visiting crews took off for the three-hour flight back to Samar.

After mid-day chow time on Samar, we joined the rest of the squadron in making final plans for a party. It was an ideal time—the 394th Squadron had no mission assigned for the next two days, so there would be time enough for hangovers.

Enlisted men went to their new club to break out their beer rations and to send delegations out to scrounge ice from the Sea Bees or the Navy.

Officers put finishing touches on the new Quonset hut officers' club we had been building. Called "Top of the Rock," it was set on the edge of a cliff with a great view of the airstrip and the palm trees beyond. With the staging crews back, July 5 was declared official opening night.

Each officer brought in a few of his own beers to put on ice, and the house provided one mixed drink, "Pacific Cocktail"—canned grapefruit juice (from Captain Wellenbrock, Mess Officer) spiked with pure ethyl alcohol (from Captain Dolce, Flight Surgeon). There was plenty on hand to get all of us drunk if we wanted. I didn't want that—I had never been drunk in my life.

For this opening night, the club directors had hired the Bomber Baron Jazz Band, a five-man group led by Captain Herring, Group Weather Officer.

By a stroke of serendipity, a boatload of U.S. Navy nurses pulled into the harbor at Samar Naval Station on this very day. Captain Davenport and friends lost no time in dashing there in a jeep to invite them all to our party. A dozen or more nurses agreed to come from eight to eleven, to give them time to get back to the Naval Hospital before midnight. Davenport spread the news to other officers in the squadron that we could see some real, live, American girls up close. I was elated to hear it.

After supper there was an unusual amount of cold-water showering and shaving (we had no water heaters in the Pacific). Then, in fresh khaki shirts and trousers, we gathered at the "Top of the Rock" to admire our freshly-painted, new facilities, and await the arrival of the musicians and the ladies. I got a beer from the bar and sipped it as I strolled around the club.

The Quonset hut, shaped like half of a barrel lying on its side, was about twenty-four by eighty feet, nearly twelve feet high along the centerline. The wide entrance, with a pair of screen doors, was in the middle of the long side; the bar was to the left of it. Pictures of lightly-clad glamorous girls decorated the walls.

On both sides of the entrance, part of the curved metal sides had been lifted up like an awning, to provide a continuous window opening. Under those long, screen-covered windows, a row of square tables and chairs furnished each side, with a wide center aisle for dancing.

The tables and chairs were soon occupied by small groups of officers talking, drinking, laughing. Others stood at the bar or moved up and down the aisle, back-slapping and visiting.

Captain Herring and his musicians arrived soon and set up their places in the band space near the bar. After warming up with "Off We Go Into the Wild Blue Yonder," they settled down to "Stardust," "Moonlight Serenade," "Don't Fence Me In," and other contemporary favorites. Their jazz was really good—sweet music to our long-deprived ears. Herring played a hot trumpet, accompanied by a clarinet, trombone, guitar, and bass fiddle. *How did he get that big bass fiddle shipped to the Pacific war zone?*

The guitarist doubled as the vocalist. He sang "You'll Never Know," and the song took my mind back to my date with Persis. I remembered dancing to that song with her.

Finishing my beer, I returned to the bar for a "Pacific Cocktail." The bartender poured grapefruit juice from a can, alcohol from a medical bottle, threw in a little ice, and handed it to me. I swallowed a gulp, and nearly choked. *Wow! Strong tinny flavor!*

I saw Captain Dolce sitting alone at one of the tables, a half-smoked cigar in hand. I ambled over to him.

"Hi, Doc! Are you waiting for someone, or can I join you?"

His bushy brown mustache curled up in a smile. He waved me to the empty chair beside him.

"Have a seat. You can keep it warm 'til the nurses arrive."

"I'm trying your Pacific Cocktail for the first time. I'm not sure I like this strange new flavor yet— maybe it'll grow on me. Thanks for providing the alcohol, anyway!"

"Be careful how fast you drink that stuff—ethyl alcohol has no flavor, but it can get you looped in a hurry!" He lit his cigar again, drew in a deep draft of smoke, then exhaled slowly.

"You're sitting here by yourself, looking at people go by—"

"What am I doing? Waiting for the women, just like you!" He laughed a good belly-laugh. "Actually, I'm practising my profession. Flight surgeons are concerned with the mental health of their men as much as the physical. I'm looking for signs of stress—hypertension–combat fatigue. You see it more in relaxed settings like this than when the men are on duty."

"Really? What are the signs?"

"A man who can't relax—stares at his drink with jaw set—rigid expression—he's probably suffering from combat fatigue."

"What we call 'flak-happy'?"

"Sure! Why do you think I pour your after-mission shot of whiskey myself, instead of letting Sergeant Simpson or another medic do it for me?"

"I've wondered about that."

"I study the face of every crew member as he takes his whiskey. He's right off the plane after the mission—if he's dangerously overstressed, I'll see it."

"What happens when you find a case?"

"I ground him temporarily—pull him off flying status! We can't let unstable crew members endanger the next mission." He crushed his cigar butt into the ashtray as he spoke

Wow! I never realized he was studying us like that!

I reminded Doc of my centipede bite twelve days earlier, and told him how a mosquito bite on the same hand in Palawan had made it swell up all over again. He looked at my hand, now normal again, and confirmed the diagnosis of residual toxins causing the second swelling. I left him to return to the bar.

The Navy nurses appeared in the double screen doors of the entrance, wearing white summer uniforms with short sleeves and knee-length skirts. Suddenly the aisles were full of men eager to invite them to a table and bring them drinks. The ladies spread themselves around the room, one or two to a table, surrounded by male admirers who had drunk enough to lose their shyness. I was not one of them—I still felt shy, so I watched from the bar.

The musicians struck up "I'm Beginning to See the Light." It didn't take long for the aisle to fill with dancers—six or eight couples at a time. When the song ended, they sat down, and other men invited the girls to try the next dance—"Begin the Beguine." So it continued all evening. Most of the women were careful not to dance too often with any one man.

After watching all the others have fun for an hour, and sipping my way through another Pacific Cocktail, I worked up my courage and moved toward the dancers. *How can I get into the action myself?* But the chairs were taken at every table, so I couldn't sit down and begin small talk with a girl.

I've got it! Intercept a couple returning to a table after a dance—invite the lady to change partners before she sits down. This was a bold move for me, but I tried it, flashing my most winsome smile at the girl. It worked!

I found myself dancing with an attractive lady with brown hair, blue eyes, and a lovely scent of perfume. I asked her name ("Helen") and told her mine. In a moment we settled into the familiar rhythm of big-band swing, driven by its pulsating tempo and melody.

The song was "Chattanooga Choo Choo," which I knew well, so I sang the words in her ear as we danced. I don't know whether she liked my singing, but I enjoyed every moment of her dancing. I held her close, intoxicated by her heady perfume and the sensation of her soft breasts against my chest. Then I felt her thighs touching mine. That quickened my pulse rate; my heart-beat pounded over the beat of the music, throbbing in my temples. I was dancing passionately in another world—dancing with Persis at the Stone Cellar in Palo Alto again, remembering her sweet, soft body close to mine, transported to the clouds.

All too soon, the song ended, bringing me down to reality. I thanked Helen, and dutifully escorted her to her table.

Feeling light-headed and flushed with triumph, I looked for

someone to share it with. Seitz was at the bar; I grabbed a beer and joined him on a bench under the window.

"Did you see me, Seitz? I danced that last number with one of the nurses! It was marvellous! You ought to try it."

"I'm a married man, Hamilton—you know that."

"So is Captain Davenport, but he's certainly entertaining the ladies tonight."

"He has his life to live, and I have mine. I wouldn't feel comfortable dancing without Doris here. Besides, I don't feel like celebrating much, since I heard the news from the 23rd Squadron."

"What news?"

"Looks like we lost our Group Commander yesterday."

"Colonel Haviland? You're kidding! What happened?"

Seitz raised his bottle and took a long swallow of beer. "While we were at Palawan, he led the other two squadrons that staged out of Morotai—the 23rd and 31st—remember?"

"Of course. So—"

"Yesterday, the last day of staging, Colonel Haviland led his group against two airfields at the southwest tip of the island of Celebes. After the strike, they returned to Morotai by individual aircraft. But the lead plane never returned."

"You don't mean it! What happened to it?"

"Nobody knows. Didn't get shot down over target. Just disappeared on the way home."

"Any radio messages? Distress calls?"

"None. Colonel Haviland and nine other crew members are listed as missing in action."

"Damn! That makes me sick!"

I paused for a long swig of beer. "Which crew was lost?"

"First Lieutenant Gurman's crew, from the 23rd Squadron. Guess you know Gurman was one of their best lead pilots."

"Why does it happen to the best? Colonel Haviland was one of my heroes!"

Seitz gave me a mournful look. "I know he was."

We paused. I put down my beer. "Who's in command now?"

"Lieutenant Colonel James was Deputy Group Commander, so he took over as Acting Group Commander right away."

"Seitz, this news sure took the pop outta my party! Guess I'll just sit and sulk a while—maybe drink more'n I should."

> ### WHAT HAPPENED TO COLONEL HAVILAND?
>
> Twenty-five years later, in 1970, U.S. officials in Indonesia identified (by the crew's dog tags) the wreckage of that B-24 at the top of 11,000-foot Mt. Rantemario on Celebes, after it was found by a native woodcutter. The plane had flown into the mountain ridge with all four engines running strong.
>
> Why was he there? I did a lot of research to find the answer: While bombing the primary target south of Makassar, the lead plane had five bombs hung up. Instead of just jettisoning them on the safe route home, our "gung-ho" Colonel flew a hundred miles north to drop them on the secondary target (fifty miles west of Cape Siwa). Flying northeast from there, toward Morotai, would carry him over the highest mountains on Celebes, which were hidden in clouds. He was climbing, but not quite high enough to clear the ridge.

My mind drifted back to the day when Colonel Haviland had personally welcomed four new crews to the Fifth Bomb Group, assigning one to each of his four squadrons. He looked like a born leader—tall, well-built, with dark hair, handsome face, square jaw and prominent chin. His earnest face reminded me of a movie star.

But it was his personality, his infectious enthusiasm, his charisma, that made me like him instantly. My memory replayed the scene.

"Let me welcome all of you to the Bomber Barons!" he had boomed. "Congratulations for joining the best team in the Thirteenth Air Force! Give yourself a round of applause!" He had led the clapping himself, with a smile. "Each one of you is an important member of this team! Be proud of it! We'll depend on every one of you to DO YOUR BEST to make it the best damn team in the whole Pacific!"

Was that just ten weeks ago? It seems like forever. But now he's gone. What a loss! What a waste! This damn war is so full of waste! He had the right stuff to become a general.

Losing a hero so soon after losing my two best friends brought back all the pain I had felt at *their* loss. On the emotional level, it was like a re-enactment of the physical trauma of my hand. Losing Colonel Haviland was like the mosquito bite—it would not have caused much effect without the residues of the much deeper trauma preceding it. Now it seemed to revive all the results of the previous wounds. Alternate waves of searing pain, rage, helplessness, anger, and numbness swept over me. First I wanted to scream, then kick somebody's ass, then beat a rapid rythm on a punching bag, then crawl in a hole and die.

I finished my beer, and sat like a stone for a while. Then I went to the bar for another Pacific Cocktail and returned to the bench to drink some more. Too much alcohol and emotional pain interacted to leave me immobilized, out of it all.

The band played sweet music until the nurses left, but it made no impression on my catatonic state. If Doc Dolce had seen me then, he would have tagged me for sure as a case of combat fatigue. Maybe I was, for a while.

The musicians packed up their instruments and left. The club felt like a Good Old Boys' preserve again. Ten or twenty officers staggered around from bar to tables, and the more raucus ones began to sing ribald songs.

That music brought me back to life. I staggered over to join them as we sang one of our favorites:

> "I want to go home—I want to go ho-o-ome!
> The B-24s, how they rumble and roar—
> Don't send me to Ba-lik-pa-pan any more!
> I'm ready to quit!—I'm ready to shit!
> Oh, my, I'm too young to die,
> I just want to go home!"

There were several more verses, but I couldn't stay for the rest, because I saw the club beginning to spin around me. *"I want to go home!" Yes, I'd better go home—while I can still make it!*

I staggered in the direction of the doors, which seemed to be moving sideways. With great effort, I somehow made it through them into the night outside. There, the darkness seemed to rotate around my head, making me feel dizzy and nauseated.

I began to stagger toward the officers' tent area somewhere in the darkness below. Then I stumbled and pitched headlong down the hill, vomiting as I fell.

I rolled over and lay on my back for quite a while, semiconscious, looking up at the midnight sky. The stars seemed to be blurred and rotating rapidly. I watched them gradually slow down their spinning motion, then stop, then slowly come into focus. Soon I recognized the big triangle directly overhead.

Deneb—Vega—and Altair! My three good friends! Help me make it home tonight!

Seeing the perfect order of the heavens seemed to quiet my disorder on earth. The stars—my familiar friends—gave me strength to make it home. I stripped and collapsed on my cot.

22. Ordeal Ahead

My head was throbbing when I woke up late next morning. I tried to sit up, felt dizzy and collapsed on my cot again, naked except for shorts.

"Ooooh—woe—no," I moaned. "I feel awful!"

"Bad hangover?" Seitz looked up from the letter he was writing. Fully dressed in the usual khaki shirt and trousers, he was sitting in the home-made easy chair Cordell had built from Sea Bee lumber. Cordell and James were out of the tent.

"Is that what this is—a hangover?" I groaned.

"You never been drunk before? I should've known. Look at your clothes piled on the floor—you puked all over 'em!"

"Yes—I vomited when I fell down the hill, coming back from the party. I'm a mess!" Growing shame and remorse mingled with the hangover to depress me. *I failed my upbringing— my no-alcohol parents. I failed Dad—*

"Don't worry—it's not fatal," Seitz said. "You just drank too much. There's a first time for everything."

"This first time will be the last time! I'll never do *that* again!"

An hour later, after a cold-water shower, shave, and aspirin, I felt well enough to attend mid-day chow with Seitz. As we sat down, the Squadron Navigator, First Lieutenant Bishop, saw me and picked up his mess kit to come over to our table.

"Mind if I join you?" he asked, plunking down his dinner.

"Be my guest," I said. "I think you know Seitz, my pilot."

"Of course," said Bishop. "Seitz is the new Assistant Operations Officer Captain Davenport just appointed."

"Really?" I asked. "Seitz, you should've told me!"

Seitz brushed his left hand over his wavy blond hair and grinned. "I figured you'd find out soon enough."

Bishop turned to face me. His hair was dark, his thin mustache black, his steel-grey eyes grave.

"Hamilton, I guess you know it's my job to review the logs of all the navigators after each mission, and confer with those who seem to be goofing off—"

"Surely Hamilton isn't in that category," Seitz said.

"Oh, no! Just the opposite! His logs are the best in the squadron!"

"Really? What do I do?" I asked.

"You print legibly—like a draftsman. And you fill in all the entries needed for a complete record. You even write in your celestial calculations. I can always reconstruct any mission of yours by studying your log."

"That's my boy!" Seitz beamed.

"You just described my professional duty," I said. "That's what all navigators are taught to do in school."

"You'd be surprised how many navigators slack off after they graduate. They're flying in formation—they know that the lead navigator'll get 'em there, so they goof off. And what some of 'em write in the log is too scribbled to read."

"That's terrible!" I said.

Bishop's thin black mustache curled up in a smile. "How would you like to be Assistant Squadron Navigator?" he asked. "I need the help, and it'll put you on track for a promotion."

"Sure, I'll give it a shot. When do I start?"

"Tomorrow. I've already cleared it with Captain Davenport and Major Luketz. Then on Monday morning, your assignment will be to join me in going through our new H2X radar school. We'll learn all the hot new techniques together."

"H2X radar! Bombing through overcast! Wow!" *I've wanted to lay my hands on that stuff ever since I first heard of it!*

Next morning was Saturday, July 8. My pilot, copilot, bombardier, and engineer flew off on a practice bombing mission. They didn't need a navigator to fly to the nearby bombing range at Sila Point, so I had the day free. I went to the 394th Operations tent on the flight line to see if Bishop needed any help. He pointed to a pile of navigator logs on his desk.

"These are the logs of our recent missions staged from Palawan," he said. "You're so good at making logs, bet you'd be good at checking 'em too. Why don't you look these over for me? Mark 'em up where they need help, and give me the bad ones to deal with in person."

"Can I sit here and do it at your desk?"

"Sure. I'll be away from it all morning, anyway."

As he left, I sat down at his desk, amazed at how important it made me feel. A sign on the desk read "Squadron Navigator." *Wow! Here I am in Squadron Operations—rubbing elbows with Captain Davenport—doing supervisory work on the flight line!*

I picked up the first log and got to work. Then I searched for my own log of the same mission, a standard to check the others against.

Three hours later, the three B-24s on the practice bombing mission landed. Three first pilots, Seitz, Wildey and Monteith, came into Operations to close their flight plans.

"Well, hello, Hamilton—what are you doing here?" Wildey looked surprised.

I tried to be nonchalant. "Oh, I'm checking navigator logs for Bishop."

"My boy's Assistant Squadron Navigator now!" Seitz beamed like a father whose kid just caught the long fly ball.

"Well, congratulations!" Wildey said.

I looked at the stack of logs I was just finishing. *That was a lot of work—but the respect I feel is worth it all!*

After supper, I felt so good about my new appointment that I went back to 394th Operations. *I'll just hang around a bit and see what goes on in the evening shift.* Captain Gaston was there as duty officer, and Corporal Capo as duty clerk.

"Not much happening now," Gaston said. "We just have one B-24 flying tonight, number 651. Lieutenant Peoples is instructing two new pilots, Ownby and Hill, in night take-offs and landings."

"Is that what I hear on the VHF radio?" I asked.

"Yeah—it's on the tower channel. They've made three take-offs and three full-stop landings, and now they're ready for the fourth take-off."

The radio came on, "Boxcar 651 from Samar Tower, cleared for take-off on runway 07, over."

"Roger, Tower, 651 taking off 07, out."

The roar of his four engines increased as he got closer. Suddenly I heard a loud "pop"— like a gunshot—as the plane swept by. I ran out of the tent to see it swerve to the left—*Oh, no! He's gonna crash!*—but then it lifted off the runway and straightened its flight path.

The radio squawked again, "Tower from 651, we have a problem, over."

I stepped inside to hear better.

"651, describe your problem, over."

"651's left main tire blew out on take-off run. Pilot got us airborne and under control, but we're wondering how to land with one tire gone—without crashing, I mean. Over."

"651, we'll refer your problem to Operations. Meanwhile, turn on landing lights, fly over tower low and slow, gear down. We'll put a spotlight on it from below, and see what's left of your wheel, over."

"Roger, tower. 651 wilco, out."

The field telephone rang. Gaston grabbed it.

"Captain Gaston here. Yeah, I heard it all on VHF. Tell him not to land—repeat, *do not land gear down*! In that condition, it'll ground-loop, crash and burn. Tell him he's got two options: He can make a gear-up landing on the runway, cut off engines and skid along on the belly 'til it stops. Or he can fly over the field on autopilot while they all bail out, and let the plane continue eastward over the ocean 'til it disappears at sea. Do you have your spotlight on his wheel yet? No? Well, call back and tell me what you see."

I went outside again to watch the bomber's lights as it flew slowly over the tower. A spotlight lit up the left main wheel. Then the phone rang and I popped back inside to listen.

"Yeah, this is Gaston. You say the left tire is still on the wheel? Looks good? Great— gives me an idea. Tell him to shoot the air out of his other good wheel. Yep, then land—gear down—on two flat tires. That's right—equal drag on both sides. Tell him to use the machine gun in the belly ball turret. That'll give 'em a good shot at the right tire. But do it over water, so we don't have bullets falling in camp."

The tower radio came on again, repeating those instructions.

"Roger, Tower. 651 will fly east over the ocean to shoot ourselves in the foot, out."

Fifteen minutes later, the radio squawked again.

"Samar tower, 651 downwind for landing."

"Roger, 651, we have emergency vehicles ready to help you."

We all left the tent to watch his landing lights circle the traffic pattern and come in to land. As soon as he passed the end of the runway, a fire truck and an ambulance turned onto the runway there to follow him, lights and sirens blazing. He touched down with a thump and rumble. Wheel rims cut the tires to bits, sending pieces flying. The plane slowed with rims howling on the runway, then stopped in an otherwise normal landing.

We spectators let out a sigh of relief, and went back into the operations tent.

"Good job!" I said to Captain Gaston.

Next morning was Sunday, July 8. I woke up to the roar of twelve bombers taking off at dawn, on their way to Balikpapen. *I'm glad our crew's not flying today.* I rolled over to relax in comfort. *Hey, that's the first time I've ever wanted NOT to fly. I must be getting old, or the missions are getting old.*

Then I realized that I was free on Sunday for the first time in many weeks; I decided to attend the Protestant church service.

The Group Chapel was a wood-frame tent-covered structure with open sides and crushed-coral floor. An outstretched parachute made a silky ceiling over the altar. Empty crates were used for seats, two hundred or more. The Catholic chaplain had an early mass before Sunday breakfast, while the Protestant chaplain, Captain George Ivey, held his service in mid-morning.

The chapel was well filled that morning, but it was only a very small part of the two thousand men in the Fifth Bomb Group. The chaplain was a lean, sun-tanned captain with sandy hair and glasses. Instead of the priestly robes worn by the Catholic, this one dressed in the same kind of open-collar khaki shirt and pants worn by the congregation. He led the singing of familiar hymns without accompaniment, since there was no organ or piano, and he prayed for the safety of the men who were flying on today's mission. Otherwise it was like any worship service at home, but it meant a lot to me to have it there, overseas, where we were.

On the way out, I saw Pieper, who had been sitting a few rows behind me. We chatted; his home church in Wisconsin was Lutheran, mine in Atlanta was Presbyterian. We agreed that it felt good to have a Sunday free to attend church.

"Take a good look at these sergeant stripes on my sleeves," he said. "This is the last time you'll ever see 'em."

"How come?" I asked. "Pieper! You didn't get busted, did you?"

"Nothing like that!" he laughed, blue eyes twinkling. "No, I got promoted! I'm a staff sergeant now!"

"Congratulations, Pieper!" I gave him a hearty handshake. "When did you get the good news?"

"Just this morning. I checked the squadron bulletin board on my way to the chapel, and there was my name on the promotion list! In fact, all six of our crew were on the list. We're all staff sergeants now!"

"Do the other guys know it yet?"

"No, not yet."

"Let's go tell 'em! Come on, I'll walk home with you, and share the good news!"

394th SQUADRON AREA
Bulletin board is on right in front of the orderly room tent.

Pieper covered his blond crew cut with his khaki overseas cap, while I put on my khaki service cap with leather visor and no grommet (for the droopy "fifty-mission crush"), and we left.

When we reached his tent, we found the other five in various stages of dress and relaxation. Gerson lay asleep on his cot, his plump, hairy body naked except for underpants. Imhof and Herrema wore only khaki shorts, their tops bare-chested and sun-tanned as they sat on a cot playing checkers. Williams and Hill wore khaki trousers and white T-shirts. Williams, tall and thin, stood smoking a cigarette as he watched his pet monkey, Shoo-Shoo, sitting on Hill's shoulder. Hill was playing solitaire, with cards laid out on his cot.

"Hi, gang!" Pieper called. "Look who I brought home."

"Hello, Hamilton!" Hill said. "Good to see you down here again. It's been a while."

"Good to be here. I met Pieper at church, and came back with him to share the good news."

"What good news?"

"You've just been promoted—you're all staff sergeants now!"

Imhof looked up from the checkerboard. "Is that for real?"

"I went by the squadron bulletin board," Pieper said. "Our names are all on the new promotion list."

"Yay, man!" said Williams, giving Pieper a clap on the back. Imhof grinned, gave Herrema a high five clap above the checker game. "Great! We'll buy new stripes at the P.X."

Williams gave the sleeping Gerson a slap on the butt. "Wake up, you lazy bum! You're a staff sergeant now!"

"Congratulations to all!" I said, shaking hands with Hill.

"Thank you, sir!" Hill said. "This is good news indeed!"

The sidewalls of the tent were rolled up to catch the breeze. Outside the tent, behind Hill's cot, I saw a big white cockatoo in a screened cage as big as a bathtub and tall as me.

"What's all this?" I asked. "You have a new pet?"

"Yes, I built a cage for Joe, my cockatoo." Hill turned to open the door of the cage. "I'll introduce you to Joe. He likes to sit on my shoulder. Come on out, Joe. Come to Papa."

The big white bird flew out of the cage, circled inside the tent and flew straight toward Hill. The monkey, Shoo-Shoo, still on Hill's shoulder, saw Joe coming and jumped down onto the bed. Joe landed on Hill's left shoulder with a friendly squawk.

"He can talk a little," Hill said. "Hi, Joe!"

"Hi, Joe!" the cockatoo squawked.

"Hi, Joe," I said.

"Hi, Joe," it echoed with a nasal squawk.

Shoo-Shoo climbed up Hill's right arm to occupy his other shoulder again. Hill turned his head from one pet to the other.

"Man, are you popular!" Imhof said.

"But not for long," Hill said. "Joe's exclusive."

As if on cue, Joe turned around, stretched his head across the back of Hill's neck, and whacked that little monkey in the back with his big yellow beak, knocking Shoo-Shoo off Hill's shoulder. The monkey fell on the bed, chattering angrily, while the cockatoo turned around again to enjoy the exclusive use of Hill's shoulder. "Hi, Joe!" he squawked again.

Everyone in the tent roared with laughter except Williams, who reached down to pick up Shoo-Shoo and lift him up to his own shoulder. "That's okay, baby, you can use my shoulder anytime!"

Just then a crew chief from the flight line strolled past the tent with his big mongrel dog that looked like a German shepherd. The dog snarled and barked at the big white bird.

Joe flew off Hill's shoulder, heading straight for the dog. The dog jumped up to catch him, but Joe swooped up and circled over the dog's head, squawking "Hi, Joe!" Then he flew slowly down the road, three feet off the ground, and the dog bounded after him, barking furiously. As the dog caught up with him, Joe flew a little faster, keeping himself a little ahead of and a bit higher than the pursuing hound. At the end of the tent row, Joe turned right, and they both disappeared behind the tents.

"Joe's leading that dog on a merry chase," Pieper said.

"Do you think he'll come back?" Herrema asked.

"Listen to where the barking is now," Imhof said. "Sounds like they're making a big circle around the tent area."

Imhof was right. Soon Joe flew into view around the other end of the tents, leading the dog toward his home tent. More men emerged from neighboring tents to watch the show. Joe didn't stop, but flew right by home and on down the road the way he went before. The dog was barking less and panting more as he ran by, his long tongue hanging out.

"That dog is slowing down," Pieper said. "Do you think he'll make it around another lap?"

"Did you hear him panting as he ran by?" Hill mimicked the sound, breathing in and out, "Huh-ah-huh-ah-huh-ah-huh!"

"He may drop dead before they make it back," said Gerson.

"I hope not!" said the dog's owner. "I'll catch him, next time around."

Soon Joe flew into view again around the end tent, with the dog following at a slower pace than before, on wobbly legs. This time Joe flew to Hill, while the crew chief grabbed his dog.

The cockatoo settled on Hill's shoulder. It cocked its head to one side, winked one eye, and squawked "Hi, Joe!"

"Look at how smug he looks," Imhof said. "That bird knew exactly what he was doing all along!"

Hill called out to the dog owner, "Better take your dog away from here, before my cockatoo kills him!"

Monday morning I started the new H2X radar school set up for the Fifth Bomb Group. It was a small class, three selected navigators and bombardiers from each squadron, a dozen students in all. From the 394th Squadron, Bishop and I were the navigators, plus Lieutenant Hackenberger, our Squadron Bombardier (member of Wildey's crew).

The instructors told us that H2X was an airborne radar system that the Eighth Air Force had used over Germany. It had a revolving antenna inside a plastic dome that protruded from the belly of a B-24 in place of the usual ball turret. The antenna rotated slowly through a full circle, sending out radar pulses and receiving the reflected signals from the earth's surface below. Those signals were displayed on a radar screen (like a round TV screen).

The circular sweep on the radar screen painted a map of the earth below the aircraft. It helped the navigator to find his location and the bombardier to release his bombs. Radar signals penetrate most clouds (except heavy rain cells), so the H2X could paint the map through an overcast below.

Compared to modern radar, these sets were very primitive. Before they could be used, the operators had to calibrate them with a complex sequence of adjustments. It took us a whole week to learn how to operate the H2X.

During that week, Lieutenant Colonel James was appointed Commanding Officer of the Fifth Bomb Group on July 10, six days after Colonel Haviland disappeared. On the following day, he led the group in a successful ground-support bombing mission to the island of Negros in the Philippines, to help the American Sixth Army overrun the enemy there.

"Did you hear about the SNAFU mission the Group P-R boys sold as a model?" Captain Davenport asked. I was relaxing with a small circle of officers in the "Top of the Rock."

"Tell us about it," said Seitz.

"Two days ago, July 10, the Fifth Bomb Group sent two squadrons—including ours—on a ground-support mission to help the Aussies at Balikpapen. Group P-R had their photographers cover every phase of the mission—before, during, and after—to show the world the story of 'A Fifth Bomb Group Tactical Mission.'

"When our twelve B-24s got there, Aussie ground control identified the target by smoke shells—enemy personnel and supplies in Kaman, a fishing port north of Balikpapen. But there was one small problem."

"What was it?" I asked.

"The lead bombardier flew a little too far to the right, and all 36,000 pounds of bombs fell into the sea, a few hundred feet right of target."

"Oh, boy!" Seitz rolled his eyes.

"Just what we need for a model mission!" Bishop chuckled.

"Instead of hurting the enemy, we increased his food supply. Innumerable freshly-killed fish floated to the surface for the Japs to retrieve."

"Didn't that kill the story?" Wildey asked.

"Oh, no—the P-R men put their photo story on display at Group Headquarters. I saw it just an hour ago. It's all true, except for one small detail. They omitted the strike photo of the July 10 target, and substituted a great strike photo taken on the June 15 mission to Balikpapen!"

Wildey groaned. "What a crock!"

"How'd you identify the substitution?" I asked.

"Easy—deciphered the numbers on the print," Davenport said.

During my week of radar training, a team of inspectors led by Major Larson from the Thirteenth Bomber Command investigated every part of the Fifth Bomb Group. All four squadron commanders urged their men to work hard to get their own squadron named as "Best in the Group." We would hear the results in the award ceremony Friday afternoon.

On Friday, July 13, amid the usual round of Friday-the-13th jokes, our H2X radar classes finished in the morning. Each squadron gained three new radar operators to fly on the one plane in each squadron equipped with all the H2X gear.

Friday afternoon, the whole Fifth Bomb Group turned out for a full-dress parade and award ceremony. Brigadier General Carl Brandt, the tall, heavy-set head of Thirteenth Bomber Command, flew in for the occasion. He stood on the reviewing stand with our group and squadron commanders as we all marched by on parade.

Then we stood at attention while the general read the citation accompanying our Air Medals:

"For meritorious achievement while participating in sustained operational flight missions in the Southwest Pacific Area, during which hostile contact was probable and expected..... The courage and devotion to duty displayed during these flights reflect great credit on the United States Army Air Forces."

He read the list of names of those who had earned medals recently. There were over two hundred receiving the Air Medal (given for surviving ten combat missions), and as many others receiving an Oak Leaf Cluster for the Air Medal (awarded for ten more combat missions). Quite a few received their second or third Oak Leaf Cluster.

On our crew, the names of all except Gerson were read on the list for the Air Medal. (Gerson had flown fewer missions since we changed to nine-man crews; he earned his medal later.) Hearing our names read that day made me feel very proud of my crew.

There were also forty others receiving the Purple Heart (given to those who shed their blood in combat). Those were mostly posthumous awards, including my two friends who crashed on take-off. When I heard their names read, my eyes filled with tears in spite of my discipline.

A few minutes later, General Brandt walked through our ranks to give the Air Medals in person to those he had named. (Oak Leaf Clusters were not presented; those named bought them at the P.X.) Two aides followed the general, each with arms piled high with boxes of medals to hand to the general one at a time.

Soon General Brandt stood in front of me, gave me the Air Medal box and a handshake. His handclasp was very firm, and he looked me squarely in the eye. He reminded me of John Wayne—big, dignified, self-assured. He made me feel very proud, not boastfully so, but satisfied to be passing a milestone.

With the medals distributed, the general returned to the stand to announce the result of the Group inspection.

"My inspectors have spent the last three days going over every aspect of the Fifth Bomb Group," his voice boomed. "From the flight line to the chow line, we wanted to see whether your group measured up to the high standards of the Thirteenth Air Force. It gives me great pleasure to announce that the Bomber Barons passed with flying colors!"

A great cheer rose from the whole assembly. (We were not standing at attention then, but at "parade rest.")

"Lieutenant Colonel Albert W. James, your new Commanding Officer, has my heartiest congratulations for this good showing!"

Colonel James, tall, thin, and smiling, stepped forward on the stand, and the general shook his hand.

"Now for the Best Squadron in the Group award. After careful evaluation of each of your four squadrons, my inspectors have informed me that the winner of this close race is—the 394th Bomb Squadron!"

Another cheer rose from our section of the parade ground.

"Major George Luketz, new Commanding Officer of the 394th Bomb Squadron, has my congratulations!" Major Luketz, small, dark and wiry, stepped forward on the stand.

"You guys did all the work, but he gets congratulated," the general said as he shook hands with the major. We all laughed.

"Now hear this news. Day after tomorrow, June 15, the Fifth Bomb Group and the whole Thirteenth Bomber Command will be reassigned to training duty for a sixty-day period." A collective gasp and moan came from the men.

"This is a compliment to your efficiency—you've worked yourselves out of a job," the general continued. "In 1942 and '43, you helped win the epic battle for Guadalcanal, which turned the tide in the South Pacific. From there, through all your jungle island bases to Samar today, you hit the enemy hard. You helped drive 'em back across the southwest Pacific. You struck the Japs so hard, there's not much left here for you to do.

"On June 15, the Royal Australian Air Force will take over future air strikes in Borneo. If they need occasional help, we'll bomb again. The campaign to retake the Philippines is now over except for some mopping up. Our infantry may need a few more strikes for that. If so, we'll bomb upon request. But combat will not be our primary mission.

"Our new assignment is to become a Combat Replacement and Training Center, like the one at Nadzab, for sixty days. We need to train new crews for the final assault against Japan. The Thirteenth Air Force will have a major role in the invasion of Japan—the greatest battle ever fought in the Pacific!

"For that battle, we need new crews to swell our ranks, and we need you to share your combat know-how with the newcomers. So do your usual outstanding job for the next sixty days, and someday soon, we may have another award ceremony on another parade ground—IN TOKYO!"

His voice soared on the final two words, igniting more cheers from the crowd.

Wow! What a stunning idea!

Next morning, six B-24s took off to practice formation bombing at the group bombing range. Seitz, Cordell, James and Pieper manned number 330, "Boomerang." Each of the six planes took turns leading the formation on a bombing run.

I was not with them—I had something far more exciting to do—my first flight with H2X radar! Wildey flew our squadron's only radar plane, number 618, with his copilot, Lieutenant Glenn Lewis, and his engineer, Tech Sergeant Frank Crow. His bombardier, Earnie Hackenberger, plus Bishop and myself, were the radar operators.

We headed for the group bombing range also, but over the clouds at ten thousand feet instead of the lower altitude used by the six-plane formation. While we circled, climbing to that height, the radar men adjusted the H2X equipment and lowered the antenna radome through the hole where the belly turret used to be.

The radar screen glowed as the green sweep painted its circular map of the earth below. We were over Leyte Gulf, west of Samar, where a formation of our warships cruised the surface.

"Look at that!" said Hackenberger. "Every single warship is there as a green dot on the screen."

"Not only that," said Bishop, "you can distinguish between the aircraft carrier and other ships by the size of the dot."

"Wow! I hadn't expected that!" I said.

The bombing range target was a tiny island off Sila Point. It showed up beautifully on the screen because it was surrounded by water which provided good contrast. (A target on land would be harder to see.) We had no difficulty setting up our radar bombing runs on that target. We took turns, so we each got to operate a bombing run. I was filled with hope and excitement by this first radar flight, and went home ready to conquer the world.

That afternoon I joined Bishop in the Operations tent.

"Want to know more about the changes General Brandt talked about?" he said.

I lit my pipe. "What happens when our Combat Replacement Training ends?"

"Beginning tomorrow, sixty days takes us to mid-September. The latest poop from the Group says that the whole 13th Air Force will move to Okinawa then."

"Okinawa! Aren't we still fighting there?"

"Our side won that battle just this week. It was a helluva fight—lasted three months. Our Tenth Army lost seven thousand men killed and thirty thousand wounded, on top of thousands of Navy and Marine Corps casualties." He jabbed his desktop with a finger to emphasize each point.

I pointed my pipe at him. "Bet we'll go back to combat duty when we get there."

"Of course. Okinawa is within B-24 strike range of Tokyo, about a thousand miles—"

"—like the distance from Samar to Balikpapen," I added. "We'll be able to reach Tokyo easily."

"Yes, but we won't be bombing Tokyo—that's a strategic target. The 20th Air Force will hit all strategic targets with their B-

29s. We're a tactical air force now—our targets are ships, trains, tanks, artillery and armies in the field."

"Good! Then I won't have to bomb civilians in cities!"

Bishop looked surprised. "You have a problem with bombing cities?"

"I don't like killing anybody! In spite of that, I can see attacking military forces that are trying to kill us—it's a form of self-defense. But when we bomb innocent civilians, it's just plain murder!"

His grey eyes turned to cold steel. "Sometimes the civilians are not so innocent. Civilian war-workers may be just as involved in the war as soldiers."

"Maybe so, but I'll be glad to leave their murder to the Strategic Air Command. I'm glad we're a tactical air force now."

"Yes, General Kenney's Far East Air Forces, the 5th, 7th, and 13th—"

"Whoa! The 7th Air Force is not in Kenney's command."

"Not yet, but it will be for the invasion. His Far East Air Forces will be the tactical air arm for the invasion of Japan."

"When?" I asked. "Dumb question—none of us know for sure."

"Not so dumb—we can guess the general time frame. Some time this fall—probably soon after we get to Okinawa. October or November."

"General Brandt said that our invasion of Japan will be the greatest battle ever fought in the Pacific! That means it'll dwarf the epic struggles over Tarawa, Iwo Jima and Okinawa!"

"There were ninety thousand Jap soldiers defending Okinawa," Bishop said. "Over eighty-seven thousand died there—only twenty-five hundred surrendered. If they fought that hard for an outpost, how much harder will they fight for their sacred homeland?"

"I shudder to think of it!"

"With that kind of fighting going on for another year, there could be a million American casualties and three or four million Japanese, before we win this war."

He's right! My hair prickled at the thought. *What a bloody ordeal we have ahead of us!*

23. Shot Down Over Borneo

"Every time I fly over Borneo," I said to Lieutenant Corrin, "I wonder what would happen if I had to bail out over that jungle. You did it, and survived. Tell me about it. You must have gone through hell out there—"

"Not quite hell, but pretty bad at times," Corrin said.

"Can you talk about it? I really want to hear what happened."

"Where should I start?"

"Well—how were you shot down?"

Second Lieutenant Phillip R. Corrin, Bombardier, sat across a small table from me in "Top of the Rock," 394th Squadron's new officers club. We were both sipping beers, enjoying the breeze blowing through the screened openings in the Quonset hut. The warm breeze kept us from sweating too much during the afternoon heat of Samar on July 18. The club was nearly empty.

Eight months earlier, in November 1944, three of our B-24s had been shot down attacking the Japanese Navy in Brunei Bay. Recently I heard that one of those crews had bailed out over Borneo and survived in the jungle for over seven months, then returned to the Fifth Bomb Group! Was it true? Who were the survivors?

I found that Lieutenant Corrin of the 23rd Bomb Squadron was the only surviving officer on that crew. I located him and asked him to tell me his story at the club. He brought along his "Borneo Log"—a sheaf of notes written on all sorts of paper.

Corrin had come to Samar a few days earlier, after treatment in the hospital on Morotai for dysentery, leech bites, jungle itch, malaria, and malnutrition. Not yet fully recovered, the bombardier spoke with hesitation at first.

"Well, let's see—it was November 16, 1944, on my eighth

combat mission," he began. "Morotai was our base then. We flew to attack a big Jap fleet in Brunei Bay—what was left of their navy after the Battle of Leyte Gulf." He paused to sip his beer.

"Were there many planes involved?" I asked, sipping mine.

"Biggest operation I ever saw! Thirteenth Air Force sent both the Bomber Barons and the Long Rangers—four squadrons from each group, plus P-38 fighter escort." He paused to bring out a pack of Camel cigarettes and light one.

"Where was your plane when it was hit?"

"In the lead squadron, third plane. Our 23rd Squadron C.O., Major Saalfield, was leading the whole strike. We were heading west over the water of Brunei Bay, flying toward the Jap fleet at 10,000 feet about 11:15 A.M. I was in the nose, setting up for the bomb run. They hit us when we were more than ten miles away."

"That far? How in the world could—"

"They had big ships—battleships and cruisers, as well as smaller ones. They aimed their big deck turret guns up at us. A huge sheet of flame lit up a ship when it fired a salvo at us. Big shells started bursting near us when we were fourteen miles away. They shot down three bombers in three minutes! Major Saalfield was hit first, then our plane, then Lieutenant Norris. The Major's plane went down with all his crew, but I heard just last week that Norris flew partway home—four members of his crew were picked up in the water by a PBY seaplane."

"What happened in your plane?"

"A big shell exploded near the pilots! Shrapnel raked the flight deck and wings. Both pilots were hit real bad—navigator killed! Number three engine knocked out—electric and hydraulic systems dead. The plane was riddled."

"Navigator killed?" *(One like me.)* "What was his name?"

Corrin's face was grim. "Lieutenant Fred Brennan. He was navigating from the flight deck, where the hit was worst. When I got there from the nose, I saw he had a huge hole in his head. Lots of blood—" His voice faded away. He lowered his head.

Sensing his suffering, I waited until he looked up again.

"Are you okay to go on?" I asked.

He nodded. "I had my hands full with the nose gunner, Corporal Eddy Haviland. His plexiglas turret shattered in his face—he was almost blind. I had to help him through the nose tunnel and up to the flight deck. Then I went to the bomb bay to get rid of the bombs. No electrical—had to release 'em all by hand."

"Hey, I know what that's like! I stood in the open bomb bay once myself, to help with that job! Howling wind all around you!"

"Pretty hairy trip!" He took a deep draft on his cigarette, then slowly exhaled.

"Who was your pilot? Was he hurt bad?"

"Lieutenant Tom Coberly—compound fractures of his right leg—bleeding real bad, and in shock. Our engineer, Corporal Jim Knoch, pulled him out of his seat—laid him down on the flight deck—gave him two shots of morphine."

"The copilot—could he still fly? Who was he?"

"Lieutenant Jerry Rosenthal—badly wounded on the right side of his face and head, though we didn't know it for a while. He turned the plane around to head back toward Morotai— kept it flying over Borneo for about twenty minutes, then yelled on the interphone, 'Bail out! Bail out!' I guess he knew he was ready to pass out.

"When we heard 'Bail out,' Dan Illerich. radio operator, went to check on the copilot, saw his head wounds, and told me that Jerry was in real bad shape. We're almost out of pilots!

"I started toward the rear to bring Waist Gunner Tom Capin up to the pilot's seat—he was the only other crew member who had enough pilot time in the cadet program to fly a plane if he had to. I saw Jim Knoch standing on the catwalk in the open bomb bay, trying to fix broken fuel lines, and told him to go get Tom. Jim entered the waist and came back to tell me that all the guys back there had bailed out already. Tom was last to go, and Jim saw him jumping out the rear hatch just as he got there—too late!"

"What a shame! If Tom had taken over as emergency pilot, he might have nursed that wounded bird all the way to Morotai!"

"Maybe partway back, but I doubt it—the plane was badly shot up, and losing lots of fuel. Anyway, Jerry died at the controls around 11:45."

"What happened then?"

"I helped Eddy out—he was still blinded—while Jim and Dan dropped the wounded pilot out the bomb bay and popped his chute for him. Then we all jumped too."

"Good! You made it safely out of the dying plane!"

"Yes, but not out of danger! Hanging in our chutes, we looked up to watch that wicked plane curl around into a spin, heading right at us! Already a coffin for Fred and Jerry, now it was trying to kill more of us! Came so close it scared the devil out of me! But it missed—spun on down to a horrible crash—exploded and burned on the jungle hillside below us. Then we were afraid of falling into the searing flames—had to pull hard on our chutes to avoid it."

"What happened to the wounded pilot?"

"He was too far gone to make it. Jim and I found his body in the jungle three days later. We gave him a decent burial."

I paused to load and light my pipe. "So—how many bailed out?"

"I was the only officer able to jump, but all six of our enlisted men bailed out. Plus another one—Sergeant Phillips, a photographer, was with us on that trip. He jumped with the guys in the waist—they saw his chute open—but he disappeared in the jungle below. Maybe he got spiked on a tree branch, or something. We searched for him repeatedly, but never saw a trace of him."

"Did you land close together?"

"Oh, no! After the first group jumped from the waist, the plane flew on for several minutes before the rest of us bailed out. That put miles between the two groups. We were separated by thick brush and even mountain ridges. Many of us landed all alone, as far as we could tell."

"How long did it take your seven survivors to get together?"

"Over four months," Corrin said. "The full reunion didn't come until March 23rd—my birthday, so I remember the date."

"What kept you apart?"

"To begin with, we were afraid to holler for each other—didn't want Jap patrols to hear us. We had been told that Japs in Borneo killed their prisoners."

"So how did you get together?"

"We were all found by Dyak natives in different places. They brought us together into three different groups—four men here, two there, and one by himself—all miles apart, with no communication. I found Dan right away—Corporal Dan Illerich, radio operator—we landed close together. The two of us carried our chutes through the mountain undergrowth downhill to a small hut beside a river. Dyaks there saw the "U.S." on our gun holsters—greeted us with 'Americano, Americano!' Then they took us to their long house. They fed us and let us sleep there that night. They wanted our parachutes to make into clothes."

"What's a long house?"

"A long native hut with many rooms—big enough for thirty people to live in. Next day the natives brought in Eddy and Jim. Jim was okay, but Eddy was hurt—still partly blind from shattered plexiglas, also bruised his ribs in landing. So four of us were together by the second day, and three of us healthy. Soon the Dyaks moved us to another long house on the edge of a river."

"What river?" I asked. "I'm a navigator, and I have to locate everything on maps. Where in Borneo did you guys land?"

"We all landed within twenty miles of Long Berang. That's a jungle village about fifty miles east of the point on your map where the borders of three states come together—British North Borneo, Sarawak, and Dutch Borneo. Long Berang is in the Dutch part, on a branch of the river that flows past Malinau into the sea near Tarakan. Rivers are the main highways of Borneo—the only good way to get through the jungle."

I nodded. *Like the rivers used to be in early America.*

"Well, Long Berang is a small native village—two hundred people—with a Malayan official in charge of the area. A few days after we arrived, he came up the river to see us."

"Who was he? Did he work with the Japs?"

"He was William Makahanap, from Celebes. Technically, he worked for the Japanese Military Government. He'd been a Malayan missionary school teacher at the American mission there before the war. When the Japs invaded in '42, Makanahap saved his life by going over to the other side. Offered to be the Area Administrator for the Japs. He could speak a little Japanese, as well as Malay, Dyak, Dutch and some English, so they took him on. But secretly he hated the Japs."

"Did he help you, or protect you?"

"He sure did! William Makahanap took us under his wing like a mother hen. Moved us by canoe down river to Long Berang. Put us up in his own well-furnished house, and his son Christian cooked some great meals for us. A few days later, he learned that Jap soldiers were on their way to Long Berang. He sneaked us out of there long after midnight—sent us up river to Long Matoiel. That's a remote village run by a chief friendly to our side. We lived near there for eight weeks."

"Did the Japs ever come close to you?"

"Sure! The very next day, they sent a messenger with a note for us—'MR. SOLDIER, I AM JAPANESE. GIVE YOUR GUNS TO THIS MAN AND COME TO LONG BERANG. R. IWASAKI.' Our friends told us that Iwasaki had fifteen Jap soldiers out looking for us."

"What did you do?"

"The friendly chief moved us to a safer place—a hut hidden in the jungle above the village. He sent us food every few days. We stayed there for weeks, until the uprising broke out."

"What uprising?"

"Local Dyaks revolted against the Japs on—let's see—the date's down here in my notes— January 19, 1945. A Jap patrol raped a Dyak woman in Long Matoiel, and the Dyaks there went on the warpath. Killed all three Japs there with blowguns—shot poison darts—then cut off their heads for trophies."

I groaned. *Head-hunters?*

"They have a thing for human heads! They got so excited, they brought us down to their longhouse to see them celebrate their head-taking with their own special ceremonies. We saw the heads smoking over the fire-pit. They smoke heads for many days to cure them before they put them on their trophy shelf.

"Their ceremonies went on for three days of dancing and chanting, and two nights of great feasting. Everyone got drunk on the local rice wine—including us. But the night events were for Dyaks only—we could only peek at them through cracks in the partitions. The four of us—Jim, Eddy, Dan and I—saw things during those days and nights that were amazing! We witnessed rituals that I'm sure no white man had ever seen before!"

What a privilege! "What did you see?"

"I don't want to go into that—it's their own private thing. Anyway, three days later, William came with news—the rebellion had spread all over the district. All the Japs in Long Berang were dead, including R. Iwasaki. William's young son Christian had stolen a Jap machine gun and killed two Japs himself!"

"Was it safe for you to come out of hiding, then?"

"Sure! William moved us back to Long Berang the next day. There we saw the Dutch flag flying where the Jap flag had been before. Christian showed us their souvenirs of victory—Jap heads, guns, pistols, and a samurai sword."

"Great souvenirs." *Except for the heads.*

"A week later—first of February—William and Christian came down from the mountains with Tom Capin! We had a great reunion!"

"Another missing crew member?"

"Yes. Corporal Tom Capin—assistant radio operator-gunner. He'd been separated from the rest of the crew until then. Landed in a more isolated place than the rest of us—followed a stream uphill into the mountains—nothing to eat for a week. Then two Dyak men found him, took him to their village. Those Dyaks sort of adopted him as part of their tribe. Tom lived with 'em—like a native—for ten weeks."

"Wow! How could he talk with 'em?"

"He learned their Dyak language by himself! Always knew Tom was smart! Told us later, if he had to live in their tribe for the rest of the war, he wanted to be the best damn tribesman he could be! So he learned to hunt with a blowgun and track wild boar with their hunters. Wore a loincloth like they did, and let them tattoo their tribal insignia under his left arm. He showed it to us—an eye-of-the-mountain tattoo, in blue dye. Part of his initiation ritual."

"Wow! He really went native!"

"Oh, yes! But he must have made a funny-looking tribesman! He was head and shoulders taller at six-foot-five, and red-headed and fair-skinned, too! Can't you see him creeping along the trail with those short, dark-skinned Dyaks? What a sight!"

Corrin's face crinkled into a broad smile, and he actually laughed. I was delighted. *Laughter is the best medicine. Maybe talking about funny things will help him heal.*

"Another funny thing," he said, "Dyaks are head-hunters—or they used to be, openly, until the Dutch government in Borneo outlawed it a few years earlier. Missionaries preached against it too, of course. But when Japs invaded their own mountains, Dyaks went back to head-hunting— with Japs as their target! Tom saw four fresh Jap heads on their trophy shelf, beside all the old native heads from long ago." Corrin laughed again, and took a long drink of beer with obvious pleasure.

"So, did Tom do any head-hunting?"

"Naw, he told 'em it was against his religion! The Dyaks thought that was funny, 'cause head-hunting is an important part of their native religion!" He was relaxed now, and smiling.

I noticed his glass was empty. "How about another beer?"

"Why not?" he said. He lit another cigarrette.

As I went for our refills, I thought about how unusual it was for a modern American, trained in technology, to adopt a primitive culture, even temporarily. What led him to do it?

I set two fresh beers on the table and sat down.

"Do you think Tom's decision to go native was due to his isolation?" I asked. "The rest of you were living with Dyaks too, and you didn't go native. But you guys had other Americans present to talk to and keep you involved in your own culture. Tom had no one around but Dyaks. If he found social acceptance at all, it had to be in the Dyak culture."

Corrin looked pensive. "Never thought of it quite like that."

"Or maybe it was the challenge of learning new things—new language, new skills like tracking game, shooting a blowgun."

He nodded. "That would appeal to Tom."

He paused to drink more beer, seemingly lost in thought. I tried to focus my mind on where the story was going next. My eyes drifted to the paintings of nude girls on the wall of the club. *How unreal they are—irrelevant to anything here.*

"So, you had five survivors together by February first," I said. "What about the other two—what happened to them when they bailed out?"

"We heard their stories later, after we all got together. Corporal John Nelson, armorer-gunner, landed in a tree in the mountains. He climbed down and followed a creek downhill to a stream, and followed that down to a native long house. There he saw a Dyak man—dark, fierce-looking, carrying a spear.

"John tried speaking to the warrior in his high-school Spanish, 'Yo soy Americano.' The Dyak laid down his spear and bowed a welcome. John pointed to the sky and said in Spanish that he had come out of an airplane. The man looked puzzled, but took him into the long house—fed him and sheltered him overnight."

Those natives are sure hospitable to Americans!

"After three days, Dyaks found our tail gunner, Staff Sergeant Frances Harrington—we call him 'Franny'—and brought him to the long house to join John. The natives didn't understand John's Spanish, so they brought out a glossary with words in Dyak and English. It had been hand-written by American missionaries—helped a lot with communication."

"Well, God bless the missionaries! What a help!"

"God bless the missionaries indeed! Our survival in Borneo

was due to the work they had done there long before we arrived!"

I paused to collect my thoughts. Corrin took another cigarette from his pack of Camels, tapped the end on the table, and lit it.

"What next for John and Franny?" I asked.

"Well, Dyaks are short people, and they couldn't get over how big we were. John said they couldn't believe we came out of an airplane. They'd seen planes high in the air—look so small up there—they could hardly believe airplanes were big enough to hold anybody—'specially people big as us!" Corrin broke into a laugh again.

"That's funny!" I laughed with him.

"Well, a few days later, John asked to see the nearest large village. He wanted to find some way to return to Allied territory. Dyaks took John and Franny to Long Naut, a village in the high mountains. They brought our guys to William Monahan, another Malayan missionary from Celebes. He was Mrs. Makahanap's brother, known to us as 'Uncle Louie.' He made room for them in his own house, and they stayed with him for quite a while."

"My parents were missionaries to China before the war," I said. "I can understand that spirit of sharing."

"The Malayan missionaries had been assistants to American missionaries before the war. Uncle Louie told John how the Japs invaded in 1942 and killed a lot of people, including five American missionary men in those very same mountain areas. They arrested all their families—took the wives and children to prison camps, but killed the men as 'spies'."

"*They killed missionaries?*" *I've heard of lots of Jap atrocities to prisoners of war, but not to missionaries!*

"Let me tell you what those bastards did! One missionary—Rev. Willfinger—was in the hills, up there at Long Naut, when the Japs killed the other four in Long Berang. The Japs really fixed him! They rounded up his native Christians in Long Berang, then sent word to Willfinger that they would kill one of his converts every day until he came in. And they started killing 'em! Soon as he heard about it, Willfinger came down and turned himself in.

Before the Japs let his people go, they cut off his head with a samurai sword, right in front of them!"

I shook my head. "Barbaric!" *More of this stuff, and I will learn to demonize the enemy, after all!*

"When Japs came prowling around Long Naut, Uncle Louie risked his own life—he moved John and Franny several times to different safe hiding places."

"Who were those five martyred missionary men?" I asked. "What group did they represent?"

"I have that somewhere in my notes." Corrin looked through several pages. "Here it is—their names were Dickson, Jeffries, Michaelson, Presswood, and Willfinger. They were from the Christian and Missionary Alliance, based in New York City."

"I have friends in the C.M.A.," I said. "Good people!"

"The natives around those Borneo hills sure respect the memory of Willfinger! He's more than a saint to them—he saved them from execution by the Japs!"

"'Greater love hath no man than this, that a man lay down his life for his friends,'" I said.

"Those missionaries planted native churches that were still carrying on without them three years later. I attended their Sunday services at several different villages in the area."

We both slowly drank more beer. I relighted my pipe.

"Do you feel like talking some more?" I asked. He nodded.

"Well, let's see if I got this right: In February, John and Franny were in Long Naut; you and four other crew members were in Long Berang, a long way off. So how did you all get together?"

"Toward the middle of February, William was afraid the Japs would send more troops to Long Berang, so he led the five of us on a four-day hike to Bang Biau—a safer village, run by a Christian chief named Sadi. We were his guests for the next five weeks. While we were there, native messengers brought us two short letters from John and Franny at Long Naut.

"The first one said that there were some U.S. Navy airmen nearby! A PB4Y (navy B-24) had been shot down near Miri—on the coast, west of us—on January 13, two months after we went down. The plane crash-landed in a rice paddy, and nine surviving crew members fled into the hills ahead of the Japs. Eight of 'em hid, while their copilot, Lieutenant Bob Graham, went up mountain trails to Long Naut to contact two army airmen—our boys, of course. He'd heard about 'em from the natives.

"When they wrote the letter, John and Franny were about to leave Long Naut to follow Graham over the ridge to Pommaton in Sarawak, where the other navy flyers waited. Then they expected to go together on a very long walk to Kudat, at the north tip of Borneo. They hoped to be rescued, somehow, at Kudat."

"Not a good plan!" I said. "The Japs have an airfield at Kudat—a strong military presence. I've seen it from the air several times myself. Why go toward a major enemy center?"

"I know—it seemed dumb to me too. But the navy men seemed to believe that if they could get to Kudat, they could be picked up at night by a U.S. Navy sub, or something like that."

"But it's too far to walk through enemy-held territory! It'd take two months! It's crazy!"

"I agree! Anyway, two weeks later—the middle of March—we got a second note from our guys in Long Naut. They had followed Graham into Sarawak and joined three of his sicker crewmen at Pommaton. The healthier ones—a party of five, led by the pilot, Lieutenant Commander Marvin Smith—had already left on the long march toward Kudat. A few days later, the rest of 'em were ready to follow along the path toward Kudat, when they got bad news. The earlier group had been ambushed by Japs and killed—all five of 'em!"

"Damn! I knew they'd never make it to Kudat!"

"That news changed their plan, of course. They all came back to Long Naut, to enjoy Uncle Louie's hospitality again. So this second letter from John and Franny said that four navy fliers were there with 'em—Lieutenant Graham and his three crewmen, named Harms, Robbins, and Shepherd. They were all sick and badly malnourished, and needed to rest and heal for quite a while."

"What made 'em sick?" I asked.

"All sorts of bugs got to us in Borneo—not a healthy place to live. Flat areas were rice paddies, ankle-deep in water—fertilized with human shit. That spread stomach ailments—diarrhea or dysentery—we came down with a lot of that. Shallow water bred swarms of mosquitoes, too— we all got malaria after our atabrine wore off. That gave us recurring chills and fever."

Never again will I complain about taking atabrine pills!

"Also, there were leeches in all the water—rice paddies, rivers, and mountain streams. Leeches cling to your bare skin and suck your blood. We'd walk along stream beds to keep from hacking our way through jungle growth, but every hour we'd have to stop and pull leeches off our legs, and wipe up the blood from their bites. Then there were skin problems we picked up somewhere—jungle itch, fungus, ulcers—kind of slow to heal. And we were all malnourished. So all of us were sick some of the time, and some were sick all the time."

"Wow! Walking the trails of Borneo was no pleasure trip!"

"Hell, no! But rivers don't go everywhere. If you couldn't get there by river boat, walking was the only way left!"

"Did the natives get sick too?"

"Yes—malnutrition was widespread, in addition to diseases. The weaker ones die young. Stronger ones develop resistance to many of the diseases over time. But the natives all had their spells of sickness too."

Corrin slumped down in his chair, looking tired.

"Don't let this talk of sickness make you sick again," I said. "Let's talk about something cheerful. When were you all reunited?"

"On March 23rd, my birthday. The day before, Christian led the five of us from Bang Biau—Dan, Eddy, Jim, Tom, and me—on a two-day walk over mountain trails to his father's hide-away at Pa Silau. At the same time, William led the guys from Long Naut—John, Franny, Lieutenant Graham, and Shepherd—to the same place. The other two navy men—Harms and Robbins—were too sick to travel, so they stayed at Long Naut.

"Pa Silau was a small village in a narrow canyon so deep the sunshine reached the valley floor only four hours a day. The trail into it was so steep we had to hang onto bushes all the way down. But it was worth the trip, because we had a grand reunion at the Makahanap home in the valley! It was great to get all seven survivors from our crew together at last!

"The whole Makahanap family was there, Christian, William and his wife—"Mama" Makahanap. Mama was a strong-willed lady, the real strength behind William. When he wavered in his loyalty toward us, she pushed him in the right direction. Well, Mama cooked us a grand feast that day. It was the best birthday of my life!" He grinned in retrospect.

His pleasure was infectious. I smiled, too. "So that's how you all got together again. But how did you get out of Borneo?"

"On April third we got some exciting news. Uncle Louie came from Long Naut to tell us that eight Australian commandos had parachuted into Sarawak nearby! Their purpose was to organize natives into guerilla bands to fight the Japs. Airplanes were dropping them supplies—they had radios! Hey, that brought the war right into our neighborhood—gave us hope for possible help! You have no idea what a difference hope makes!"

"Hope recharges your batteries in a hurry!"

"I wrote a note to the Aussie commander, and William took it. He was anxious to meet the man because William already had a band of Dyak guerrillas fighting the Japs. He came back a week later with a note from a Major Harrisson of the Australian Reconnaissance Corps! The Major said one of his missions in Borneo was to evacuate downed flyers, so he would HELP US GET OUT!" Corrin's eyebrows rose with his voice, and his eyes shone.

"Great!" I said. *Aussies to the rescue! Trumpet fanfare!*

"The Major sent us gifts—medicines, cigarettes, chewing gum. He wanted to recruit our radio operators—Dan and Tom—to work with his 'Z-Forces' as radiomen—"

"'Z-Forces!' Sounds like a movie script!"

"—and he wanted me, as an officer, to lead one of his guerrilla bands. So Dan, Tom, and I left the next day—April 10—with William and Christian, to start a long trek westward to meet the Major in Sarawak. We spent the nights in native huts of many villages along the way."

Corrin paused to refer to his notes again. "We finally found the Major's headquarters at Bareo, in Sarawak, on April 21." Corrin looked up again, bright-eyed. "Major Harrisson really is a swell guy. He gave us all the news we hadn't heard for months—even told us what would happen next—Australians were going to invade Tarakan about a week later, and then invade Brunei Bay soon after—"

"I remember three invasions," I said. "Tarakan, May first—Brunei Bay, June tenth— Balikpapan, July first. Our Bomber Barons bombed the landing beaches in front of all three invasions, and I flew on the Brunei Bay invasion myself."

"We were really shocked when the Major told us that President Roosevelt had just died!"

"That shocked all of us, too."

"Roosevelt had been President for as long as I could remember—elected four times! It's hard to get used to Truman as President!"

It sure is! "Was the Major from Australia?"

"No, he was from England. Professor Tom Harrisson, Ph.D., had been a scientist before the war—wrote several books, travelled around the world doing scientific studies for Oxford University. For a year he lived on an island in New Hebrides with savages who eat human flesh. They initiated him into their secret tribal rituals. He showed me tattoos they made on his body. Hollywood almost made a movie about his life—Douglas Fairbanks wanted to do it."

Wow! Quite a character!

"The Major set up five platoons of guerillas from the natives available, under his officers—Captain Rick Edmonds from New Zealand with the First Platoon, Warrant Officer Rod Cusack from Brisbane, Australia, with the Second, and Warrant Officer Hurst with the Third. He put me in charge of the Fourth Platoon—twenty-three men, ten armed with blowguns, eight with rifles, five with hand grenades and spears. And he told me to train these guys, turn 'em into soldiers." He waved his arms in frustration, and lit another Camel.

"Hey, this Borneo experience really got you guys into new and different activities. Tom, a radio operator, spent weeks creeping around jungle trails as a Dyak warrior, and you, a bombardier, joined the ground forces to lead a platoon of natives armed with blowguns, rifles, hand grenades and spears!"

"Better than sitting on my ass waiting for rescue!"

"Right—you were active in the war effort. And this whole war experience changes all of us in more ways than we know."

"Nothing will ever be the same again," Corrin said. We both paused to sip more beer as we thought about that. I reloaded my pipe with aromatic tobacco, and lit it again.

"Let's finish the story," I said. What happened next?"

"Major Harrisson gave William a field commission as an auxiliary officer—recognition for his earlier leadership against the Japs. 'Lieutenant' Makahanap led the Fifth Platoon away to Long Berang, to defend it against a Jap attack."

"Makahanap really deserved some recognition!" I added.

"A week later, a B-24 from the Royal Australian Air Force flew over to parachute in ten big packs of weapons and supplies. With that equipment, the Major sent Captain Edmonds and his First Platoon to the Trusan River in north Sarawak to kill Japs there. And he sent me and the Fourth Platoon off to Long Berang with twenty extra rifles and more ammunition, to reinforce William at Long Berang."

They expected the Japs to attack there for sure.

"The walk to Long Berang was an eight-day trek, but after six days I had to stop—too sick to go on. I was weak from malnutrition, my feet were leech-bitten and swollen, my stomach had dysentery, my skin had the itch, and my head had a cold!"

"Man, you were really a sad sack then!" I said.

"Too sad for words! So I sent the guns and men on to Long Berang while I stayed a week at a Malayan Christian school-teacher's house at Long Sempayan. I finally reached Long Berang on May 15, and found the rest of the gang there, too—except for Tom and Dan, of course—they were still doing radio work for the Major in Bareo."

"I hope you stayed there long enough to rest and heal."

"I did, for over two weeks. Then on June first, we got a message from the Major that eight more Australian commandos had parachuted into Belawit to prepare a way to evacuate us by air! That was hard to believe! I had gone through Belawit on my last trek—it's in a broad flat valley full of wet rice fields—no solid ground to land an airplane anywhere!"

"So how did Major Harrisson get you out?"

"By air, sure enough! His men, and the natives they hired to do the work, used split bamboo strips to weave large bamboo mats. They laid the bamboo matting over the mud of a rice paddy near Belawit. It made a runway four hundred feet long by thirty feet wide—strong enough to support a light plane. 'Harrisson Field' took a couple of weeks to build."

"A bamboo airstrip! Of all things! Pretty darn clever!"

"They built it to evacuate the Z-Forces, too, of course, but we got to use it first. On June 7, I got orders from the Major to bring Jim and Robbins to Belawit, so we left the next day."

"What kind of plane could land at Belawit?"

"Australian light plane called the 'Auster.' It was a high-wing two-seater, a lot like our L-5. The back seat folded down to make room for a stretcher. Some of us were pretty sick pups by then, and needed the stretcher."

"So they flew you out one at a time?"

"Yes, over a space of several weeks, after the Brunei Bay invasion secured Labuan Island. First out was the sickest one—Harms, of the navy crew. Dyaks carried him down to Belawit on a stretcher—he flew out on June 10. I got to Belawit on June 14, with our Jim, and Robbins of the navy. The rest of the guys at Long Berang were also on their way down by then. My turn to leave came on June 23."

"Where did they fly you?"

"North to Labuan Island in Brunei Bay—a one-hour hop in the Auster. A week later— July first—we caught a C-47 flight to Morotai, where they put us in the hospital. They let me out just a few days ago to fly here."

Lieutenant Corrin slumped in his chair, suddenly tired. Telling about his experience must have been like reliving it. *I hope it did him good to talk about it.*

"Thanks so much for sharing your amazing story," I said. "Let me get you another beer."

"Why not? I don't have anything better to do now."

When I returned, I asked, "What do you expect to do next?"

"I want to find all the enlisted men from my crew, and see how they're doing. I think most of 'em are here by now, but I haven't had the strength to find 'em all yet."

"Will you do some more flying with us here?"

"Oh, no—we're all grounded, and scheduled for rotation real soon. In a couple of weeks, they'll send us to Clark Field, Manila, and then back to the States." Corrin's face lit up with pleasure. "I'll go home to mother's house in Glendale, California, in the good old U.S.A.!"

"Glad to hear it! If anyone deserves to go home, you do!"*

>*(This chapter has been checked for accuracy by using the written primary sources—the official 23rd Bomb Squadron History for October 1944, Phil Corrin's 6,500 word "Borneo Log," and John Nelson's 1,700-word "Mission to Brunei Bay," and also by personal consultation with five of the survivors of the Borneo ordeal who remain alive today—Tom Capin, Dan Illerich, Jim Knoch, John Nelson, and Robert John Graham. Also contacted were Phil Corrin's wife, Jean, and mother, Ruby, who just turned 100 years old).

24. Victory!

"What do you mean, we gotta serve ground duty?" Hill said at a meeting of our crew near the mess hall. "We're combat flyers!"

"Yeah," Gerson said, "Flyers risk their lives in combat, and ground-pounders do all the support work."

Williams put out his arm to lean against a palm tree. "It's always been like that!"

"Until now," Seitz said. "But wars are full of changes. The new policy says that all enlisted combat personnel are subject to ground duty when not flying or in classes."

Herrema lit a cigarette. "What kind of ground duty?"

"It goes with your special skills," Seitz answered. "You and Gerson are armorers, so you'll work in the armament section, loading bombs and ammunition. Engineers will help the mechanics on the flight line, so Pieper'll get his hands dirty. Radiomen like Imhof will work in radio maintenance or communications. And regular gunners, like Hill and Williams, will help out in the mess hall."

"K.P. again! Of all miserable things!" Williams groaned.

"My special skill was never peeling potatoes!" Hill added.

"Use your trigger finger to peel 'em, Hotshot," Cordell laughed. "Don't get burned up yet. We have enough crews here so you won't be drafted more'n once or twice a week."

The reason for this new policy was the shortage of ground personnel because of rotation. On July 19, sixteen of our 394th Squadron's high-time "ground-pounders" (non-flying personnel) were rescued by the army rotation plan, returning to the U.S.A. They had been sweating through life on jungle islands for two or three years, so they deserved it. But their replacements had not come in. To beef up needed services, some flight crew members were drafted for shifts of ground duty.

Just when we lost some of our mechanics, our need for maintenance increased. The new training program had three time slots for flying—morning, afternoon, and night, each four hours. The same planes were often scheduled to fly three times a day, which required more maintenance than the old days when a plane flew only one combat mission a day.

"Boy, oh boy! Do we ever have a juicy new target!" Bishop said to me after meeting with Major Luketz.

"What is it?" I asked, eager for a change in routine.

"Formosa!" His thin black mustache curled up in a smile. "It's a new Bomber Barons campaign—we've never been there."

"Great! We'll pioneer a new route. When do we start?"

"August first, day after tomorrow. We may get a dozen strikes there in the next two weeks."

"Wow! That's a welcome change! A lot of the men are bored."

"Yes," he agreed. "All this training stuff gets old pretty quick, compared to combat. And guess what else is new—"

"What?"

"We've been authorized to use H2X! Summer weather over Formosa is pretty cloudy, but we can now bomb by radar. We'll carry two navigators in the lead plane, one as lead navigator, one as radar operator."

"Hot dog! Who gets to go first?"

"Everybody wants to get in on the first mission, of course. Major Luketz will fly as squadron leader, with Captain Campbell as copilot, Hackenberger as bombardier. I'll be radar operator and you'll be lead navigator."

"Lead navigator!" *My first time! I wouldn't miss this trip for all the tea in China!*

That afternoon, I started feeling sick. Stomach cramps led to diarrhea, with frequent hasty trots to the nearest latrine. Then a feeling of weakness—I left the flight line and wobbled home to flop on my cot.

Seitz returned from the flight line with news.

"Hey, Hamilton, we have a mission to Negros tomorrow."

"I know, but I can't make it. I've got the G.I. trots."

"When did it start?"

I covered my eyes with an arm. "Soon after lunch."

"Good old army chow! Hope it's not an epidemic."

"Get a replacement navigator for tomorrow's mission, Seitz. I just hope I'm well enough to fly the next day, on the first mission to Formosa. My first trip as lead navigator!"

"Great! Hope you do get to make that one!"

Next morning, my crew members flew with another navigator on a three-and-a-half-hour bombing mission to Negros Island in the central Philippines. I skipped breakfast and went to the squadron dispensary to be first in line for sick call. A couple of dozen more men had joined the line by the time Sergeant Simpson and Corporal Mulroy came to open shop. Clipboard in hand, the good-looking sergeant wrote down everyone's name, rank, and ailment. Captain Dolce arrived a little later, and sick call began.

"What do you have for jungle diarrhea, Doc?" I asked Dolce. "I've got to get over it before tomorrow! I'm lead navigator on the big new mission to Formosa!"

"Diarrhea's our most common ailment, and we give 'em all a chalky fluid called Kaopectate. Take two spoonfuls every four hours, and you might be over the trots by morning."

"Sure hope so."

"Sergeant, give this man a bottle of Kaopectate."

"Thanks, Doc." I took the bottle and left.

The rest of that day was misery for me. I lay on my cot, feeling weak, skipping meals to empty my body. I took three spoonfuls of the medicine instead of two, every three hours instead of four, hoping that overdosing would speed recovery. It seemed to work, because my trots to the latrine had subsided by evening, and I found the strength to go to the briefing tent.

At briefing we learned that our targets were at the city of "Takao" (now called Kaohsiung) in southwestern Formosa, the large island off the east coast of China now called Taiwan. The primary target was the railroad marshalling yard north of the city, and if clouds hid that scene, the secondary target was a Japanese army storage depot southeast of the city. Neither of these targets would show up on the H2X radar screen (low contrast), but if both were covered by clouds, we could bomb the secondary by a special technique called "H2X offset bombing."

All four squadrons of Bomber Barons were going. Lieutenant Colonel James would lead his old 72nd Squadron at the front of the group; the 394th Squadron was second. Each squadron had a radar plane and crew in its lead position, a first for the Fifth Bomb Group.

We were told to expect plenty of opposition. There were dozens of enemy aircraft on Formosa, and heavy-caliber flak guns could easily reach our bombing altitude of 12,000 feet. *This mission may be dangerous as well as exciting!*

In the darkness of early morning, the lead crew arrived at our plane to discover that it was not 618, our familiar radar airplane. It was 845, "Stardust," which I had never seen before.

"Where's 618, our radar ship?" Major Luketz asked the crew chief.

"It's laid up for maintenance—engine change," he answered. "But 845 here is another radar plane we borrowed from the 31st Squadron—they had two of 'em. We loaned them 673, 'Wild Irish Rose,' in exchange."

"Bishop, go through this plane to make sure it's a real radar plane with everything you need on board," Luketz said.

He did it rapidly. "Yep, it's real—got it all."

In the darkness, we climbed on board through the open bomb

bays, where Hackenberger paused to check the seven bombs hanging there—six 500-pound regulars and one air-marking smoke bomb. I took my equipment to the navigator station in the nose, while Bishop took his to the radar position on the flight deck. Then the pilots and other crew members completed their usual checks by the dim interior lights.

"Have a good mission!" the crew chief called to the pilot.

"We will," Luketz replied through his open side window. "We'll bring her back to you!"

At the first light of dawn, the airfield reverberated to the sound of ninety-six big engines starting. Soon the dispatcher's flashlight waved us onto the taxiway to join the stream of bombers creeping toward the runway. As lead plane in the second squadron, we were seventh out of twenty-four to take off.

One after another, the six big bombers ahead of us took off at one-minute intervals, each with an earth-shaking roar. Our turn came at 6:10 A.M.; the tower flashed us a green light, and we roared down the runway as the engineer called out airspeeds. Standing behind the pilots with Bishop and Hackenberger, I began to sweat as the overloaded airplane used up all the runway. Just before the end, the rumble of wheels ceased; we lifted off into the glare of the rising sun on our nose. Like a circus performer walking a tightrope, the pilot eased the plane along, twenty feet above the ocean waves for the first mile, as we slowly gained airspeed enough to begin climbing.

"Navigator, what's our heading?" Major Luketz called out.

"335 degrees," I cried above the engine noise.

Luketz rolled the wheel to the left, and we turned to fly northward along the east coast of Samar. The beaches below us were going our way, a golden pathway in the morning sunlight, contrasting vividly with the dark green hillsides rising to our left, and with the several shades of blue water on our right. With a strong impression of the beauty of the scene below, I left the flight deck and crawled through the tunnel to the nose to start navigating.

At seven we left the north end of Samar behind, and half an

hour later passed Catanduanas Island, continuing on our northwesterly course over the dark blue Pacific. Flying as individual planes en route to an assembly point two more hours away, we could see the planes ahead of us at three mile intervals. We were like twenty-four giant silver beads in a string seventy miles long, suspended over a dark velvet sea.

By nine A.M. I could see the mountains of northern Luzon, the largest island in the Philippines, coming into view on our left as we drew closer to its coastline. At 9:44 we reached the assembly point, Cape Engaño at the northeast tip of Luzon. We joined the planes already circling there, waiting for the ones behind to arrive, gradually finding assigned places in squadron and group formations. By 9:55 the whole group had assembled, with "Able," "Baker," Charlie," and "Dog" squadrons in sequence as we flew on toward Formosa. We were leading "Baker Squadron."

Now there were only two more hours to the target, the hardest ones. The formation climbed to 12,000 feet and we put on oxygen masks. The air inside grew colder.

The nose gunner waived "Hi!" as he passed me to enter his turret, and Hackenberger came forward to set up his Norden bombsight. He put on his mask and plugged into the oxygen outlet.

"Do you think you'll be able to use that bombsight for visual aiming today?" I asked him through my oxygen mask.

"Maybe so," he replied. "Weather's been good so far."

"But it's forecast to be messy over target."

"We'll just have to wait and see."

The wait was brief. We flew through a weather front between Luzon and Formosa, and on the north side of the front, clouds stretched out in solid layers both above and below our altitude of 12,000 feet. It was also very cold. Outside air had been a chilly 38 degrees Fahrenheit south of the front, but on this side it dropped twenty degrees to a frigid 18. There were no heaters on B-24's, so the inside air was nearly that cold. We all put on our fleece-lined leather jackets, trousers, boots and gloves.

"Pilot to Radar, over," Major Luketz said on interphone.

"Radar to Pilot, go ahead," Bishop's voice replied.

"Did you see that P-38 go by? It was a weather-recco F-5 just back from the target. He told us that the target is fully covered with undercast—we will need a radar bomb run, for sure."

"Roger, that means we hit the secondary target. I've got the radar gear warmed up and ready."

I continued to plot loran fixes to determine our position, which told me that the winds aloft had shifted significantly at the weather front. Here we had a strong crosswind from the east, 090 degrees at 32 knots.

"Pilot to Crew, Colonel James just turned over group lead to us. His H2X unit burned out, so he can't lead a radar bomb run. He's leading his whole squadron around in a big circle to the tail end of the group. You can see 'em going by our left wing."

I looked out the navigator's left side window. There they were, the 72nd Squadron—six bombers flying toward the rear, wheeling around to become the fourth squadron in the group. *The first shall be last! We are now leading the whole group!*

"Radar to Navigator, the southern tip of Formosa is now on screen, range twenty miles at forty degrees azimuth, over."

"Nav to Radar, that checks with my loran position. We're on course for secondary target, groundspeed 152 knots, ETA 11:48."

"Pilot to all Gunners, test fire your weapons now." The plane shook as eight .50-caliber machine guns fired short bursts.

The solid layer of cumulus clouds below hid all of Formosa (Taiwan) except its central range of mountains, which rose up through the clouds in a line of peaks stretching northward. Two snow-capped heights towered above the rest, Kuan Shan, fifty miles inland, reached our 12,000-foot level, and more distant Tung Shan, over 13,000 feet high. *Those snow-covered peaks sure would make a pretty picture postcard!*

"Radar to Bombardier, the target's too flat to pick up, so we'll make the bomb run on a coastal promontory that shows up on our radar screen. It's 8,000 feet ahead of the target, so delay bomb release 31 seconds to cover it."

"Roger," said Hackenberger. He set the delay, and waited.

"Bombs away!" Hackenberger called over the interphone. The first bomb out was a special air-marking smoke bomb which burst below our plane to mark the spot where the other planes behind us would release their bombs as they flew past the smoke.

"No Jap fighters!" said a gunner on interphone. "Wonder where the Zeros are?"

"Maybe these clouds go down to the ground," another voice answered. "If the field is socked in, they can't take off."

"No flak, either," said a third voice. "How come?"

"I can answer that," said Bishop. "The clouds blocked visual aiming, and radar aiming was confused by the chaff we dumped. All during the bomb run, the planes behind us tossed bundles of tinfoil streamers through the bomb bay doors. That stuff reflects radar—it messed 'em up!"

"Why didn't it mess up our own H2X radar?" asked another.

"Our H2X was aimed ahead—the chaff was all behind us."

The return flight was uneventful and brief, nearly an hour shorter than the outbound leg. We landed at 4:35 P.M.—total time, ten and a half hours. All the way back, I felt a warm glow of pride. *I finally led the whole parade!*

We were eating lunch on Monday, August 6, when the mess hall loudspeaker came on with amazing news:

"Now hear this! Armed Forces Radio brings you this special bulletin: At 8:15 this morning, Tokyo time, the city of Hiroshima, on the Japanese island of Honshu, was completely destroyed by a single atomic bomb carried by one B-29. The atomic bomb is a new and revolutionary secret weapon, unleashed today for the first time. It released the kind of energy that fuels the sun itself. That single atomic bomb produced a giant fireball equal to twenty thousand tons of conventional explosives.

"President Truman urges the Japanese High Command to accept the Allied Armed Forces demand for unconditional surrender, to keep other Japanese cities from suffering the fate of Hiroshima."

We were stunned. Like most Americans, none of us had ever heard of even the possibility of such a weapon. I sat there in silence, trying to finish eating, while my mind raced to attempt to grasp what had happened. *One plane, one bomb, one city!*

Armed Forces Radio repeated that brief bulletin six times in the next half hour. My mind dwelt on the phrases, "the kind of energy that fuels the sun itself," and "a giant fireball equal to twenty thousand tons of conventional explosives." I felt sure that a new and fearful era had begun. I was glad that it was the Americans, not the Germans or the Japanese, who had developed the super weapon first. No one knew then how close both Germany and Japan (especially Japan) had come to beating us in that nuclear race.

THE JAPANESE ATOMIC BOMB

Japan detonated its own experimental atomic bomb on a tiny island in the Sea of Japan at sunrise on August 12, 1945, just six days after our first atomic bomb destroyed Hiroshima. It was a U-235 uranium bomb of about the same power as ours, developed by Dr. Yoshio Nishina at a secret plant in Konan, Korea, according to David Snell, reporter for the *Atlanta Constitution*, who interviewed the Japanese officer in charge of security at Konan. Japan planned to use their atomic bomb to destroy our invasion fleet. (See "Undercover" in *World War II* magazine, July 1995).

"Hey, Hamilton, you want to go to Manila?" Captain Davenport called to me from his desk in the Squadron Operations tent, telephone in hand.

"Sure," I replied, laying some navigator logs on Bishop's desk. "When?"

"Right now. Major Lewis, of Fifth Group staff, wants to fly there in the B-25, but he needs a navigator. Grab your stuff and report to him in Group Operations."

"Yes, sir!" I said, throwing my E6B computer and plotter into my navigation case. *A B-25! I've never flown in one!*

I found the twin-engine medium bomber parked on the flight line in front of Group Operations. With two rudders in the tail, it looked somewhat like a smaller version of our B-24s. This one had a broad blue stripe painted from the pilot's window to the tail, and under the pilot's window was "Bomber Barons Airliner." It was used as an executive transport by the Fifth Bomb Group.

"Hamilton, this trip is to ferry a high-time combat crew to Manila for rest leave," said Major Lewis.

"Whose crew got so lucky?" I asked.

"First Lieutenant Newsom, from your own squadron."

"We'll take 'em to Clark Field, won't we?"

"Of course. We'll stop there for lunch, refuel, and fly back this afternoon."

"Yes, sir," I said. "The heading is northwest, 313 degrees, and the trip should take a bit less than two hours each way."

It was exciting for me to fly in a new kind of plane, and also to see fresh scenery on a new route. The greenhouse nose of the B-25 gave the navigator-bombardier a wonderful view, much better than I was used to, and it was beautiful that day in the central Philippines. Lush green islands bordered by sandy beaches made vivid contrasts with several shades of blue water.

We flew over the large city of Manila both going and coming. It gave me an eyeful of the destruction of war. Burned-out buildings and rubble cried out their memories of the soldiers who died in the streets fiercely contesting every block. Flying over the historic old town, the Intramuros, I looked down into churches without roofs. *How many innocent people died when those roofs collapsed?* It made me sick to think of the human agony that accompanied the long, brutal struggle to drive out the Japanese.

Only recently, Hill told me the sad news of the death of his brother-in-law. His wife, Anne, wrote that her brother, Charles, in the 37th Infantry Division from Ohio, had been killed in action in this battle, and was buried in a military cemetery nearby only five months ago.

How would Hill feel if he were with me here, looking at the very scene where Charles died? It hits you so much harder when you see it in person!

I returned to Samar in a somber mood.

Next morning, August 8, Captain Davenport took off at sunrise in our newly-added second radar plane, 735 "Sweet Sue." He had our lead team with him—Bishop for radar, Hackenberger as bombardier, and I was lead navigator again. We led both our squadron and the whole group on this third mission to Formosa. Seitz was number three to take off in 199, "Daisy Mae," with his own crew, except for a replacement navigator.

This trip repeated the first mission as far as the group rendezvous at Cape Engaño, where we circled from 9:10 to 9:40 assembling the group combat box formation. From that north tip of Luzon, I led the group on a true course of 349 degrees, which went over the mountainous center of Formosa to our target, the airfield at the city of "Shinchiku" (now called Hsinchu). On the way, we climbed to our bombing altitude of 17,000 feet, to reduce the flak expected over target. Only our fleece-lined flying suits kept us from freezing.

At noon, black bursts of flak informed us that the target was near. The flak began a thousand feet below us, but got closer with every shot. A flash of memory brought back the time shrapnel hit my helmet and flak vest over Balikpapen. I felt the mental shock all over again.

The airfield was straight ahead, partly covered by clouds, but visible enough for Hackenberger to aim through his bombsight visually. At 12:04 he called "Bombs away!"

"They didn't drop out!" I shouted. "Your panel lights are still on!" Six green lights on his bombardier panel glowed.

"Aw, shit!" he said. "Some damn malfunction!" He turned his bombsight control backwards, and suddenly it worked—the panel lights went out one after another as bombs dropped.

"Too late," he said. "They'll be 3,000 feet beyond target."

Flak bursts nearby rocked the airplane.

"Too close for comfort! Let's get out of here!" Davenport said on interphone. He led the breakaway turn to the left, over the Formosa Strait. We flew over the water a few miles offshore, following the west coast of Formosa to its southern tip.

"Where are all the Jap fighters?" a gunner asked on interphone. "They said there were lots of 'em on this island."

"Maybe they flew them back to Japan to defend Tokyo."

"Break out the lunch," said Davenport. "I'll take us down to 10,000 feet so we can take off these oxygen masks and eat."

It was a lot warmer at the lower level. We stripped out of the heavy flying suits and masks, and ate the canned C-rations. They always tasted better in the air, after six or eight hours of flying, than they ever did on the ground.

I led the formation straight to the tip of Luzon, where the planes peeled off to fly back to Samar on their own. The sun was setting as we landed on Samar at 6:15 P.M.—total time 12:20.

At lunch on August 9, Armed Forces Radio brought us another special news bulletin:

"This morning the city of Nagasaki, on the southern Japanese island of Kyushu, was completely destroyed by a single atomic bomb carried by one B-29. This is the second Japanese city in four days to be obliterated by these amazing weapons of mass destruction. Although this bomb was a very different model, it also had the power of twenty thousand tons of T.N.T. Its giant fireball left a mushroom-shaped cloud towering 20,000 feet high.

"President Truman again called on Japan to surrender unconditionally, to save other Japanese cities from meeting the fate of Hiroshima and Nagasaki.

"In other news, at midnight last night, Russia declared war against Japan, and the Red Army immediately invaded Manchuria. They crossed the Amur and Ussuri Rivers and penetrated fourteen miles on a wide front, capturing many towns. The Japanese Army in Manchuria is reported to be fighting fiercely, but appears to be overwhelmed by the sudden onslaught."

The crowd in the mess hall was not stunned this time.

"A different kind of atomic bomb," Seitz said, "but still twenty thousand tons of explosive power!"

"You know how many B-24s it would take to carry that much?" I asked. "Maximum four tons each, so you'd need five thousand!"

"Can you imagine five thousand B-24s flying over Nagasaki and all dropping their full load at the same time?" James said.

"And that other news," Cordell said. "Russia's in it, too!"

"They sure waited long enough!" Seitz said. "Those jackals came in at the last minute just to get a piece of the kill!"

"Well, it might help persuade Japan to surrender," I said. "Russia, and the second atomic bomb, both on the same day."

"Maybe we won't have to invade Japan after all," Cordell added. "Maybe the war'll end before it comes to that."

The mess hall loudspeaker came on again. "Now hear this: Major Luketz has ordered all 394th Squadron personnel to turn in all firearms to the Personal Equipment building, effective immediately. This includes combat flyers' .45 caliber pistols. Turn them in today! That is all."

"Damn! Why does Luketz want to take my .45?" Cordell moaned.

"Maybe he's afraid we'll have a shooting orgy celebrating the end of the war," I said.

"Whatever the reason, we have to turn 'em in," Seitz said. "Orders are orders."

Captain Davenport left the 394th Squadron on August 10, promoted to Fifth Group Operations. First Lieutenant Seitz, his former assistant, stepped into his shoes to become the new Operations Officer for our squadron.

"My first act as Operations Officer is to schedule myself to lead the squadron on tomorrow's mission to Formosa with my own crew," Seitz told us at lunch.

"Good move," Cordell said.

"And I scheduled Hamilton as lead navigator. Now that I'm Operations Officer, maybe I can get this hotshot lead navigator to fly with *me* again." He sounded serious, but he smiled.

"Anytime," I chuckled. "Just twist my arm."

Late that night, the outdoor movie was stopped in mid-scene for an announcement: "Now hear this: Domei News (in Japan) has just reported that the Japanese are willing to accept the surrender terms—"

Whoops and screams interrupted the announcement as most of the audience heard no more, but rushed out, cheering, to celebrate.

Earlier, my crew had attended the briefing for tomorrow's mission, and then gone to bed. We were awakened by distant gunshots, bedlam from the officers' and enlisted men's clubs, and radios blaring news in many tents near and far. We heard so many gunshots that it sounded like a battle zone, and rockets and flares soared over the palm trees.

"The war must be over," Cordell said. "What else would cause a celebration like this?"

"It's a good thing Luketz did collect the firearms in our squadron. All the shooting is in other squadron areas."

"If the war's over, there'll be no mission tomorrow," James said. "Let's go for a beer and celebrate!"

"Wait till I find out whether that's true," Seitz ordered, pulling on clothes and leaving. A few minutes later he returned, looking grim.

"The war's *not* over, and we *do* have the mission tomorrow. The Japs announced that they were willing to surrender—*if* they could keep their emperor. But that's a condition, and we demand unconditional surrender. Our side has not agreed—not yet."

We went back to bed to get what little sleep we could. The noise of misguided celebrating continued well beyond three A.M., our wake-up call time for the dawn takeoff. After our early breakfast, we found that quite a few men seemed to think that the mission was canceled. Sleepy gunners delayed some crew trucks, making their crews late at the flight line. Even some crew chiefs were late getting to their airplanes. The Personal Equipment men failed to report at all; we flyers had to crawl under a locked gate to get our parachutes and life vests.

The sun was just rising as Seitz led the 394th Squadron takeoff in number 649, "Hubba Hubba." The mission got off on time in spite of the difficulties. We were "Charlie Squadron" today, third of four in the group. We followed the usual route to the south end of Formosa, where our target was the aircraft factory at "Heito" (now called Pingtung). We approached at 14,300 feet. Black bursts of flak greeted us, but no fighters appeared. The flak got close enough to rock the plane. Sweat dripped from my face in spite of the frigid air; it wet my oxygen mask.

"James, this is your moment of glory," Seitz said on interphone, "your first time as lead bombardier. Make it a good one."

He did. Imhof's strike photos showed that more than half of the fifty-four 500-pound bombs from our squadron hit the target. Six large factory buildings and two smaller ones were completely destroyed, others damaged; surrounding shops were blazing. Black smoke rose high in the air.

"Let's have lunch," Seitz said as we were homeward bound. "This may be our final mission—if so, it's a good one."

We landed at 4:30 P.M. after ten hours twenty minutes of flying.

Next morning, August 12, twenty-four bombers took off at dawn for the seventh (and last) Bomber Barons mission to Formosa. Major Luketz led both our squadron and the group in radar plane 618, with Hackenberger as lead bombardier. Wildey was next in 401 with his own crew except for a replacement bombardier, followed by Lieutenants Ownby in 406, Ellenbecker in 474, Sershen in 380, and Walsh in 366. The group flew to southern Formosa. The primary target was the airfield at "Kagi" (now called Kang Shan).

The airfield was largely covered by clouds, but Luketz led a bomb run over an open patch. Ten seconds before release, clouds covered the aiming point; Hackenberger stopped the bomb release. Two other bombardiers did not stop it, so eighteen 500-pound bombs dropped there. (Later photos showed half of them hit the runway.) Neither flak nor fighters came up at Kagi.

Luketz led the group to the secondary target, the railroad marshalling yard at "Takao" (Kaohsiung). Here, too, no planes came up to contest the skies. Heavy flak rocked our bombers, but none of them were shot down.

The railroad yard had fewer clouds, permitting visually-aimed bombing. The results were unusually good—95 percent of all remaining bombs hit the target. Two direct hits completely destroyed the roundhouse, while others demolished three large buildings, the turntable, railroad tracks, freight cars, and one locomotive ("blown clean off the track!" said Hackenberger). It was a great final mission for the Bomber Barons.

On August 13, Bomber Command canceled the eighth mission to Formosa, for which our crews had been briefed the night before. Instead, the same crews and planes were sent on a ferry mission, leaving behind all gunners and bombardiers to save weight. The planes flew empty to Clark Field, Manila, where each picked up twenty soldiers and their equipment, then ferried them to Okinawa, where the Army of Occupation for Japan was being assembled. Many other aircraft of all shapes and sizes were also making the six-hour ferry flight from Manila to Okinawa. Our crews stayed overnight at Okinawa, then returned their empty planes to Samar on the 14th.

On Tuesday, August 14, in the early afternoon, came the long-expected announcement that Japan had agreed to accept the terms of surrender. This brought jubilation and cheers at our base, but no wild celebration—too much premature celebrating had left our men burned out. Our celebrations now were after-supper gatherings for "beers and cheers" in the "Top of the Rock," and also at the Enlisted Men's Club, where free ice cream sodas and sundaes made a big hit.

The next day, Sunday, August 15, official cease-fire orders went out from the highest officials on both sides to their forces in the field. Ours was a teletype from Commander, Thirteenth Air Force (Major General Paul Wurt-Smith) to the Fifth Bomb Group, received at 8:45 A.M.: "STOP ALL STRIKES AGAINST JAPANESE. CALL BACK ALL MISSIONS NOW IN PROGRESS. RADIO TIME AND DETAILS OF YOUR LAST MISSION PERFORMED."

At last it was official! I felt profoundly grateful that the killing had stopped. *No invasion of Japan will be needed! World War Two is finally over!*

25. Peace in the Pacific

"WILD PEACE CELEBRATIONS" in America followed the radio news flash that Japan had agreed to surrender. That was a headline in the August 15, *Bomber Baronet,* our mimeographed news sheet.

"This is outrageous!" I said to Seitz. "In San Francisco, thousands of soldiers and sailors— in uniform—marched down Market Street in an unplanned peace parade. But rowdy ones fell out and smashed windows in thirty liquor stores to loot the booze! Then they turned cars over and set bonfires on Market Street!"

Seitz took the paper and read it. "What an ugly scene! They ought to be busted out of the service—dishonorable discharge—the whole lot of' em!"

"I agree! This is more than just 'boys will be boys.'"

"But troops need opportunities to celebrate in controlled situations, so they can blow off steam without rioting."

"Sounds like this event advertised for our outdoor theater: 'Victory Celebration Tonight: NAVY BASE BAND, at 7:15. Later, the movie—*Cinderella Jones,* starring Joan Leslie.'"

That was the first of a series of official celebrations, from Cease-Fire Day to V-J Day. Next came an official holiday for all mechanics and other flight line workers on Friday, August 17. (No planes had flown after the cease-fire anyway, except Wildey's frequent cargo flights to Leyte in the C-47.) Then came a dinner celebration in our 394th Squadron mess hall. For that, a written invitation was posted:

"The Mess Personnel cordially invite you to attend a V-J SUPPER at YE OLDE SQUADRONE MESSE HALLE, 18 August

1945 (Saturday), 1600 to 1800." The menu followed, featuring roast beef Southern style, potatoes and brown gravy, peas in butter, creamed corn, bread, butter and jam, orangeade and coffee, with "George Washington Pie" and "Victory Ice Cream."

"Best meal I ever ate in this mess hall!" said Cordell.

"Ditto," James burped appreciatively.

"They're celebrating my birthday a little early," Seitz said with a wink. "Nice birthday dinner!"

"Really?" I said. "When's your birthday?"

"How old will you be?" asked James.

"Tomorrow I'll turn twenty-three."

"Well, congratulations, old man!" Cordell said. "You're catching up, but I'm still a year older."

That evening I went to the officers' club to make Seitz a birthday card. I folded a sheet of letter paper in half, sketched an ink-line drawing of a blond pilot in front of a B-24 on the first page, above these words: "HAPPY BIRTHDAY TO OUR PILOT!" Inside, I wrote a poem, signed my name, and made the rounds of my crew to ask each one to sign the card.

Next morning, Sunday, August 19, the reveille bugle call woke up the four of us in our officers' crew tent. As Seitz got up, I said, "Happy Birthday, old man!"

"Well, thanks, Hamilton." He buttoned his shirt, smiling.

"Here's a card from the whole crew." I handed it to him. He looked at the front with a broad smile, then opened it to read:

"Happy Birthday, Marvin Seitz!
 Now's the time for peaceful flights!
  Thanks for PILOTing your crew
   Through the mess of World War Two!"

Below the verse, signatures flowed at all sorts of angles: "Bob Hamilton, Jim Cordell, Howard James, Bob Pieper, Tony Imhof, Jim Hill, Richard Herrema, Ben Gerson, Bob Williams."

"Thanks, fellows," Seitz said. "These names mean a lot!"

After breakfast, I was free to attend Protestant church at the group chapel. Chaplain Ivey's good service gave me a mellow feeling, so after church, I took my writing kit to a table in the officers' club to write letters to my family and three girl friends, Pauline, Sandy, and Persis. Writing them all at the same time made composing each letter easier; the news was the same, with variations in the terms of endearment.

I told them how glad I was that the bombing and killing was over: how my twenty-third mission was just before the cease-fire, how we had problems getting off on time because of the premature peace celebrations and wild parties the night before. I asked each what happened when she saw the end of the war.

With the writing finished, I lit my pipe and leaned back for a quiet smoke in a contemplative mood. *Pauline—Sandy—Persis—*I visualized each one, slowly, lovingly, longingly. My memories of each enriched my life in a special way. *Why does my mind dwell on Persis more than the others? That's not being fair. I ought to give'em equal time.*

New questions floated through my mind: *Am I old enough, or mature enough, to consider marriage soon? If so, which one should I share my life with? I ought to give'em all an equal opportunity.*

Later that day, Seitz received a "Happy Birthday!" letter from his wife, Doris, enclosing a snapshot of their baby, Marvin Junior. He showed it to us at chow time with a proud father's beaming smile. "Look at my great kid!"

"He's one to keep, all right!" Cordell said.

"Can't believe it arrived right on your birthday!" I said.

"Doris has an uncanny sense of timing," Seitz added.

Next day I saw Imhof and Pieper in the chow line. Both were sporting new stripes on their sleeves.

"Well, look at those pretty new stripes! TWO rockers under your sergeant stripes!"

"Yep, we're technical sergeants now!" said Pieper, looking proud.

"Did the whole crew get promoted again?" I asked.

"No, staff sergeant is as high as gunners can go," Imhof replied. "Only engineers and radio operators can reach the tech level, and we just did it."

"Congratulations! Now the whole crew has gone as high as each one can go." I said.

"True for the enlisted men, but what about the officers? When will any of you guys get promoted?" Imhof asked.

"Wish I knew, but I don't. Hope it's soon."

The training program, interrupted by the missions to Formosa and the end of the war, resumed now. *They're just giving us something to do in this transition to peace.* Five B-24s from our squadron flew to the practice bombing range to give pilots a try at using the bombsight. Seitz hit the tiny island target eight times out of ten separate practice bombs he dropped, amazing everyone, especially James.

"You'd make a hotshot bombardier!" James said.

"Just beginner's luck," Seitz replied.

"Wish I could do that well—I'm no beginner."

A few days later, the Bomber Barons sent a fleet of B-24s to Manila, four from each squadron, carrying the first wave of our high-time men to Clark Field, where they would be processed for return to the States. Demobilization began with "bringing the boys home"; discharge followed soon thereafter. The first to go home were the envy of all the rest of the group.

I enjoyed a new dividend of peace on Sunday, August 26—a day of fishing on the PT boat used by the Bomber Barons as the "crash boat" to pick up survivors when our planes fell into the sea. The powerful torpedo-boat throttled back to trolling speed for a leisurely deep-sea fishing trip for a deck full of men from our group.

What a beautiful day! The waves were gentle, the sky blue, and the tropical sun hot; most of us peeled off clothes down to shorts to add to our suntans. I felt like I didn't have a care in the world.

My Uncle Liston in Florida had taught me how to make good fishing lures; on this trip I got to try out a new game-fish lure I had made after the cease-fire. A two-foot-long silver mackerel struck it and gave me an exciting run before I brought him in. *What a beauty! Biggest fish for me since that big drumfish I got in Florida with Uncle Liston!* All the fish caught were taken to the mess halls for food, but our pride in catching them lingered on for many bragging sessions.

On August 25, the Bomber Barons began a new task of patrolling the south China seas for Japanese ship movements, to detect possible violations of the cease-fire agreements. The area covered was divided into four sectors: (1) Hong Kong to Swatow, (2) Swatow to Amoy, (3) Amoy to Foochow to Formosa, (4) Formosa to Myako Jima. Each squadron sent two bombers daily to one of the sectors, so all four were covered every day.

Major Luketz led in 735, "Sweet Sue," and Lieutenant Hill followed in 406, "Hubba Hubba," on the first day's patrol of sector one, reporting a fleet of 38 schooners and one SLC (small landing craft) near Swatow. These turned out to be authorized vessels, so our planes did not attack them.

On Thursday, August 30, Seitz led the China coast patrol in 735, "Sweet Sue," with me as his radar navigator. Lieutenant Ownby followed in 330, "Boomerang." Both planes carried full crews, including gunners, to add more eyes to the search.

We took off at six A.M. and followed the familiar route to the northern tip of Luzon, where we turned northwest to Swatow. Our altitude was 5,000 feet, low enough to see any ships moving along the surface. We were told to report all ships by radio at once; if they were unauthorized Japanese vessels, radio orders to attack would follow. Each plane carried ten bombs and plenty of bullets to cover such an attack if necessary. This counted as a combat mission (my twenty-fourth) since it came before the official V-J Day.

We reached the China coast at noon, and turned northeast to follow it toward Amoy. Swatow was off the left wing about ten miles away, where the Han river flowed into the sea. The China coast was quite irregular here—a series of bays, large and small, with little islands in them, traditional hangouts for oriental pirates through the centuries. We saw many native fishing boats, junks and sampans, but nothing large enough to be Japanese military transports, so we made no radio report.

Further inland were darkly forested hills and mountains, while the whole length of the coastal plain glowed with the vivid green of rice plants growing in the shallow water of rice paddies. *How familiar it all looks!* This was my China, land of my birth, where I had spent most of my life until age sixteen. This was the closest I had come to returning since leaving it four years ago. Seeing it so near made me feel nostalgic and pensive. I reached for my pipe and lit it.

What about my application for transfer to Army Intelligence in China? If it were approved now, would I want it? The war's over, so I don't need to fret about killing people any more. I'd like to see China again, this time as an adult. On the other hand, would I rather go home for discharge? I'm not sure.

We flew past the port of Amoy and Quemoy Island, then turned southeast across the Formosa Strait toward Tainan, Formosa.

"Pilot to Bombardier," I heard on interphone, "we've left China behind—might as well dump our bombs and go home."

"Roger, I'll drop 'em on safety, in train."

James adjusted his intervalometer for one-second intervals and squeezed his bomb release. Ten glowing lights on his panel went out one after another.

"Bombs away!" James called. But they were not dropped in anger; they were jettisoned at sea in peace. *Peace in the Pacific.*

The trip home, past southern Formosa, Luzon and Samar, was

scenic but uneventful. Sunset and twilight went by before we made a night landing at 6:45 P.M.

The day after the mission, I got two "sugar reports," one from Pauline, the other from Sandy. Both told about cease-fire celebrations in their small towns as something special. Pauline said she thought her twin brother, Paul, was on a navy ship headed to Tokyo Bay for the surrender ceremony. He hoped to come home soon after that, and she hoped I would too. Sandy said how excited she was to see the end of civilian rationing—shoes, tires, gasoline, canned goods, and coffee would all be plentiful again very soon—"the better to welcome you home!"

Next day a "sugar report" came from Persis. My heart beat faster when I saw her name, and I ripped open the envelope eagerly to read—how happy she was, spending the summer in a mountain cabin in the Sierras, where her father ran a sawmill. The nearest city, Sonora, had less than three thousand people, but those lumberjacks put on quite a celebration when the cease-fire came, drinking and dancing in the streets. She'd be leaving in September for Stanford University School of Nursing in San Francisco, where she'd like to see me whenever I came through there on my way home.

I'd love to see you, Persis! But—am I ready to go home yet? Maybe I'll go to China in Intelligence, and have a career in the postwar army. Maybe you'll even be through nursing school before I get back.

I wrote Persis a cheerful letter telling her about my deep-sea fishing trip, and how I thought that she was a wonderful, lovely, happy girl I'd like to have around. But I didn't mention coming home. *Bob, you have some major decisions you need to make, and soon!*

Sunday, September 2, 1945, was the day appointed for the final ceremony of the war. Tokyo Bay was the setting, with a large fleet of American warships anchored there. The stage was the open deck of the battleship U.S.S. Missouri; the players were dozens of high-ranking officers from all the nations involved in the Pacific war.

The show was brief, only twenty-two minutes, beginning at 8:30 a.m. Tokyo time (7:30 Philippine time). I listened to it, along with many other Bomber Barons, on the radio in the mess hall during a prolonged breakfast.

"Americans have the largest group here," said the radio reporter. "We have many officers from every branch of service on the deck of this great ship. All are wearing khaki field uniforms, open collar, no tie, no jacket. Seems to be a fashion statement that this is just a working day for us. In contrast, all the other officials—Australian, British, Canadian, Chinese, Dutch, French, New Zealander, and Japanese—are wearing formal uniforms with ties and jackets. The three Japanese diplomats are decked out in full tuxedos with top hats and white gloves!"

The radio reporter went on to describe how everyone stood at rigid attention while General MacArthur stepped up to the microphones to read a brief speech. The general said that he had been appointed Supreme Commander of Allied Powers (American, British, Chinese, and Russian) for the occupation of Japan, and that everyone in Japan, including the Emperor, will obey his orders for the duration of that occupation. He also said that he will rule the Japanese people with justice and tolerance.

He sat down on one side of a large velvet-covered table to begin the signing ceremony. Without a word, Japanese Foreign Minister Shigemitsu sat down on the other side of the table and signed the surrender document for the Japanese government. He was followed by General Umezo for the Japanese Army, and Admiral Tomioka for the Japanese Navy. General MacArthur signed as Supreme Commander of Allied Powers (SCAP), then Admiral Nimitz for the United States, followed by officers from China, Britain, Russia, Australia, Canada, France, Netherlands, and New Zealand, in that order.

MacArthur then returned to the microphones for a closing speech:

"It is my earnest hope—indeed, the hope of all mankind—that from this solemn occasion a better world shall emerge out of the blood and carnage of the past, a world founded upon faith and understanding, a world dedicated to the dignity of man and the fulfillment of his most cherished wish for freedom, tolerance and justice." He paused to look around at the officials present, adding, "Let us pray that peace be now restored to the world, and that God will preserve it always."

When that ceremony was over, the radio network switched us to Washington, where President Truman proclaimed September second as "V-J Day," to be remembered ever after for our victory over Japan. "We should not forget Pearl Harbor," he said; "the Japanese militarists will not forget the U.S.S. Missouri." (Missouri was President Truman's home state. For the surrender ceremony, that battleship was selected to honor him.)

My brother David's a sailor on the battleship Missouri—wonder if he got to see the ceremony first-hand? I'll write to ask him.

Seitz poured himself another cup of breakfast coffee. "That's it, guys. It's all over now."

"Hard to believe," I said. "World War Two is finally over."

Cordell lit a cigarette. "Sooner 'n we expected."

"Thanks to two atomic bombs," said James.

"You got that right, buddy," I said. "Without those two bombs we would've had to launch the great invasion of Japan."

"And that would've been one helluva scrap!" Cordell said.

"Yessirree! General Brandt told us that the invasion of Japan would be the greatest battle ever fought in the Pacific!" I said. "It could've doubled the cost of the whole Pacific war from Pearl Harbor to the present—cost in lives, effort, time, equipment, and treasure."

"Speaking of cost in lives—better include our own lives there. We were slated to be in the thick of that battle. We could've been wiped out easily in the course of it," Seitz said.

Cordell looked grave. "Those atom bombs saved *our* lives! Never thought of *that* before."

"Yep, we sure dodged the bullet on that number," James said.

"Thank God for the atomic bomb!" I said.

The conversation paused for a minute while its implications sank in.

> ## THE PLANNED INVASION OF JAPAN
>
> The invasion of Japan was code-named "Operation Downfall," with two major steps. After the secrets were declassified, we learned that the first step, "Operation Olympic," would have been the massive invasion of southern Kyushu scheduled for November 1, 1945. When Kyushu was secured, the Far East Air Forces (including the 13th) would have moved from Okinawa to newly captured bases on Kyushu, to cover the second step, "Operation Coronet," an even larger invasion of the beaches of central Honshu (near Tokyo) on March 1, 1946.
>
> All the military units and their commanders were named in the Pentagon's plan, and the forces were being moved into position for the assault, when our atomic bombs brought a surprise ending to the war. Invasion casualty estimates ranged from a low of a quarter-million Americans and a million Japanese, to a high of one million Americans and four million Japanese. All those lives were spared by using two atomic bombs on two smaller cities, convincing Japan of the need to surrender. ("Greatest Battle Never Fought: The Invasion of Japan," *World War II*, July 1995)

"Well, now that the war's over, how many of us are planning to stay in the army?" Seitz asked.

"Are you kidding?" James laughed. "I'd never stay in—not one hot minute longer than they make me!"

"Our enlisted men would probably agree with you," I said.

"I'd like an Air Force career, but not as a Flight Officer," Cordell said. "It's very hard to get promoted out of that rank."

"I've been debating whether to stay in or not," Seitz said. "I enjoy the military life, and I've done well in it, both in the Infantry and the Air Corps—"

"You're a natural officer," I said, "my idea of what a good officer should be."

"That goes for me too," said James.

"Really, Seitz, if you stay in, there's no limit to how high you might go!" Cordell said.

"But my wife doesn't like the travel or the separations. You guys are all single, so you don't have that problem. I feel torn. I'll probably go back to civilian life in Iowa for the sake of Doris and Marvin Junior."

"I'm debating whether to stay in or get out, too," I said. "I like Army life—don't mind the discipline. If my request for transfer to Intelligence in China comes through, I'd be tempted to stay in. On the other hand, I've always wanted to be a teacher—"

"I thought so!" James said. "Always giving us lectures on everything under the sun."

"—and for that, I need to finish both college and graduate school. And—I might want to get married soon. And then—there's just something nice about going home."

That evening the Fifth Bomb Group staged its own V-J Day Ceremony at the outdoor theater. On stage sat Colonel James, Chaplain Ivey, and the Bomber Barons Band led by Captain Herring.

First we stood to sing two verses of "America" to the music of the band. Chaplain Ivey then gave a short sermon on "The Blessing of Peace." We stood and sang "God Bless America." Colonel James gave a brief speech on "The Significance of V-J Day," pointing out the pride we could take in the achievements of the Army

Air Forces in winning the Pacific war. Then we closed by singing two verses of "The Star Spangled Banner."

I enjoyed the whole ceremony. It gave me a warm glow of pride in my country and my army unit, and it gave me a sense of closure on the war. My future was still as unsettled as ever, and my romantic life unresolved. But I felt peace of mind about where I was, and what I was doing then, on that first day of official peace in the Pacific.

Most of the crowd stayed for the movie which followed, *The Wizard of Oz*, starring Judy Garland, one of the very few films in color circulating during World War II. "Somewhere, over the rainbow" lay the Emerald City. With the end of the war, I felt that it was almost within reach.

26. Off-Base Adventures

"Time for a pass off base!" I said to Bishop in the Operations tent. "I haven't visited any part of these Philippine Islands except this little south end of Samar."

"Why don't you start with a visit to Leyte?" he replied. "The officers club at Tacloban is a nice place for a brief R-and-R."

"How do I do that?"

"Phone ahead for a reservation, get your pass from the orderly room, then hitch a ride on the next C-47 flight across the bay."

The Gulf of Leyte stretched out below the "Bomber Barons Airliner" as it flew from Samar westward to Tacloban. In the cabin were bags of outgoing mail, other cargo, and several hitch-hikers—enlisted men and officers. Wildey sat in the pilot's seat, watching his copilot, Lieutenant Lewis, fly the plane. I sat in the jump seat behind them, enjoying the view on this clear, sunny morning. Ahead to the left, I saw the dark green foliage of Mount Cancajana on Leyte, the highest peak nearby, over 4400 feet. It was balanced by other mountains on the right, rising in the distance in northern Samar, with the U.S. naval base at their feet on the north shore of the gulf. Dead ahead was the runway of Tacloban Army Airfield, and a few miles south of it, the runway at Tanauan, where my friends were buried in the military cemetery nearby. *Maybe I could drop by the cemetery to see where they're buried. I think I'd like that.*

The plane landed at Tacloban after a twenty-minute flight. I waved farewell to Wildey and walked, bag in hand, to the transient officers' quarters (a series of tents). After checking in there, I hiked to the officers club on a hilltop nearby.

The club was a spacious building with wood trusses overhead

and walls with generous open window screening to entice the hilltop breezes to flow through it. This was the officers club for a major headquarters (Thirteenth Air Service Command), larger and more luxurious than our own Quonset-hut club. This one included a dining hall with meals considerably better than the canned C-rations that formed the bulk of our squadron mess hall offerings. The dining hall drew me in immediately to enjoy my best midday meal since leaving America.

Contented and happy, I stepped through double screen doors on the far side onto a large balcony overlooking San Pedro Bay, the major anchorage for Leyte. Beyond the blue water, the green hills of Samar rose in the distance. The bay was full of ships and landing craft of all shapes and sizes, some moving but most at anchor. From the near shore, the runway at Tacloban stretched northward into the bay, with its toy-sized airplanes flying low over the ships.

I lit my pipe and settled back in a chair to enjoy the scene. Feeling mellow, I wanted to share the view with a friend. I thought of my tail gunner, whose artistic eye would appreciate its color and beauty. *Too bad Hill isn't an officer—sure wish I could bring him next time I come.*

"Quite a view, isn't it?" I looked behind me to see a big blond Air Corps major.

"Yes, sir, it sure is!" I saw at a glance that he was no flyer—his khaki shirt had no wings, and he wore glasses. (All flyers had 20-20 vision without glasses.)

"Did you know that you're looking at the place where the U.S. invasion of the Philippines took place?" he asked.

"No, Major. Can you tell me about it?"

"October 20, 1944—San Pedro Bay here was crowded with the invasion fleet, and another naval task force steamed in Leyte Gulf, off to the right. The warships shelled the coast from Tacloban south to Dulag—twenty-two miles—beginning at dawn. B-24s from the Fifth and Thirteenth Air Forces bombed all Jap airstrips nearby, and our B-25s hit their defenses on the beaches before the landing craft swarmed in. Navy fighters from carriers in the Gulf tangled with Jap fighters in the air, and strafed the beaches in front of the landings."

"Where was the beachhead?"

"At Tanauan, ten miles south of here. The Japs had built three airstrips along this coast, at Tacloban, Tanauan, and Dulag. We wanted to seize them first and put them to immediate use for our fighters. The Sixth Army soon poured ashore along the whole twenty mile stretch."

"So here's where MacArthur's famous return to the Philippines began," I said.

He laughed. "After the beachhead was well secured, the general waded ashore in front of the cameras."

"Old 'Dugout Doug' never fails to stand up and claim all the credit."

"He's a glory hound all right," the major agreed. "Did you hear the fictitious quote attributed to Big Mac?" He paused, struck a pompous pose, and boomed, "'With the help of God, (and a few marines), I HAVE RETURNED to the Philippines!'"

That afternoon I hiked to the beach wearing a T-shirt and swimming shorts. The sun was hot, but the water cooled me, and I enjoyed alternating between swimming and sun-bathing. Then a group of men playing volleyball in the sand needed more players, so I got sucked into the game. It was a carefree afternoon.

Dinner at sunset in the officers club was a gourmet treat compared to my usual fare. After dessert and coffee, I retired to the bar. There I saw the major who had told me about the invasion, sitting alone at a small table. His glass was half drunk, and he looked like he was, too.

"Hi, Major," I said. "May I join you?"

"Sure, Lieutenant," he replied.

"Thanks for telling me about the invasion here. I love history, and like to learn what happened at any historic place I visit."

"This area's historic for another reason, too," said the major, slurring his speech slightly.

"What's that?"

"Three days after the invasion, the Jap fleet steamed this way to challenge our navy here. The Battle of Leyte Gulf—October 23 to 26—broke the back of the Jap navy. Our navy paid a heavy price, but we beat 'em bad! It was a historic turning point of the war." He drained his glass.

"What're you drinking? I'll buy you another."

"Gin and tonic." That was a drink I had never tried. I brought back two of them.

"No hard liquor's available at our squadron bar," I said. "I'm surprised they have it here."

"Not much choice, though—just gin or whiskey. But here's to you, pal." He raised his glass with an unsteady hand.

"Cheers," I said, clinking his glass. Then a sip—the taste reminded me of turpentine. "Wow! This drink tastes like pine tree sap! It'll take some getting used to!"

"You never had gin before?" His bushy blond eyebrows arched, wide-eyed. "Well, Lieutenant, you do have some growing up to do."

"I had a sheltered life—preacher's kid—never tasted alcohol 'til I joined the army. But every kind of liquor seems strange at first sip. Liking any of it is an acquired taste. First beer I had reminded me of horse piss, but now I've grown to like the stuff. My first sip of whiskey puckered my mouth like battery acid, but now I drink a straight two-ounce shot after every mission."

"This gin will grow on you, too, with more experience." He drank his glass halfway down. "Experience is what makes us grow up. The more we have, the faster we mature."

"Which is why war makes us grow up so fast. It crams us full of life-or-death experiences."

"Yeah. But it's not just facing death—it's all kinds of situations—involving discipline, honor, responsibility, travel, sex—remember your first sexual experience?"

I hesitated. *Well, why not tell him?* "I haven't had it yet. I'm still a virgin." *In vino veritas.*

"Lordy, you have been sheltered!" He smirked. "I had my first sex at fourteen!"

"Fourteen! Wow! Incredibly young! What happened?"

"I grew up in a li'l country village in Nebraska. No fancy school there—just a one-room schoolhouse where a single middle-age woman taught all the kids in grades one to eight. I was always big for my age—big, blond, husky Swede, taller 'n my old man at fourteen. Teacher started asking me to stay after school to help her with the chores—bringing in coal for the pot-bellied stove, sweeping the floor, washing the blackboards—all that sort o' stuff."

"One-room school teachers were also their own janitors, I see."

"Yeah. Well, she gave me hugs to thank me for my help, and the hugs gradually got longer and cosier. Then hugs led to kisses—they grew more passionate each day. Then one day her hand slipped down inside my pants—"

I felt a hot, prickly sensation behind my ears. *This story is making me very uncomfortable!*

"Next thing I knew, she pulled me into the little toilet, pulled down my pants, and initiated me into the world of sex." He paused for another long drink.

I was stunned. Never in my life had I heard of such a thing—a teacher taking advantage of an eighth-grade student! (If tabloid papers existed in the 1940's, I had never seen one.)

"Did—did she have a family? Husband? Boy friend?" I asked.

"Naw—just an old maid schoolteacher with a room in Mrs. Jensen's boarding house."

"Weren't your parents suspicious? I mean—staying after school, day after day?"

"They thought it was great that I was helping teacher! Thought she might teach me a few things more if I hung around. Boy, did she ever! If they only knew!"

"How did this affair make you feel?"

"Made me feel grown-up and proud, at first—excited to have a big secret life. But by spring, it got boring to me. I only went on with it to satisfy her needs, and much less frequently."

"It was sex without love—just animal gratification," I said.

"Then something she said—on the last day of school—let me guess that she had done the same damn thing with another big eighth-grader the previous year—and also with a different one the year before that. I remembered she'd asked 'em to help her after school—one each year. Then I got mad—not a sudden rush, but a slow burn—made me more and more angry over time!"

"What'd you do about it?"

"Never said a thing 'bout her, 'cause I didn't want my parents to know 'bout me! Instead, years later, I got revenge on all her sisters—took out my anger on every woman I could date! I used 'em, abused 'em, and ditched 'em! I still do!" His face was flushed and scowling. "I live by the four F's—'Find 'em, Feel 'em, Fuck 'em, and Forget 'em!'"

My mind revolted in anger, then I just felt sick. I had heard soldiers talk like that before, but always as a joke. Here was a man who was dead serious. *He was a victim as a child, yes—but that doesn't give him license to victimize others! I hate the bastard!* To think that such a predator could be my fellow officer made me feel degraded and depressed. "I gotta go," I said, and left.

Next morning, I decided to visit the military cemetery at Tanauan. I caught the G.I. bus that shuttled up and down the east coast of Leyte between the many U.S. military camps and bases from Tacloban south to Dulag. Tanauan was nearly halfway at ten miles. The rutted dirt road offered spectacular views of Leyte Gulf most of the way. The sun rising higher over Samar Island brought forth a reflected trail of sunlight that shimmered on the waves, silhouetting the palm trees passing my window as we rolled along. But the occasional army trucks and other vehicles we saw stirred up clouds of dust that marred the beauty of the scene. Whenever one passed, we choked on dust that flew in through windows left open to relieve the tropical heat.

When we stopped at Palo, a market town halfway to Tanauan,

I saw beside us the rickety old civilian bus used by the Filipinos. It was jam-packed with people and small farm animals. Those I could see near the open windows were holding chickens, ducks, or small pigs in their laps. *Boy, am I glad I don't have to fight for standing room on THAT bus! I know how it smells—like the crowded, smelly place where I grew up in China, "the land of pagodas and pig odors."*

At Tanauan I left the bus, shook the dust off my khaki shirt and overseas cap, and strolled to the cemetery, which I could see from the road. It was a gently rolling hill rising out of the rice paddies all around, covered with small white crosses, row after row. I walked up the dirt driveway to the entrance, past a large, neatly-painted sign reading:

> **U. S. MILITARY CEMETERY**
>
> Here Americans landed 20 October 1944
> to liberate the Philippine Islands.
> Hallowed by the blood they shed,
> this place is dedicated to their memory.
> May they rest in peace.

I strolled along the driveway past hundreds of white crosses on both sides. Identified only by a dog-tag at the top, they all looked alike except where an occasional six-pointed Star of David indicated a Jewish burial. The driveway led to the back end of the cemetery where the newest graves were located. Some of them looked quite fresh. In this area of more recent burials lay the bodies of the crews we lost in the crashes on take-off, including my two best friends. I read one dog-tag after another looking for their names. There was no alphabetical order, just the sequence of burial. Finally I found their crew members, then my two navigator friends themselves.

Holding my cap over my heart, I said a prayer for each of

them, hoping it would give me a sense of closure on their loss. Suddenly I realized how heavy was the burden of grief I had repressed too long. Then I wept, tears mingling with dust on my face to make mud stains. Gradually I felt the burden lifting. I left with a new feeling of release, glad that I had made this pilgrimage.

After another good lunch at the Tacloban Officers Club, I caught an afternoon flight back to Samar. *I'm so spoiled by those good meals, I hate to go back to our squadron mess. I'll sure come back here again—when I can—and bring a friend. If only Hill could be an officer—*

September 8 (Saturday)—Seitz and crew led the daily reconnaissance mission to the coast of China. We flew in radar plane 618, while Lieutenant Monteith followed in 330. We covered Sector Two again, from Swatow to Amoy, like our last mission on August 30, but this flight did not count as a combat mission because it came after V-J day. *Combat flights are gone for good!*

The bomb load we carried was just reduced from ten bombs to two. That makes sense—we have not yet had to drop a single bomb on any enemy target since these surveillance flights began. The Japanese seem to be observing the terms of the cease-fire as ordered.

Our longer-serving men, both ground personnel and combat crews, were now leaving the squadron at the rate of thirty per week. We flew them to Clark Field, Manila, to be shipped home to the states either by sea or air. At the current rate, the whole squadron would be gone in less than four months. Meanwhile, rotation had cut our supply of mechanics to the point that our flight engineers worked a shift on the flight line when not flying. So Pieper was busier than ever.

Our crew ought to be eligible for rotation any day now. We heard rumors that the 307th Bomb Group, the other B-24 group in the 13th Air Force, had already sent home all of its crews who had 200 hours of combat flying time. Seitz' crew and many others in our Fifth Bomb Group have more than that (I have 250 hours myself), but we still wait for rotation. Such unfair practices put a big damper on morale for lots of Bomber Barons. But not for me, because—*I still haven't decided whether I want to stay in or get out of the army. I need more time to think about it.*

September 12 (Wednesday)—Seitz and crew again led the China sea sweep in 618, followed by Lieutenant Sandifer in 380. This time we covered Sector One, the China coast from Hong Kong to Swatow—a longer distance, so our flying time was more than fourteen hours. Seeing China again renewed my unresolved debate over whether or not to stay in the army, creating internal anxiety again. *What should I do?*

That was the last China mission using two B-24s. Beginning the next day, only one plane would patrol each sector. And the bomb size would shrink to the smallest we have, 100-pounders.

September 15 (Saturday). At lunch in the mess hall, I noticed something new about Seitz—captain's bars on his collar!

"Well, hello, *Captain* Seitz! When did you get promoted?" I asked.

Seitz put down his fork. "Orders came through just this morning." He beamed.

"Congratulations, Captain!" I snapped him a salute. He returned it, blushing.

James spread jam on a piece of hard toast. "Operations Officer should be a captain.'"

"You sure didn't waste any time getting to the P.X. to buy new captain's bars!" I said.

"Well, I've been waiting for this for a long time. Sort of expected it."

Cordell lifted his coffee cup. "Bet you've had those new bars in your pocket for a month!"

"Not quite!" Seitz laughed. "But I do have another cheerful bit of news. Last night I completed my night landing check in the C-47. Now I'm a fully qualified C-47 pilot."

James took a big bite of toast, saying through a full mouth, "Congratulations, old man!"

I took a sip of coffee. "In less than a month, you've become Operations Officer, a captain, and a C-47 pilot. Any more goals left?"

"Just one more—to see my wife and little boy again."

A week went by before our crew was scheduled to fly again. On Tuesday, September 25, our full crew was aboard 618, flying over the South China Sea toward Hong Kong to patrol Sector One again. Seitz' voice came over the interphone.

"Listen up, men. This is our last China mission together. These patrols will terminate September 30, and I've already posted all flight crew lists through the end of the month. So enjoy this flight—the last of its kind for us." He changed his voice tone. "This is your Captain speaking. Be sure to ask the stewardess for in-flight drinks and snacks. We thank you for choosing to fly Uncle Sam Airlines."

Then came a high-pitched voice: "This is the stewardess speaking. We have drinks and snacks for everyone in the waist section. Come to the waist and see my waist! Ooo, la la!"

Another falsetto voice came on: "This is the tail stewardess. Uncle Sam Airliners have lots of tail. Come to the tail and see my tail! Ooo, la la, indeed!"

Half an hour later, the wide mouth of the Pearl River came into view ahead. The Portugese colony of Macao sprawled on its west bank, to our left, while on our right, the British island of Hong Kong rose up out of the bay to its apex, Victoria Peak. We turned right to follow the China coast northeast to Swatow. The low coastal mountain range paralleled our heading, a few miles off our left wing. On a four thousand foot peak, I saw a beautiful six-storied pagoda. It brought to mind Dad's phrase, "land of pagodas and pig odors," which encapsulated the paradox of China. On the mountaintop stood the pagoda, alone, beautiful and beckoning, while at the foot of the hill lay the city of Pinghai, crowded with people and repulsive pig odors. Suddenly I thought of the crowded

Filipino bus I had seen on Leyte, and felt a wave of revulsion that resolved my indecision about China—I did not want to go back there, after all. I just wanted to go home to the comfortable civilization I had left behind. *Bob, I think you just made a major decision! Finally!*

This long, final mission lasted fourteen and one-half hours. On the homeward leg, Seitz spoke on the interphone again.

"Pilot to all crew members, I have an announcement. After considerable soul-searching, I decided to leave the army and request rotation back to the good old U.S.A. Yesterday I resigned as Squadron Operations Officer and recommended my assistant, First Lieutenant Benjamin Hill, to fill my shoes. When we land tonight, your skipper will be just a regular pilot again, on his way home to his wife and son."

"Navigator to Pilot, congratulations on your decision! I've been doing some similar soul-searching, and today I decided that the view I just had of the China coast was all I want to see of China for quite a while. I'm getting out of the army, too."

"Copilot to Navigator, durn if this ain't a coincidence! I've been soul-searchin' too, and today I decided to go back to civilian life! Maybe I can get a job flyin' for an airline."

"Engineer to Pilot, I'm amazed that you guys had to search your souls to decide whether to get out or not! Speaking for all the enlisted crew members, we knew right away what to do. We joined the army to win the war, and now that we won it, we want out! What could be simpler?"

"Tail Gunner to Engineer, well said! Three cheers and Amen!"

Two days later, September 27, promotion orders were posted for both James and me.

"Hey, Hamilton, we're both first lieutenants now!" James crowed like a bantam rooster.

"That's swell! We can both buy silver bars instead of gold."

Wonder what I'll do with my gold bars? Give them away? To whom?

On the following day, I celebrated my promotion by getting a three-day pass and hitching a plane ride to Manila's Clark Field, just two and a half hours away. I spent Friday night and Saturday night in transient officers' housing on base, and caught the G.I. bus to Manila for sight-seeing and souvenir-shopping by day. I walked all through the historic Intramuros, the old Spanish city within walls three centuries old. On Sunday, I hitched a plane ride back to Samar.

Next day, a letter from Persis arrived:
"Dear Bob, It's Thursday night, 9/20/45, and I'm writing from room 437 in my new home, the student nurses' dormitory. Just got back from a "pajama party"—a handful of friends gather in one of our dorm rooms for a quick party just before bedtime. Such fun we girls have!

"My first year of nursing school is off to a good start. I love my work in the hospital—it's so very interesting! More about that later, when I have more time to write. I've been wanting to get a letter off to you ever since we arrived here last week. You seem to bring out the deeper side in me, and I value that link with you.

"Now that the war is over, shouldn't you be coming home soon? You didn't mention that in your last letter. I hope it'll be soon! I'd love to show you some of downtown San Francisco—such a quaint and interesting city—and my hospital and dormitory—I have a great view of the bay from my window, since we're on such a hill.

"Whenever you get here, just give me I call, and I'll give you directions on how to get here. My number is JUniper 4-8603-extension 437. Goodnight for now. Sweet thoughts always, Persis."

I went to the officers' club to write a reply:
"Oct. 1, 1945. Dear Persis, Your swell letter reached me this evening, and I enjoyed it very much. I'm glad that you've found your new work so interesting. Those pajama parties must be like the midnight feasts we used to have in my dorm at college—a little food and a lot of fun.

"Guess what—I'm coming home pretty soon! I know I'll make it by late November (Thanksgiving), and if I fly, I may be there before Halloween. I think I'll fly my own plane back, so you might watch for those B-24's as they fly over the Golden Gate. If you see one with a black diamond on the tail (our squadron insignia) and somebody waving a white flag out the rear side window, you'll know it's me. If you see that, expect your telephone to ring within an hour. Yep, I intend to see room 437.

"Here's a little souvenir to remind you of me until I get back. It's a decorated handkerchief that I bought in Manila yesterday. It's more delicate than your gauze bandages, since it's woven from a native plant fiber, so don't blow your nose too hard!

"That was quite an interesting trip to Manila. I live on Samar (southern tip), an island about four hundred miles from "the Pearl City of the Orient," but the planes I hitch-hike on cover that in two and a half hours. I saw Manila on a three-day pass.

"I was most impressed by the Intramuros, the original walled city built by the Spanish in the seventeenth century. Our artillery had tragically destroyed most of the ancient landmarks during the battle for Manila, but you could tell from the empty shells of buildings still standing how great had been the glory of the many old cathedrals and churches and public buildings. Great oak gates carved with ornate figures three centuries old stood in the doorway of the Cathedral of the Immaculate Conception, and there were many beautiful statues in the inset niches high in the walls of the Church of Saint Augustine. The roof had been blown out of one church, and the south wing was destroyed in another.

"There was one church that had been topped by three beautiful domes—one large, in the center, and two small ones in the front towers. The whole building was demolished except the three domes and their supporting pillars, so the domes are still standing, with almost nothing beneath them. It looked as if they were held up by faith alone!

"I'm glad that I bring out the deeper side in you. You need an outlet for some of the very real things in life that you may not have a chance to discuss in your everyday routine of living with others. I'm always interested in you.

"You really are on your own now—everything that you think, do, or say is independent of all your family. What you do in the big city, and in all your life ahead, is up to you. You've been pushed over the edge of the nest, to try your own wings. I want to see you fly!

"Goodnight for now, sweet Persis. Always yours, Bob."

In the interest of fair play, I next wrote letters to Pauline and Sandy with similar descriptions of my trip to Manila. I told each of them that I hoped to be back in California by Thanksgiving, but that I didn't know when or where I would be released from the army, or how soon I could see them again. I hoped that it wouldn't be too long before I could get over to Illinois to see Pauline (or Arkansas to see Sandy). *I'm definitely going to visit all three girls again, before I do something rash—like getting engaged to any one of them!*

While catching up on my routine duties during the next three days, I got a sudden brainstorm—I knew what to do with my old gold bars. At the next chow call, I found Hill in the mess hall and asked him to meet me at the bulletin board—I had something to show him.

"Here I am," Hill said as he arrived. "What d' you want to show me?"

"These gold bars," I said, bringing them out of a pocket. "Since I got promoted to silver bars, I have no use for the old ones. I thought of giving them to you."

"Thanks," he laughed. "What would I ever do with those things?"

"A month ago, I flew to Leyte for an overnight visit to the officers' club at Tacloban. They serve food like you won't believe—a lot better 'n what we get here."

"Anything's better 'n what Snafu serves here!" (They called our cook "Snafu.")

"Their bar serves real gin and whiskey as well as beer, and the spacious club is cool and elegant. I'd like to go again soon, and take a good friend along as a companion. I mean you!"

"Me? You know they don't let staff sergeants visit officers' clubs!"

"That's why I'm giving you these gold bars. You won't be a staff sergeant—you'll be Second Lieutenant James C. Hill, U.S. Army Air Corps, welcome at any officers' club."

Hill's mouth dropped open, and he sucked in air with an audible gasp. "Are you telling me to impersonate an officer? Isn't that a federal crime?"

"Not telling you—inviting you. I know we'll have fun together, and I know we'll get away with it! No one interrogates the guests there—how could we get caught?"

"What's the plan? How would we pull this off?"

"Do you have a khaki shirt without staff sergeant stripes? Like you wear under a jacket?"

"Yeah," Hill nodded, with a questioning look on his face.

"Use pins to fasten some loose stripes to the sleeves. That'll cover you while we fly over on a Bomber Barons C-47, where the crew will know you. Then, at Tacloban, where no one knows you, we'll find a private place where you can remove the stripes and put the gold bars on your collar and overseas cap. Then we two officers will walk up the hill to the officers' club."

Hill's face slowly crinkled into a broad grin. "You know, that just might be fun!"

Saturday morning, October 6, the two conspirators met on the flight line.

"All set?" Hill asked.

"Yep," I replied. "I telephoned ahead for reservations for Lieutenants Hamilton and Hill."

"I have the gold bars in my pocket," he said.

"And I see that your stripes are pinned on your sleeves. Now all we need to do is hitch a ride to Tacloban. Let's see what's scheduled in Operations."

On the board we saw that the pilot for the first flight was Major Luketz instead of Wildey. We waited until he arrived, and hitched a ride, along with several other men from our squadron. Hill and I sat inconspicuously with the others on the mail sacks and cargo crates in the cabin, so as not to attract attention from our C.O. Twenty minutes later, we got out at Tacloban airstrip.

We walked to the far end of the row of planes parked there. Hidden behind the tail of a fat-bellied C-46, Hill unpinned his stripes and put them in his shirt pocket. Then I pinned a gold bar on his right collar and the Air Corps winged propeller pin on his left collar. Hill pinned the other gold bar to his overseas cap and put it back on his head.

"Stand straight and tall, Lieutenant Hill" I said, saluting him. "You're every inch an officer."

"Yes *sir*!" He returned the salute.

"As we walk along, every G.I. we meet will throw us a salute. Get in the habit of saluting back. I remember my first few days as a second looey, how strange it felt to be saluted."

We walked around the plane, down the ramp, and headed toward the transient officers quarters. Sure enough, several times we passed enlisted men of various ranks who promptly saluted us. The first time Hill was slow in returning the salute, but after that he was quicker than I was.

"You're right, it does feel strange to be saluted," Hill said. "On that first one, I thought, 'Who, me?'"

"They salute the rank, of course, not the person. But it doesn't take long for your ego to grow to match the rank. Then you feel it only right for them to salute *you*."

"My ego is growing already," Hill chuckled. "Now I'll put a little swagger in my walk."

"Attaboy! That's the spirit! Soon you'll develop the natural arrogance of rank."

After registering at Transient Officers' Quarters, we left our bags by our cots and walked up the hill to the Officers' Club. Walking into the spacious bar and lounge, Hill looked around at the high ceiling, the wood roof trusses, and generous open screened window areas, with an awe-struck expression. "Very nice!"

"What would you like to drink?" I asked. "They have whiskey, gin and beer, and most importantly, they have ice."

"Ice is nice, but not for beer. I'll have something we can't get at home—whiskey and soda."

"Sounds good to me, too. I'll buy this round."

We took our drinks to a small table.

"To your health!" Hill raised his glass.

"And cheers to you!" I raised mine for a clink.

We sipped, looked around at the view, and sipped again. The morning sunlight shimmered on San Pedro Bay to the east, silhouetting a multitude of ships. The green hills of Samar rose like a painted backdrop beyond.

"Isn't that view just great?" I exclaimed.

"Beautiful!" Hill raised his hand to point. "The sheen of shimmering sunlight on the waves throws an iridescent cast over the whole scene."

"Well said! The first time I came here, I wanted to share this scenery with you. Your artistic eye can really appreciate it."

"Thanks for thinking of me. In spite of our difference in rank, I've thought of you as my friend ever since our days in Tonopah."

"True," I said, "I share the same feeling."

"And we shared that life raft adventure, back in New Guinea. Man, that was some trip!"

"Here's to life on a life raft!" We clinked glasses again, and drank some more.

"I think we're ready for a refill," Hill said. "My turn to buy."

We spent a nostalgic morning relaxing in the bar, sipping drinks and reminiscing. Then we moved to the dining hall and had what seemed like a gourmet meal compared to our usual lunch. After that we decided to walk to the beach and take a nap while we sunbathed. Soon we were lying on the sand, cooking in the tropical afternoon. Whenever we got too hot, we jumped into the waves for a cooling swim, then stretched out on the sand again. We had no idea how damaging to our skin this solar radiation could be.

"I can't believe how relaxed I feel," Hill said as he rolled over.

"I've done this very same thing on the beach on Samar, and didn't feel half as relaxed."

"Why do we have to get away from home to really relax?"

"As long as we hang around home, we're always subject to possible interruption by an emergency or someone's change of plans," I said. "Whether we're interrupted or not, we know subconsciously that it could happen, so we never really let go. When we leave town, we can relax."

The outdoor cold-water shower felt good on my lobster-baked skin. Then we returned to the officers' club for a drink before dinner, a great meal, and another drink after dinner.

"I'm feeling so good now, I'd like to do something exciting," I said over our drinks.

"Impersonating an officer and getting away with it is exciting enough for me."

"Wouldn't it be more exciting to drive to downtown Tacloban and see what kind of night life they have? I wonder if they have flashy neon signs?"

"Or girls beckoning from upstairs balconies? You can't be serious about driving to town. We haven't driven anything—anywhere—since coming overseas."

"I did, back in Nadzab—I drove a jeep that I borrowed from the motor pool to check out the river for our rafting trip. And I discovered that jeeps have no keys! Anybody could steal one!"

"Steal one? Steal a jeep? Wouldn't that stretch the envelope of luck a bit too much?"

"We've gotten away with so much already, I think we're on a roll."

"Are you the same missionary's son I started my overseas tour with?"

"The same, only full of mischief tonight. I feel adventurous!"

"Full of the devil, or whiskey, or both. But where could we find a jeep to steal?"

"On the flight line—I saw several jeeps parked there. Besides, we won't *steal* it—we'll just *borrow* it for the evening! We'll go to town for a while, then return it to the very same spot. I bet it'll never be missed!"

"Well, 'borrow' does sound a lot better than 'steal'! Count me in! Let's go to town!"

Night had darkened the world when we left the club. Down the hill and over to the flight line we walked, then around the corner to the front of the Quonset hut Operations office. The number of jeeps parked there had been greatly reduced since I saw it earlier; only two remained. One was painted white, with "MILITARY POLICE" stenciled in bold black letters. The other was painted the usual olive drab.

"Don't take the white one!" Hill whispered. "We don't want to upset the M.P.'s!"

"Of course not!" I gave him a withering look. "We'll just walk up to the other one and get in as if it belonged to us, then start it up and drive away. Acting bold will dispel suspicion."

Boldly we strode up to the jeep, with a little joking and laughter to add to our bravado. Casually I opened the door and sat in the driver's seat while Hill cheerily plopped into the passenger side. I started it, backed out turning, gunned the motor, then drove away at a casual rate of speed.

"That was easy," Hill said. "Now, which way to the city?"

"On the map, Tacloban town is three miles northwest of the airstrip, but first we have to go south a mile to get off base. This is a north-south runway, and I can see by looking up at the stars that we're heading south right now, so we are on course to exit the base."

"Good to have a navigator on board!"

Driving felt wonderful! The warm breeze blowing over the open top bathed my sunbaked face with soothing comfort. The stars overhead beckoned me like old friends. The sense of power I felt from driving this responsive vehicle fed my liquor-induced euphoria to an absolute high. *I'm invincible! I'm flying! I'm as high as the stars—*

A loud, wailing siren behind me interrupted my reverie. We both swivelled our heads around to see flashing red lights on another jeep roaring toward us at twice our speed. Hill spewed a string of unprintable profanity, while I felt my stomach, made of lead, sinking down through my guts. I braked to a stop as the white jeep zipped around me in a half-spin that placed him crosswise to the road, blocking my path. A burly corporal jumped out, flashlight in hand, wearing an M.P. armband and garrison cap, army 45 automatic in holster. His flashlight beam scanned our faces and the interior of the jeep.

"What's the matter, Corporal? Was I driving too fast?" I decided to be bold.

"No, sir—but is this your vehicle?" His flashlight returned to my face.

"Of course not, Corporal. All army vehicles belong to Uncle Sam, not to me, or you, or any other person." *I'm really sharp tonight!*

"Don't get smart, sir! Is this vehicle assigned to you for your use?"

"This vehicle became available to me tonight, so I was using it to show Lieutenant Hill the sights of the fair city of Tacloban, and if you'll kindly back your jeep out of the way, we'll continue our journey."

"Sir, you'll have to turn around and drive back to Operations. Tell your story to the captain. Park the jeep in the same place it was before. I'll follow you all the way."

"What a waste of time!" I barked, but backed the jeep into a 180-degree turn and headed north to Operations. The M.P. followed hard on our tail.

I've got to take full responsibility for this incident—distract them from paying any attention to Hill—protect him from discovery. I'll have to confess, act up, or do anything to keep him from being charged with impersonating an officer! I can't let that happen to my friend!

We were ushered in to see a tough-looking captain. He was old–maybe even forty.

"Show me your dogtags," he snarled. I pulled at the chain around my neck, and the aluminum tags popped out from under my shirt. He looked at mine, then at Hill's. "Hamilton and Hill, I see. What units are you assigned to?"

"Fifth Bomb Group, 394th Squadron, based on Samar, across bay," I said.

The captain pickup up the microphone of the VHF radio on his desk. "Samar Ground Control, this is Tacloban Base Command, over."

"Tacloban, Samar reads you loud and clear, over."

"Samar, check your roster, please. Do you have a Lieutenant Hamilton and a Lieutenant Hill assigned to the 394th Squadron? Over." *Oh, no! Here it comes! Hill's goose is cooked!*

"Affirmative, Tacloban. Lieutenant Hamilton is Assistant Squadron Navigator, and Lieutenant Hill is the newly-appointed Operations Officer, over." *That's First Lieutenant Ben Hill!* "Thank you, Samar, Tacloban out." *Saved—by an incredible coincidence of last names!*

"Lieutenant Hill—Operations Officer, eh? Mighty responsible position to be stealing the Major's jeep!" *Oh, oh! I've got to do something—anything—to get him off Hill's case!*

"Sir, I confess!" I burst out. "It was all my idea—Hill had nothing to do with it!"

"So it was you, Hamilton—you take full responsibility for this crime?"

"Yes, sir! But I didn't *steal* the jeep—I just *borrowed* it for the evening to explore the city—I intended to return it to the very same spot before midnight."

"You intended—the road to hell is paved with good intentions! How old are you?"

"Twenty, sir."

"Attens-HUT!" the captain barked, his dark eyebrows pinched in a scowl. "Pop to attention, both of you! No—straighter than that! Shoulders back! Chest out! Suck in that gut! Didn't they teach you how to pop to attention in cadet school? You're going to get a refresher course here tonight! Hold that posture—until *I* give you further orders! You young whippersnapper! Your generation is going to hell in a handbasket! What does your father do, Hamilton?"

"He's a Presbyterian minister in Knoxville, sir."

"A minister! You're another preacher's kid gone bad! What do you think your father would say about what you did tonight?"

"He would condemn it, sir."

"Damn right he'd condemn it! His Bible says, 'THOU SHALL NOT STEAL!' Didn't they teach you that in Sunday School? You say you didn't steal it, you just 'borrowed' it? The Articles of War state that any unauthorized use of government property is tantamount to stealing, so legally, you STOLE the Major's jeep! That's a federal crime! I could throw your ass in jail and they'd ship you off to Alcatraz! You've read the Articles of War, haven't you? No? An officer in the U.S. Army, and you haven't read the Articles of War! You're a disgrace to the uniform!"

Just then a door opened, and the major I met last month stepped out of an inner office.

Oh, no! He's the owner of the jeep! As if I needed any more bad news! That ruthless sonovabitch will really cut me down!

27. Sunset and the Golden Gate

"What's going on here, Captain?" the major asked. "Sounds like a royal ass-chewing."

"Yes sir, it is! This young flyboy stole your jeep to go sightseeing in town!"

Hill and I were both still braced at attention.

"Which one did it?"

"The taller one, Lieutenant Hamilton."

The major looked closely at me. His eyes told me that he recognized me from last month.

"Lieutenant, how many combat bombing missions did you fly in the war?" the major asked with a straight face.

"Twenty-four, sir."

"Any awards and decorations?"

"Air medal with oak leaf cluster, Philippine liberation ribbon with two battle stars, and Pacific theater ribbon with five battle stars."

The major gave the captain a look that made him squirm.

"At ease, men," said the major.

Hill and I dropped the brace position with sighs of relief.

"Captain, I know this man from prior experience. I'll vouch for him. And as for his little joy ride, haven't you already punished him enough?—gave him a good ass-chewing, didn't you?"

"Well—" the captain began.

"He certainly did, sir!" I said. "He chewed out my ass so thoroughly, I have nothing left to sit down on!"

"Then drop all charges, and let these men walk out," the major told the captain.

"Yes, sir!" the captain said. "I was just about to do that, when you—"

"Lieutenant!" the major interrupted. "Remember when we talked about experiences that make you grow up? Make sure this is one of those learning experiences."

"Yes, *sir!*" I said. "I've already learned my lesson."

"Dismissed!"

Hill and I both saluted, turned on our heels, and walked out into the clean night air. I drew in three deep breaths to clear my head. Hill lit a cigarette and inhaled deeply.

"The last time I saw that major, I thought he was a real sonovabitch!" I said.

"Well, the sonovabitch turned out to be a straight-shooter after all."

"Hallelujah!" I clapped Hill on the back. "They just let us through the pearly gates!"

After a good night's sleep and a leisurely breakfast at the officers club, Hill and I went down to the flight line to wait for the next plane from Samar. Before it arrived, we strolled beyond the last plane to find a private place to change Hill's emblems of rank. Off came the gold bars and winged-propeller collar-pin. Hill took his stripes out of his pocket and pinned them on his khaki shirt sleeves.

"Well, Hill, you're a staff sergeant again, all ready for the flight home."

"Yep! Cinderella's coach just turned back into a pumpkin," he replied. "Here are your gold bars back."

"I'll never need those again. Why don't you keep 'em as a souvenir of our escapade? After all, how often do you impersonate an officer and get away with it?"

"That's right—you got busted for stealing the jeep, but I got away with the other business altogether! That's something to celebrate."

Back on Samar, nothing local seemed very important to me after I made the decision to leave the army. Our crew waited our turn for rotation to the states, and the month of October crept by more slowly than usual. Fifteen million men in service could not be discharged overnight. They filled the pipeline to the major "reception centers" set up in several regions of America, where their processing for discharge took time. But to those of us overseas, time seemed to stand still until we were finally on our way by plane or ship, homeward bound.

A tropical cyclone swept over the Philippines in mid-October, kicking off the annual rainy season. Our flying, reduced by the end of the war, was further decreased by nasty weather. Drizzle and fog depressed our spirits, too, but the hope of going home was the silver lining we looked for behind every cloud.

By chance I ran into Ensign Jim Ethridge, a friend of my sister, Minnie, whom she met in Atlanta while she attended Agnes Scott College. Commissioned in the U.S. Navy, he was assigned to an LST (landing ship, tank) docked then at the naval station on Samar. Jim invited me to dine with him at the Naval Officers Club there. It was an elegant experience, with white tablecloths, real cloth napkins, glassware and silverware I had not seen for years. The food, too, was good enough to be worthy of all those trimmings. Best of all, there was no chow line! Instead, we had Negro waiters in starched white jackets who came to our table to take orders and serve us.

"Who are these waiters?" I asked. "Did the navy hire servants and ship them overseas?"

"Oh, no," Jim said with a laugh. "They're enlisted men in the navy. Negroes in the navy are limited to service roles like stevedores, cooks and mess stewards. It's just our tradition." (That tradition ended soon after the war, with the racial integration of all the armed services by President Truman's executive order in 1949.)

The "Sunset Project," unveiled October 18 in the 13th Air Force, offered more rapid rotation by dealing with individual flyers instead of crews. We were all dumped into a common pot, and high-time names drawn out at random to create temporary aircrews for the flight home. This broke up our combat crews, which gave us one more thing to gripe about. I would have preferred waiting a little longer to fly home with the same crewmates who flew all those combat missions with me, but that was not an option. Our last flight together, as Seitz' crew, was the China coast surveillance mission we had flown on September 25. I bade a fond farewell to each of my combat crew members there on Samar.

On October 21, my air travel orders under the Sunset Project attached me to seven other assorted crew members from the 394th Squadron who had never flown together, to make up a new crew to ferry an airplane home. The other three officers were all second lieutenants, Pilot Robert Prall from Scranton, Pennsylvania, Copilot Mike M'Gillycuddy from Rapid City, South Dakota, and Bombardier Frank Storment from Los Angeles, California. We had two tech sergeants, Radio Operator Jack Young from Burlingame, California, and Engineer Raymond Jones from Rochester, New York, and also two staff sergeant gunners, George Marsh from Pittsburg, Pennsylvania, and James Dalton from Downers Grove, Illinois.

Eight days later, this new ferry crew flew B-24 number 845, "Stardust," to Clark Field for remodeling, and waited there a week for departure clearance. To save weight, the plane was stripped of all machine guns and armor, and the ball turret removed. A sheet of plywood covered the hole it left in the floor.

During the wait, our temporary crew members got acquainted with each other. Prall, the pilot, was a small, slump-shouldered man with a grown-out blond crew cut that reminded me of a cock's comb; a matter-of-fact man who said little. M'Gillycuddy, copilot, was a big dark-haired Irishman with a ready sense of humor—he loved to laugh. Storment, bombardier, was a medium-sized young man with movie-star good looks and wavy blond hair, carefully combed. He loved to talk, mostly about the amazing beauty of California and the wonders of his home town of L.A., which included Hollywood, of course, and all the stars, glamor and glories of tinsel-town. His sentences came out of his mouth with built-in exclamation points. He was a one-man chamber of commerce.

Lest I jump to the conclusion that all Californians were braggarts like Texans, the radio operator, Technical Sergeant Young, told me to consider the source.

"Storment's from *southern* California–the land of fruits and nuts," Young said. "I'm from Burlingame, on the San Francisco peninsula. *Northern* California is like a different country–we have real people living there."

"I know that already," I replied. "I have a girl friend in northern California–at Stanford University. She's the 'realest' person I ever met."

It was nice to think about Persis again, and nicer still to realize that in a few more days, I could see her again. That thought made my heart beat faster and my head feel lighter. *Whoa there, Bob! You have three girl friends, not just one! Don't get light-headed over the first one you see. Remember, you said that you were going to visit all three— Persis and Sandy and Pauline— before you get engaged to any of them!*

Dawn was breaking over Clark Field as "Stardust" took off at six A.M. on Sunday, November 4. Rain pelted the windshield as another tropical cyclone tried vainly to delay our trip. Through the mist I caught my last glimpse of Manila off the right wingtip as we headed east across Luzon. By the time we had flown ten hours to Guam, the rainy weather was behind us. We had also flown through two time zones, so the sun was setting already as we landed at Agana airfield at six P.M. local time.

"Number four engine was acting up the last two hours," Prall said as we unloaded. "Ran too hot, backfired, burned oil—I just about shut the durn thing down."

"I was wondering when you would," M'Gillycuddy replied.

"Sure, and we'll have to tarry now on this Pacific paradise until Engineering can fix it or change it."

We spent two nights and two days on Guam waiting for our engine change to be completed. During that time, I hitched a ride to North Field to see the famous B-29s. They were the newest and biggest bombers in the world. They impressed me as giant works of art—their clean lines and graceful curves were beautiful. And awesome, too, as I thought of their cargoes of death and destruction that had ended the war. B-29's had firebombed Tokyo, and carried the atomic bomb to Hiroshima and also to Nagasaki.

Finally, at 10:20 P.M. on Tuesday, November 6, we left the runway lights of Agana behind us, and headed east through the night across an ink-black ocean. The autumn stars were out in all their glory, allowing me to plot our course by celestial fixes all night long. Celestial navigation was the highest skill in my field, but I seldom had a chance to use it, because all of our B-24 missions had been daylight flights. This night gave me a glow of pride in my work.

Then the sunrise, straight ahead, dissolved the night in a burst of radiant color that thrilled me with its unexpected splendor. Three hours later, we landed at Kwajalein Atoll at 9:20 local time Wednesday morning, after a ten hour flight.

On Thursday, November 8, we got up in early morning darkness to take off from Kwajalein at four A.M. local time, heading east-northeast toward Honolulu. Four and a half hours later, we crossed the 180th meridian, the International Date Line, and suddenly the day became Wednesday, November 7. As we approached local noon, I used three successive sun shots with my octant, spaced at half-hour intervals (while the sun's direction swung through 90 degrees, from southeast to southwest), to develop a celestial noonday fix, plotting our position in that empty stretch of ocean. Hours later, the sun set behind us long before we reached the island of Oahu after a fourteen hour flight. We landed at Hickam Field at

8:30 P.M. Hawaiian time on Wednesday, so datewise, we landed a day earlier than the day we took off.

The sun was setting on Thursday, November 8, as we took off from Hickam Air Force Base at 5:40 P.M. for an all-night flight to California. It was one more opportunity for me to practice the high art of celestial navigation. Since we were flying east through two and a half time zones, the night ended long before our fourteen-hour flight did.

At 9:55 A.M. California time, we flew right over the Golden Gate bridge. What a breath-taking sight! Beyond the red steel lace of the bridge, the wooded hills of Alcatraz Island lay to the right, the curving bay of Tiberon to the left. The beautiful, dark blue San Francisco Bay stretched out all around us as we headed for Sacramento. There we landed at Mather Field at 10:20 A.M., Friday, November 9, 1945. It was hard to believe that only eight months and one week had elapsed since I had left California—that seemed like a lifetime ago.

As soon as I got near a pay phone in the terminal building, I called Persis. There was no answer in her dorm room. *It's late morning, and she'd be in class, of course.* I left a message with the switchboard lady, to be put in Persis' box, that I was back from the war, and would call her again that evening. Then I called my parents in Knoxville, to let them know I was here.

We stayed only a few hours at Mather Field. That very afternoon, we were put on a bus to Camp Stoneman at Pittsburg, California, about fifty miles east of San Francisco. There we shed our tropical khakis and changed into winter uniforms. We would stay there about a week, until we were sent individually to reception centers in different regions of the country for processing for discharge. Our ferry crew disbanded; its members said farewell to each other. No longer were we members of any recognizable military unit; we were just individuals in a vast holding pool of soldiers milling around until we became civilians again.

That evening Persis answered her dorm room phone on the first ring.

"Hello, Persis! Guess who this is!"

"Hello, Bob, you crazy nut! As if I haven't been waiting for your call!"

"It's so good to hear your voice again! I can't tell you how glad I am to be back!"

"And I'm so glad to have you back! What are your plans?"

"I think I can get free tomorrow. How about a date—dinner and dancing at some nice place in San Francisco?"

"Wonderful! The best dance bands are in the big hotels. I'll make reservations for us. Tomorrow's Saturday—we couldn't get in without a reservation."

"Great! I'm in Camp Stoneman at Pittsburg. I'll catch a Greyhound Bus to San Francisco. Can you give me directions from the bus station to your place?"

"Of course—grab a pencil and start writing."

I jotted down her directions, becoming more excited all the time.

Saturday afternoon, I dressed in my best winter uniform, pinkish-grey gabardine trousers and dark green jacket over a tan shirt and tie, with dark green garrison cap without grommet (for that "fifty-mission crush"), wearing my silver wings and two rows of service ribbons. I caught the Greyhound for a ninety-minute ride from Pittsburg to San Francisco. Leaving the Seventh Street Greyhound Terminal, I walked down Market Street past Sixth and then Fifth Street, crossing Market to the cable car turntable at the end of Powell Street. Beside the turntable was a vendor selling flowers from a pushcart. *What a good idea!* I bought a bouquet to take to Persis.

In a few minutes I saw one of the famed cable cars I had read about in Persis' letters. It came downhill on Powell toward me, looking like a little "Toonerville Trolley" painted dark red with gold, black and green trim. I heard its bell clang noisily at every

First Lieutenant Bob Hamilton,
November, 1945

intersection. It was small, only half as long as a full-size city bus or streetcar. In front of the turntable, it stopped. Two men in black uniforms got off, rotated the turntable to align the track, and pushed the cable car to roll it onto the turntable. They turned the car all the way around, and rolled it off onto the uphill track. Then people waiting all around me started jumping onto the car through the open sides. I followed their example, grabbing a seat near the front. Quite a few men in uniform were on board, all treated in very friendly ways by the civilians around them.

One of the crew sat down in the gripman's seat up front, pulling a chain with one hand to clang the bright brass bell overhead, while his other hand pulled the big grip lever to start the car rolling forward. The other man, the conductor, moved up and down the aisle to collect fares from all the passengers. He wore a metal coin holder over his belly to sort coins and make change.

We were passing a large, sloping park on the right, surrounded by tall buildings.

"What's this park called?" I asked.

"Union Square," the conductor said. "Sort of the hub of the city."

The car stopped at the end of every block, and more people piled on while few got off. Every seat was taken and the aisle was full of standees. Now people were hanging onto the outside of the car, standing on the running boards and holding on to metal posts. Another cable car approached on the downhill side of Powell Street, loaded with as many people as ours. I watched in amazement as the two cars passed each other—on both cars, the outer layer of hanging-on passengers sucked in their butts as they passed with only inches between them.

After a few more blocks, the tracks made a left turn onto Jackson Street, which was lined at first with small shops under apartments, and then with more and more homes. We lost our outer layer of passengers and the crowd continued to thin out as we went along. We crossed broad Van Ness Avenue and continued westward on Jackson through a residential neighborhood. (In 1945, cable cars still ran the full length of the routes laid out in 1873 by Andrew Hallidie. The Washington-Jackson line ran west to Fillmore, the California line ran all the way to Arguello. Today, no cable cars cross Van Ness. Buses made them obsolete, except as tourist attractions.)

The houses were three stories high and only twenty-five feet wide, stepped down the hillsides to match the sloping sidewalk. There were no side yards between houses—they touched their neighbors, wall on wall. *What a way to build a city! I've never seen anything like this!*

Following Persis' instructions, I got off at Webster Street, and walked south two blocks to Clay. On one side of Clay Street was the Stanford-Lane Hospital, and on the other side, the School of Nursing, with its dormitory. Up the steps I went and through the large door.

A grey-haired receptionist turned away from her telephone switchboard to greet me.

"I'm here to see Persis Mary Tangemann," I said.

She looked me over with a motherly smile. "I'll call her room. What's your name?"

"Bob Hamilton."

She dialed her switchboard unit. "Hello, Persis? You have a visitor—handsome young officer with wings and ribbons—Bob Hamilton..... Okay, I'll tell him." Turning to me, she said, "She was late getting away from the hospital. She'll be ready in half an hour. Why don't you wait in the lounge?"

"Thanks. She's worth waiting for."

I strolled into the small lounge, still carrying my bouquet of mixed flowers. and sat down to wait. Until now, I had been a tourist on my first day in San Francisco, too distracted by the sights to think of much else. Now I thought about Persis, and how she might respond to me. The longer I waited, the less confident I became. *Will she remember our first date? That was so long ago. So much happened in my overseas tour. Will she like what I've become?*

I got up and paced the floor to regain self-confidence, then strolled around, looking at the pictures on the wall. Then the elevator door opened, and out came Persis. She was wearing a dark red evening dress, ankle-length, with a fur coat over one arm. Her round face had an innocent, open look, framed by shoulder-length honey-blonde hair. We stood there, twenty feet apart, for a moment, as our eyes moved up and down, taking in the whole person.

"Persis," I broke the silence, "you look lovelier than I remembered!"

"Bob—you look mighty good yourself."

We moved toward each other. I held out my bouquet. "Here are some flowers I picked up on my way. Hope you like 'em."

"Oh, I do! Let's put 'em in some water." She led the way to a small kitchen, where she found an empty glass vase and filled it with water, then put the flowers into it.

"Let's leave it here for now. I can take it up to my room later."

"Then we're ready to go. Shall I call a cab?"

"Don't be silly—it's only a block to the cable car line. Let's walk."

At the door, I helped her into her fur coat, and she held my arm as we went down the steps. I liked the feeling it gave me. Then we held hands as we walked one block to Washington to catch the east-bound cable car. The sun had just set, and the street lights glowed in the twilight. Looking farther down the hill, I was surprised to see the lights disappearing into fog.

"Look!" I said, pointing. "The whole bay is covered with a blanket of fog! I don't remember seeing that when I came up the hill."

"Welcome to San Francisco! The fog comes here in late afternoon almost every day. It rolls through the Golden Gate from the ocean, and spreads out over the whole bay."

The cable car came, and we climbed on board. It was nearly empty, but more people got on at every stop. We plunged into the fog, which felt cold and clammy in the open car. But soon we came out the bottom side of the fog, which became an overcast above us. By the time we got downtown, the air was chilly but not wet.

"Let's get off at Union Square," Persis said. "Our reservations are at the Saint Francis Hotel ballroom." She led the way off the car and into the hotel lobby, where we took the elevator to the penthouse level. I checked her coat and my hat at the checkroom, and soon we were seated at a small table in the dining area of the ballroom. A big band was playing the beautiful swing music of that era. Tommy Dorsey's "I'll Be Seeing You" floated into our ears.

The wine steward came by for our order.

I turned to Persis. "Would you like a drink before dinner?"

"We drank rum and coca-cola on our first date. Shall we try it again?"

"Let's raise that to champagne, to celebrate! Bring us a bottle of pink champagne."

Persis turned to me as the man left. "Okay, what are we celebrating?"

"Two things—my return from the war in one piece, and our reunion tonight!"

"I'll drink to both of those—when the champagne comes."

"Meanwhile, we're wasting good swing music. Let's dance a few while we wait."

I led her onto the dance floor to the strains of "Sentimental Journey," and we settled into moving together to its easy rhythm. I held her loosely at first—didn't want to seem too eager, or make her feel crowded. We stayed on the floor through two other numbers, "Boogie Woogie" and "I'm Beginning to See the Light," before returning to the table.

The champagne had arrived. We drank our toasts and ordered dinners, prime rib of beef for me and veal cordon bleu for Persis. Between every course, we went back to the dance floor for two or three more numbers, feeling looser and more comfortable with each other all the time. Persis was a good dancer, flowing easily with the rhythm and beat, a pleasure to dance with.

Our leisurely dinner finally ended. The dishes were removed, the table cleared except for the champagne bottle in its ice bucket, our champagne glasses, and the candle-lit centerpiece.

I lit my pipe and smoked a while. We stayed on, sipping champagne and dancing, for hours. The dance floor became more crowded as the hour grew later. The other couples dancing on all sides pushed us closer to each other than ever before. It legitimized full body contact that I was ready for now—gentle, firm, top-to-bottom contact that felt so soft, warm, enticing, exciting, fulfilling—absolutely wonderful! It made me feel very light-headed—I was on "cloud nine."

"Did you know it's after midnight?" Persis said, looking at her watch. "If I'm not home by one-thirty, I'll be locked out and punished severely."

"Can't let that happen! Time to go home."

I retrieved her fur coat and my cap from the checkroom, and we rode the elevator down.

"I'm going to take you home in a taxi," I said.

"At this hour, that sounds very nice."

A line of cabs waited outside the entrance, and we climbed into the nearest one.

"2340 Clay Street," I told the cabbie. "Stanford Nurses Dormitory."

The taxi ride was quick and comfortable. As we climbed the steps to the dorm entrance, Persis held my arm. It was a gesture of dependency that pleased me.

Inside, she led me toward one of the "sitting rooms" near the lobby.

"No men are allowed above the first floor, so I can't show you my room. But we can visit here in semi-privacy."

We entered a small parlor with well-worn living-room furniture. She opened the heavy draperies around the major window. "Look at the view from this hilltop."

"The light's too bright—all I see is reflections of the room."

"Of course! Let me turn off the light. Now, what can you see?"

I stepped up to the window. "Oh, wow! What a great view of the whole bay—all covered with that thin sheet of fog— with the city lights underneath it making it glow, like the luminescence on tropical seas that I saw in the south Pacific. And look at that beautiful moonlight shining on the bridge rising up through the mist!"

"Oh, that's so poetic!" She slipped her arm around my waist. "I love what you said."

I turned toward her, and put my arms around her waist. "And I love what I'm seeing."

Slowly, gently, our faces came closer, and our lips found each other in a kiss—then another. Then our arms moved to grasp each other with greater strength, and we shared a long, passionate kiss. *Why are you afraid to tell her how much you really love her?*

We released our grip, and I took both her hands in mine. We looked into each other's eyes silently for a while, in the glow of moonlight.

"How soon can I see you again?" I asked softly.

"My nursing schedule is crammed, but I'll be free Wednesday night."

"I'll be here before sunset, and take you out to dinner." One goodby kiss, and I left.

Back in Camp Stoneman, I slept until late Sunday afternoon. I was troubled with a gut-level reaction against the date with Persis. Yes, I had enjoyed every minute, but my logical mind told me that we were moving too fast. The relationship was growing like a big snowball rolling downhill—things were getting out of hand! *If things keep going like they did last night, you'll be engaged to Persis before you ever get to visit Sandy and Pauline again! Whoa, Bob! Slow it down. You'll violate your sense of fair play if you don't visit **all three girls** before settling on any one of them.*

Suddenly I got a bright idea—*why not use long-distance telephone to call Sandy and Pauline right now?* Talking to them would refresh my memories of each one, and help insulate me against an overdose of Persis. *Hey, I'll do it!*

"Hello, Sandy! This is Bob!"

"Oh, Bob! Is it really you? Where are you, and what're you doing?"

"I'm in Camp Stoneman, California, near San Francisco, waiting for discharge. I just found out that I'll be sent to Camp Chaffee, Arkansas, to be discharged there."

"That's wonderful! Does that mean that I'll get to see you soon?"

"Of course! I don't know where Camp Chaffee is, but it's somewhere in your state. Soon as I get discharged, I'll find my way to Pine Bluff to see you on my way home."

"I can hardly wait! It's so good to talk to you again!"

"I love to hear your voice, too, but this is long distance, and we can't talk forever."

"Of course. Thanks so much for calling. I love you!"

My mind flooded with sweet memories of Sandy. She was in high school and I a cadet in navigation school when we met. A medium-size girl, a little shorter than Persis, she also had blue eyes and honey-blonde hair, nice figure, and a fun-loving, upbeat personality. She was out of high school now, of course, with a full-time job as teller-trainee at the local bank, but still very young. Talking to her brought her back to life for me.

"Hello, Pauline—is that you? This is Bob, calling from California!"

"Bob? In California? Whoopee! I've been waiting for this! Are you okay? In one piece?"

"Sure—I came through the war just fine. How are you, after all this time?"

"I'm fine—still working at the Hallmark Shop downtown. When can you come to see me?"

"Not right away, I'm afraid. First I have to go to a reception center in Arkansas to be discharged, and then I need to go home to Knoxville, Tennessee, to visit my family for a while. That may get into Christmas, which I really ought to spend with my family. But I'll come to Illinois to see you, soon as I can!"

"You better do that, or I'll have your scalp! I can't wait to see you! It's been two years!"

"I miss you, too. But this is long-distance, and we ought not to talk too long."

"I know. It's so good to hear your voice again! Remember—I love you, young rascal!"

Now memories of Pauline flooded my mind. A petite, five-foot brunette with gleaming dark eyes and curly black hair, she was two years older than I. That had seemed like a big age difference when she was twenty and I only eighteen. But now that we were both in our twenties, it no longer seemed like a barrier. I loved her sunny, upbeat personality, always good for a laugh. Though older than Sandy, Pauline was like her in education and experience.

Then I thought of Persis, and realized the difference between her and them. Persis had higher goals in life—Stanford University education, professional career, service to others. In a word, she had class! I fully expected to complete my higher education and become a teacher. *Which girl would be more compatible with my professional life? Persis, of course. Which one do you love? I love all three. But who do you love most of all? Which one really turns you on the most? Honestly, that's also Persis. Well then, dummy, what are you waiting for?*

Wednesday afternoon was a replay of Saturday P.M. Dressed in the same uniform, I caught the same bus to San Francisco, and walked to the same cable car turntable. But I passed by the flower vendor without buying any—tonight I wanted to lower the level of romance. The cable car took me up Powell past Union Square and the Saint Francis Hotel again, reviving memories of Saturday night. *What delicious memories!* But tonight I planned a different kind of date.

At the dormitory, Persis came down without delay, wearing a

light blue, knee-length dress that matched her eyes and showed off her blonde hair nicely. She carried a black fabric coat.

"Let's do something different tonight," I said. "How do we get to Chinatown?"

"That's easy—just walk two blocks to California, and catch the California Street cable car eastbound. It goes straight down the hill past Chinatown."

"How would you like a good Chinese dinner? I haven't had one for a long time."

"Fine! It's been a while for me, too."

The California Street cable car looked much like the ones on the other line, though the color scheme was different. It plunged down through the evening fog and came out below it.

"We'll get off at Grant Street, just before Saint Mary's Square," Persis said.

Northward we walked on Grant Street, pausing to peek at window displays of many interesting shops selling fine silks, carved jade and ivory art, Ming porcelains, teakwood furniture, and curios from all over the orient. The storefronts featured red and gold painted columns and projecting green tile roofs with turned-up corners like pagodas. The street lights were shaped like Chinese lanterns, casting their own oriental spell. Food stores displayed pickled fish, smoked meats, tofu, herbs, roots and other oriental delicacies. Cocktail lounges had American jazz music coming from them, but other shops featured distinctively Chinese music, with external speakers to add atmosphere to the sidewalk scene.

We entered a fine restaurant called the China Palace.

"Look at the food display in the foyer," I pointed. "Is that real cooked food, or mockups?"

"Probably mockups, but very realistic. They show what their whole menu looks like."

I helped her out of her coat. "So we just find some good-looking dishes, and order by the numbers. Which ones appeal to you?"

She bent over the showcases. "Number five looks like almond

chicken with broccoli—I love that! And number nineteen looks like a good shrimp and veggie dish."

"And let's have a sweet-and-sour pork dish—number fourteen."

"Yes, and start with sizzling rice soup, number three."

Inside, we were seated at a red lacquered dining table. A wall carving of a gilded dragon glared down on us. We sipped Chinese tea while we waited for our orders.

"Can't stay out as late tonight as last time," Persis said. "This is a weeknight, and I have to be back by ten-thirty."

I smiled. "Can't win 'em all. But look at the bright side—we still have three and a half more hours to lavish on each other."

She laughed. "Always the optimist, aren't you?"

"Always. And so are you; I can tell."

She flashed her charming smile. "It doesn't cost any more to be happy than sad."

"I like your philosophy—in fact, I like everything about you—more than you know."

Our soup came, and then the other courses. I showed her just how to hold chopsticks to use them most efficiently, an art I had learned in Shanghai. We talked about my China heritage, and I shared stories from my childhood there, including the pranks I had pulled in high school at the Shanghai American School. The Chinese music permeating the room reinforced the setting for my tales. Persis was a wonderful conversationalist—she encouraged me to talk about my favorite subject, myself. She drew me toward herself with an invisible web of words and smiles.

I had planned an unromantic evening with Persis to slow down the snowballing romance, but it didn't work. Just being with her turned me on, and filled me with a great longing for more. The ongoing struggle between my head and my heart was no contest in her magical presence—my heart won, hands down. I realized then that I was really in love.

"It's only nine, Persis. Let's finish the evening with a romantic flourish—go to our old hotel for an after-dinner drink and a little more dancing to that beautiful big-band music."

"Why not try the Mark Hopkins Hotel on Nob Hill? It's close to the California Street cable car line. They have a swell band. This is mid-week—I think we can get in without reservations."

The cable car took us within sight of the tall hotel, and a short walk put us inside. We took the elevator up to the "Top of the Mark" ballroom, where the band was beginning "That Old Black Magic." We wasted no time getting out on the dance floor.

"That's what it is, Persis—'That Old Black Magic has me in its spell' whenever you're near. 'Round and round I go, in a spin, loving the spin I'm in, under that old black magic called *love*."

"Nice words, aren't they?"

"More than nice—they're powerful words. You weave a web of magic around my heart, Persis—bonds of love stronger than steel cables."

A new song started. A willowy blonde singer crooned, "You'll never *know* just how much I love you. You'll never *know* just how much I care...."

Persis whispered in my ear, "This is the first song we danced to on our first date, so long ago. And while you were gone, I thought of this song whenever I thought of you."

"What a sweet memory to share with me!" I drew Persis very close. *As long as I've lost the struggle against romance, I might as well enjoy the result.*

The song went on, "You went away and my heart went with you—I breathe your name in my every prayer. If there is some other way to tell you I love you, I swear I don't know how. You'll never know if you don't know now!" *That's got to be our special song from now on.*

It seemed like only a few songs later that my watch said ten-fifteen. "Time to go—now!"

We caught a cab in the hotel driveway and settled into the back seat. I drew her close and kissed her thoroughly. *Bob, you big dummy—you know Persis is the one you want. Why wait? Make the decision now!*

"Persis—I love you!—I really love you! Will you marry me?"

She sucked in her breath, and paused for a moment that seemed like forever.

"Yes, Bob—I will marry you!" We fell into each other's arms for another long kiss.

The cab stopped moving. We were there. I paid the cabbie, and we skipped up the steps.

Persis rushed through the door excitedly and ran toward the motherly switchboard lady. "Guess what! We're engaged!" She grabbed both my hands and swung us around a circle like a child's dance, singing, "We're engaged—we're engaged—we're engaged!"

"That's wonderful, Persis," came the motherly reply, "but now it's ten twenty-nine, and you'd better dance your man right through that door before it locks."

I stretched my arms like wings and flew down the steps, joyful, exuberant. I ran the block to Washington Street and jumped on the approaching cable car before it could stop. My face was beaming with the biggest smile of my life. I danced up and down the aisle, chanting a mantra:

"I'm engaged! My sweetheart said 'Yes'! We're engaged!"

"Congratulations!" "Way to go, man!" "Great!" Everyone on the car started to celebrate with me. A dozen people, including the conductor and gripman, started laughing with each other, cracking jokes about brides and grooms, clapping hands and celebrating. Half of the passengers were servicemen—soldiers, sailors and marines, probably returning from dates themselves; they joined me in singing all our familiar marching songs—"Off we go, into the wild blue yonder....." "Over hill, over dale, we have hit the dusty trail....." "Anchors aweigh, my boys, anchors aweigh....." "From the halls of Montezuma...."

"Stop the car!" I shouted to the gripman. "That's a cigar store on the corner! Wait right here while I dash in and out!" He held the car on the corner, and I was back in one minute flat with the first box of cigars I saw. Opening it now, I handed one to each person. We all lit up to celebrate–even two ladies who were there.

The celebration continued down Powell, past Union Square, growing noisier all along.

The car stopped in front of the turntable at Market Street, and everyone jumped off. The servicemen hung around, still singing, while the two crewmen rolled the car onto the turntable.

"Let's help these boys turn the car around!" I shouted. The other men in uniform leaped in to help with cries of approval, and the cable car started going around, and around, and around.

"One more time for the Army!" shouted a soldier. Around again it went.

"One more time for the Navy!" some sailors called. We pushed it around again..

"One more time for the Marines!" said a burly, red-headed marine. Around again it went.

"One final time for the *13th Air Force!*" I called in conclusion. We spun it once more, and gave it back to the cable car crew.

Then my newly-found comrades-in-arms and I dispersed into the civilian crowds around us, like the millions then being discharged. We were glad we had won the war, glad to be home again, glad for the celebration we had just shared, and glad that the best years of our lives lay ahead of us in the second half of the twentieth century, which at that time seemed to stretch on, and on, and on, ahead—forever.

– The End –

POSTSCRIPT

What has happened to the ten young men in my bomber crew since the end of World War II? For many years, we were all too busy pursuing our own separate goals to give much thought to the others. As the century wore on, and the fortieth and fiftieth anniversaries of World War II were celebrated by the nation, many of us were caught up by the general nostalgia, and began to seek out other members of the crew. Gradually, we started learning of each other's locations.

The first mini-reunion of Pilot, Copilot, and Radio Operator (and their wives) took place in 1988 at Pilot Seitz's home in Glenwood, Iowa. The next, a reunion of Navigator, Engineer, Radio Operator, Ball Gunner, and Tail Gunner (and their wives), was held in October 1997 in Canton, Ohio, centered on the home of Tail Gunner Hill. The third, bringing together Copilot, Navigator, Engineer, Radio Operator, and Ball Gunner (and their wives), occurred in April 1999 in the mountains of western North Carolina where Copilot Cordell has a cabin near Fontana Lake. We enjoyed the nostalgia each time, retelling our old war stories (many of which appear in this book).

Here's a thumbnail sketch of how each of us spent the half-century since the war:

Pilot Marvin Seitz settled in Glenwood, Iowa, where he worked briefly for a railroad, and then went into his career with the Post Office, rising from Letter Carrier to Assistant Postmaster. He built a large, four-engine, radio-control, flying model of his beloved B-24, which is still in his home. He died on January 3, 1989, at age 66, survived by his wife, Doris, four children, eight grandchildren, and (now) five great-grandchildren.

Copilot Jim Cordell attended the University of North Carolina, joined the Air Force Reserve as second lieutenant, was called to active duty for the Korean War and stayed on for an Air Force career as pilot of many types of bomber and transport aircraft, retiring in 1967 as a major. He had a second career as pilot of corporate airplanes, especially the MU-2. Jim has four children and six grandchildren. He lives with his wife, Polly, in Palm Bay, Florida, and visits their mountain cabin in North Carolina.

Navigator Bob Hamilton settled in northern California with his wife, Persis, for twenty-eight years, generating three children and two grandchildren. He flew the Pacific as airline navigator for four years, graduated from the University of California at Berkeley, earned advanced degrees from that school and Dallas Theological Seminary, and taught History and Philosophy at three colleges. Persis also taught at three other colleges and authored textbooks on Nursing. Bob retired in 1985, and lives with his wife, Jeanne, on the shore of Jackson Lake near Atlanta. They often visit her nearby four children, ten grandchildren, and two great-grandchildren.

Bombardier Howard James returned to his home town, Topeka, Kansas, where he was living in 1957, but we have been unable to trace him beyond that point.

Engineer Bob Pieper settled in Wausau, Wisconsin, where he had a career with the Police Department, rising from Patrolman to Senior Investigator. After retiring, he had a second career as a private security officer. He continues to live in Wasau with his wife, Cecelia, enjoying frequent visits with their five children and eight grandchildren.

Radio Operator Tony Imhof settled in Saint Louis, Missouri, with his wife, Marian. He studied architectural drafting, but his major career was with the U.S. Army Aviation Purchasing Command, where he was a civilian Personnel Specialist. He retired in 1977, designed and built two successive homes for his family, and travels frequently, visiting his four children and ten grandchildren.

Nose gunner Robert Williams returned to Canton, Ohio, where he lived with his wife, Donna, and their child. He pursued a career as a salesman of building products, and died in Canton on May 26, 1994, at age 71.

Armorer-gunner Benjamin Gerson returned to his home town, Brooklyn, New York, after the war, but we have not been able to locate him since then.

Ball Gunner Richard Herrema settled in his familiar part of Michigan near Grand Rapids and Holland. He pursued a career first as a house painter, then as Painting and Siding Contractor. He lives with his wife, Lorraine, in Byron Center, Michigan, surrounded by their five children and twelve grandchildren.

Tail Gunner Jim Hill returned to his home town, Canton, Ohio, where he put his artistic ability to work both full-time, in his career as Media Specialist for Timken Roller Bearing Company, and also part-time, as a painter of portraits, well-known in his community. He continues to live in Canton with his wife, Anne, who is a published poet. Their five children and seven grandchildren visit them frequently.

These ten men have had rather typical American lives—postman, pilot, teacher, policeman, office worker, salesman, house painter, graphic artist—but think of how many other lives would be different (or non-existent) today, if this crew had failed to return from World War II. We salute our fallen comrades-in-arms, and honor and cherish their memory. What we all did in World War II, the defining event of the twentieth century, changed the world forever. The world of the new century and new millennium owes a debt of gratitude to the special generation who stayed on course to victory.

Finally, if Howard C. James or Benjamin V. Gerson are still alive and read this, please call your old navigator at (770) 775-0713, or e-mail him at hamiltonbob@juno.com and we'll include you in our next reunion, now planned for April, 2000 A.D.

BIBLIOGRAPHY

The chief sources of data for this book have been the secret official monthly squadron and group histories written during the war for Far East Air Forces Headquarters, declassified in 1983, available on microfilm or as unbound original documents in the Air Force Historical Records Agency, Maxwell Air Force Base, Montgomery, Alabama. In addition to those documents, the following brief bibliography was helpful to the author:

I. BOOKS:

Arnold, (Gen.) Henry H., *Global Mission*. New York, Harper, 1949.
Birdsall, Steve, *Log of the Liberators*. New York, Doubleday, 1973.
Birdsall, Steve, *The B-24 Liberator*. New York, Arco Publ., 1968.
Blue, Allan G., *The B-24 Liberator*. London, Ian Allan, 1976.
Boeman, John, *Morotai: A Memoir of War*. Manhatten, KS, Sunflower University Press, 1981.
Bowman, Martin W., *B-24 Liberator 1939-45*. Wellingborough, U.K., Patrick Stevens, Ltd., 1989.
Carigan, William, *Ad Lib: Flying the B-24 Liberator in World War II*. Manhatten, KS, Sunflower University Press, 1988.
Craven, W.F., and J.L. Cate, *The Army Air Forces in World War II* (7 vols.). Chicago, University of Chicago Press, 1948-58.
Davies, Al E.(editor), *Pictorial History of the Second World War* (4 vols.). New York, Veterans of Foreign Wars, 1944-46.
Hammond Historical World Atlas (2 vols). New York, Hammond, 1991.
Harris, Brooklyn, *Bill: a Pilot's Story*. Klamath Falls, OR, Graphic Press, 1995.

Haugland, Vern, *The AAF Against Japan*. New York, 1948.
Howard, Clive, and Joe Whitley, *One Damned Island After Another*. Chapel Hill, NC, University of North Carolina Press, 1946.
Lester, John R. (Bob), *Frontline Airline: Troop Carrier Pilot in World War II*. Manhatten, KS, Sunflower University Press, 1994.
Lippincott, Benjamin, *From Fiji to the Philippines with the Thirteenth Air Force* (with paintings by Robert A. Laessig). New York, Macmillan, 1948.
Mander, Alexander J., *The Story of the Fifth Bombardment Group*. Raleigh, NC, Hillsborough House, 1946.
Maurer, Maurer, *Air Force Combat Units of World War II*. New York, Franklin Watts, 1963.
Odgers, George, *Air War Against Japan*. Canberra, Australian War Memorial, 1957.
Perkins, Paul, and Michelle Crean, *The Soldier*. Charlottesville, VA, Howell Press, 1994.
Rust, Ken C., and Dana Bell, *Thirteenth Air Force Story in World War II*. Terre Haut, IN, Sun Shine House, 1981.

II. VIDEOS:

"Airmen of World War II." Atlas Video, 1991.
"B-24 Liberator, View from the Cockpit." History of Air Combat, Publishers Choice Video, NSI-XZ7.
"B-24s at War in the Pacific." American Sound & Video, V-5885.
"The B-24 Story." American Sound & Video, V-5884.

III. OTHER SOURCES:

Corrin, Phil, "Borneo Log," unpublished manuscript copied from notes written in the jungle. U.S. Air Force Historical Research Agency, Maxwell A.F.B., Montgomery, AL, 1945.
Doyland, Russ, "The Last Task Force: the Mission to Brunei Bay," *Friends Journal*, Winter 97/98.

Nelson, John R., "Mission to Brunei Bay, November 16, 1944," unpublished manuscript. U.S. Air Force Historical Research Agency, Maxwell A.F.B., Montgomery, AL, 1993.

Hemingway, Al, "Did the Japanese successfully test-fire their own atomic bomb shortly after American A-bombs fell on Japan?" ("Undercover" column) *World War II*, July 1995.

"Survival Saga in Borneo," *Naval Aviation News*, February, 1960.

Walker, Ansil L., "Greatest Battle Never Fought: the Invasion of Japan," *World War II*, July 1995.